This volume provides an up-to-date critical reflection of a range of initiatives and interventions across diverse experiences and perspectives, with a strong inter-disciplinary approach to the spatial implications of the profound socio-economic changes impacting contemporary urbanism.

Frank Gaffikin, Emeritus Professor and former Director of Research from Queen's University, Belfast

PUBLIC SPACE/CONTESTED SPACE

It is not possible to be alive today in the United States without feeling the influence of the political climate on the spaces in which people live, work, and form communities. *Public Space/Contested Space* illustrates the ways in which creative interventions in public space have constituted a significant dimension of contemporary political action, and how this space can both reflect and spur economic and cultural change.

Drawing insight from a range of disciplines and fields, the essays in this volume assess the effectiveness of protest movements that deploy bodies in urban space, and social projects that build communities while also exposing inequalities and presenting new political narratives. With sections exploring the built environment, artists, and activists and public space, the book brings together diverse voices to reveal the complexities and politicization of public space within the United States.

Public Space/Contested Space provides a significant contribution to an understudied dimension of contemporary political action and will be a resource to students of urban studies and planning, architecture, sociology, art history, and human geography.

Kevin D. Murphy is Andrew W. Mellon Chair in the Humanities and Professor and Chair of the Department of History of Art at Vanderbilt University. Previously, he was on the faculty of the CUNY Graduate Center and the University of Virginia School of Architecture.

Sally O'Driscoll is Professor of English and Women's, Gender, and Sexuality Studies at Fairfield University. Her work on 18th-century literature and culture has appeared in such journals as *Signs, Tulsa Studies in Women's Literature,* and *Eighteenth-Century: Theory and Interpretation.*

THE METROPOLIS AND MODERN LIFE

A Routledge series
Edited by Zachary P. Neal, Michigan State University

This series brings original perspectives on key topics in urban research to today's students in a series of short accessible texts, guided readers, and practical handbooks. Each volume examines how long-standing urban phenomena continue to be relevant in an increasingly urban and global world and, in doing so, connects the best new scholarship with the wider concerns of students seeking to understand life in the 21st-century metropolis.

Books in the Series:

Common Ground? Reading and Reflections on Public Space edited by Anthony Orum and Zachary P. Neal
The Gentrification Debates edited by Japonica Brown-Saracino
The Power of Urban Ethnic Places: Cultural Heritage and Community Life by Jan Lin
Urban Tourism and Urban Change: Cities in a Global Economy by Costas Spirou
The Connected City by Zachary Neal
The World's Cities edited by A.J. Jacobs
Ethnography and the City edited by Richard Ocejo
Comparative Urban Studies by Hilary Silver
Housing America: Issues and Debates by Emily Tumpson Molina
Urban Empires by Edward Glaeser, Karima Kourtit and Peter Nijkamp
Experiencing Cities, 4th edition by Mark Hutter
Public Space/Contested Space, edited by Kevin D. Murphy and Sally O'Driscoll

PUBLIC SPACE/ CONTESTED SPACE

Imagination and Occupation

Edited by Kevin D. Murphy and Sally O'Driscoll

First published 2021
by Routledge
52 Vanderbilt Avenue, New York, NY 10017

and by Routledge
2 Park Square, Milton Park, Abingdon, Oxon OX14 4RN

Routledge is an imprint of the Taylor & Francis Group, an informa business

© 2021 selection and editorial matter, Kevin D. Murphy and Sally O'Driscoll;
individual chapters, the contributors

The right of Kevin D. Murphy and Sally O'Driscoll to be identified as the authors of the
editorial material, and of the authors for their individual chapters, has been asserted in
accordance with sections 77 and 78 of the Copyright, Designs and Patents Act 1988.

All rights reserved. No part of this book may be reprinted or reproduced or utilised
in any form or by any electronic, mechanical, or other means, now known or
hereafter invented, including photocopying and recording, or in any information
storage or retrieval system, without permission in writing from the publishers.

Trademark notice: Product or corporate names may be trademarks or registered trademarks,
and are used only for identification and explanation without intent to infringe.

Library of Congress Cataloging-in-Publication Data
Names: Murphy, Kevin D, editor. | O'Driscoll, Sally, editor.
Title: Public space/contested space: imagination and occupation /
edited by Kevin D Murphy and Sally O'Driscoll.
Description: 1 Edition. | New York City: Routledge, 2021. |
Series: Metropolis and modern life |
Includes bibliographical references and index.
Identifiers: LCCN 2020038321 (print) | LCCN 2020038322 (ebook) |
ISBN 9780367558123 (hardback) | ISBN 9780367558116 (paperback) |
ISBN 9781003095262 (ebook)
Subjects: LCSH: Public spaces–United States. | Community development–United States. |
Social movements–Political aspects–United States. |
City planning–Political aspects–United States.
Classification: LCC HT123.P83 2021 (print) | LCC HT123 (ebook) |
DDC 303.48/40973–dc23 LC record available at https://lccn.loc.gov/2020038321
LC ebook record available at https://lccn.loc.gov/2020038322

ISBN: 978-0-367-55812-3 (hbk)
ISBN: 978-0-367-55811-6 (pbk)
ISBN: 978-1-003-09526-2 (ebk)

Typeset in Bembo
by Newgen Publishing UK

To all those architects, activists, artists, and academics who have put their bodies in the streets and used their creative skills to reimagine a different future for public space. And to the activists of Black Lives Matter, who are challenging the boundaries of public space and public discourse as this book goes to press.

CONTENTS

List of Figures and Table	*xi*
Contributor Biographies	*xviii*

1	Introduction: Public Space/Contested Space *Kevin D. Murphy and Sally O'Driscoll*	1

SECTION 1
The Built Environment   **17**

2	Process, Product, Program: The Architect as Facilitator of Social Change *Garrett Nelli, AIA*	19
3	"The Search for New Forms": Black Power and the Making of the Postmodern City *Brian D. Goldstein*	45
4	Centro Cultural Móvil: Critical Service Learning and Design with Latinx Farmworkers *Silvina Lopez Barrera and Erin Sassin*	78
5	Inside Out: Private Space on Public Display in Modern and Contemporary Demolition Art *Kevin D. Murphy*	94

x Contents

SECTION 2
Artists and Public Space   **121**

6 Intervention: Indigo   123
   Laura Anderson Barbata

7 "No Matter Where We Move, We Look at the Same Moon":
   A Half-Century Between the Pacific and Stars   134
   Jerome Reyes and tammy ko Robinson

8 Silenced Subversions: *Critical Messages* Exhibition at
   Artemisia Gallery, Chicago (1985)   155
   Joanna Gardner-Huggett

9 International Revolution by Design: The Art of Tanya
   Aguiñiga   184
   Sheila Pepe

SECTION 3
Activists and Urban Space   **193**

10 Occupying Domesticity: Reproductive Labor in
    Zuccotti Park   195
    Susan Fraiman

11 Occupy Wall Street: Mapping a Movement   217
    Marlisa Wise

12 Tent City, USA: The Growth of America's Homeless
    Encampments and How Communities are Responding   224
    Maria Foscarinis and Eric Tars

13 Bodies in Space: A Conversation with L.A. Kauffman   241
    L.A. Kauffman with Sally O'Driscoll

Index   *261*

FIGURES AND TABLE

1.1 Property line marker on public sidewalk, Fifth Avenue and
41st Street, NYC. Courtesy of Katherine Gleason   2

2.1 El Guadual Children Center, Designed by Daniel Feldman and
Ivan Dario Quiñones, Photography by Ivan Dario Quiñones.
Courtesy of Ivan Dario Quiñones Sanchez   25

2.2 El Guadual Children Center, Designed by Daniel Feldman and
Ivan Dario Quiñones, Photography by Ivan Dario Quiñones.
Courtesy of Ivan Dario Quiñones Sanchez   26

2.3 Dreamhamar, Designed by Ecosistema Urbano, Photography by
Emilio P. Doiztua. Courtesy of Emilio P. Doiztua   28

2.4 Children Village, Designed by Aleph Zero and Rosenbaum,
Photography by Leonardo Finotti. Courtesy of Leonardo Finotti   30

2.5 Children Village, Designed by Aleph Zero and Rosenbaum,
Photography by Leonardo Finotti. Courtesy of Leonardo Finotti   32

2.6 National Memorial for Peace and Justice, Designed by MASS
Design Group, Photography by Alan Karchmer/OTTO.
Courtesy of Alan Karchmer/OTTO   33

2.7 National Memorial for Peace and Justice, Designed by MASS
Design Group, Photography by Alan Karchmer/OTTO.
Courtesy of Alan Karchmer/OTTO   34

2.8 Common-unity, Designed by Rozana Montiel Estudio de
Arquitectura, Photography by Sandra Pereznieto. Courtesy of
Sandra Pereznieto   37

2.9 Common-unity, Designed by Rozana Montiel Estudio de
Arquitectura, Photography by Sandra Pereznieto. Courtesy of
Sandra Pereznieto   38

xii List of Figures and Table

2.10 Stage, Designed by Stage Dnipro Community, Photography by Alexandr Burlaka. Courtesy of Alexandr Burlaka and Stage Dnipro Community   39

2.11 Stage, Designed by Stage Dnipro Community, Photography by Katerina Kovacheva. Courtesy Katerina Kovacheva and Stage Dnipro Community   41

3.1 Conceptual plan prepared in August 1968 by ARCH and the Community Association of the East Harlem Triangle, showing a mixture of land uses within the East Harlem Triangle neighborhood and community and social services at its "heart." Madison Avenue defines the western boundary of this diagram, while 125th Street forms its southern boundary. From ARCH, East Harlem Triangle Plan (New York: ARCH, 1968). Courtesy of Arthur L. Symes   63

3.2 ARCH's August 1968 rendering showing "Triangle Commons," the community and social service complex to be located at the center of the East Harlem Triangle neighborhood. Planners envisioned its plaza as a vibrant public space that maintained Harlem's civic life. From ARCH, East Harlem Triangle Plan. Drawing by E. Donald Van Purnell. Courtesy of Arthur L. Symes   64

3.3 Rendering showing residents on the plaza intended for the cleared gymnasium site in Morningside Park. The image, from September 1968, suggests ARCH and WHCO's vision of this as an inclusive space welcoming of all Harlemites and supportive of the era's radical politics. Signage includes the advice, "Read Muhammed Speaks" and "Support Black Panthers." From ARCH and WHCO, West Harlem Morningside: A Community Proposal (New York: ARCH and WHCO, 1968), 34. Drawing by E. Donald Van Purnell. Courtesy of Arthur L. Symes   65

3.4 ARCH's rendering of 125th Street, from its East Harlem Triangle Plan completed in August 1968. ARCH used the same drawing to represent Eighth Avenue in its West Harlem Morningside plan of the same year, suggesting this as an ideal type symbolizing the organization's vision for Harlem's major boulevards. Eclectic buildings align to define a public realm in which residents gather, converse, and display symbols of the Black Power Movement. Drawing by E. Donald Van Purnell. Courtesy of Arthur L. Symes   66

3.5 By the late 20th century, new development in Harlem typically retained, repaired, or sensitively replaced the neighborhood's built fabric, but the residents of such housing were increasingly affluent. Pictured here are two examples, both on West 131st Street: a rehabilitated building completed in 1993 (left) and Harlem Sol, a privately developed condominium involving restoration of a historic

List of Figures and Table **xiii**

brownstone and contextual new construction, completed in 2011 (right). Photographs by author. Courtesy of Brian Goldstein 70

4.1 Participatory design process diagram. Author: Silvina Lopez Barrera. Courtesy of the author 88

4.2 Storyboards produced in participatory design meetings. Photograph by Silvina Lopez Barrera and Oliver Oglesby. Courtesy of the photographers 88

4.3 Drawing by Shan Zeng, Yihao (Lyra) Ding, and Zihan (Selena) Ling. Courtesy of the artists 89

5.1 Eugène Atget, *Maison. Vue en perspective du percement de la rue Domat, Paris 05*, 1900. Photograph, Ministère de la Culture (France) 97

5.2 John Marin, Woolworth Building (The Dance), 1913, plate: 12 13/16 × 10½ in, sheet: 17 15/16 × 13 7/16 in © Estate of John Marin/ Artist Rights Society (ARS), New York. Courtesy of Philadelphia Museum of Art, The Alfred Stieglitz Collection, 1949, 1949-18-28 99

5.3 Childe Hassam, *The Hovel and the Skyscraper*, 1904. Oil on canvas, 34¾ × 31 in. Courtesy of the Pennsylvania Academy of the Fine Arts, Philadelphia. The Vivian O. and Meyer P. Potamkin Collection, Bequest of Vivian O. Potamkin. Acc. No.: 2003.1.5 100

5.4 Dox Thrash, Demolition, c. 1944. Oil on canvas board, 26 × 20 in. Courtesy of the Philadelphia Museum of Art, Purchased with the Katharine Levin Farrell Fund, 2002. 2002-97-1 101

5.5 Gordon Matta-Clark, *Conical Intersect 3 (documentation of the action 'Conical Intersect' made in 1975 in Paris, France)*, 1975, printed 1977. Gelatin silver print. Sheet: 10 x 8 in.; image: 9¾ x 6 15/16 in. Gift of Harold Berg. Inv. N.: 2017.128. New York, Whitney Museum of American Art. © Digital image Whitney Museum of Art/Licensed by Scala © Photograph SCALA, Florence 105

5.6 Rachel Whiteread, *Ghost*, 1990 © Rachel Whiteread. Courtesy of the artist, Luhring Augustine, New York, Galleria Lorcan O'Neill, Rome, and Gagosian Gallery 108

5.7 Rachel Whiteread, *House*, 1993 © Rachel Whiteread. Courtesy of the artist, Luhring Augustine, New York, Galleria Lorcan O'Neill, Rome, and Gagosian Gallery 109

5.8 George Shaw, *The End of Care*, 2013. Humbrol enamel on board 36 × 47 in. Courtesy of the artist and Anthony Wilkinson Gallery, London 114

5.9 Zhang Dali, *Demolition, Forbidden City*, 1998. Chromogenic color print. Denver Art Museum, Gift from Vicki and Kent Logan to the Collection of the Denver Art Museum, 2015.659. © Zhang Dali. Photography courtesy Denver Art Museum 116

6.1 Indigo Queen, Intervention: Indigo, Bushwick, New York, 2015. Photograph courtesy of Rene Cervantes 124

xiv List of Figures and Table

6.2 The Brooklyn Jumbies, *Intervention: Indigo*, Bushwick, New York, 2015. Photograph courtesy of Rene Cervantes   125

6.3 Little Jaguar, portrayed by Laura Anderson Barbata. *Intervention: Indigo*, Bushwick, New York, 2015. Photograph courtesy of Rene Cervantes   126

6.4 *Intervención: Índigo*, Mexico City, 2020. Photograph courtesy of Erik Tlaseca   127

6.5 Indigo King portrayed by Najja Codrington, and Los Diablos de la Costa de Guerrero portrayed by Jarana Beat. *Intervention: Indigo*, Bushwick, New York, 2015. Photograph courtesy of Rene Cervantes   128

6.6 Indigo Angel portrayed by Ali Sylvester, and Indigo King portrayed by Najja Codrington. *Intervention: Indigo*, Bushwick, New York, 2015. Photograph courtesy of Rene Cervantes   129

6.7 Rolling Calf portrayed by Chris Walker. Photograph courtesy of Rene Cervantes   130

6.8 The Brooklyn Jumbies and Laura Anderson Barbata. *Intervention: Wall Street, New York*. Photograph courtesy of Frank Veronsky   132

6.9 Rolling Calf portrayed by Chris Walker, and Los Diablos de la Costa Chica, Los Rebeldes de El Capricho. Intervención: Índigo, Mexico City, 2020. Photograph courtesy of Erik Tlaseca   133

7.1 Jerome Reyes, *Abeyance (Draves y Robles y Vargas)*, 2017. Yerba Buena Center for the Arts. Photograph courtesy of Jeremy Keith Villaluz   135

7.2 Daniel Phil Gonzales in San Francisco, Commercial Street and Leidesdorff Alley. 1971. Photograph courtesy of Linda Palaby Gonzales   136

7.3 Protesters linking arms in front of the International Hotel at 848 Kearny Street near Jackson Street in San Francisco, California on August 4, 1977. Photograph by Nancy Wong. Courtesy of Creative Commons   137

7.4 Installation image of exhibition *Contact Points: Field Notes Towards Freedom*, 2006–2016. Courtesy of tammy ko Robinson and Jerome Reyes   138

7.5 *Routes and Seasons (After Carlos Villa's quilt of hope)*, 2010. Cast fedora made of International Hotel brick debris, fedora bird feather made with brick dust (accumulated from transporting and protecting the last remaining ton of I-Hotel bricks, as a promise to the activists not to break any of them), raw wood table designed from tenant interviews, 2,005 bird feathers covered in brick dust. 8 × 8 ft (floor), 30 × 20 × 24 in (table) 9 × 7 × 7 in (hat). Courtesy of Jerome Reyes   141

7.6 *Analgesia (and Armament)*, 2009. High definition video 8 × 6 ft floor projection, 4 min. 45 sec. Courtesy of Jerome Reyes   141

7.7	Dr. Estella Habal during video shoot. Courtesy of Jerome Reyes	142
7.8	Jerome Reyes in collaboration with Alexa Drapiza. Russ Street, 2016 (excerpt). Audio file and sound installation on front steps of 50 Russ Street, South of Market San Francisco. Courtesy of Jerome Reyes	146
7.9	2017 Formal ribbon cutting ceremony with (left to right) Jerold Yu, Mary Claire Amable, Alexa A. Drapiza, Philip Maverick Rostrata Ruiz, Raymond Castillo, Tony Robles, Dr. Estella Habal, Daniel Phil Gonzales JD and project curator Katya Min at Yerba Buena Center for the Arts. Courtesy of Jerome Reyes	148
7.10	*The horizon toward which we move always recedes before us*, 2018–ongoing. Drafting ink, corrective fluid, sprayed housepaint, painter's tape on vellum, 21.5 × 34 in. Courtesy of Jerome Reyes	151
8.1	Barbara Jo Revelle, *How to Look at Women*, *Critical Messages* exhibition, Artemisia Gallery, 1985. Elevated train platform billboard, 46 × 30 in. Courtesy of Barbara Jo Revelle	160
8.2	Rebecca Michaels, Untitled, *Critical Messages* exhibition, Artemisia Gallery, 1985. Bus ad placard, 11 × 28 in. Courtesy of Rebecca Michaels	161
8.3	Kay Rosen, Untitled, *Critical Messages* exhibition, Artemisia Gallery, 1985. Bus ad placard, 11 × 28 in. Courtesy of Kay Rosen	161
8.4	Jenny Holzer, *Survival: UNEX sign*, 1984. Electronic sign. 30.5 × 113.5 × 12 in.; 77.5 × 288.3 × 30.5 cm. Text: *Survival*, 1983–1985 © 2020 Jenny Holzer, member Artists Rights Society (ARS), New York	162
8.5	Sheila Pinkel, "Fear is Our Gross National Product" from the *Thermonuclear Garden* series (1982–1991). Elevated train platform billboard, 46 × 30 in. *Critical Messages* exhibition, Artemisia Gallery, 1985. Courtesy of Sheila Pinkel	163
8.6	Silvia Malagrino, "A Rain of Ruins" from the series *A Bomb Desert*, 1982. Silver print photograph, 20 × 24 in. Elevated train platform billboard, 46 × 30 in., *Critical Messages* exhibition, Artemisia Gallery, 1985. Courtesy of Silvia Malagrino	164
8.7	Ilona Granet, Untitled (Dear Men, While on the streets … Maintain 5 feet of distance), 1985. Hand-painted sign, collection of Barry Holden. Photograph by Barry Holden. Courtesy of Ilona Granet	165
8.8	Installation photograph of Anne Turyn, *Critical Messages: Life Story*, 1985. Bus placard, 11 × 28 in., *Critical Messages* exhibition, Artemisia Gallery, 1985. © Anne Turyn. Photograph courtesy of Artemisia Gallery Fund. Courtesy of Anne Turyn	165
8.9	Nancy Bless, *Manifestation at 12th and Vine*, c. 1982. Elevated train platform billboard, 46 × 30 in., *Critical Messages* exhibition, Artemisia Gallery, 1985. Courtesy of Nancy Bless	166

xvi List of Figures and Table

8.10 *SisterSerpents, For All You Folks Who Consider a Fetus*, 1989. Poster, 23⅙ × 18⅞ in. Courtesy of Loyola University Chicago, Women and Leadership Archives, SisterSerpents Records   174

8.11 Unleash the Fury of Women as a Mighty Force for Revolution, Women's March, Chicago, January 20, 2018. Banner. Photograph courtesy of Joanna Gardner-Huggett   177

8.12 *SisterSerpents, Piss on Passivity, Piss on Patriarchy*, 1992. Banner. Courtesy of Loyola University Chicago, Women and Leadership Archives, SisterSerpents Records   177

9.1 *Border Quipu / Quipu Fronterizo* (AMBOS Project). Commuter participant postcard. Courtesy of AMBOS Project   185

9.2 *Border Quipu / Quipu Fronterizo* (AMBOS Project), 2016. Commuter participation documentation at the San Ysidro Port of Entry. Photograph by Gina Clyne. Courtesy of AMBOS Project   186

9.3 *Border Quipu / Quipu Fronterizo* (AMBOS Project), 2016. Commuter participation documentation at the San Ysidro Port of Entry. Photograph by Gina Clyne. Courtesy of AMBOS Project   187

9.4 *Border Quipu / Quipu Fronterizo* (AMBOS Project), 2016. Installation of quipu on billboard at the San Ysidro Port of Entry market. Photograph by Gina Clyne. Courtesy of AMBOS Project   190

9.5 *Tension* (AMBOS Project), 2017. Performed by Tanya Aguiniga and Jackie Amezquita at the Douglas, Arizona/Agua Prieta, Sonora in constant view of the US Border Patrol. Photograph by Gina Clyne. Courtesy of AMBOS Project   191

11.1 Benedict Clouette and Marlisa Wise. Map 1: OWS in Lower Manhattan   219

11.2 Benedict Clouette and Marlisa Wise. Map 2: OWS in New York City   220

12.1 Tent City, USA: The Growth of America's Homeless Encampments and How Communities are Responding. Report by National Law Center on Homelessness and Poverty, 2017. Image courtesy of the National Law Center on Homelessness and Poverty   225

12.2 "The number of homeless encampments reported by the media has increased by 1,342% in the last ten years … but two-thirds of this growth came after the Recession of 2007–2012 was declared over." Graphic included in the "Tent City, USA" report by the National Law Center on Homelessness and Poverty, 2017. Image courtesy of the National Law Center on Homelessness and Poverty   227

12.3 "Total Encampments Reported" graph published in the "Tent City, USA" report by the National Law Center on Homelessness and Poverty, 2017. Image courtesy of the National Law Center on Homelessness and Poverty   228

List of Figures and Table **xvii**

12.4 "Many Cities are Failing to Protect Encampment Residents" info-graphic published in the "Tent City, USA" report by the National Law Center on Homelessness and Poverty, 2017. Image courtesy of the National Law Center on Homelessness and Poverty 229

12.5 Homeless encampment by the Arroyo Seco, South Pasadena CA, almost entirely abandoned following a sweep by police. Photograph by Levi Clancy, September 25, 2012. Image courtesy of the photographer 231

12.6 "Percent of Homeless Population With and Without Available Shelter Beds," graph published in the "Tent City, USA" report by the National Law Center on Homelessness and Poverty, 2017. Image courtesy of the National Law Center on Homelessness and Poverty 232

12.7 Notice of Violation at the Arroyo Seco Homeless Encampment. Photograph by Levi Clancy, September 25, 2012. Image courtesy of the photographer 234

12.8 Quotation from Martin v. Boise, 9th Cir. (September 4, 2018) Decision. Image courtesy of the National Law Center on Homelessness and Poverty 237

13.1 Panoramic view of the January 2017 Women's March in Washington, DC, one of the largest demonstrations in US history. Photograph by L.A. Kauffman. Courtesy of L.A. Kauffman 242

13.2 The most important impact of the Women's Marches of 2017 was how they inspired participants to take up other kinds of organizing work afterwards. Photograph by L.A. Kauffman. Courtesy of L.A. Kauffman 245

Table

4.1 Hispanic Population by County in Vermont, 2000–2018 80

CONTRIBUTOR BIOGRAPHIES

Laura Anderson Barbata was born in Mexico City, and works in Brooklyn and Mexico City. She has initiated projects in the Amazon of Venezuela, Trinidad and Tobago, Mexico, Norway, and the US. Her drawings, photographs, and projects have received awards from the Institute of Bellas Artes FONCA, the Lindbergh Foundation, the Carnival Commission of Trinidad and Tobago, and the New York Foundation for the Arts. Her work is included in many private and public collections. She has been featured in *The New York Times*, *Sculpture Today*, *Kunstforum* Germany, *ARTnews*, *Art in America*, *ArtNexus*, and *160 Años de Fotografía en México-INBA*, among others.

Silvina Lopez Barrera is Assistant Professor in the School of Architecture at Mississippi State University. She is a licensed architect in Uruguay, and holds a Master of Architecture degree from Iowa State University. Her research is at the intersection of architecture, urban studies, and spatial justice. Professor Lopez Barrera's current academic interests include informal urbanism and housing inequality, public interest design and participatory design to develop sustainable alternatives for rural-urban communities and food systems, and transnationalism (particularly in creating connections between Latin America and the US). She is a member of the Uruguayan Society of Architects and an associate member of the American Institute of Architects.

Maria Foscarinis is founder and Executive Director of the National Homelessness Law Center, previously known as the National Law Center on Homelessness and Poverty, a not-for-profit organization based in Washington, DC, and the only national organization dedicated to using the power of the law to end homelessness in America. Foscarinis has advocated for solutions to homelessness at the national level since 1985, when she left her career at a major law firm to become an advocate for homeless people. She is a primary architect of the McKinney-Vento Act, the first major federal legislation addressing homelessness, and has led successful litigation to secure the legal rights of homeless persons. Foscarinis has published dozens of articles, book chapters, and opinion pieces; speaks regularly about legal and policy issues affecting homeless and poor persons; and is frequently quoted in national and local media. Foscarinis is the recipient of the 2006 Public Interest Achievement Award from the Public Interest Law Foundation at Columbia Law School and the 2016 Katharine and George Alexander Law Prize from Santa Clara University's School of Law.

Susan Fraiman is Professor of English at the University of Virginia. Her primary interest is in the politics of gender and sexuality. Notable articles include "Jane Austen and Edward Said: Gender, Culture, and Imperialism" (1995) and "Pussy Panic versus Liking Animals: Tracking Gender in Animal Studies" (2012), both in *Critical Inquiry*. She writes frequently about Austen and is editor of the Norton Critical *Northanger Abbey* (2004). Her most recent book, *Extreme Domesticity: A View from the Margins* (Columbia University Press, 2017), takes up accounts of unorthodox homemakers (queer, feminist, immigrant, working-class, homeless). Two of its key goals are reiterated by her essay in this volume: to make visible and value the work of reproducing daily life; to recognize forms of domestic labor tied to progressive rather than conservative ideologies. As an academic committed to activism, she was honored by the chance occasioned by this essay to interview some founding members of the Occupy Wall Street movement.

Joanna Gardner-Huggett is Associate Professor and Chair of History of Art and Architecture at DePaul University, where she teaches courses on 20th-century art and feminist theory. Gardner-Huggett's research focuses on the intersection between feminism and arts activism and has been published in the journals *Artl@s Bulletin, British Art Journal, Frontiers: A Journal of Women's Studies, Historical Geography*, and *Woman's Art Journal*. Her most recent scholarship explores the history of the Guerrilla Girls, the Feminist Art Workers, and the origins of the women artists' cooperatives Artemisia Gallery in Chicago (1973–2003) and ARC (1973–present).

Brian Goldstein is a historian of the American built environment and Assistant Professor at Swarthmore College. Previously, he was Assistant Professor in the School of Architecture and Planning at the University of New Mexico and an Andrew W. Mellon Postdoctoral Fellow in the Center for the Humanities and the Department of History at the University of Wisconsin-Madison. He received his PhD from Harvard University in 2013. Goldstein is the author of *The Roots of Urban Renaissance: Gentrification and the Struggle Over Harlem* (Harvard University Press, 2017).

xx Contributor Biographies

L.A. Kauffman has been an activist for more than 35 years, and has been involved in organizing some of the largest public protests ever held in the US, such as the New York protest against the Iraq War in 2003 (which drew an estimated one million people) and the 2004 protest at the Republican Convention in New York. Her two recent books offer detailed historical accounts of protests in the US: *Direct Action: Protest and the Reinvention of American Radicalism* (2017) and *How to Read a Protest* (2018).

Kevin D. Murphy is Andrew W. Mellon Chair in the Humanities and Professor and Chair of the Department of History of Art at Vanderbilt University. Previously, he was on the faculty of the CUNY Graduate Center and the University of Virginia School of Architecture. Murphy is the author of several books and articles and co-editor with Sally O'Driscoll of *Studies in Ephemera: Text and Image in Eighteenth-Century Print* (Bucknell University Press, 2013).

Garrett Nelli, AIA, LEED AP BD+C, is a practicing architect based in Seattle, WA, whose passion exists at the intersection of architecture, sociology, and activism. With an emphasis on articulating spaces that promote social cohesion and empowerment, Garrett believes architects have the potential and responsibility to address the broader issues of a global society through thoughtful community-engaged design solutions. He has worked on the design of an Infant Rescue Center in Burkina Faso, in collaboration with Architects Without Borders-Seattle; a design-build led by the University of Tennessee addressing the lack of clean drinking water in rural Appalachia; and several public works throughout Seattle that have led to state and national recognition. Nelli's independent research into the emergence of public interest design was awarded the *2017 AIA Seattle Emerging Professionals Travel Scholarship,* which allowed him to catalog the societal influence of international community-based architectural projects. His research findings titled "In the Public Interest: Redefining the Architect's Role and Responsibility" have been exhibited in Seattle and Boston.

Sally O'Driscoll is Professor of English and Women's, Gender, and Sexuality Studies at Fairfield University. Her work on 18th-century literature and culture has appeared in such journals as *Signs, Tulsa Studies in Women's Literature,* and *Eighteenth-Century: Theory and Interpretation.* She is co-editor with Kevin D. Murphy of *Studies in Ephemera: Text and Image in Eighteenth-Century Print* (Bucknell University Press, 2013).

Sheila Pepe is an artist and educator known for her large-scale, ephemeral installations and sculptures made from domestic and industrial materials. For over 20 years, she has used lesbian feminist and craft traditions to counter systems of power in institutions of art and education. Because Pepe's works are often site-dependent, there is a critical relationship to traditional boundaries of

Contributor Biographies   **xxi**

museum display that is essential to her sculptural practice. Pepe has exhibited widely throughout the United States and abroad in solo and group exhibitions. Venues include the MoMA PS1, the Weatherspoon Art Museum, Chapel Hill, and OCAT, Shenzhen, for the 8th Sculpture Biennale. Her mid-career retrospective, *Hot Mess Formalism*, originated at the Phoenix Art Museum and traveled to the Everson Museum of Art and the Bemis Center for Contemporary Arts, and the DeCordova Sculpture Park and Museum through spring 2019. Pepe has taught since 1995 at a variety of universities including Bard, Columbia, RISD, VCU, Williams College, and Yale.

Jerome Reyes, who lives and works between Seoul, Korea, and his native San Francisco, is an artist, researcher, and educator who addresses ideas of architecture, public space, and cultural difference. He is on the faculty at Stanford University's Institute for Diversity in the Arts. He has an MFA from Stanford University and has made projects for the Prospect.3 Biennial, San Francisco Museum of Modern Art and Yerba Buena Center for the Arts. He has been awarded residencies at the National Museum for Modern and Contemporary Art, Korea, Gwangju Biennale Foundation, Asia Culture Center, Seoul Museum of Art, and he received the 2016 Artist-in-Residence Award at the Yerba Buena Center for the Arts. He has received support from the National Endowment for the Arts and awards from the Joan Mitchell Foundation, Art Matters Foundation, Creative Work Fund, and Center for Cultural Innovation. Recent projects include Asia Art Archive, Hong Kong, KADIST, and upcoming artist publication with Ala Ebtekar for the Third Line in Dubai, UAE.

tammy ko Robinson is an artist-researcher based in Seoul. Her body of work explores decoloniality and the stewardship of airwaves, land, and water through videos, installations, and archive creation. ko Robinson's works have been exhibited at ArtSonje, Bongsan Art Center, Kukje Gallery, San Francisco Museum of Modern Art, and the Seoul Museum of Art, among others. Her writings have been published in *The Hankyoreh, Pressian, SPACE Magazine, Asia-Pacific Journal, ArtAsiaPacific, KoreAm, Flash Art*, and *InSEA*. Formerly faculty of the School of the Art Institute Chicago and the San Francisco Art Institute, she now serves as an Associate Professor at Hanyang University where she teaches cinema and new media.

Erin Sassin is Assistant Professor of History of Art and Architecture at Middlebury College. She received her PhD in the History of Architecture from Brown University in 2012. Her research is closely linked to her teaching interests: she has published articles on the public/private world of middle-class women in the German Empire and the intersection of architecture, power, and ethnicity in Upper Silesia. Her book, *Single People and Mass Housing in Germany and Beyond (1850–1930): (No) Home Away from Home,* is forthcoming from Bloomsbury

xxii Contributor Biographies

Academic Press in 2020. Awarded a 2019 fellowship from the Graham Foundation for Advanced Studies in the Fine Arts, it is the first complete study of single-person mass housing in Germany and the pivotal role this class- and gender-specific building type played for pre-war German architectural culture and society, the transnational Progressive reform movement, and architectural Modernism in the 1920s, as well as its continued relevance. She has presented her research at CAA, GSA, SAH, and VAF, among other forums.

Eric Tars is Legal Director at the National Homelessness Law Center, previously known as the National Law Center on Homelessness and Poverty. He received his JD magna cum laude as a Global Law Scholar at the Georgetown University Law Center. He received his BA magna cum laude in political science from Haverford College and studied international human rights in Vienna at the Institute for European Studies and at the University of Vienna. Tars also teaches human rights advocacy as an adjunct professor at Drexel University Kline School of Law.

Marlisa Wise is an architect and writer whose work focuses on the social effects of design. As co-founder of the collaborative Interval Projects, she has worked as an architect in post-disaster and post-conflict situations. Her work has been published by *Domus*, *Volume*, *San Rocco*, and *The New York Times*, among others. Since 2011, she has been a faculty member at Parsons, the New School for Design. She is a graduate of Columbia University and Brown University.

INTRODUCTION

Public Space/Contested Space

Kevin D. Murphy and Sally O'Driscoll

Public space is fragile: it is a delicate bubble being pressed in on from all sides. Just how vulnerable public space is to being appropriated by private entities has become increasingly evident in the West since the 1980s. Powerful forces constantly try to fill public space with private enterprises, to repurpose it, to limit its possibilities (see Figure 1.1); defenders of the space push back from the inside. Public space is not static, but exists as a delicate equilibrium, balanced between two dynamic tensions that move in different directions: one outward, one inward. Once we understand this, we see why it is a contested space, one worth fighting over. If there is no pushback from its center, then public space will disappear. What will be lost with it? Our suspicion is that the disappearance of public space will lead to a disastrous decline in public life in Western democracies and, in particular, the withering of resistance to government and corporate power. Thus, we ask: how best to maintain the boundaries of the bubble? That is the fundamental question to which the essays in this book offer some exploratory responses.

The authors assembled here – architects, activists, artists, and academics – all respond to spatial circumstances brought about by neoliberal policies in the industrialized, capitalist West (see Harvey 2005). Neoliberalism, as David Harvey emphasizes, was a program put in place by corporate elites to support their interests over those of organized labor in the late 1970s and early 1980s:

> Overall I think this period was defined by a broad movement across many fronts, ideological and political. And the only way you can explain that broad movement is by recognizing the relatively high degree of solidarity in the corporate capitalist class. Capital reorganized its power in a desperate attempt to recover its economic wealth and its influence, which had been seriously eroded from the end of the 1960s into the 1970s.
>
> *(Harvey 2016)*

2 Kevin D. Murphy and Sally O'Driscoll

FIGURE 1.1 Property line marker on public sidewalk, Fifth Avenue and 41st Street, NYC. Courtesy of Katherine Gleason

In this context, public space – particularly public *urban* space – was increasingly privatized to enhance profit-making by corporations; where it remained ostensibly accessible, it was increasingly policed to prevent uses that had the potential to disrupt commerce. The heavy-handed neoliberal control over physical space exerted by Western governments on behalf of powerful economic interests creates a situation in which the disenfranchised are forced to attempt to wrest back control over public space, ideally to control it, but at least to preserve its use by a broad range of constituents.

Although neoliberal policies have been put in place by governments throughout the West, notably in Great Britain under Prime Minister Margaret Thatcher (1979–1990) and in the US under President Ronald Reagan (1981–1989), this book focuses primarily on the situation in the United States from the 1990s through the early 2000s. Yet, looking at issues around public space in the US necessarily entails consideration of the other nations with which it shares a continent: Canada and Mexico. The southern border, in particular, has become a politically and socially contested space as an especially heated discourse around immigration has emerged during the presidency of Donald Trump. At the same time, many of the artists and architects who are considered in this book operate on an international, and even global, stage. Thus, the book frequently looks beyond North America to spatial politics elsewhere in the world. The works of art, architectural projects, and other interventions in public space that are treated in this volume collectively express a broadly felt need to rethink contemporary cities from many angles. As Toni L. Griffin, Ariella Cohen, and David Maddox write:

> Over the past decade, there have been numerous conversations about the "livable city," "green city," "sustainable city" and, most recently, the "resilient city." At the same time, today's headlines – from Ferguson to Baltimore, Paris to Johannesburg – resound with the need for frank dialogue about the structures and processes that affect the quality of life and livelihoods of urban residents. Issues of equity, inclusion, race, access, and ownership remain unresolved in many communities around the world, even as we begin to address the challenges of affordability, climate change adaptation and resilience.
>
> *(Griffin, Cohen, and Maddox 2015, 4)*

All of these urban issues are critical at this moment; the sheer access to public space is central – a fact that was driven home in early summer 2020 when the administration of President Trump attempted to use the US military to prevent legal and peaceful demonstrations for racial justice across the country and especially in the capital.

The importance of the struggle for public space derives from the fact that space is not only materially crucial, but also symbolically important. Resistance takes many forms, as the following essays demonstrate, from buildings to mass demonstrations to small-scale, isolated art projects. Their means can be simple or complex; some projects require massive mobilization of resources, others are improvised with minimal investment. Some forms of resistance aim to restructure access to public space and permanently safeguard accessibility on behalf of disenfranchised populations; other interventions are temporary and serve mainly to raise awareness of the ways that ostensibly available public spaces are in fact policed, surveilled, or are made off limits to certain groups (Peterson 2006, 356–359). Restricting access to public space imposes a particular hardship on the disenfranchised, for whom Saskia Sassen argues the "global street" is their only political outlet: "By *global street*, I mean a space not only for making claims but also for making the social and the political by those who lack access to formal instruments of power" (Sassen 2012, 68).

It is well understood by now that all space is a construction, and is also constructive: it is defined by social relations and defines social relations. Further, "spaces have political effects, and politics have spatial effects" (Wendel 2015, 11). The concept of public space, though, is loaded with the especially heavy weight of meaning carried by the word *public*: that word holds the promise of democracy, freedom from control, and popular rights, and thus the contest over how to use and inhabit public space is the external sign of a struggle to the death over those fundamental issues. Even when the argument seems to be about a purportedly practical issue such as keeping streets free of homeless people, or obtaining police permits to hold a protest march, the contest over public space is always, fundamentally, about the rights of all people to be present in such spaces. Given the degree to which, with neoliberalism, governments work to defend private property interests, struggles over space often pit the rights of the people against the rights of the government. Spatial contests are about power in the public sphere.[1]

The sheer fact of being able to occupy or control public space holds deep symbolic significance; having the right to be present and visible in public is tantamount to being recognized as a person. Conversely, being excluded from public space, being made invisible, means being robbed of one's personhood and value. The symbolic meaning of space needs to be interrogated in its nuance and complexity; there are multiple layers of meaning that must be teased out. Doing so is important because our public spaces – be they village greens or urban squares, streets or parks – remain crucial venues for expressing the presence of individuals or groups whose very existence threatens dominant ideologies. There is nothing so powerful as publicly expressing – on a street or in a park – one's "difference" in solidarity with others, however much online communities can facilitate alliances that would not have been possible before the Digital Age. For instance, Mark Robbins describes a 1996 art installation in Adelaide, Australia, *TellTale*, that marked an area along the banks of the River Torrens as a long-established gay cruising ground. Robbins argues that despite apps that now bring gay men (and other groups) together, the constitution of communities in space, and the representation of their presence, remains significant: "Asserting one's presence in a public sphere (whether virtual or actual) continues despite predictions of its demise, and electronic devices provide yet another tool to locate oneself among others" (Robbins 2018, 261).

It is important to point out that public space is real rather than virtual. The metaphorical use of the term *space* has almost overwhelmed its original meaning, especially as information science and computing have seized upon spatial metaphors, as in "information space" and "cyberspace" (Coyne 1999, 165). Furthermore, there is a current casual assumption that the Internet provides a virtual public space, available to all. This misperception gives the ongoing war about public space a particular urgency at this moment. In fact, the space of the Internet turns out to be strictly mediated and controlled; Saskia Sassen observes that

> Thus while in principle many of the key features of the Internet do indeed have the capacity to enhance democracy, its openness and its technology also contain possibilities for significant indirect control and limitations on access, including once inside the Internet. Furthermore, a large share of electronic networks are private and inaccessible to non-members, among which wholesale financial electronic networks are perhaps the most significant example. There are, then, limitations on what many have considered the inherently democratic character of digital networks.[2]

Even in instances where Internet communication assists in mobilizing action in the material realm, or where local activists use the digital to place their struggles in global context,[3] virtual space has *not* replaced actual three-dimensional public space, whose importance continues to be vital. One of the things the essays in this collection address is the unique nature of what happens when actual physical bodies are mobilized in actual physical space. The boundaries of the hard space (architecture) matter; they define how the space is physically shaped. In that real space, communities are formed, in a way that is fundamentally different from how they are established on the Internet. As L.A. Kauffman says in her contribution here, the point about putting bodies in space is to hold open the space of dissent; and although the Internet is a useful tool for communication, as a way to help get bodies to go to the space, it is only the physical space that has this power – the power to protect the boundaries around the space for dissent.

However much virtual communities have become critical to political life around the world – from the so-called "Twitter Revolution" and "Facebook Revolution" to grassroots fundraising for American political campaigns – politicians and activists across the ideological spectrum continue to believe in the power of bodies in space. For instance, while the Women's March in January 2017 was extremely important for leftists to participate in following the inauguration of Donald Trump, the newly elected US president continued to argue with record keepers, among them the government's own National Park Service, about the number of people who attended his inauguration on the National Mall in Washington, DC. He has continued to insist, despite ample evidence to the contrary, that it was the largest crowd assembled to witness an inauguration, ever. Trump and his associates went so far as to pressure a government photographer to crop out empty space in the inauguration photographs "where the crowd ended" to make it seem larger, as *The Guardian* and other newspapers later reported.[4] There is no doubt that Trump has a substantial number of supporters nationwide, but their physical representation in the space of the Mall holds a symbolic significance for the president that is far out of proportion to its actual political importance.

In Western democracies, there is an ideology about public space and its relationship to democracy: such space has been ideologically freighted with the notion that all citizens enjoy free access to it. It serves as a spatial marker for a set of freedoms that citizens of democratic states believe they enjoy: the freedom to walk wherever they wish, to go about their business in the pursuit of happiness, to make autonomous choices about what they do in their lives. The belief that one has access to such freedom becomes paradoxically stronger as one is forced to trade away the reality: in the contemporary West, we have little choice but to submit to surveillance and control, while stridently insisting that we remain free; instead, we internalize the outside forces that pen us in.

Thus the ideology of the freedom of public space is in an important sense a myth: in reality, in the direct sense, public space is always controlled through a variety of mechanisms, from the police force to "public-private partnerships" that

6 Kevin D. Murphy and Sally O'Driscoll

give corporations control over ostensibly public spaces; most public space is also now under constant electronic surveillance. Ingrid Burrington's experience in New York could doubtless be replicated in many other cities:

> I go for a walk literally anywhere in the city. In the span of about three city blocks I can usually figure out where there's buried fiber optic cable (and, sometimes, who owns that cable), which devices hanging above traffic intersections are talking to one another, how many cell towers are in the area, and whether I'm currently under surveillance (by the NYPD or a private observer).
>
> *(Burrington 2016, n.p)*

Indirectly, government control over the citizenry is strong, and we have less and less autonomy over our own lives.

The gap between the mythic symbolic ideology and the material reality of public space needs to be examined, since it makes the space itself even more important. Paradoxically, the ideology of freedom, no longer linked to a real, existing public space that truly belongs to the people, takes on even more cultural power as its existence is less rooted in reality. While neoliberal thought purportedly espouses freedom – for markets, for corporations, and from government control – in fact, the state operates in support of such private entities. Occupying public space means taking possession of that which is, ostensibly, the property of the people. In fact, however, access to public space is tightly controlled and never uncontested.

The fact that political struggle takes place in physical spaces is so obvious as to hardly need stating. Especially in the modern period, taking to the streets and controlling public space – both outdoor places like New York's Liberty Plaza Park (now called Zuccotti Park), "occupied" in 2011, or the university administration buildings taken over by student movements in the 1960s – have been the means by which political change has mostly happened. Yet it is important to remember that space can be reappropriated, and that in doing so activists can hope to deter domination by the state and its allies. Doing so is especially significant given that we have become attuned, by Michel Foucault and other poststructuralist critics, to the ways that architectural and urban space have been instrumentalized by governments and capitalists since the 18th century to produce docile bodies.[5]

The work of the leading urban theorists of our time, including Edward W. Soja, David Harvey, and Richard Sennett, provides the conceptual means to understand the politics of urban space in the contemporary situation. For example, Soja's *Seeking Spatial Justice* (2010) theorizes the relationship between urban space and social justice in the context of contemporary Los Angeles. Sennett's *Building and Dwelling: Ethics for the City* (2018) diagnoses the economic policies that have produced highly controlled cities in which non-elites struggle for spaces in which to express dissent or even to live.

The impact of neoliberal policies on urban space has been addressed more directly by David Harvey than by any other scholar. His writing on the "right to the city" has inspired our own work (Harvey 2012; Erdi and Şentürk 2017). The Occupy movement, which is a major focus of several contributions to this volume, remains an important example of how the fundamental right to express oneself in public urban space can be asserted in defiance of exclusionary policies.

In our current state of utter control over space (which is a metaphor for the general control of the state over every aspect of our lives), a whole array of strategies is devised to resist control. The battle over public space is then both a real struggle to maintain access to a real physical space, and also a metaphorical struggle in which the attempt to maintain the public-ness of public space represents resistance to government and corporate control writ large. This is where activists of all kinds take on particular significance: the artists, architects, activists, and academics who contribute to this book demonstrate creative ways to address the problem of access to public space. In a range of actions, they show how citizens can push back from inside the bubble, to maintain a fragile place of freedom for dissent. The projects they describe intervene in a variety of ways to regain control, running the gamut from attempts at institutional transformation through architectural production to ephemeral art projects.

The interventions work, on one hand, to rebuff government policies; sometimes they do this directly, by causing public outrage that reverses a policy, and sometimes less directly, by changing or opening up the discourse. On another level, they create the sensation, for the individual, of refuting the compromise we have all made. Putting bodies in space matters not only because those bodies reify the threatened boundary of public space, but also because the experience of acting in this way transforms the people who participate. It is gratifying to participate in such resistance; it is also pleasurable and satisfying, because the creative spark of radical intervention literally empowers participants who have felt crushed by the experience of constant government control. Thus, resistance begets further resistance:

> "If you look at 2017, I think it becomes an historic year of the woman," said Anita Dunn, who served as communications director for President Barack Obama. She said it began with the Women's March, where the scale of the movement showed great potential for continued engagement. "Then the year is ending on this note of women who are stepping forward, finding their voices, in many ways doing the classic 'we are mad as hell and we aren't going to take it anymore.' It's sort of a primal scream."[6]

Many women used their participation in the 2017 women's marches to move directly into political organizing, some of them for the first time.

The Women's March created an atmosphere in which a more diverse group of political leaders felt empowered to step forward. That was a nationwide sentiment

8 Kevin D. Murphy and Sally O'Driscoll

that grew out of the "microclimates" produced by the collected individuals who participated in demonstrations in public spaces throughout the United States. The concept of atmosphere is an effective way of capturing how, during the 2020 protests of police brutality spurred by the murder of George Floyd in Minneapolis, people coming together in the streets produced a political moment when repressive state institutions could be challenged. Ben Anderson observes that "atmospheres are generated by bodies – of multiple types – affecting one another as some form of 'envelopment' is produced" (Anderson 2009, 80). As bodies are enveloped in an atmosphere, it exerts an important – yet ineffable – force on society.

Action, Praxis, Representation: A Unified Approach

This book deals with people who are actually mobilizing in real space, and also people who are representing it: in other words, our book is about action, praxis (a theorizing of action), and representation of action. Some of the interventions described in these essays are about permanent change – the building of new public spaces to enhance community life. Others consider ephemeral interventions: consciousness-raising exercises that both take up space and articulate resistance. Such ephemeral interventions can be particularly significant, since they represent public space in a way that challenges government control, and can be conveyed to audiences who may not yet have understood that message. In other words, they create a narrative. This kind of representation of public space is especially meaningful; if we doubt that, we only need to consider how President Trump speaks of the US/Mexican border as a public space that he longs to privatize, rather than the backdrop for a policy on immigration; his obsession with the border focuses on it as a place with symbolic significance, a meaning that he himself wishes to define as a buffer zone of protection for pure Americans to save them from the marauding hordes of foreigners. Like his claims about the crowds on the Mall at his inauguration, Trump's rhetoric around the border conjures a heroic narrative designed to appeal to the voting public. The narrative that one can tell about public space, the way it is represented, is extraordinarily powerful. Part of the struggle over public space, then, is the struggle to claim and control the narrative, or for progressives, to make room for multiple narratives about public space. The contributors to this volume recognize and explore that phenomenon.

Public space has already received a great deal of scholarly attention; however, most of the work being done approaches the issue from the perspective of urban studies/sociology, or architecture and planning, or policy, or activism – from one perspective only. No one has yet integrated an approach that is not only interdisciplinary but also extra-academic; activists and artists have not yet been drawn fully into the conversation. Yet the battle over public space operates on many levels and in different discursive registers, and a conversation that invites different constituencies to speak to each other can explore it more effectively.

The control of public space at this moment is a consequence or manifestation of neoliberal spatial urbanism; that is the underlying economic structure against which all of these projects strain, at the same time that they all illuminate aspects of its ramifications. That restraining force often feels homogenizing, oppressive, and deadening. The sheer complexity of the mechanisms by which it operates – through land-use policies, surveillance, policing, and more – invites a creative, multi-level response.

The Essays

The essays in this collection approach all aspects of the struggle around public space: how to create it, how to use it or act in it, how to represent it, and how to protect it from predatory forces.

The essays in the first section focus on the built environment: on the act of planning and designing actual buildings, and considering how they affect the space they are placed in and the people who use them. Garrett Nelli, in "Process, Product, Program: The Architect as Facilitator of Social Change" (Chapter 2), describes what happens when an architect consciously decides to work with the people who will use a space, in order to build a hardscape that facilitates liberation rather than reinscribing inequality. Here the concept of the construction of space is both literal and theoretical – Nelli's design process enables the users of space to creatively imagine buildings that will produce a liberation that doesn't yet exist.

In "'The Search for New Forms': Black Power and the Making of the Postmodern City" (Chapter 3), Brian D. Goldstein argues that for Black Power activists in New York City in the 1960s, the challenges of urban renewal and of rehabilitating urban housing actually offered an opportunity to reimagine the future. The attempts of Harlem's residents to plan their own community, rather than have designs imposed from outside, were an expression of racial self-determination and self-reliance. Just as Nelli argues that architects who consult with those who will live in their buildings can help create a better future, Goldstein demonstrates that Black Power advocates had the same idea, but filtered through a specific racial/political lens. They tried to transform and maintain inner-city low-income neighborhoods rather than sweep them away in urban renewal plans, along with their residents and their existing community support structures. Theirs was a uto-pian vision of transforming urban public space, of allowing residents to control the areas they occupied. Goldstein argues that the Black Power ideals of urban space gained a partial victory – enough to halt the bulldozer of wholesale urban renewal, but not enough, later on, to protect the area from the onslaught of gentrification and its emptying out of utopian ideals.

As Silvina Lopez Barrera and Erin Sassin demonstrate in "*Centro Cultural Móvil*: Critical Service Learning and Design with Latinx Farmworkers" (Chapter 4), students too can learn the process of socially conscious design; their essay addresses the nitty-gritty process of engaging in dialogue with those who

10 Kevin D. Murphy and Sally O'Driscoll

will use the planned space in order to produce a meaningful design. In the project described here, Lopez Barrera and Sassin's students worked with migrant farm laborers to meet some of the needs they articulated, and created space in imaginative ways (a roaming trailer designed to serve as a social services center). However, as they demonstrate, socially conscious design cannot control the long-term consequences of making visible a population who is at legal risk. To enter into public space, to make oneself visible to those who would control it, is to take a risk – in this case, it meant to put oneself at risk of deportation.

Kevin D. Murphy's essay, "Inside Out: Private Space on Public Display in Modern and Contemporary Demolition Art" (Chapter 5), considers both the creation of public space and its representation. He begins by focusing on the increasing control government entities have taken over public space, using 19th- and 20th-century Paris as an example. He then shows how artists Gordon Matta-Clark, Rachel Whiteread, and others created artworks that showed graphically the effects of demolishing older housing to create strictly controlled new spaces: what was lost in this violent reorganization of space? By putting private space on display – the private spaces of people who were too powerless to resist government plans – these artists force viewers to contemplate the boundaries between public and private, and the powers that can create or destroy those boundaries. As spectators, we must see and acknowledge the violence involved in nonconsensual demarcation of space.

The second section of essays continues to explore the methods that artists/activists use to turn public space into an arena for what we have previously called an "ephemeral intervention" but now might label by the broader term of "engaged resistant representation" – a combination of action, praxis, and representation: action that works together with its conceptualization (praxis), and then moves on to representation.[7] Each essay digs into the details of specific places and times of interventions, and shows the relationships between the formation of community and the representation of democratic discourse.

Laura Anderson Barbata's photo essay (Chapter 6) recreates for readers the ephemeral act of a vibrant intervention, which she titled "Intervention: Indigo." This action wove together deep-rooted traditions from West Africa, Trinidad, and Mexico – the symbolic use of indigo dye, ceremonial masks worn by those charged with protecting the communities, and stilt-walkers who are also protectors. The participants formed a procession that marched through a contested area – Bushwick, Brooklyn – to draw attention to the neglect of communities of color and police violence against those same communities. In this intervention, long-standing cultural traditions are brought back and presented to the diaspora communities in the New World, to reconnect them to cultural foundations they have been cut off from by the violent history of colonization and the slave trade. Stills from the video of this intervention show a mesmerized audience of bystanders, who are drawn into the visceral meaning of the procession. "Intervention: Indigo" is a remarkable example of reclaiming the public streetspace to catalyze resistance, teach, and build community.

Jerome Reyes draws our attention to complex art projects in urban spaces in "'No Matter Where We Move, We Look at the Same Moon': A Half-Century Between the Pacific and Stars" (Chapter 7). Living and working in San Francisco, and considering its ethnic past at the very moment of rapid gentrification, Reyes and his collaborator tammy ko Robinson look minutely at the past in order to both honor and build on the power of collaborations between artists and the communities in which they live. Reyes and Robinson's work is a blueprint for engaged resistant representation: they lay out a variety of representational forms that can do the work of representing the communities they are situated in, and use that representation to create change. Billboards, radio shows, art education, public projections – all this and more are discussed in an essay that both honors the history of the community activism of people of color in the Bay Area, and recognizes the tools that artists offer to be part of that activism.

Joanna Gardner-Huggett, in "Silenced Subversions: *Critical Messages* Exhibition at Artemisia Gallery, Chicago (1985)" (Chapter 8), describes a less successful artistic intervention, from which much can still be learned: this was a failed attempt to create dialogue in public space, an attempt that was censored. In this case, an artists' collective wanted to put political art by women into the public space of the Chicago transit system. They were blocked by the CTA, who deemed the work obscene because it violated commercial norms of representation for the female body. These artist/activists were engaged in the same kind of engaged resistant representation that Reyes and Robinson describe; they put work out in public in an attempt to make visible a discourse that resists and challenges the status quo. The story of their failure is instructive in laying bare the power that pushes against the fragile bubble of public space.

Sheila Pepe's essay, "International Revolution by Design" (Chapter 9), brings us straight to a locus of intense political conflict: the border between the US and Mexico. Here, Pepe contextualizes the work of an artist who focuses on exploring the significance of that border: Tanya Aguiñiga. Aguiñiga addresses commuters caught in the snail-slow daily crossing in their cars: she draws them into conversation, and then quantifies and reifies the exchanges by creating *quipus* out of colored wool skeins attached to the commuters' postcard-size responses – the *quipu* was an indigenous Central American form of mathematical calculation, and one that when aggregated creates a colorful, tactile image of the border crossings. Through this work Aguiñiga makes visible and tangible a much more legitimate reality of the border: a place where barriers now obstruct what was once a productive exchange between countries, turning the public space of the border into a conflict zone. Her work challenges the narrative of border as combat zone and rehumanizes those who must occupy it.

In the third section of the book, the essays move in a different direction – away from the exploration and celebration of (sometimes) successful interventions that opened up public space for communities in creative and enriching ways, and toward an examination of the difficulties of rejecting long-standing oppressive forms of social organization, and the discussion of various forms of the repressive power of government. In this section, the focus is on activism: the sustained praxis of resistance.

Susan Fraiman's essay, "Occupying Domesticity" (Chapter 10), works hand in hand with Marlisa Wise's visual representation of it, "Occupy Wall Street: Mapping a Movement" (Chapter 11). Fraiman brings our attention to the way even radical movements such as Occupy Wall Street can reproduce the same gendered inequalities they purport to move beyond. What she makes visible is the infrastructure of Occupy: that infrastructure – the basic elements of life such as food, washing, and elimination – supported the occupiers and enabled them to stay. Yet its vaunted modeling of a new form of democracy actually reproduced an old, sexist model that rendered women's domestic work illegible, invisible, and unimportant. Domestic work was needed to sustain the occupation – which was, after all, a temporary home, with all the needs that involves; but her essay reminds us that simply occupying public space is not all that is required for a radical reorganization of society.

Marlisa Wise brings Fraiman's argument to life by literally mapping the spaces that were required to sustain the occupation; her maps make visible the different kinds of physical spaces that were needed to provide for the needs of the occupiers. The very act of making visible the hidden infrastructure of creating life in a space where such occupation had been denied reminds us tangibly of the repressive counter-energy deployed in everyday life to make that work invisible and to deem it insignificant.

The next essay focuses on responses to vilified populations whose attempts to occupy public space are attacked through laws. In "Tent City, USA: The Growth of America's Homeless Encampments and How Communities are Responding" (Chapter 12), Maria Foscarinis and Eric Tars document the rising numbers of people lacking traditional shelter who now, by necessity, live in public space. More specifically, they focus on the efforts municipal governments have been making to criminalize that use of space; as the numbers of the homeless rise, so does the attempt to refuse them access to public space. As activists who fight these legal battles, Foscarinis and Tars make legible the consequences of repressive control of public space, especially on those who have no alternatives. Their essay is a reminder of exactly what is at stake when the needs of vulnerable people are matched against the sensibilities of wealthier citizens. What Occupy Wall Street made symbolically clear, Foscarinis's work elucidates as an ongoing challenge of material survival.

The book ends with a thoughtful reflection on why public space matters so much, and brings us back to the questions we began with. In an interview, L.A. Kauffman (Chapter 13) ponders one of the central questions of the deliberate taking over of public space for democratic political protests: does it really matter if people gather in the streets to make a point? Her thinking is the very essence of praxis: a fully theorized model of action. Building on her more

Introduction: Public Space/Contested Space **13**

than three decades of work as an activist, and on her two books analyzing the planning and effectiveness of well-known protests, Kauffman expands on her published analyses of why protests still matter – even when neither participants nor organizers can point to any clear objective that was gained. Her detailed discussion of how protests work and why they can be effective is the best possible spur to protest; as she points out, we may not know – in the moment or later – whether a protest had any effect. But, at the very least, the act of deliberately putting bodies in space to make a political point both energizes the participants and holds open – literally and symbolically – the space for dissent. It is one of the most effective tools we have for pushing back from inside the bubble to hold it steady against predatory forces.

The battle for public space is here viewed from a wide variety of vantage points. While the interests of the contributors in space are – variously – historical, political, professional, artistic, and more, together they cohere as a provocation to consider how important it still is that citizens of a democracy are able to come together physically. By mobilizing online, 21st-century citizens can connect with one another to agitate for nearly limitless political causes. The Internet enables debates on a national – even global – scale that would be practically impossible in the real world. Nevertheless, access to public space, and with it to the empowerment that comes from being able to carry out quotidian tasks, as well as to assemble and demand a voice in shaping our collective destiny, has never been more important.

Notes

1 The terms "public sphere" and "public space" are not synonymous; however, the three-dimensional, real-world manifestation of the former in the latter is part of a larger philosophical and historical debate that has been unfolding for nearly a half-century. One way into the major protagonists is Benhabib 1997. Among the important contributors to the debate over the significance of public space in modern democracies and cities are Richard Sennett, starting with *The Fall of Public Man* (1977) and continuing through his recent *Building and Dwelling: Ethics for the City* (2018), and Sorkin 1992.

2 Sassen 2008, 289. See also Benkler 2016.

3 As discussed by Sassen 2008, who writes that

> Individuals and groups that have historically been excluded from formal political systems and whose struggles can be partly enacted outside those systems can find in cyberspace an enabling environment both for their emergence as nonformal political actors and for their struggles.
>
> *(318)*

4 *The Guardian*, September 6, 2018.

5 For instance, see Foucault's (1977) *Discipline and Punish: The Birth of the Prison* and Anthony Vidler's (1987) development of Foucault's discussion of architecture in *The Writing of the Walls: Architectural Theory in the Late Enlightenment*.

6 "Outraged and Inspired, Women Join the Political Fray," *New York Times,* December 5, 2017, 10.
7 The concept of an ephemeral intervention is discussed in our article, Murphy and O'Driscoll 2015.

References

Anderson, Ben. 2009. "Affective Atmospheres." *Emotion, Space and Society* 2: 77–81.
Benhabib, Seyla. 1997. "The Embattled Public Sphere: Hannah Arendt, Jurgen Habermas, and Beyond." *Theoria* 90 (Dec.): 1–24.
Benkler, Yochai. 2016. "Degrees of Freedom, Dimensions of Power." *Daedalus* 145 (1) (Winter): 18–32.
Burrington, Ingrid. 2016. *Networks of New York: An Illustrated Field Guide to Urban Internet Infrastructure.* Brooklyn: Melville House.
Coyne, Richard. 1999. *Technoromanticism: Digital Narrative, Holism, and the Romance of the Real.* Cambridge: MIT Press.
Erdi, Gülçin, and Yıldırım Şentürk, eds. 2017. *Identity, Justice and Resistance in the Neoliberal City.* London: Palgrave Macmillan.
Foucault, Michel. 1977. *Discipline and Punish: The Birth of the Prison.* New York: Pantheon Books.
Griffin, Toni L., Ariella Cohen, and David Maddox. 2015. "Introduction," in *The Just City Essays: 26 Visions for Urban Equity, Inclusion and Opportunity Vol. 1,* edited by Griffin, Cohen, and Maddox. New York: J. Max Bond Center on Design for the Just City at the Spitzer School of Architecture, City College of New York.
Harvey, David. 2005. *A Brief History of Neoliberalism.* Oxford: Oxford University Press.
Harvey, David. 2012. *Rebel Cities: From the Right to the City to the Urban Revolution.* London: Verso.
Harvey, David. 2016. "Neoliberalism is a Political Project," *Jacobin* (July 23, 2016), www.jacobinmag.com/2016/07/david-harvey-neoliberalism-capitalism-labor-crisis-resistance
Murphy, Kevin D., and Sally O'Driscoll. 2015. "The Art/History of Resistance: Visual Ephemera in Public Space." *Space and Culture* 18 (4): 328–357.
Peterson, Marina. 2006. "Patrolling the Plaza: Privatized Public Space and the Neoliberal State in Downtown Los Angeles." *Urban Anthropology and Studies of Cultural Systems and World Economic Development,* 35 (4), Anthropologies of Urbanization (Winter): 356–359.
Robbins, Mark. 2018. "Marking Time and the Critical Reading of Space." *Change Over Time* 8 (2): 248–263.
Sassen, Saskia. 2008. *Territory, Authority, Rights: From Medieval to Global Assemblages,* rev. ed. Princeton: Princeton University Press. E-book.
Sassen, Saskia. 2012. "To Occupy." In *Beyond Zucotti Park: Freedom of Assembly and the Occupation of Public Space,* edited by Ron Shiffman, Rick Bell, Lance Jay Brown, and Lynne Elizabeth. Oakland, CA: New Village Press, 67–69.
Sennett, Richard. 1977. *The Fall of Public Man.* New York: Knopf.
Sennett, Richard. 2018. *Building and Dwelling: Ethics for the City.* London: Allen Lane.
Soja, Edward W. *Seeking Spatial Justice.* 2010. Minneapolis: University of Minnesota Press.
Sorkin, Michael, ed. 1992. *Variations on a Theme Park: The New American City and the End of Public Space.* New York: Hill and Wang.

Vidler, Anthony. 1987. *The Writing of the Walls: Architectural Theory in the Late Enlightenment.* New York: Princeton Architectural Press.

Wendel, Delia Duong Ba. 2015. "Introduction: Toward a Spatial Epistemology of Politics." In *Spatializing Politics: Essays on Power and Place,* edited by Delia Duong Ba Wendel and Fallon Samuels Aidoo. Cambridge, MA: Harvard Graduate School of Design.

SECTION 1
The Built Environment

The built environment is the starting point for a consideration of public space: the essays in this section discuss how architects and others can intervene in the process of creating that environment to reflect the needs of communities who use it. The essays discuss the results of deliberate attempts to involve communities in planning and design, and the subsequent effects on civic life once those designs have been built. Garrett Nelli shows case histories of community-engaged architecture and the effects they have on the communities they were built for: the projects he describes focus less on the architect as star and more on careful prior discussion with all the people who will use, and live in or near, the built structure. Nelli's essay is an eloquent plea for architects to consider the primary stakeholders as they design and build, and to use their profession as an agent of social change. Brian D. Goldstein focuses on a particular historical moment, when the Black Power activists of the 1960s articulated that the redevelopment of Harlem needed to be planned with input from the community who lived there and who did not wish to be displaced in the wholesale urban renewal projects that had destroyed communities. Goldstein demonstrates how politics interact with decisions about urban design, and can change the course of city-building. Silvina Lopez Barrera and Erin Sassin turn to architecture students and consider their training: they describe a course that teaches fledgling architects to understand how community-engaged design can have an impact on people's lives. In this case, the community involved is even more invisible than most: migrant workers in rural areas, whose communities are rarely recognized as such because they are mobile and mostly spread out in isolated farms. Finally, Kevin D. Murphy shows how artists can render the built environment (and its deliberate destruction through urban renewal) visible to onlookers, thus opening up a conversation about how urban renewal affects the lives of those whose environment and community have been destroyed. The essays

18 The Built Environment

share an understanding that the built environment shapes the people who live there, and is not just shaped by them. The key question is which groups of people will have the power to intervene in the design process, and shape it according to their own needs: the poor and racial minorities have too often been ignored in the process, and these essays demonstrate why that matters.

2

PROCESS, PRODUCT, PROGRAM

The Architect as Facilitator of Social Change

Garrett Nelli, AIA

The Role of Architects in Our Lives

Around the world, architects are recognizing the latent potential of the architectural profession to serve their communities in a far greater capacity. Bold new designers are harnessing their influence as facilitators, organizers, and provocateurs, alongside their existing roles as builders, to realize the true disruptive potential in assisting communities to realize profound social change. At its most fundamental level architecture is social – a tool for engaging in politics, economics, aesthetics, and culture. As architectural historian Spiro Kostof puts it, "architecture is a social act and the material theater for human activity" (Kostof 1985, 10). For much of the profession's history, aesthetics has been the primary acknowledgment and obsession of the architectural profession, but a new generation of socially minded designers are leveraging their full professional capabilities to use architecture as a transformative tool for progressive change.

Architecture evolved as a response to the relationship between human needs (shelter, security, community, and the creation of the social fabric) and skills, materials, and knowledge. As this collective practice materialized and was formalized through tradition, that craft became recognized as architecture, and architects were society's master builders. Architects were tasked with the primordial responsibility of sheltering humanity, and these edifices began to aspire to greater significance, striving for the sanctity of purer geometry, artistry, astrology, and psychology to satisfy the evolving human spirit. Cultures across the world altered their environments to better reflect their most intimate desires and, in doing so, associated collective meaning to what they had built. Through this existential lens, architecture became the backdrop for human existence, charged with immense consequence in the eyes of the beholder. The separation between culture and our built environment blurred, as did the roles and responsibilities of the architect.

Born from this ambiguity, a line of inquiry into the "correctness" of architecture developed: a philosophical questioning of the proper approach to constructing buildings and having consideration for the people served. These questions prompted society to examine architecture as more than geometric form, seeing it instead as a primary driver of culture and social evolution. Through this association grew a desire for the architect to impose certain ethics, values, and aesthetics onto space. This evolution of the architectural profession and realized cultural relevance of architecture reveals the primary query for this essay: how do we assess the quality of our built environment, and how does that quality impact our collective and individual lives?

Firmitas (durability), *Utilitas* (utility), *Venustas* (beauty): these are the three tenets of architecture as defined by Marcus Vitruvius Pollio, an architect and military engineer from ancient Rome, whose text *De Architectura* (c. 30-15 BCE) served as a guide for the Roman Empire's construction projects – bridges, forums, baths, etc. – and is one of the sole surviving texts on architecture from antiquity. His work sought to address the ethos of architecture, grounding the practice in an ethical and pragmatic framework that ensured a successful and healthy built project: it must be a self-supporting structure (*Firmitas*), it must have appropriate spatial consideration (*Utilitas*), and it must appease the eye through clear ordering, shapeliness, and symmetry (*Venustas*) (Rowland and Howe 1999, 45). The former two are considered prerequisites to achieving the latter. There is academic consensus regarding the original meaning of *Firmitas* and *Venustas*, but what is unclear is the underlying considerations of *Utilitas,* the appropriateness of spatial consideration. Vitruvius outlines that "the principle of *Utilitas* will be observed if the design allows for faultless, unimpeded use through the disposition of the spaces, and the allocation of each type of space is properly oriented, appropriate, and comfortable." Important to this text is the phrase "faultless, unimpeded use," which points toward a belief that in the Roman Empire architecture was a civic amenity for the use of the civitas, the social body of citizens. This provision's implications are twofold – that architecture is a public infrastructure available to all members of the society, and that the functional needs of those people who inhabit the building and those who are affected by its presence should be considered equally.

"Our Western architectural psyche deals with Vitruvius' shadow in one way or another – honoring or critiquing 'durability-utility-beauty,'" as Gregory Palermo puts it (Palermo 1999, 190). Early in architectural studies, these values for assessing a building's efficacy are impressed upon the student as foundational teachings. In many ways, these values serve as the bedrock for the profession, establishing a rudimentary understanding of the built environment and its role in our lives. Vitruvius's writings lay the groundwork for a thesis that the social, psychological, and cultural impacts of our constructed world extend beyond the building footprint.

Throughout history there have been debates about the public utility of architecture. Renaissance architect Leon Battista Alberti states,

> let it be said that the security, dignity, and honor of the republic depend greatly upon the architect: it is he who is responsible for our delight, entertainment, and health while at leisure, and our profit and advantage while at work, and in short, that we live in a dignified manner, free from any danger.
> *(Lewis 2016, 165)*

John Ruskin's seminal text *The Seven Lamps of Architecture* (1849) states: "Architecture is the art which so disposes and adorns the edifices raised by man that the sight of them contributes to his mental health, power and pleasure" (Ruskin 1989, 8). This basis of beliefs illustrates a direct link between societal wellbeing and the condition of our constructed world. The role of the architect not only encompasses the creation of structural, functional, and aesthetically appealing buildings, but expands its purview to ensure the health – both physical and mental – of an entire population. As such, should this not demand an ethical and civic obligation by architects to design in the public's best interest?

The American Institute of Architects (AIA) has attempted to address this requirement within their Code of Ethics as a contemporary pseudo-reinterpretation of Vitruvius's seminal triad. It is noted under Canon 1 – General Obligations, "Members should employ their professional knowledge and skill to design buildings and spaces that will enhance and facilitate human dignity and the health, safety, and welfare of the individual and the public" (AIA Code). This commitment demonstrates an intention and understanding that the profession bears a responsibility to serve the social welfare. Let's break down these remarks in further detail. "Facilitating human dignity and health" is a declaration to provide equity in design: that wealthy neighborhoods will receive a school as well designed and equitable in function as one built in a low-income neighborhood, as well as ensuring that a building will support healthy interior environments so as to not be detrimental to its inhabitants or neighbors. In many ways, this canon has a direct connection to *Venustas* as it too seeks to create a sense of dignity and delight, to design in a manner that elevates the human spirit. Second, "safety" remains unaltered from the *Firmitas* of 2,000 years ago as both require safe inhabitation of all buildings. Our contemporary use of *Utilitas* is also intriguing: defined as to "enhance and facilitate welfare of the individual and the public," it points toward an architecture self-aware of its potential and responsibility to inspire positive social change. This statement also reasserts the architect's role as civil servant rather than hired hand. Sadly, this Code of Ethics, although its aspirations are true, is merely an internal self-audit of sorts, rather than a strict moral code that projects are measured by and held to. Throughout its history the architectural profession has shown a general understanding of what it could be but has yet to take ownership over what it must be. This raises the question of why it is important that

The Role of Architecture in Our Lives

a profession whose contractual obligation is to design buildings for individual clients be held responsible for the society as a whole.

The Role of Architecture in Our Lives

Architecture acts as an ideological mirror that reflects aspects of society and layers of human information. It also stands as a monument to the zeitgeist. Whether it represents a society divided between the ideas of the past and the prospect of a new future, as was the case with the Berlin Wall, the buildings around us deeply influence and reinforce the mainstream culture. These structures literally and subliminally impact the collective, shifting the societal pendulum in a specific ideological direction.

Architecture propagates ideas. As the primary authors, architects carry a substantial responsibility to transfer that presiding culture into the work they design. Up until now, the work carried out by architects rarely included the influence of the greater population, which made it more a tool for authoritarian rule rather than the reflection of a collective democratic voice. This is evident in the many grand palaces, cathedrals, and monuments that served the few but are still unanimously celebrated today. Still, architecture is nothing but social, yet this social practice has both supported and reinforced hierarchies and has operated, more often than not, as a mechanism of oppression: a practice that has been adopted by the presiding power structure to dominate and further personal gain. This is a troubling truth that our contemporary world and architectural practice are both founded upon. When approached as such, architecture will only be used as a tool for suppression as opposed to liberation.

Critical to architecture's tool kit is understanding the primary mechanism that associates meaning to buildings: built knowledge. Built knowledge is comprised of the ideas and philosophies embedded in or associated with an architecture as viewed through the human condition (Salingaros and Madsen 2017, 97). This includes the means and methods that were used to construct it (whether it be slave labor or union wages), the ideological message that is expressed through its form (such as the civic demeanor of the white marble US Capitol building or a softer community-oriented expression of a neighborhood pub), and the character of activities that surround it. Each of these facets contributes to the complete life of a building. The sum of this built knowledge comprises our built environment, which contributes significantly to defining and altering our collective conscience. This collective conscience, a fundamental sociological concept that refers to the set of shared beliefs, ideas, attitudes, and knowledge that are common to a society, is the very underpinning that defines culture and our understanding of our self within it (Sennett 1992, 71).

Environmental psychologists describe the culmination of built knowledge as place identity, meaning "essentially that the foremost building blocks of our sense of self are actually the spaces in which we live, work, and play" (Cary 2017, 17). At its best, architecture is a physical celebration of the human spirit. At its worst, it has a submissive quality that reinforces inequality and the degradation of self-value. Understanding that the built environment has a profound ability to shape the "self" should be viewed as liberating, as it points to a future where the inclusion of a greater public into a design process must be the solution to defining a zeitgeist that is reflective of the many. By stacking these layers of human psychology, we recognize that the world we have created is integral to the world that exists within us. It reveals a truth that if architecture, built knowledge, and place identity contribute to the shaping of our collective conscience then architects are by nature social engineers with the responsibility to ensure that what is built benefits the collective.

In 1968, Whitney M. Young Jr., executive director of the National Urban League, famously chastized the AIA at its national convention for its lack of influence in the areas of social welfare and inequity. Young explained,

> As a profession, you are not a profession that has distinguished itself by your social and civic contributions to the cause of civil rights, and I am sure this has not come to you as any shock. You are most distinguished by your thunderous silence and complete irrelevance.
>
> *(Betsky 2018)*

It was an unequivocal critique of a profession that largely was aware of the truth in Young's remarks but unwilling to take ownership for their misbehaviors. Today, 50 years later, the profession has gained little ground in the realms of social impact, but an emerging movement within the architectural field is galvanizing behind Young's declaration.

To finish his address, Young brought his point home with this statement: "It took a great deal of skill and creativity and imagination to build the kind of situation we have, and it is going to take skill and imagination and creativity to change it" (Betsky 2018). This was a direct call to action for architects to resist the status quo and to reshape a more just world, recognizing that the built environment of the past was used malevolently but that a more equitable future can be achieved. Bryan C. Lee, Jr, architect, advocate, and cofounder of Colloqate Design, has coined a similar sentiment for the design justice movement: "For every injustice in the world, there is an architecture that has been planned and designed to perpetuate it" (Lee 2020). Let us further rally around the truth that for every political and social movement that will dismantle the inequities of the past, there will be an architecture that manifests it.

What follows is a survey of contemporary projects that have accepted the challenge as a call to action: an architecture aware of its role as provocateur and architects who are shifting pedagogy from focusing on product to impact. These emerging architects are utilizing every facet of the design process to empower communities in elevating their condition. This is a new era for architecture: a

24 Garrett Nelli, AIA

socially conscious architecture that transcends the built environment to catalyze progressive societal change; an architecture that unearths hidden possibilities and reveals new capacities. When the time is taken to form real relationships and connections with communities, architecture, planning, and design can become transformative engines for profound social change.

Design as Process

Traditionally, the design process has been considered a single act of artistic inspiration by a sole individual, the architect, but in reality this effort is far more collaborative. In a prototypical built project the key contributors to its shaping are the owner, architect, builder, and – in some novel circumstances – the end user. This reveals the tragedy of the traditional and antiquated design process. If there is acknowledgment that our built environment has a profound impact on the health, psychology, and identity of our communities, then why not seek the input of stakeholders to ensure that all are benefiting? If place-making projects aspire to contribute positive change in communities, the desires, connections, and accumulated wisdom of those communities must be a driving factor in the design process (Goldhagen 2017, 43). In this participatory model the architect acts less as the hierarchical designer but rather is tasked with the responsibility of compiling collective input into a coherent vision: a coherence born from its diversity. This shift in approach not only democratizes input, but stimulates greater consensus and ownership among stakeholders, ensuring long-term impact. The more individuals can participate in the process of design, the more authentic their connection and relation with that building will be. Conversely, a lack of participation leads to a lack of direct experience, which results in detachment and indifference (Canizaro 2007, 27). As David Harvey, the professor of anthropology, so aptly describes, "The freedom to make and remake our cities and ourselves is, I want to argue, one of the most precious yet most neglected of our human rights" (Harvey 2012, 4).

Architectural expertise, when guided by local knowledge and experience, can envision spaces that truly unlock the potential capacities of a community. This is best observed at the individual level: when we are engaged within our locale there is a direct increase in our sense of community, altruism, neighborhood pride, and political activism. By unlocking these hidden dimensions within ourselves and sharing them with others, we find our communities become far more resilient and interconnected. When a community is connected, its capacity for self-mobilization is unlocked. In truth, most do not realize that they deserve better or that better is even a possibility because they have never been given the space to dream of a more prosperous future. That is why it is paramount for architects to activate a process where collectively we can aspire to those unimagined possibilities. Architecture is not only a product, but a process – a process that instills the tools and critical awareness for individuals to envision the radical possibilities of a future crafted by their own deepest desires and aspirations.

Process, Product, Program **25**

FIGURE 2.1 El Guadual Children Center, Designed by Daniel Feldman and Ivan Dario Quiñones, Photography by Ivan Dario Quiñones. Courtesy of Ivan Dario Quiñones Sanchez

El Guadal Children Center, Villa Rica, Colombia

In the war-torn Cauca region of Colombia, among the dense streets and sugarcane fields of Villa Rica, is the El Guadual Children Center (see Figure 2.1). This center is the product of the national integral early youth attention strategy, *de Cero a Siempre,* established to provide food, education, and recreation services to children, newborns, and pregnant mothers across the country (Sykes 2015). Young Colombian architects Daniel Feldman and Ivan Dario Quiñones were chosen to lead the design efforts for this pilot program on the site of a former makeshift soccer field, donated by the mayor. Both designers saw this initative as an opportunity to revitalize a derelict community through an integrated design process that would prioritize civic pride and community ownership. The ensuing three years of workshops, community events, and construction would be a hallmark of the participatory design process, demonstrating the potential for designers to promote positive social change through an integrated collective design process.

Villa Rica is a city of 16,000 residents with high levels of unemployment and few opportunities for economic growth. The influx of federal funding into Villa Rica for the Children Center brought the potential for new economies to the city, but only if the process prioritized the importance of local labor. Feldman and Quiñones worked as designers and community liaisons, holding workshops with representatives of the multiple stakeholder groups the new center would serve.

These discussions led to the inclusion of auxiliary architectural features such as first aid stations, a community garden, meeting halls, and an outdoor cinema and catwalk requested by local teens to activate the exterior facade for community events. During construction, 60 local tradesmen were employed and trained specifically to construct the 16,450-square-foot complex over a nine-month period. Made primarily of reinforced concrete cast in split bamboo, the center's textured exterior walls absorb the intense midday heat to keep the interior cool in an extremely volatile environment. Construction techniques such as these merged the use of traditional building techniques from locals with the efficiencies of modern technologies introduced by the architects (see Figure 2.2). These new learned skills empower local laborers to implement current best practices on future projects that lead to economic gain across the region. Thirty local women were similarly selected and trained in youth education, certified and hired to be the daily workforce for the center (DesignBoom 2014). This methodology placed the social responsibility for fostering the city's youth on the shoulders of Villa Rica's residents, which further galvanized the community through a sense of collective ownership for the next generation. The design team leveraged their capacity as master builders to ensure that the knowledge, resources, and capacities generated from this public project remained within the community.

The impacts of this participatory design effort can be felt far beyond the extent of the project's property line. El Guadual Children Center has become an anchor in a blooming cultural zone of Villa Rica, which now includes plans for a sports

FIGURE 2.2 El Guadual Children Center, Designed by Daniel Feldman and Ivan Dario Quiñones, Photography by Ivan Dario Quiñones. Courtesy of Ivan Dario Quiñones Sanchez

complex and hospital. "With its communal spaces used by the kids and the community, El Guadual has become a hotspot for the many groups that now come to this part of town," says Feldman. "We wanted to create a dynamic public block to set an example for future institutions" (Keskeys n.d.). The wide array of public amenities, influenced by collective feedback, has made of El Guadual a new locus for civic activity within the Villa Rica community.

Across the country as a whole El Guadual stands as a model for the *de Cero a Siempre* program. Thirty towns in war-affected areas have begun to build children's centers through similar participatory methods, each tailored to the community's specific needs. Indeed, in process and outcome, El Guadual sets a new national standard for childhood development and community capacity building. For Villa Rica, this project illustrates how two young designers leveraged their role to usher in positive social change through participation in the design and construction of significant community projects.

Dreamhamar, Hamar, Norway

Dreamhamar is a networked design process whose aim was to reimagine an existing parking lot in Hamar, Norway, as a new, vibrant public square. Through creating novel opportunities to engage in the visioning process, the architects invited citizens to collectively reimagine the character of this square in an effort to bring greater democracy and activation to Hamar's public realm. Studio Ecosistema Urbano, a design firm whose focus lies at the intersection of urbanism, architecture, and participatory design, pioneered a revolutionary design approach for this project that expands the architect's and urban designer's tool kit to engage the public in the modern era ("Network Design" n.d.).

Ecosistema Urbano deployed a four-pronged approach to a collective brainstorming process for redesigning Stortorget Square: Physical Lab, Urban Action, Digital Lab, and Academic Networks. The Physical Lab (place) consisted of a permanent space located centrally in Hamar that hosted lectures, workshops, and public discussion (see Figure 2.3). Its open-door policy encouraged spontaneous contributions and activation from a diverse audience of passersby. Events organized at the Physical Lab focused around technology, activities, environment, people, and climate strategies as relating to the town and its future square. The Lab quickly became a landmark in Hamar for stakeholders to share, collect, and experiment with ideas. Urban Action (intervention) served as planned events in which 1:1 scaled mock-ups of potential design interventions were installed onsite to aid the visualization of the possibilities for future programming. These included temporary street paintings, moveable benches, and pop-up markets. The publicity and spectacle surrounding these events injected an energy and imagination into the possibilities for the square redesign. The Innovative Digital Lab (connection) employed new technologies to aid in gathering feedback and connecting residents. Because the designers used a web-based platform to gather the community under a single virtual roof, local and global stakeholders had access to project

FIGURE 2.3 Dreamhamar, Designed by Ecosistema Urbano, Photography by Emilio P. Doiztua. Courtesy of Emilio P. Doiztua

content, online workshops, and avenues for sharing their feedback. An active blog, Dreamhamar.org, kept the collective discussion ongoing with live construction updates while an open-source phone-based app allowed residents to propose and share geo-referenced ideas for the city at large. Lastly, academic studios (education) from across Europe used Dreamhamar as a practical case study for research in urbanism and participatory design. Over 1,200 students were able to contribute to this uniquely democratic process through university-led design studios. This academic framework allowed Ecosistema Urbano to test conceptual ideas in an academic setting before presenting them to the Dreamhamar community at large (Furuto n.d.).

The resulting built project is an authentic reflection of the myriad responses collected across the totality of the design process. The new Stortorget Public Square is defined by a series of flexible architectural elements ranging from benches, ground painting, a multipurpose fountain that can be activated during winter months as an ice-skating rink, and an open area for temporary events. A revived civic spirit exists within the Dreamhamar community, which was revealed and showcased through this design process. Critical to the success of this process was the level of transparency that was established from the onset. Ecosistema Urbano saw a unique opportunity to amplify connectivity by creating a variety of public platforms that spurred consensus rather than concealing information behind red tape. This combination of analog and digital activity illustrates the possibilities for a variety of emerging forms of participation critical to engaging a wider cross-section of the population. While some individuals may find the in-person, on-site workshops most helpful, a separate group of the community may find the ease and accessibility of a web platform to be the most comfortable outlet for their engagement. This combination of approaches allowed for a larger pool of participants to reimagine the identity of their community, and thus new ways for occupying their city.

Design as Product

Buildings are as tightly connected and deeply intertwined a feature of our social fabric as any element in our daily lives. In antiquity, the grandest temples were dedicated to the most holy of ideas, materializing humans' mortality and fascination for the phenomenological in stone. In the same way today, culture is projected onto the built environment, and the built environment reinforces and reflects that culture back. Architecture is a manifestation and extension of culture. When, as a community, we propose building, we are making a greater statement than that of just brick and mortar: we are materializing those ideologies supported by that institution in physical form. The environmental psychologist Roger Barker studied the correlation between habitation and the human experience. His findings followed youth throughout their day to determine which factors were most likely to alter their behaviors. He discovered that the most consistent indicator of behavior was not an individual's personal psychology (i.e., background and demographics) but rather the space they inhabited. In sum, students in a library were more attuned to be calm and attentive as opposed to those in a cafeteria or playground where they were geared for activity. These findings reinforce a foundational theory that the built environment is not a supporting framework for human existence but rather an active agent in the shaping of human development, identity, and well-being (Goldhagen 2017, 197). French writer Noël Arnaud so appropriately declared, "I am the space where I am."[1] Understanding this ethical responsibility demands that architects adhere to a more conscientious professional obligation: what we build today will memorialize our society's values for future generations. In that light, no architecture is neutral, innocent, or passive. A building actively reasserts existing boundaries and typologies and/or reassesses those same relationships and patterns: the onus is on the architect to decide whether to stabilize the dominant power structure in stone or dismantle it through collective action.

Children Village, Formoso do Araguaia, Brazil

When the Brazilian Bank's Bradesco Foundation approached Aleph Zero to design their newest boarding school in the remote and densely forested region of Formoso do Araguaia, Brazil, they were taking a chance on young and fairly unknown architects. As the bank director put it, "We chose the architects precisely because they are not the kind who think they know everything"; that was a deciding factor in choosing an architect who would be working with an agrarian community living on the fringes of society.[2] The facility would provide boarding and support facilities for 540 students traveling from remote communities, mostly by horse on unpaved roads, to attend the Canuanã boarding school. For students making this long commute, the facility was an important transition between the natural beauty and folkloric traditions of their remote communities and the modern approach to education being taught. In response, Aleph Zero saw this as an opportunity to monumentalize the natural site, indigenous memories, local techniques, and vernacular aesthetics to instill a sense of self-pride for students while still providing a modern education important to childhood development. This project's success is rooted in its sensitive approach to celebrating local cultural values without overshadowing them with a false sense of modernity (see Figure 2.4).

Aleph Zero began the design process with an intensive 10-day program of workshops and activities to connect with teachers, students, and families of Formoso do Araguaia. Two primary challenges came to the forefront from these ongoing discussions. First was creating an environment that felt welcoming and inspiring to students while acknowledging that many see the traditions of the past as old-fashioned in comparison to what is portrayed on social media. Second was the challenge of building in such a remote region: the means and methods for procuring material were a concern in terms of both time and transportation. This dilemma lent itself to a two-for-one solution that utilized local materials and

FIGURE 2.4 Children Village, Designed by Aleph Zero and Rosenbaum, Photography by Leonardo Finotti. Courtesy of Leonardo Finotti.

craft to express regional identity and mitigate the need for transporting imported materials long distances. Aleph Zero cofounder Gustavo Utrabo states, "The challenge was to convince the students and teachers that the local materials of earth, bricks, and timber could represent progress – that being modern didn't have to mean glass, steel and air-conditioning" (Wainwright 2018). This dichotomy became the crux of the project, and led to its ultimate success.

Aleph Zero understood the need to both physically and ideologically monumentalize the facilities, place, and people in an architecture that sensitively melded tradition and modernity. As one approaches the building, the forest of eucalyptus columns supporting the razor-thin roof line appears as a modernist extension of the surrounding Brazilian savannah: life and nature existing harmoniously beneath its canopy. The hot and humid climate demands that one "build the shade" through means of an expansive roof that drastically cools the spaces below. Locally sourced glue-laminated eucalyptus was chosen as the primary structural material for its versatility and potential for prefabricated assembly, while the base was grounded with stabilized earthen blocks that subdivide the interior spaces (the blocks are a popular traditional building material composed of nearby soils). This brick provides excellent thermal qualities as it absorbs the sun's heat throughout the day, while openings in the walls allow for cross ventilation to cool the eight interior dormitory blocks.[3] The contextual approach of this design navigates an architecture that is truly economically and environmentally sustainable. The final resolution is neither of the past nor alien to its context, neither traditional nor a symbol of modernism. It delicately occupies the space in between.

The programming of the school plays a pivotal role in the wellbeing of the students (see Figure 2.5). Beneath the large roof canopy are two primary housing masses opposite one another, one for boys and one for girls, stretching 165 x 65 meters. Each mass is comprised of living pods, which are shared by six students, that face toward a central social courtyard. These living pods are connected by upper-floor walkways and gathering spaces that further integrate the individual student within the larger community. In the previous boarding facilities, up to 40 students were placed in a single living pod. The decrease in the size of the housing pods in the new facility has sparked a new level of intimacy among students that further strengthens their bonds with one another as well as their general comfort with being away from home. This comfort has transitioned into the classroom as teachers have noted that students appear calmer and more focused on their studies. Encompassing the boarding school is a veranda composed of eucalyptus columns that acts as a threshold between the interior academic program and the infinity of the exterior lush landscape. Designed as a flexible "in-between space," the veranda now regularly hosts Pilates, acting lessons, and after-school play (Wainwright 2018).

Ultimately, the design for the Children Village aims to increase the children's self-esteem, individuality, sense of belonging, and overall academic performance, by materializing an ongoing dialogue between indigenous traditions and

FIGURE 2.5 Children Village, Designed by Aleph Zero and Rosenbaum, Photography by Leonardo Finotti. Courtesy of Leonardo Finotti

contemporary desires. Thus, students are provided with a familiar space to explore and dream in a manner contextualized to their own unique experience. Co-architect Utrabo describes the experiential quality best as "a place that feels like a home away from home for the kids," for home is the genesis for dreaming. Aleph Zero's sensitive resolution has brought international recognition to Children Village, garnering it the highly sought after biannual RIBA (Royal Institute of British Architects) Prize for Building of the Year Award (Goldberg 2018). Such accolades illustrate the shift in support for socially conscious architecture by the professional elite, which will only help produce more emerging architects such as Aleph Zero.

Equal Justice Initiative, Memorial for Peace and Justice

> *Fred Rochelle, 16, was burned alive in a public spectacle lynching before thousands in Polk County, Florida, in 1901.*
>
> *After Calvin Mike voted in Calhoun County, Georgia, in 1884, a white mob attacked and burned his home, lynching his elderly mother and his two young daughters, Emma and Lillie.*[4]

Eight hundred devastating accounts similar to these are made visible by the Alabama-based Equal Justice Initiative (EJI), whose National Memorial for

FIGURE 2.6 National Memorial for Peace and Justice, Designed by MASS Design Group, Photography by Alan Karchmer/OTTO. Courtesy of Alan Karchmer/OTTO

Peace and Justice memorializes the more than 4,400 victims of lynchings across the southern United States (see Figure 2.6). In direct contrast to memorials designed to console and soothe, this building presents somber accounts of domestic terrorism that serve as a jarring reminder of the horrors imposed on black Americans by white Americans. Visitors are compelled through this architecture to confront and acknowledge the atrocities of the past and the pervasive ethical narrative of racial discrimination that still runs rampant in America today (Robertson 2018).

Bryan Stevenson, the founder of the Equal Justice Initiative (EJI), has spearheaded civil rights efforts through his writings, including his bestselling memoir *Mercy*, but in 2013 when the EJI began erecting physical markers recognizing the slave trade in Montgomery, Alabama, in protest against the many memorials to the Confederacy already in place, Stevenson was blown away by the massive public interest (Bernstein 2018). As a result, when the EJI released a comprehensive report on lynching in America, Stevenson knew that they needed to memorialize one of America's greatest tragedies in physical form. The EJI's answer was to develop a highly public space in Montgomery that would stand in defiance of the presiding power structures that oversaw and condoned those horrific acts. A six-acre plot of land centrally located in downtown Montgomery was chosen. To solidify it as an act of rebellion, the memorial sits atop a hill that looks directly down toward the Alabama Capitol Building and the nine-foot-high bronze statue of Jefferson Davis, the president of the Confederacy, that adorns its front steps – the very same steps where Alabama governor George Wallace declared in 1963 for an entire nation to hear, "Segregation now, segregation forever!"

34 Garrett Nelli, AIA

At the time when EJI's findings were released, Michael Murphy, cofounder of MASS Design Group (Model of Architecture Serving Society), was struck by the gravity of Bryan Stevenson's vision. Murphy saw this effort as one of the most important contemporary built projects America could invest in, so he decided to cold-call Stevenson to ask whether the EJI had selected an architect for their memorial. MASS Design Group, a radical architecture firm in its own right, had primarily experienced designing with and for disadvantaged communities across Africa, garnering them international recognition, but were yet to build on their home soil in America. Both Murphy and Stevenson saw this project as more than a static memorial, but rather a necessary step in the healing of a city and nation. Immediately, Stevenson responded to Murphy's inquiry and invited him and his team to Montgomery to be a part of his vision (Murphy 2016).

The memorial consists of a large pavilion atop a hill, similar in prominence to the ancient Greek Parthenon, overlooking the city, demanding reverence and respect. Beneath its roof rest 800 six-foot-tall corten steel tablets, each of which is inscribed with a state and county within that state, and the names of those African Americans who were lynched in that county (Figure 2.7). As visitors enter the pavilion space, they are greeted on-grade by these mini-memorials which are tightly packed together to evoke the feeling of compression, similar to that experienced on boats en route from Africa during the transatlantic slave trade. As visitors move through the colonnaded structure, the ground beneath begins to drop down as the viewer's perception of the pavilion and tablets shifts. Each tablet

FIGURE 2.7 National Memorial for Peace and Justice, Designed by MASS Design Group, Photography by Alan Karchmer/OTTO. Courtesy of Alan Karchmer/OTTO

rises into the air as the visitor moves deeper into the memorial. At their most visceral, the tablets rise well above the visitor, suspended from the ceiling, to evoke the emotions of witnessing the very lynchings this architecture is memorializing. As the visitor exits the pavilion, 800 identical tablets lie outside the pavilion stacked like caskets for the 800 individuals who were never laid to rest. The EJI hopes that as a national act of remembrance and reconciliation, those counties whose names are engraved on the tablets will erect these monuments in their original locations until all have been relocated to their final resting place (Bernstein 2018). The goal is both to spread awareness about our collective suppression of the past and to honor those victims of horrific racism. Whether the monuments will be adopted, and when, and by whom, remains to be seen, but the EJI hopes that this act of healing can bring solace to a broken nation.

The National Memorial for Peace and Justice is a brutal reminder that American history is filled with acts of unthinkable inequity and hate, and that these acts still persist today. At its core, this memorial makes physical our collective capacity to acknowledge, remember, and reconcile with our past. Lynching was more than an act of terror: it was an act of civic discord and unlawful occupation of public space by white bodies. Often occurring in public squares, the heinous visual act demonstrated the complete oppression of one group of people by another. By location and by stature, the National Memorial for Peace and Justice stands in direct opposition to those underlying spatial implications. Now occupying a space once presided over by discrimination, it stands as a public gesture committed to remembering those once-forgotten victims in hopes of creating an even greater disruptive force toward racial equity. Over time, the absences of the individual tablets as they are relocated across the United States will provide new opportunities for the reclaiming of public spaces that bear the scar of America's founding sin. Michael Murphy describes this relationship between ourselves, our aspirations, and space: "great architecture can give us hope, great architecture can heal" (Murphy 2016).

Design as Program

Without question, space has played an active role in the evolution of culture and the significance of historical events. From Occupy Wall Street to the devastating white nationalist march at the University of Virginia campus in 2017, place serves as a rallying point that pulls activity into its atmosphere, either by form, stature, or purpose. Winston Churchill understood this when he proposed that the UK House of Commons chamber of Parliament be rebuilt in its identical preexisting rectilinear form after being damaged by Nazi airstrikes during World War II. Churchill insisted that the duality of the rectilinear form was reflective of the two-party system in England, representing the essence of parliamentary democracy. In both literal and subliminal ways, the built environment is the backdrop for the human condition. It sets the stage for the very nature of activities that will persist in the foreground. Churchill recognized this when he so famously declared, "We shape our buildings, and afterward our buildings shape us."[5] If understood and harnessed, it can be used to sequester and sterilize civic uprising, but if unleashed, it can catalyze and mobilize movement. Like a meticulous gardener, the architect must tend and cultivate the ideal circumstances for space to produce radical thought and activity. The programs that persist within buildings are thus the key indicators of the health and success of space as a social generator. Only through the organic assembly of bodies and ideas can architecture self-mobilize communities. It is the responsibility of the architect to redefine the built environment from one of inclusivity and isolation to one of democracy and mobilization that compels civic occupation and duty.

Common-unity, San Pablo Xalpa, Mexico

Infonavit, a social housing lender and manager, has long been operating as a government institution tasked with producing and supporting housing for low-income families across Mexico. Its projects have been considered low quality, with little regard given to social enterprise or environmental standards. This all shifted in 2012 when Infonavit changed internal leadership to the son of a former Mexican president, Carlos Zedillo Velasco. With this shift in leadership came a shift in practice, from focusing on the construction of new housing blocks to the reuse and rehabilitation of their existing stock. This effort concentrated on upgrading building exteriors, surroundings, and basic amenities to a standard that all inhabitants deserve. As part of this overhaul process, Rozana Montiel, an emerging Mexican architect, and her studio were tasked with the rehabilitation and reimagination of the San Pablo Xalpa housing block's exterior spaces. Montiel understood that a place-making approach, focused on the transformation of the underused and discarded spaces surrounding the block, could become the framework through which inhabitants could connect, strengthen communal bonds, and better understand their socioeconomic condition (Montiel n.d.).

Montiel and her team used participatory action research to determine the most appropriate way to reuse the public realm. She observed that tenants would extend the private space of their apartments into the courtyards in the form of temporary tents and other makeshift shelters to host parties and family gatherings. Montiel saw a unique occupation of space taking place that caused her redesign to center on elevating these preexisting activities. In order to expand these functions, Montiel's first task was to convince a small percentage of the approximately 7,000 inhabitants, who had over the years privatized parts of the public space by erecting vertical barriers, to remove their fences for the greater good. She was able to persuade them by explaining the benefits that would come to the greater community through improved shared amenities at the expense of their individual needs.

FIGURE 2.8 Common-unity, Designed by Rozana Montiel Estudio de Arquitectura, Photography by Sandra Pereznieto. Courtesy of Sandra Pereznieto

Residents agreed to remove 90 percent of the barriers. In their place, a series of lightweight interventions were erected for informal and formal gathering (Betsky 2018). These simple steel structures are clad with slatted wood ceilings and metal roofs to offer shade but left open-aired for visible opportunities for communal interaction (see Figures 2.8 and 2.9).

The flexibility of Montiel's design, Common-unity, illustrates the potential that even minimal architectural means have to rejuvenate communities. Montiel's philosophy throughout the process was to "work around the physical barriers created by the residents in common areas to make them permeable, democratic, and meaningful" (Betsky 2018). Her design response established a series of visual anchors, occupying reclaimed public space, that would offer new avenues for interaction. Today, a variety of public programs persist, including exercise classes, open-air cinema, an active climbing wall, chess games, a small lending library, tutoring, and Zumba classes. Even the inclusion of free Wi-Fi has provided a new hub for people to work in a café-like atmosphere. Through participatory planning, existing vertical dividers that were intended to fragment were replaced with a democratic horizontal fabric that has united the inhabitants in an open, flexible, and economical manner. In what was once a depressed, overgrown, and divided space, a vibrant civic life now exists, supporting previous and new programs.

FIGURE 2.9 Common-unity, Designed by Rozana Montiel Estudio de Arquitectura, Photography by Sandra Pereznieto. Courtesy of Sandra Pereznieto

Common-unity has facilitated a unique form of ownership and appropriation among the San Pablo Xalpo housing block, one that redistributed agency from the individual to the collective. Montiel describes this phenomenon:

> People sweep the space early in the morning, young people come and exercise, ladies sit with their knitting club, old folk play chess, and at night there are open-air cinema shows. The spaces were designed to engage people in daily routines of rapport and exchange that give them a sense of pride and ownership.
>
> *(Betsky 2018)*

Relationships that were latent have been nurtured and maintained through thoughtful place-making: as Montiel added, "Our horizontal intervention of common spaces creates a democratic horizon: it rebuilds society as a whole." Rozana Montiel's innovative approach to place-making earned Common-unity the 2018 Mies Crown Hall Americas Prize for Emerging Architecture, a biennial prize awarded to recently built work in the Americas that demonstrates the highest standard of design in response to today's changing environment. This is yet another prestigious award that further encourages the profession to expand its creative potential to rethink public space and support social movements. It is worth noting that Montiel is among a number of Central and South American architects, like Aleph Zero, who are demonstrating the value architects and architecture can contribute to society at large. A provocative article in *Architect Magazine*, a publication by the AIA, summarizes this movement occurring below the border best: "The message seems to be, to be a good architect, do the right thing and build (for) community – and, for now, look to the south" (Betsky 2018).

Stage, Dnipro, Ukraine

Situated on the site of an abandoned Soviet-era amphitheater in Dnipro, Ukraine, sits Stage, a multipurpose pavilion that embodies the collective creative energy of the community by which it was envisioned. Designed, built, and occupied solely through crowdsourced methods, Stage represents the potent potential for grassroots efforts to reclaim and repurpose public space. Ukraine is a nation once defined by collective ideology during communist rule, but this communal notion has lain dormant since the fall of the Soviet Union (Hatherley 2018). Stage is a comprehensive effort to redefine this collective through critical reflection and radical action, which has manifested itself as a truly unique civic space for the Dnipro community (Figure 2.10).

In 2017, the old Soviet theater at the Leisure and Culture Park in Dnipro became the site of interest for reactivating a network of social and artist movements that had emerged three years prior during the Euromaidan demonstrations. Euromaidan was a series of protests across Ukraine to oppose the decision by President Viktor Yanukovych to align Ukraine's interest with the Eurasian Economic Union and

FIGURE 2.10 Stage, Designed by Stage Dnipro Community, Photography by Alexandr Burlaka. Courtesy of Alexandr Burlaka and Stage Dnipro Community

40 Garrett Nelli, AIA

Russia rather than the European Union. Many saw this as an abuse of power, fueled by government corruption, which could lead Ukraine to fall back into the oppressive society that persisted during Soviet rule. This movement motivated a group of artists, designers, musicians, and thinkers, self-titled Kultura Medialna, to occupy an abandoned Stalinist-era amphitheater in Dnipro's central park as an act of creative rebellion ("Stage" 2018). In an attempt to galvanize the movement beyond the Euromaidan demonstrations, the group prompted the community at large to speculate new ways of occupying the old theater for uses that would reflect the desires of a freer, more diverse society. An online questionnaire was distributed by Kultura Medialna to residents requesting 25 possible uses of the space, which crowdsourced over 1,000 responses. The consensus was to construct a new stage on the site of the old Stalinist one that could accommodate a myriad of flexible community-led programs: a stage that would host critical reflection and open debate, where all forms of artistic and cultural expression would be welcomed, standing in direct contrast to the propagandistic functions of its oppressive predecessor.

A coalition of architects, engineers, and artists collaborated online to design the stage. Concurrently, activists on the ground mobilized by gathering supplies and clearing the existing site for construction. An overwhelming sense of ownership grew among the participants, who were inspired by the collective process to be a part of a larger movement. Materials, costs, and construction labor were all crowdsourced from the local community, culminating in Stage's completion nearly one year after inception. This level of commitment to the cause during and after construction is best illustrated by the sheer quantity of public events that Stage hosted in its first summer of operation. In a span of two months, over 60 grassroots events occurred, ranging from outdoor concerts to talks, dances, and cinema (Snopek 2018). Each event was operated independently, and the variety of content curated ensured that all Dnipro residents would be welcome. Whoever wanted to organize an event could do so freely. The totality of this effort is a robust mechanism for social cohesion manifested in the reclamation of public space energized by collective action (see Figure 2.11).

This unique design effort required the lead designer, Tomasz Świetlik, to release his authority as lead designer in favor of being a design facilitator. His primary task was to take the potpourri of responses and weave them into a synchronized legible gesture. To achieve this effect, he sought to "make each creative contribution clearly articulated in the design, while preserving the coherence of the whole structure" (Snopek 2018). The structure itself, made from simple materials like dimensional lumber and plywood sheets, includes a stage for performance, a lounge space and storage, a small garden, and a megaphone – all of which were elements designed and crowdsourced by individual request. During Soviet rule, Dnipro was considered "Rocket City" for its role as a top-secret site for major ballistic missile production. This industry led to a city largely defined by big bombastic spaces intended for enforcing and instilling civic valor, whereas conversely

Process, Product, Program   41

FIGURE 2.11 Stage, Designed by Stage Dnipro Community, Photography by Katerina Kovacheva. Courtesy Katerina Kovacheva and Stage Dnipro Community

today, the greatest need for community is for greater intimacy and individual flexibility. Stage put architectural form to this desire. In many ways the intimate scale of the project is a political act of defiance.

Stage was recognized for its novel collective approach by being selected as one of the five projects awarded the prestigious 2018 European Prize for Urban Public Space. This level of acknowledgment counters the preconceived notion that great design requires singular authorship. Stage argues to the contrary, and illustrates the possibility for exceptional design to be a performative process with many actors. In the case of Stage, both design and function were completely public and transparent. The Dnipro community was given agency to be a part of something larger than themselves, which in turn resulted in a collective spirit that has manifested a new public space for civic discourse.

The Public Architecture of Tomorrow

The essence of this essay is to illustrate that what we build, how we build, and the life of our buildings have profound importance to who we are and what we value. The built environment is not just a supporting framework for life but an active agent in shaping human development, individual identity, and the society at large. It is time to view the task of architecture as more than the creation of objects for habitation and instead to see it in its totality, as an ideological, monumental, and disruptive tool waiting to be harnessed. If we want to shape a future

42 Garrett Nelli, AIA

that is crafted by ideas of connection, flexibility, and the many, we must repurpose this tool to satisfy those specific needs. Architecture is a critical tool for engaging in economics, politics, and social reform and an untapped resource that should no longer be ignored by the architectural profession or public.

The case studies described above illustrate the potential for the architectural profession to have a profound impact on the larger sociopolitical condition through the design process and reveal novel ways for how a public architecture can be made manifest. At its core, this process requires an open dialogue between architects, owners, stakeholders, and the public that includes, rather than isolates or belittles, in order to channel the ideas and values of all into architectural form. If we can recognize the potential of our built environment, and catalyze our collective voice to demand much more, we will find an architectural profession that rises to meet those needs. Architecture is a service, and the architect's professional obligation is to serve. Now architects need to answer the question of what they are working in service of and for. To whom much is given, much is required. A higher standard of moral and civic obligation must be demanded from a profession that contributes disproportionately to our shared human experience. In an ever-changing future, growing ever more connected through emerging technologies, one cannot predict how the profession will respond to this challenge. As the world grows more fluid, and public space becomes more ambiguous and contentious, there is a need to establish more robust open dialogue surrounding our built environment. My hope and belief is that the Internet of things, along with the democratization of information, will only create a stronger conduit between designers and the public. Emerging trends such as crowdsourcing and open-sourcing, along with the pervasive nature of social media, will reinforce a growing demand to involve a wider pool of thought into architectural discourse. Architects must further promote these avenues that allow lay individuals to realize that they have the competency to question and be critical of what is built around them. Most recently, social media has been bombarded with proposals for the controversial reconstruction of the roof and spire atop the Notre Dame Cathedral, which caught fire during renovations in April 2019. Quick to criticize or celebrate these architectural proposals have been the voices of a truly global community concerned with the appropriate way to preserve and reevaluate the significance of an architectural totem. This may very well be one of the first moments in human history when millions will have the opportunity to openly debate the value of the built environment. This is a pivotal moment in architectural history, a moment that could have an impact on every project that is to follow – an opening of Pandora's box that cannot be reversed.

The challenge is for all to find opportunities to plug in to these discussions at the local, regional, national, and global level. So I ask: share your values and beliefs. Think actively and critically about your surroundings. If you seek high and low, yet are unable to see your desires reflected in what is surrounding you, stand up and demand more. Lay the groundwork for others to harness your energy to find their voice. Let's fight for the future, one that is defined by the collective, collaborative, and public, rather than be doomed to the individual, isolated, and privatized world we see today. For when we all take an active role in shaping our built environment, we will find a world emerge that is far more reflective of our collective human aspirations, and a landscape far more fit to support the diversity of ideas that endure.

Notes

1 Quoted in Gaston Bachelard, 1958, *The Poetics of Space* (Boston: Beacon Press) 206.
2 https://gustavoutrabo.com.
3 https://gustavoutrabo.com.
4 The National Memorial for Peace and Justice: https://museumandmemorial.eji.org/memorial.
5 "Churchill and the Commons Chamber," n.d. www.parliament.uk/about/living-heritage/building/palace/architecture/palacestructure/churchill.

References

AIA Code of Professional Conduct. www.aia.org/pages/3296-code-of-ethics-and-professional-conduct
Bernstein, Fred A. 2018. "Step Inside the New National Memorial for Peace and Justice." *Architectural Digest* April 26, 2018. www.architecturaldigest.com/story/national-memorial-for-peace-and-justice
Betsky, Aaron. 2018. "Glittering Prizes for Sober Buildings." *Architect* 107, no. 5 (May 2018).
Canizaro, Vincent B. 2007. *Architectural Regionalism: Collected Writings on Place, Identity, Modernity, and Tradition*. New York: Princeton Architectural Press.
Cary, John. 2017. *Design for Good*. Washington, DC: Island Press.
DesignBoom. "Feldman + Quinones Construct Bamboo Childhood Center in Colombia." www.designboom.com/architecture/feldman-quinones-el-guadual-school-colombia-08-04-2014
Furuto, Alison. n.d. "Citizens Redesign Their City in Dreamhamar / Ecosistema Urbano." *ArchDaily*. www.archdaily.com/175516/citizens-redesign-their-city-in-dreamhamar-ecosistema-urbano
Goldberg, Mackenzie. 2018. "Meet Aleph Zero, the Young Architects Behind This Year's Best New Building." *Architect*, November 21, 2018. https://archinect.com/features/article/150096943/meet-aleph-zero-the-young-architects-behind-this-year-s-best-new-building
Goldhagen, Sarah Williams. 2017. *Welcome to Your World: How the Built Environment Shapes Our Lives*. New York: Harper Collins.
Harvey, David. 2012. *Rebel Cities: From the Right to the Urban Revolution*. London: Verso.
Hatherley, Owen 2018. "The Future of Ukrainian Architecture Could Be Collective, Lightweight and Public." *DeZeen*. September 7, 2018. www.dezeen.com/2018/09/07/ukraine-architecture-collective-lightweight-public-owen-hatherley-opinion/?li_source=LI&li_medium=rhs_block_1
Keskeys, Paul. n.d. "Brilliant Bamboo: How Participatory Design Can Produce Amazing Architecture." https://architizer.com/blog/inspiration/industry/brilliant-bamboo

Kostof, Spiro. 1985. *A History of Architecture: Settings and Rituals*. New York: Oxford University Press.

Lee, Bryan C. 2020. "American Cities Were Designed to Oppress." Bloomberg Citylab. www.citylab.com/perspective/2020/06/george-floyd-protest-urban-design-history-racism-architecture/612622

Lewis, Michael J. 2016. "Architects and Citizenship." In *The Professions and Civic Life*, edited by Gary Schmitt, 161–174. Lanham, Boulder, New York, London: Lexington Books.

Montiel, Rozana. n.d. http://rozanamontiel.com/en/proyectos/common-unity

Murphy, Michael. 2016. TED2016, "Architecture That's Built to Heal." www.ted.com/talks/michael_murphy_architecture_that_s_built_to_heal?language=en

"Network Design: Dream Your City." n.d. Harvard *Design Magazine* 37. "Urbanism's Core?" www.harvarddesignmagazine.org/issues/37/network-design-dream-your-city

Palermo, Gregory. 1999. *Exploring Ethical Grounding for Architecture: Four Lenses*. Minneapolis: ACSA.

Robertson, Campbell. 2018. "A Lynching Memorial Is Opening. The Country Has Never Seen Anything Like It." *New York Times,* April 25, 2018. www.nytimes.com/2018/04/25/us/lynching-memorial-alabama.html

Rowland, Ingrid D., and Thomas Noble Howe. 1999. *Vitruvius: Ten Books of Architecture*. Cambridge: Cambridge University Press.

Ruskin, John. 1989. *The Seven Lamps of Architecture*. New York: Dover Publications.

Salingaros, Nikos A., and Kenneth G. Madsen. 2017. *The Science of Intelligent Architecture*. Krakow: Teka Komisji Urbanistyki i Architektury.

Sennett, Richard. 1992. *The Conscience of the Eye: The Design and Social Life of Cities*. New York: W.W. Norton.

Snopek, Kuba. 2018. TEDxKiev, "Collective Design for Better Architecture." https://tedxkyiv.com/en/speakers/kuba-snopek

"Stage, Dnipro, Ukraine, 2018." 2018. *Publicspace*. www.publicspace.org/works/-/project/k299-stage

Sykes, Krista. 2015. *Contract Design Network*. "El Guadual Early Childhood Development Center." March 5, 2015. www.contractdesign.com/projects/education/el-guadual-early-childhood-development-center

Wainwright, Oliver. 2018. "The World's Best Building? A Remote Brazilian School Made out of Wood." *The Guardian*, US edition. November 20, 2018. www.theguardian.com/artanddesign/2018/nov/21/children-village-brazilian-school-riba-international-prize-best-building-in-the-world

3

"THE SEARCH FOR NEW FORMS"

Black Power and the Making of the Postmodern City

Brian D. Goldstein

In the landmark manifesto *Black Power,* Stokely Carmichael and Charles V. Hamilton titled their final chapter "The Search for New Forms." In it they called for African Americans to take control of their schools, reclaim their homes from negligent absentee landlords, insist that local businesses reinvest profits in their communities, and reshape the political institutions that served them. "We must begin to think of the black community as a base of organization to control institutions in that community," they wrote, capturing the ideals of "community control" and neighborhood self-determination at the center of the radical shift in the civil rights movement in the late 1960s. In invoking "forms," the authors had in mind ways that those goals could be put into practice: through independent political candidates or through parents demanding authority over local school districts. Yet the term *forms* was also quite apt for its physical connotations, as Black Power was a movement with fundamentally spatial origins and ambitions (Carmichael and Hamilton 1967, 164–177).

Indeed, physical space played an essential role in the rise of Black Power. The movement grew from the historical process of urban spatial segregation, which had produced the sorts of racially homogeneous communities that inspired and incubated it. In such communities, Black Power proponents saw the possibility of racial autonomy, a dream fueled by the recent history of African decolonization. As activists explained in the late 1960s, spatially distinct places such as Harlem were akin to colonies, without adequate representation and vulnerable to the whims of outsiders. "Colonial subjects have their political decisions made for them by the colonial masters, and those decisions are handed down directly or through a process of 'indirect rule,'" wrote Carmichael and Hamilton. Like colonies, too, such "ghettos" bore the power to seize control over their fate, to become engines of self-governance (Carmichael and Hamilton 1967, 6).

46 Brian D. Goldstein

Scholars have acknowledged the critical function of space as a metaphor and a foundation for the self-conception, philosophy, and goals of Black Power (Self 2003, 1, 217–233; Sugrue 2008, 313–355). Yet, as this essay will explain, space also played a material role in the Black Power movement. The fact of spatial segregation gave rise to Black Power, but urban space and the built environment also served as the medium through which Black Power adherents expressed their vision of the alternative future that would follow from racial self-determination. Community control would not only provide democratic participation and self-reliance in neighborhoods that had lacked both, it would also, activists argued, produce a better, more humane city that valued local decision-making, existing inhabitants, and their vibrant neighborhoods and everyday lives.

This idea unfolded as a reaction to the large-scale, clearance-oriented urban redevelopment strategies that had reshaped American inner cities in the postwar period. These practices, known as "urban renewal," typically followed the belief that urban transformation required the excision of existing residents in predominantly poor, majority-minority neighborhoods. The Black Power movement suggested the possibility of a different mode of development, however, that rested fundamentally on the persistence of the very residents that modernist redevelopment had sought to displace. This vision grew out of the larger context of the movement, with proponents arguing that civil rights gains depended not on the thus far elusive goal of racial desegregation but on tapping the intrinsic power of predominantly African American communities. Black radicals inspired by Carmichael and Hamilton's appreciation of "the potential power of the ghettos" saw the African American residents in communities such as Harlem, Watts, and Chicago's South Side not as the cause of the urban crisis but as its solution. They placed blame for widespread poverty and daily misery on the decisions that outsiders had imposed on neighborhoods, including the urban renewal projects that had reshaped such communities in broad strokes of vast clearance and monumental reconstruction. In confronting officials who backed that approach to neighborhood change, Black Power advocates argued that residents could do a better job themselves by controlling the full spectrum of decisions that affected them, including those regarding education, political representation, and, crucially, the built environment (Carmichael and Hamilton 1967, 177).

Interpreting Black Power through the lens of the built environment, specifically through architecture and urban planning, and interpreting the architectural and urban history of this era through the lens of the Black Power movement yields several insights into both Black Power and the built environment. First, such interpretation extends the cultural history of the movement into a new sphere. Historians have uncovered the influence of racial self-determination on the visual arts, theater, music, and literature but so far have yet to examine how those professionally and personally invested in shaping the built environment translated Black Power's theoretical ideas into new conceptions via the medium of urban space. Second, understanding the breadth of this vision provides yet more

"The Search for New Forms" **47**

evidence that Black Power was more than a negative denouement to a heroic civil rights movement or simply a reactive, violent break from that movement. Utopian ambitions marked a proactive vision of a better world that valued people often taken for granted, displaced, or ignored by urban development. Lastly, bringing the history of Black Power into conversation with the history of architecture and urbanism broadens, expands, and diversifies the picture of the participants who not only took part in the project of criticizing and rejecting modernist conceptions of the built environment but also in proposing postmodern alternatives to them. Among many other sites, postmodern urbanism was born in the social history of predominantly African American neighborhoods in this decade, in the people who inhabited them, and in the work of the architects and planners who came to their aid; these origins historians have yet to explore.[1]

Harlem provides a particularly vital terrain on which to examine these issues. Segregation assumed different forms across regional contexts, and, as such, Black Power's visions and ambitions also took different forms. Yet Harlem's history proved especially influential. As the most mythologized African American community, Harlem offered a symbolic and physical space that attracted and inspired activists who sought to articulate the parameters of a black utopia and actualize goals of autonomy and self-determination. This essay focuses on one exceptionally significant effort toward those goals. When the Architects' Renewal Committee in Harlem (ARCH) opened in 1964, it became the first community design center – a new vehicle for citizen participation that would soon proliferate across all major American cities. Over the latter half of the 1960s, ARCH assisted Harlemites who sought to resist and revise official urban redevelopment plans, even as the organization transformed amid the changing racial politics of the era. The architect J. Max Bond Jr., became the first African American director of ARCH in 1967, shifting the organization's work toward the radical aims of Black Power. With Bond at the helm of ARCH, activist planners and architects and their community partners joined in the effort to trace Black Power's spatial implications. In Harlem's streets and communities, they articulated an alternative future in the language of the design disciplines.

Carmichael and Hamilton admitted the undeniable utopianism that suffused such a "search for new forms," asking, "If these proposals … sound impractical, utopian, then we ask: what other real alternatives exist?" The answer, they explained, was that "there are none" (Carmichael and Hamilton 1967, 177). Yet an irony of the search for new forms, at least in the realm of urban space, was that very often those forms were not new. In keeping with Black Power's appreciation of majority-minority communities, architects and planners inspired by community control celebrated and sought to preserve the traditional streetscape, mixed land use, and eclectic built environment of places such as Harlem. Moreover, the spatial vision that proponents advanced was as much concerned with the people who lived in Harlem's buildings as with the built form itself. Activist architects and planners idealized and strove to maintain the everyday life of those communities,

48 Brian D. Goldstein

insisting that such places be rebuilt by and for the benefit of their existing residents. If this effort to preserve the landscape and people of Harlem marked a certain restraint in activists' vision, however, the idea remained quite radical in its refutation of the social and physical ambitions of modernist redevelopment. Indeed, their vision helped end modernist urban renewal and usher in a new emphasis on the human scale and traditional urban fabric that characterized postmodernism. Yet the twofold nature of their formal vision, concerned equally with buildings and the people who inhabited them, and the seeming contradiction in focusing on preservation but for radical ends, would also be unintended obstacles to fully realizing the utopian ambitions of Black Power.

Reforming Urban Renewal

Bond assumed the top post of ARCH during a public demonstration led by militant activists on the organization's front steps at 306 Lenox Avenue in the summer of 1967. The son of a prominent family of educators, Harvard University-trained, and an expatriate in liberated Ghana, Bond had recently returned to the United States. His installation denoted the new ambitions that swept through Harlem with the rise of Black Power. Yet while Bond's ascent brought a symbolic and strategic shift in ARCH's work toward the goals of racial self-determination, this new direction would unfold within an institutional framework that had been put into place by his predecessor, C. Richard Hatch, a white architect who had founded ARCH three years earlier. Hatch had launched the organization in 1964 in response to Harlem's history as a site of constant postwar redevelopment. Through ARCH, Hatch sought to provide architectural and planning services to a community that had few resources to oppose disruptive modernist planning. Instead of simply stopping urban renewal, however, ARCH volunteers hoped to reorient redevelopment for the benefit of Harlem's predominantly low-income residents. Nevertheless, the advocacy approach that Hatch espoused would soon run against the demands of the emerging Black Power movement. Despite supporting community control, Hatch found his position increasingly untenable in a new era. In launching ARCH, however, he had created a platform that would soon come to support Bond's more radical approach to community-based urbanism.

Harlem was by no means the only New York City community transformed by urban renewal in the 1950s and 1960s, but it represented a favored site for officials seeking ambitious redevelopment of the built environment. Urban renewal underwrote the transformation of hundreds of Harlem's acres in the postwar era. It also brought the displacement of thousands of the neighborhood's residents. Central Harlem, for example, was the site of three new public housing complexes in these decades – the Polo Grounds Houses, Colonial Park Houses, and St. Nicholas Houses – and two middle-income housing developments that remade 24 acres along the neighborhood's Lenox Avenue. In West Harlem, officials built another middle-income complex, Morningside Gardens, and two adjacent public housing developments. The transformation of East Harlem unfolded on an even larger scale. Here, New York City invested over $250 million to build a string of projects housing 62,400 residents. These developments claimed massive spaces within the grid. The James Weldon Johnson Houses, for example, which opened in 1948, encompassed six city blocks. Their scale was grand but not atypical. By the time of the completion of the 15th public housing project in East Harlem, the city had reconstructed 162 of its acres.[2]

Such efforts grew from a range of motivations, many quite benign, but with devastating social consequences. Officials hoped that redevelopment would keep cities viable amid widespread suburbanization, would reverse physical deterioration, and would decently house a wide range of New Yorkers. This approach embodied a mid-century liberal faith in the merits of governmental intervention and monumental thinking. The public good exceeded the potential disruption to individuals, officials argued, in a view embodied most famously by Robert Moses, the power broker who remade vast stretches of New York City. Yet harm to people and communities could be profound, and the broad promises of redevelopment projects often fell short. Residents watched their neighborhoods deteriorate amid the delays that preceded clearance, were frequently displaced without sufficient rehousing assistance, did not qualify for new housing, or waited years for a spot to open in new developments. Public housing, underfunded and undermaintained, became rife with physical and social problems. By the mid-1960s commentators, policy-makers, and residents widely agreed that urban renewal had often worsened the conditions it promised to improve. Critics argued that large-scale redevelopment had only decreased affordable housing, created isolated urban enclaves, undermined and undervalued the social structure of existing neighborhoods, and failed in its promise to enhance the physical environment of cities.[3]

Though architects and planners had done well by urban renewal, many younger designers joined the growing critique of its means and ends. Hatch, who had called an October 1964 meeting of the New York chapter of the American Institute of Architects, leading to the formation of ARCH, agreed with many observers that the gap between design expertise and the public had grown too vast. As a result, most urban plans followed textbook orthodoxy but did not meet the needs of actual city residents. Hatch acknowledged the faults of his profession, hoping to direct knowledge to new ends. "We in the profession who have followed the pattern of urban renewal (or Negro removal, as it is sometimes called) across the country know what Harlem residents are up against," he explained. "We know that technical knowledge equal to or superior to that of the government agencies is necessary to a successful fight. We hope to be able to provide that assistance." Hatch proposed a new kind of practice that promised to combine professional expertise with Harlemites' vision for their community.[4]

Architects and planners conscious of the paradoxes of the liberal aspirations of renewal had offered their services to communities in Harlem and elsewhere on a limited basis since the late 1950s. But ARCH was most likely the first effort to

50 Brian D. Goldstein

institutionalize this function, to provide a physical space accessible to an entire neighborhood where residents affected by official plans could access professional services otherwise out of reach. This concept would come to be known as the "community design center." Its role in Harlem was revealed in the preposition that Hatch had chosen for the organization's name. ARCH was not "of" Harlem but "in" Harlem. Staffed with architects and planners who came from throughout the city, ARCH pledged to be accessible to residents, at their service and in their midst.

Hatch's vision for ARCH had roots in a range of sources. One was a personal motivation, informed by the broader context of the mounting African American freedom struggle. Hatch had grown up in a conservative Long Island family but maintained far-left sympathies, representing the American Labor party in Great Neck and documenting poverty in the town for the *Suffolk County News* in the late 1940s. He studied architecture at Harvard College and the University of Pennsylvania in the 1950s, and in the 1960s he became involved with the Student Nonviolent Coordinating Committee and the Mississippi Freedom Democratic Party. Hatch watched tides of young people leave to join the civil rights movement in the South but realized the extent of the problems that persisted in the North – an awareness that focused his energies on New York City, where he was working as an architect. In 1963 and 1964 Hatch became acquainted with Harlem civil rights leaders such as James Farmer, Jesse Gray, Marshall England, and Roy Innis. In this milieu, he began to consider alternatives to renewal in its typical form.[5]

Hatch likewise drew from the broader public discourse on participation that was gaining momentum at this time. President Lyndon B. Johnson had signed the Economic Opportunity Act of 1964 in August, bringing the Community Action Program to reality along with the promise to ensure "the maximum feasible participation of the poor and members of the groups served" in its activities. While several months would pass before the first War on Poverty money reached Harlem, Hatch, like his fellow activists across American cities, found in Johnson's initiative both a political opening for his civil rights ambitions and new financial support that would help efforts such as ARCH get under way. The War on Poverty fueled experiments in participatory democracy and new campaigns for local autonomy not only by residents of diverse racial and ethnic backgrounds but also by outsiders such as Hatch, who sought to organize communities that had suffered without self-determination. Many of these efforts took on radical dimensions over time, as would be the case in Harlem. In these early days, however, ARCH's mission and work shared the larger aspiration of the Great Society to respond to demands for grassroots democracy without fundamentally overturning existing institutions.[6]

To this end, Hatch and the activist planners and architects who made up the founding ARCH staff, most of whom were white, collaborated with Harlemites to confront disruptive redevelopment proposals. In already-mobilized communities, residents requested ARCH's assistance in drafting alternative plans that reoriented urban renewal for their benefit. West Harlem, where in 1964 the city announced a plan to clear most of the blocks east of Morningside Park as part of a larger redevelopment effort, offers a representative example. Here, where 99 percent of residents were African American, city planners claimed that an astounding 375 of the 393 structures were unsound and unworthy of rehabilitation. They envisioned clearing nearly 80 percent of this stretch of West Harlem. Faced with their demise, community groups turned to the recently formed ARCH. While acknowledging the need for reinvestment in a neighborhood with decades-old homes that had deteriorated without adequate upkeep, ARCH staff opposed the widespread use of demolition. With its community partners ARCH prepared an alternate plan that called for the expansion of the redevelopment area so the potential benefits of reconstruction would encompass more Harlemites. But ARCH embraced physical rehabilitation, not clearance, as a means of upgrading West Harlem's homes, estimating that three-quarters of the neighborhood's buildings required only code enforcement or modest reconstruction to enable residents to remain in place.[7]

In West Harlem and other neighborhoods – such as the East Harlem Triangle, a predominantly African American, low-income community north of 125th Street that officials planned to bulldoze to build an industrial park – ARCH joined Harlemites in pursuing alternatives to disruptive redevelopment from within the structure of urban renewal. Similarly, while calling for a new democratization of planning, ARCH maintained a central role for professional expertise. As Hatch explained in 1965, his objective was "to turn the consumers of architectural goods – the poor – into clients." ARCH staff would "develop their ideas into physical plans and concrete proposals for social action." Architects and planners would retain a primary responsibility as intermediaries in the process, "as advocates for the poor." His words anticipated those of the planner Paul Davidoff, whose seminal November 1965 article "Advocacy and Pluralism in Planning" set out the principles of what came to be widely known as "advocacy planning." "The planner should do more than explicate the values underlying his prescriptions for courses of action," Davidoff argued. "He should affirm them; he should be an advocate for what he deems proper."[8]

This approach offered a new vision for planning that provided avenues for participation while reinforcing the importance of the professional expert. In the case of the East Harlem Triangle, for example, long-standing community leaders frustrated with the city's disruptive plans and the neighborhood's continued deterioration decided to take on planning themselves. In mid-1966 they asked ARCH to serve as their consultant. ARCH, in turn, asked residents to form a planning committee, a nine-member group that met with an ARCH staff member daily throughout the summer. This committee symbolized the broader community, with mostly low-income members, several receiving welfare assistance or living in landlord-abandoned buildings. As they crafted a vision for their 14-block neighborhood focused on retaining and rebuilding low-income housing, their process embodied the ideal of the advocacy model. ARCH's planner, June Fields, who had previously worked in the New York City Department of City Planning, translated residents' ideas into concepts and forms.[9]

52 Brian D. Goldstein

Advocacy planning enabled Harlemites to resist official proposals with plans communicating their own interests, but ARCH's embrace of this approach would become problematic as the decade progressed. Harlem was a hotbed for the emergence of Black Power and the pursuit of community control. Indeed, the 1966 protests over community control of schools, a seminal battle in which demands for racial self-determination broke to the surface, unfolded in the East Harlem Triangle, the very neighborhood that ARCH was assisting, and included many of the community leaders with whom ARCH worked. Those protests, sparked by parents' demands for control over Intermediate School 201, attracted Stokely Carmichael to Harlem. The arrival of Black Power's symbolic leader demonstrated the degree to which radical ideals had already become widespread in the neighborhood. But Black Power's emerging calls for racial self-determination and community control did not coexist easily alongside the advocacy model practiced under Hatch. The persistent role of white expertise in ARCH's work – exemplified by its leader – clashed with rising demands for radical participatory democracy and the movement's heightened racial politics.[10]

As the wave of Black Power rose in Harlem, it soon lapped at the base of ARCH. The organization was an ally of many of the most vociferous proponents of Black Power's ideals and likewise espoused an appreciation for the residents of Harlem. Even so, Hatch understood that the transforming civil rights movement required that ARCH transform too. At first this evolution was gradual. Hatch sought to diversify the organization's leadership and joined efforts to introduce new institutional models that would support local movements for self-determination. In 1967 Hatch invited Kenneth Simmons, an African American architect from San Francisco, to join ARCH. Simmons hailed from an affluent Oklahoma family and had attended Harvard College with Hatch, but he brought a new perspective to ARCH. In San Francisco he was, as ARCH staff announced, "a CORE [Congress of Racial Equality] militant." He held a distinctly nationalist vision. "We are a group apart and obviously we are an interest group. We have our survival as a common interest," Simmons wrote. He also channeled the discourse of community control. "We must also control our land; control our geographic community."[11]

Likewise, in 1967 ARCH staff joined many Black Power movement leaders, including Preston Wilcox – an intellectual father of community control – and Roy Innis, who had overseen the radicalization of CORE, to found Harlem's first community development corporation (CDC). The Harlem Commonwealth Council (HCC), as the corporation would be called, was to raise capital through the sale of modest five-dollar voting shares to low-income Harlemites; the money would fund business ventures to create employment and fill unmet retail needs in the neighborhood. In time, founders imagined, the effort would extend to housing, education, and social services, creating an alternative to public aid. HCC was one of more than 70 urban CDCs that grew out of the Black Power movement by the early 1970s, alongside other early efforts in Brooklyn, Cleveland, and

Philadelphia. Though individual CDCs differed in their strategies and ventures, they aligned in their efforts to foster economic self-sufficiency and neighborhood autonomy. CDCs offered a means of institutionalizing Black Power's most ambitious principles, putting community control and self-reliance within reach.[12]

If radical activists agreed with Hatch and others that Harlem could be both a thriving community and one that belonged to its low-income residents, however, they disagreed over who would see it to that point. The most radical voices in Harlem were no longer willing to wait for gradual transition. Amid the growing influence of Black Power, Hatch had begun to feel out of place. He sensed suspicion from community members who had once welcomed ARCH. In June 1967 Hatch appointed Simmons as the co-director of the organization. Hatch soon reached out to Max Bond, suggesting that he return from Ghana to become ARCH's sole director. While Hatch hoped for a peaceful succession, however, Simmons had grown impatient with the pace of change. In late summer, therefore, Simmons staged a boisterous demonstration – a "palace coup," Hatch called it – outside the organization's front door. Assembling protesters for the spectacle and attracting a crowd, Simmons installed Bond as the first African American director of ARCH.[13]

"The People Cannot Do a Worse Job Than Architects Have Done"

Bond's arrival brought both a symbolic change to ARCH and a reorientation toward the radical aspirations of the Black Power movement. Shaped by his own experience in postcolonial Ghana, Bond sought to realize the movement's central objective of community control by creating new means for Harlemites to shape their built environment. While in many ways maintaining ARCH's long-standing approach and its emphasis on the role of expertise, Bond embraced new strategies that he hoped would put architecture and planning in the hands of the African American residents of neighborhoods such as Harlem. For Bond, this goal held more than a desire for democratic participation; it also promised the creation of a new kind of city.

With Bond leading ARCH, the language and goals of Black Power came to suffuse the organization's daily work. Bond launched a new monthly publication, for example, that encompassed a broad range of issues related to race, not just urban planning, and espoused a viewpoint resolutely focused on the objective of community control. Early issues of *Harlem News* featured articles on the lack of job opportunities for black contractors and continued battles over school decentralization. Under the headline "Black $$$ Power," Innis wrote, "one of the great needs of black people is for control of their own institutions." Invoking Black Power's liberatory perspective in an editorial, Bond criticized the "continued colonialism" he found in policy approaches to Harlem and similar neighborhoods. "It seems to us that the key issue in housing, in the economic development of our

54 Brian D. Goldstein

communities, in planning our neighborhoods and in educating our children is not simply what decisions are made but who makes them," he wrote. Bond argued for the central goal of self-determination in all facets of Harlem's public life, especially its built environment.[14]

Bond was perhaps an unlikely candidate to lead the radical architectural vanguard in Harlem in the late 1960s, but his biography helps explain how a member of one of the 20th century's most distinguished families came into this role. Born in Louisville in 1935, Bond moved frequently, as his father, J. Max Bond Sr., manned academic posts at Dillard University and Tuskegee Institute, an educational post for the US government in Haiti, and the presidency of the University of Liberia. Bond's mother, Ruth Clement Bond, was also an academic and played an instrumental role in modernizing the artform of the quilt through her work with the Tennessee Valley Authority. Max Sr.'s brother, Horace Mann Bond, led Lincoln University in Philadelphia, and his brother-in-law, Rufus Clement, served for two decades as president of Atlanta University. Horace Mann Bond's son, Julian Bond, would become a major civil rights leader, and he remained close to his first cousin Max Jr.[15]

Despite his exceptional family, Bond's experience as an undergraduate and architecture graduate student at Harvard in the 1950s was difficult at times due to his status as one of the few African Americans at the university. Other students burned a cross outside the dorm where he and eight other African American freshmen lived in 1952. An architecture professor instructed him to choose a different profession – architecture was not for African Americans, he said. Yet Bond also maintained leadership positions in the Harvard Society for Minority Rights, the college's National Association for the Advancement of Colored People affiliate. He moved to France to begin his career in architecture, received a series of interviews at prominent New York City firms upon his return, and then a series of rejections upon showing up. Few firms would make room for an African American designer, even one as highly trained as Bond. In 1964, inspired by a liberated Ghana, Bond joined Kwame Nkrumah's government as an architect – a "palace architect" in Bond's words – who designed state buildings and an addition to Nkrumah's estate.[16]

On moving to Ghana Bond joined a vibrant expatriate community that shaped his worldview. As one of the first African states to escape colonial status, Ghana attracted an international audience from the moment of its independence. The Americans who settled there typically skewed toward the more radical end of the political spectrum, compelled to cross the Atlantic Ocean by choice or often by necessity. The Harlem writer and activist Julian Mayfield and the scholar and activist W.E.B. Du Bois moved to Ghana when their search for alternatives to racial liberalism brought increasing state repression. However, many others expatriated electively with the same frustrations in mind. When Bond and his wife, Jean Carey Bond, moved to Ghana, they became part of a group of intellectuals and artists – including Maya Angelou – pursuing the goal of a newly liberated state run by

"The Search for New Forms" **55**

black leaders, promising collectivism and openness to socialist ideas (Gaines 2006, 4–5, 136–178).

In postcolonial Ghana these expatriates found a living example of the idea that a united people could claim the right to self-determination and self-rule. Nkrumah described his nation as the center of an international movement toward the liberation of black people, a pan-African idea that appealed to African Americans frustrated with the slow progress and failed promise of racial integration in the United States. Bond and his contemporaries drew parallels between the history of decolonization in Africa and the so-called ghettos in America. Ghanaians had taken control of their destiny, gaining the right of independence from the British Commonwealth. Segregated neighborhoods such as Harlem were also the products of forces outside their control. If segregation marked the outcome of disadvantage and discrimination, advocates reasoned, so too could it seed a seizure of power akin to Ghana's. "The ghetto, this fact of American town planning (and let no one call it an accident) invariably strikes back at the nation and, as evidenced by the recent upheavals, may yet prove to be its undoing," Bond wrote in early 1967.[17]

By the time Bond arrived in Harlem to lead ARCH he had matured as a designer – "As an architect, I sort of grew up in Ghana," he later recalled – but also politically. Rising demands for racial self-determination issued a challenge to ARCH's identity – strongly enough to unseat Hatch – but Bond navigated the inherent tensions between the desire for broad participation and the persistence of experts leading ARCH with a new racialized sensibility. In the charged climate of Black Power, the simple fact of ARCH's racial transition offered a crucial means of bridging this potential divide. Though Bond was not a Harlem native and claimed expertise that made him unusual among the people he served, he (and ARCH's increasingly African American staff) identified with Harlem not as supportive outsider but as a member of the community. This meant that advocacy planning largely continued as the status quo but with new faces in charge. For example, when East Harlem Triangle activists won the city contract to oversee redevelopment planning for their neighborhood in mid-1967, they retained ARCH as their consultant. Residents maintained their role as the involved client, while ARCH turned their ambitions into plans. At the same time, ARCH embraced a new commitment to strategies that staff hoped would expand African American representation among those who reshaped Harlem and would give Harlemites greater control over their built environment.[18]

The organization took several approaches to this task. One strategy involved a dramatic change to ARCH's board of directors, which had only one African American member among the architects, planners, sociologists, and engineers who filled its seats. In early 1968 Bond doubled the board's size to add eight new members, all African American. Unlike earlier board members, none were professional designers and all had prominent reputations as Harlem-based activists. Many, including Innis, Wilcox, and Simmons, had direct ties to the Black Power

56 Brian D. Goldstein

movement. They not only provided what ARCH claimed was "a strong position within the community but [also gave] the community a controlling influence on ARCH's policies and programs." Bond sought to ensure that from top to bottom ARCH was increasingly of, rather than simply in, the community it served.[19]

Secondly, while ARCH staff continued to provide technical assistance with planning projects, they also became more directly involved in vocal, sometimes militant opposition as a means to seize control over projects that frustrated Harlemites. Active protest became a planning strategy that found ARCH and residents together at the ramparts. When the city announced plans to build a sewage plant on the Hudson River in West Harlem, for example, ARCH supported angry Harlemites in words and actions. At an April 4, 1968, hearing on the $70 million plant, 28 residents testified. Edward Taylor joined them on behalf of ARCH, alluding to the violence of recent "long hot summers" in Harlem, Newark, and Detroit. "You want a riot this summer, you build the plant!" he proclaimed, voicing a threat that surely took on new urgency as word spread that evening that an assassin had killed Martin Luther King Jr. and as civil unrest broke out across American cities. The *Harlem News* offered an equally impassioned editorial that also revealed the extent to which ARCH staff identified with and as Harlemites. "We as black people in Harlem want and will not settle for less than the RIGHT of SELF-DETERMINATION," staff wrote.

> We have the right as citizens of this community to say what will be and what will NOT be placed in our midst and we will exert this right. Harlem does not want the plant, Harlem does not need the plant, and Harlem will not have the plant.

Even as an advocacy-based approach persisted in the day-to-day work of ARCH, these newly confrontational tactics offered a means of achieving community control that was more direct and immediate.[20]

Lastly, ARCH's leaders pursued new efforts focused on increasing minority representation among the experts who guided the design process. Bond hoped that greater racial and ethnic diversity would generate more enlightened plans. To compile a list of like-minded designers, he issued a broad call to other minority professionals, touting ARCH's accomplishments. ARCH staff also looked to address the issue of racial representation at its roots by starting a design-oriented training program for Harlemites and area residents. The Architecture in the Neighborhoods program began in the summer of 1968, targeting young African Americans and Puerto Ricans – especially those who had not completed high school. Participants enrolled in an intensive course that included design instruction by minority architects and planners, counseling, and General Education Development (GED) test preparation. The curriculum stressed the potential positive impact of design competency in predominantly minority communities. While students apprenticed in leading architectural firms, ARCH staff intended that participants would bring their talents back home. "Specific emphasis will be given to developing skills which can be used not only in traditional planning or architecture studios," they reported, "but also by advocacy planning groups (such as ARCH), by community groups, or in the implementation of governmental programs in urban areas." As the program director Arthur L. Symes explained, "Architecture and planning are just too important to be omitted from the lives of people who happen to be poor." Such efforts sought to grow the ranks of trained designers, giving control to those who had typically been excluded.[21]

Intrinsic to these shifts in ARCH's work after Bond's arrival was the idea that a designer's race or ethnicity mattered tremendously, that people of color – whether professionals or amateur activists – were particularly attuned to the needs of neighborhoods such as Harlem and could thus uniquely determine the future of those communities. The goal of diversifying and expanding participation in the design process grew from the assumption that doing so would produce a different sort of city than that wrought by urban renewal. This project of participatory democracy remained decidedly utopian, but to ARCH and its collaborators utopia seemed worth a try in a world where urban redevelopment had caused much harm. "There is no great danger in seeing whether other ways of determining architecture might work," Bond said. "The people cannot do a worse job than architects have done. How could the people possibly be more parochial and less sensitive to real human needs and concerns?" (Tucker 1969, 268). The question remained what such a city might look like.

Black Power Utopia

In attempting to discern the nature of this future city, ARCH participated in the broader project of defining the cultural implications of Black Power. While artists, poets, writers, and playwrights involved with the contemporaneous Black Arts Movement argued for the existence and necessity of a "black aesthetic," Bond and the members of ARCH extended this discourse into the realm of the built environment through words and plans. Yet their vision of the ideal city spatialized Black Power in a form with revolutionary ambitions sheathed in an outwardly conservative approach. Proponents sought to preserve the existing streets, blocks, and building types in Harlem, if not always the buildings themselves. They identified this traditional urban fabric with a vital, collective, and authentic vernacular culture that they romanticized. At the same time, they sought to preserve the existing residents of Harlem, in whom Black Power adherents saw value and potential, and build on their basic needs and demands as the foundation for the neighborhood's renaissance. Both ambitions turned modernist urban redevelopment – and its privileging of predominantly white middle-class interests and monumental forms – on its head.

Though not the only place where activists articulated the spatial implications of community control, Harlem formed a particularly vital realm for such pursuits.

58 Brian D. Goldstein

In part this role grew from the community's iconic status as the capital of black culture in America, but it also grew from the presence of ARCH, which brought the broader concerns of Black Power discourse together with its specific interest in design and planning, and from Bond, who proved a passionate evangelist for the possibility of an alternative urban ideal. Indeed, Bond's articulation of this ideal drew directly from his experiences in uniquely racialized spaces, especially Ghana and Harlem. Fundamentally, Bond believed that form – as much as power – could derive from the fact of segregation, and that race played a crucial role in determining the shape of the city. "The idea of a Black expression in architecture is … something that is scoffed at, for which there is little respect," he noted. "This, in the face of the many distinctive contributions that Afro-Americans have made to music, literature, and world culture." If critics attributed Gothic form to the culture of its makers, or the appearance of Japanese architecture to the nationality of its designers, Bond wondered why cities designed by African Americans should not also evince fundamental differences. "It seems reasonable … to expect that were Black Americans in a position to express their particular condition and values through understanding architects and planners, distinctive buildings and plans would result," he argued.[22]

Bond's claim mirrored broader debates in Harlem at this time, especially among those active within the Black Arts Movement. The movement, described in the critic Larry Neal's 1968 manifesto as "the aesthetic and spiritual sister of the Black Power concept," brought the era's nationalist goals into the realm of the written, visual, and performing arts. Its range of protagonists – including Amiri Baraka, Nikki Giovanni, and Ishmael Reed, most famously – pursued an array of goals as diverse as their respective media and geographic locales. A search for a "black aesthetic" marked one common strain in their work, however. As Neal explained, "A main tenet of Black Power is the necessity for Black people to define the world in their own terms. The Black artist has made the same point in the context of aesthetics." Neal contended that the black and white worlds were intrinsically different, "in fact and in spirit." Frustrated with the prospects for African Americans within what he perceived as an often-contradictory, white-dominated world, Neal argued for the necessity of abandoning Western cultural models. "Implicit in this re-evaluation is the need to develop a 'black aesthetic,'" he wrote. Addison Gayle Jr., another critical interpreter of the Black Arts Movement, explained in terms similar to Bond's "that unique experiences produce unique cultural artifacts, and that art is a product of such cultural experiences."[23]

The possibility of a black aesthetic rested in a fundamental conception of the "community" as the *genius loci* of creativity. "The Black Arts Movement is radically opposed to any concept of the artist that alienates him from his community," Neal wrote to open his manifesto. His proclamation reflected a ubiquitous tendency throughout the work of the Black Arts Movement – a focus on authenticity that participants discerned in the vernacular culture of economically impoverished African American communities. Proponents of the Black Arts

"The Search for New Forms" **59**

Movement rejected both the idea that the cultural vanguard would consist of highly trained intellectuals and the expectation that the raw material of cultural production would derive from or lead to "high" forms. Instead, proponents drew their inspiration from popular culture and daily life in communities similar to Harlem, where a predominantly African American and low-income population defined the neighborhood's identity for insiders and outsiders. For cultural producers in the age of Black Power, as with those who took Black Power into political realms, the identity of segregated communities was a source of inspiration, not a weakness (Neal 1971, 272; Ongiri 2010, 7, 22, 105; Smethurst 2005, 67).

Similarly, in articulating the spatial vision of Black Power, Bond pointed to informal urban settlements, with a vernacular culture and a seeming self-determination that he idealized. Bond romanticized the thriving public realms he identified with such places, describing spaces shaped collectively by "the people," without professional experts' mediation. "In considering what a 'people-planned' city would be," Bond said,

> I think we have to relate to the current fad among architects for studying Greek towns, anything built by the people. In every case we find not only a coherent expression, but one full of individual variety, full of richness, full of life.

If ancient civilizations offered one example, however, Bond noted similar qualities in contemporary, often economically impoverished settings. "What we are trying to capture is not Brasilia but that shantytown next to Brasilia; not Tema (Ghana's new city), but Ashaiman, the shantytown next to it," Bond explained, raising juxtapositions all the more interesting for their comparison of highly planned modernist new towns with the unplanned settlements on their margins.

> They are shantytowns only because they do not have the public services and facilities that Brasilia or Tema have, but they do possess the spirit and life of an urban place that Brasilia and Tema lack. They are in fact the people's creation, full of the vibrancy and color that go with life.

Bond condemned Tema for its contrasting emphasis on private ownership and individualism.[24]

Though Bond knew Tema well from his time in Ghana, he did not need to look to Africa to find a cooperatively shaped utopian ideal. Indeed, Bond found similarly idyllic qualities outside ARCH's door, on the streets of Harlem. "Physically, Harlem is terrific," Bond explained. In a description that echoed the Black Arts Movement, Bond celebrated Harlem's streets as the stage on which Harlemites protected each other and participated in the neighborhood's civic culture. "You can send your children out to play and the neighborhood will take care of them," he said. If Bond's description recalled Jane Jacobs's "ballet of the good city sidewalk,"

60 Brian D. Goldstein

it also suggested the uniquely racialized space in which participants performed, as well as the political potential latent within. "The streets are informal, they're real. They're the place where your friends are, but where the enemy (the police) is too," Bond continued. "Black people enjoy the streets; they like to go for walks. Everyone is at home outdoors." Harlem's streets revealed its contemporary life as well as its radical history, Bond noted. "Many corners are symbolic places – 125th Street and Seventh Avenue where Malcolm X used to speak, Michau[x]'s bookshop used to be – in the struggle for equality, for liberation." Despite Harlem's poverty, Bond argued, its built environment and its residents exhibited an everyday, collectivist vitality (Tucker 1969, 266–267; Jacobs 1961, 50–54).

Thus, Bond sought to retain the architectural diversity, mixed land use, and small scale that he celebrated in gazing upon Harlem's blocks – a complexity embodied in the neighborhood's traditional urban fabric. This marked a significant turn from the tenets of modernist planning, which had depended on the notion of the *tabula rasa,* joining the symbolic potential of the clean slate to the physical possibilities of wholesale reconstruction. The modernist city, embodied in the vast projects of urban renewal, prioritized massive, austere forms and the segregation of land uses. If redevelopment was not wholly anti-urban, it nonetheless largely devalued the city as it had grown over time. Bond, on the other hand, celebrated the messiness of urban life, the eclecticism of land use he discovered in Harlem, and the culture he identified as a consequence of that diversity – qualities he hoped to maintain. "I imagine that the Black city would be like a very rich fabric," Bond explained.

> It would not be a fabric with a superimposed pattern but one with multi-color threads running through it. A great mix of housing, social facilities, and working places, rather than a series of distinct zones, each separate, each pure, each Puritanical.

Bond positioned this vision against the monumentality of urban renewal. "A Lincoln Center, pompous and dull and completely aloof from the surrounding blocks, simply could not happen in a Black city," Bond argued. As he later told Ishmael Reed, this dichotomy reflected two tendencies – one grounded in popular culture, one in an elite vision that Bond rejected. He referred to the performances of the Miles Davis Quintet in the late 1950s: "Their stuff is so urban it really conveys the sense of the urban environment, and *without the pretense.*" Bond concluded, "and that's the fundamental difference between what the black art forms are doing and the establishment culture – they really deal with what the people are." In drawing an alternative to urban renewal's massive creations, Bond argued for the possibility of a people-centered urbanism.[25]

Despite their disdain for modernist redevelopment, however, Bond, ARCH, and their community collaborators did not fully eschew the tool of demolition. In some neighborhoods, they argued, physical reconstruction was necessary. Yet

"The Search for New Forms" **61**

even where they anticipated replacing deteriorated buildings, they nonetheless explicitly sought to preserve Harlem's characteristic urban forms and its residents, both disregarded by urban renewal. This mentality was evident in the plans that ARCH staff and their partners completed in 1968 for both West Harlem and the East Harlem Triangle, the two neighborhoods in which the organization had long worked. The former served as a conceptual response to the city's redevelopment plans for West Harlem and Columbia University's long-running proposal to build a gymnasium in nearby Morningside Park. The latter was an official document submitted to the city by the Community Association of the East Harlem Triangle, the activists who had opposed disruptive redevelopment, won the right to plan for themselves, and enlisted ARCH in their cause. The West Harlem plan took a dramatically different approach from – even, in a sense, rejecting – ARCH's earlier, rehabilitation-oriented 1966 plan. "For hundreds of years, Black and poor people in America have settled for secondhand possessions while the more affluent sector had the better things in life," the plan read. "Let us not be fooled by Establishment types who try to cop out on their responsibility by only offering 'rehabilitation' because it is still secondhand housing." The plan restricted rehabilitation to the neighborhood's most distinctive homes, its brownstones and post-1920s apartment buildings, and called for the wide use of federal subsidies to reconstruct West Harlem's blocks. In the East Harlem Triangle, plans depicted the extensive reconstruction of the neighborhood's homes, limiting rehabilitation to only a few small rows. This marked both a practical response to structures that had physically declined through landlord neglect and a symbolic insistence on housing quality regardless of class – a statement that Harlemites deserved equal treatment no matter their income.[26]

Indeed, even as both plans acknowledged a need for sensitive reconstruction, they intensified ARCH's focus on the low-income residents of Harlem, emphasizing not just preventing displacement but also rebuilding the neighborhood on a low-income foundation. "With few exceptions, West Harlem must be rebuilt entirely, but this time for the present residents," staff wrote. In the East Harlem Triangle, planners described a population increasingly desperate for improvement. "The people in the Triangle know something is wrong," they wrote. "They simply are not 'bettering themselves.'" Their daily barriers extended to nearly every realm of life. "Men and women cannot find decent jobs providing a living wage scale. Children are growing up diseased in mind and body for want of better social services … Housing just can't seem to get built for the poor." But optimism for the future of the East Harlem Triangle lay with the low-income residents who had opposed the proposal to demolish their neighborhood and gained the opportunity to replan it. "The Triangle Association believes there is a breath of hope remaining; that breath of hope is themselves," the plan read. "They know they must somehow deliver what all poor people need. Nothing less would suffice."[27]

Here ARCH diverged most significantly from other contemporary critics of modernist redevelopment. In voicing an ideal of small-scale, diverse urbanism in

62 Brian D. Goldstein

neighborhoods that had suffered disproportionately from the bulldozer, ARCH shared the architectural paradigm of figures such as Jacobs, articulated most famously in her landmark 1961 work, *The Death and Life of Great American Cities*. Bond differed dramatically in his social conception of this future city, however. Jacobs's view of ideal urban development in predominantly low-income communities –what she called "slums" – was predicated on economic upscaling or "unslumming": "self-diversification" of the existing residents that she did not detail. ARCH's plans, conversely, proposed the radical idea that Harlem did not need class transformation, whether from within or without, to succeed as a community but could flourish by housing and serving its existing residents, however poor they may be. Moreover, while Jacobs's limited discussion of race centered on the objective of desegregation as a prerequisite for "unslumming," Bond's vision of Black Power urbanism celebrated blackness and the potential he found in segregated populations such as this one (Jacobs 1961, 270–290).

The needs of these Harlemites stood at the center of the reconstructed neighborhoods that ARCH and its community partners envisioned. The plan for the East Harlem Triangle displayed the attributes espoused by Bond in his description of the city as "a very rich fabric" – especially the varied land uses that had long characterized the small community. Plans maintained a mixture of industry and residence in the East Harlem Triangle, for example, delineating an industrial zone along its western flank intended to provide employment for residents near their homes (see Figure 3.1). Instead of hiding residents' unique and often-acute social service requirements, ARCH and its East Harlem Triangle partners located an innovative center called the "Triangle Commons" directly in what they described as the "heart" of the rebuilt neighborhood. This center was to provide a home for the full range of services that residents required, including welfare and employment assistance, legal services, recreation, addiction treatment, day care, and special education. "An integral part of the whole concept plan is the programming of specific services to meet specific needs of the Triangle community," planners explained.[28]

Likewise, despite emphasizing new construction throughout both neighborhoods, planners sought to retain and reproduce the vernacular character that Bond had so admired on the streets of Harlem. The plan for the East Harlem Triangle rejected the "aloof" monumental structures of urban renewal that Bond denounced. Buildings instead took a smaller, variegated form and maintained the neighborhood's existing grid. Where plans called for closed streets, pedestrian pathways kept the gridiron intact. In new public spaces, planners offered hopeful visions that the civic life of the neighborhood would thrive. One illustration depicted the Triangle Commons as a lively center, with a modern plaza surrounding a low glass building, children playing, and adults socializing (see Figure 3.2).

In Morningside Park, on the clearing that was to have become the controversial Columbia University gymnasium, ARCH and its community partner, the

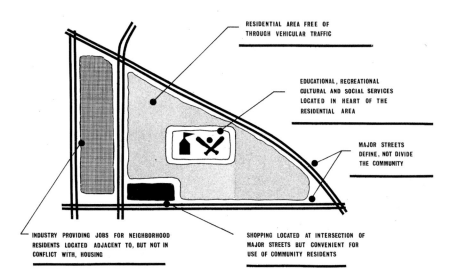

FIGURE 3.1 Conceptual plan prepared in August 1968 by ARCH and the Community Association of the East Harlem Triangle, showing a mixture of land uses within the East Harlem Triangle neighborhood and community and social services at its "heart." Madison Avenue defines the western boundary of this diagram, while 125th Street forms its southern boundary. From ARCH, East Harlem Triangle Plan (New York: ARCH, 1968). Courtesy of Arthur L. Symes

West Harlem Community Organization, envisioned a stage set celebrating the cultural and political currents of Black Power. A multiuse amphitheater was to "feature performances by Motown artists, the Negro Ensemble Company, the New Heritage Repertory Theatre, and local musical, singing, and acting groups of all ages," the organizations explained. Plans included space to accommodate "avant-garde theater," an "African museum," the production and exhibition of "black culture and crafts," and a "soul food garden." The plan's authors imagined a welcoming plaza where all of Harlem's residents – including children, couples, political radicals, and even a neighborhood inebriate – would find space to act out their civic roles (see Figure 3.3).[29]

Above all, idealized visions of Harlem's future preserved the street-side dynamism that Black Power adherents emphasized as the neighborhood's defining feature. Planners tied that quotidian activity to the diverse uses typical of Harlem's boulevards. "The strip of residential-commercial uses along Eighth Avenue has a vitality that should be retained in any rebuilding scheme," they argued in the West Harlem plan. They feared the transformation of Harlem's major axes into bland single-use business districts. "All the other crosstown streets are anonymous. What

FIGURE 3.2 ARCH's August 1968 rendering showing "Triangle Commons," the community and social service complex to be located at the center of the East Harlem Triangle neighborhood. Planners envisioned its plaza as a vibrant public space that maintained Harlem's civic life. From ARCH, East Harlem Triangle Plan. Drawing by E. Donald Van Purnell. Courtesy of Arthur L. Symes

has happened to 8th Street is a good example of what we don't want," Bond said, referring to 125th Street. ARCH's aim, he argued, was to retain the "Main Street quality" of Harlem's iconic thoroughfare, to prevent the duplication here of what one observer sympathetic to ARCH called "Sixth Avenue stoneland," filled with "maximum-land-utilization office blockbusters." To avoid this fate, the plan for the East Harlem Triangle described a mixture of commercial and residential uses in high-, mid-, and low-rise buildings along 125th Street.[30]

ARCH employed a single illustration to depict both 125th Street and Eighth Avenue, a rendering that stood as an ideal type representing aspirations for the neighborhood's famous boulevards (see Figure 3.4). The streetscape's unique qualities became immediately apparent. A divided road offered two lanes for buses, taxis, and local traffic. All other vehicles were to be diverted to secondary streets. "Read *Muhammad Speaks*," a sign on the bus urged, touting the official organ of the Nation of Islam. Signifiers of Black Power fashion abounded: passersby raised fists in greeting and wore natural hairstyles. One man sported a dashiki. Yet more

FIGURE 3.3 Rendering showing residents on the plaza intended for the cleared gymnasium site in Morningside Park. The image, from September 1968, suggests ARCH and WHCO's vision of this as an inclusive space welcoming of all Harlemites and supportive of the era's radical politics. Signage includes the advice, "Read Muhammed Speaks" and "Support Black Panthers." From ARCH and WHCO, West Harlem Morningside: A Community Proposal (New York: ARCH and WHCO, 1968), 34. Drawing by E. Donald Van Purnell. Courtesy of Arthur L. Symes

evident was the normalcy of the scene. Though new buildings faced the avenue alongside historic predecessors, they aligned to define an active public space and an eclectic but unified streetscape. A lush canopy of trees framed the sidewalk, the bearer of the street life celebrated by both Bond and the proponents of the Black Arts Movement, and vividly represented here.[31]

Such portraits of Harlem's major streets, not as the problem-filled places that outsiders often described but as a lively public realm – functional and thriving, heterogeneous and intact – with Harlem's African American residents in place, offered an approach to redevelopment founded in the preservation and reproduction of an idealized urbanity that Black Power proponents celebrated. Though this may have seemed a modest ideal, it was actually quite radical. For decades planners

66 Brian D. Goldstein

FIGURE 3.4 ARCH's rendering of 125th Street, from its East Harlem Triangle Plan completed in August 1968. ARCH used the same drawing to represent Eighth Avenue in its West Harlem Morningside plan of the same year, suggesting this as an ideal type symbolizing the organization's vision for Harlem's major boulevards. Eclectic buildings align to define a public realm in which residents gather, converse, and display symbols of the Black Power Movement. Drawing by E. Donald Van Purnell. Courtesy of Arthur L. Symes

had connected the revival of neighborhoods such as Harlem to the transformation of their built fabric and their residents. Rather than changing, hiding, or uprooting such residents and their unique needs, however, Bond, ARCH, their community partners, and fellow activists in the Black Power movement celebrated both, even putting them at center stage. Like Black Power, this vision proposed the revolutionary idea that Harlemites were not the cause of, but the solution to, the urban crisis of the late 1960s. They were the foundation for Harlem's revitalization.

Unintended Consequences

ARCH's translation of Black Power's principles into spatial form held seemingly contradictory ideas in tension. Proponents tapped the existing physical and social landscape of Harlem for transformative, even radical ends. And, in the short term, this vision would bring considerable accomplishments for Harlemites who previously had little influence over their built environment. In West Harlem and the East Harlem Triangle, ARCH and its community partners voiced alternatives that provided a counterweight to official plans or that became official plans. Both neighborhoods used these efforts to resist the destructive large-scale reconstruction that officials had intended. In the East Harlem Triangle, residents even brought much of their vision to life, building a social service center and hundreds of affordable housing units in the following years. They did so in part by rehabilitating historic buildings or, where they employed new construction, generally maintaining the existing street grid of the neighborhood. While they did not achieve every aspiration of their ambitious 1968 plan, they accomplished their objective of rebuilding the community on a low-income foundation. West Harlemites never realized the goals of sensitive reconstruction that they set out in their plan, but neither did redevelopment uproot their neighborhood. A resistant community with a vision for the future outlasted the officials who had planned disruptive urban renewal, leaving their homes and blocks intact.[32]

Through such efforts, Harlemites helped ensure that modernist urbanism – the approach that had dominated the transformation of American inner cities for nearly 25 years – would cease to be a viable strategy in this era. By the early 1970s, large-scale, clearance-oriented, and top-down redevelopment had been widely discredited as a method of city rebuilding. Likewise, young architects such as Bond and their community partners played a crucial role in articulating the parameters of a new urbanism in its place. A new sensitivity to the human scale, to the needs and desires of residents at the grassroots, and to eclectic and informal urban landscapes all became central to the practices of architecture and planning in the years that followed. These ideas represented one corner of the larger project of postmodernism. Urbanists with Black Power inclinations were not the only actors who inspired this transformation, but their effort to craft an alternative urban vision in one of the neighborhoods most dramatically transformed by modernism in the symbolic center of black America, and amid the nation's largest city, provided a key chapter in this story. Postmodernism was more than a theoretical project; it also had roots in local contexts such as this one. ARCH, the nation's first community design center, served as one site where the dominance of urban renewal came undone and was one of the actors offering an alternative.

Indeed, the spatial vision of Black Power was not simply oppositional but was also proactive – a fact exemplified by its direct and indirect influence on the built environment in subsequent years. ARCH became a model for advocacy-oriented institutions that emerged throughout American cities to help communities realize a more humane approach to urbanism. Dozens of community design centers opened in the late 1960s and after, assisting residents with alternate planning, low-income housing rehabilitation, and other small-scale design projects that reflected the neighborhood orientation and physical ideals of ARCH's work.

68 Brian D. Goldstein

Bond, too, carried this experience forward into a long architectural career in which he designed projects such as Harlem's Schomburg Center for Research in Black Culture, which were formally innovative yet complementary to their physical and social contexts. Likewise, he continued to insist on more engaged, inclusive approaches to design training, especially in his roles as an educator and administrator at Columbia University and the City College of New York. Black Power's urban vision also inspired further grassroots efforts to realize its physical and social goals, particularly in a low-income "urban homesteading" movement that emerged in Harlem amid the widespread housing abandonment of the 1970s. African American residents sought to rehabilitate historic brownstones and aging but still viable tenements through their own sweat equity, carrying forward the goal of restoring Harlem's built environment for the benefit of its existing residents while seeking the objective of community control.[33]

Yet the tensions intrinsic to Black Power's vision would also contribute to the incomplete attainment of its ideals over time. Black Power proponents sought to preserve or deferentially modify the landscape of Harlem for radical ends, but in doing so they took a physically conservative approach that often had unintended consequences. Bond celebrated Harlem's streets and blocks as models because he associated them with a vernacular culture that he idealized as authentic, natural, vital, and real. His physical ideal was always tightly bound up with a social ideal. The buildings and the people of Harlem represented equal components of a transformative vision of the future city. In time, however, it proved relatively simple for many who came in the wake of Black Power to unbind the movement's democratic aspirations from the cover under which they had arrived. In other words, successors frequently maintained the outward appearance of Black Power's ideals while transforming the objectives within. As a result, the physical ambitions of Black Power often persisted without the social ambitions at their core.

The conservative tendencies of ARCH's expertise-driven approach likewise bore much of the responsibility for this outcome. As much as Bond identified with Harlemites and as much as he and his African American peers sought to throw open the doors of their professional ranks to new voices, their vision nonetheless depended fundamentally on retaining a central role for highly trained figures such as Bond, who translated the information they received from residents into the language of architecture and planning. This emphasis on expertise, intrinsic to the nature of the design professions, evinced a belief in the power of plans and images as vehicles for political and social change. ARCH's community partners shared this belief as participants in an advocacy-based process that sought to produce alternate plans as counterpoints to official plans. Yet the gains of such efforts were ultimately circumscribed, because physical representations were mutable in a way that broad movement building or ambitious structural transformation would not have been.[34]

This dilemma and the unintended consequences that followed were endemic throughout the afterlife of Black Power. The iconic closed fist that symbolized

"The Search for New Forms" **69**

the movement provided one example – a compelling image with a fashionable ubiquity that obscured the critical project at the heart of Black Power. The new kinds of community-based organizations that grew out of Black Power offered a parallel example – not as physical representations but as institutional shells that could likewise be inhabited by a wide range of ideological interests. Community development corporations (CDCs), for instance, an outgrowth that ARCH had helped launch in Harlem, often emerged proposing that predominantly African American, low-income communities should pool their modest resources to become economic engines. Proponents imagined that CDCs, as cooperatively owned business ventures, would return their profits to the community. But CDCs appealed equally to federal officials who sought to devolve urban policy to the local level and promote a strategy of "black capitalism," and to community-based moderates who likewise saw these entities not as a means for upheaval but as a convenient vehicle for profits and as an end in themselves. President Richard M. Nixon, who embraced CDCs as part of his policy tool kit, symbolized the former tendency. He provided funding support that enabled CDCs to acquire businesses and expand, but such action also distanced them from the community that was to have invested in their success. Freed from cooperative governance, many CDC leaders pursued top-down approaches to economic development. This was the case for the Harlem Commonwealth Council, with a leader who shed the founding goal of community stock ownership for a paternalistic approach based on his assurances that the gains of the multimillion-dollar corporation would reach the community. Harlem was not alone as CDCs in other cities likewise shifted away from their initially communitarian ideals. Such organizations were meaningful and lasting legacies of Black Power, but their complicated afterlife and internal transformations suggest the incomplete victories that often followed the late 1960s.[35]

In the case of Black Power's spatial vision, ARCH contributed to the broader downfall of architectural modernism and the introduction of a more sensitive alternative, but ultimately that vision took an ironic turn in the years that followed. Just as the architectural language of once-utopian modernism could be deployed for socially harmful purposes in the most egregious cases of urban redevelopment, so too could the appreciation of the urban fabric of the postmodern era serve a variety of different, even opposing ideological goals in the late 20th century. Bond's and ARCH's visions aligned easily with other superficially similar visions in this era, though their intended ends differed greatly. There was perhaps no better example of such strange bedfellows than the typically white, middle-class "brownstoners" who, in pursuit of an ideal of urban authenticity, bought and restored historic housing throughout New York City's predominantly low-income neighborhoods (including Harlem) during these decades. They could be allies of longstanding residents when objectives converged, but more frequently they followed their own political and economic interests, which often conflicted with or undermined those of their poorer neighbors. As postmodernism took hold, then, urbanists of all stripes broadly agreed with physical ideas quite like those Bond and ARCH had voiced, including the celebration of the traditional urban streetscape and street grid, existing buildings, mixed land use, and architectural eclecticism. But few such efforts maintained the social vision that had formed the core of Bond's ideal – that the current residents in places such as Harlem were already enough for a successful, vital, and prosperous community.[36]

In Harlem and elsewhere, the block-clearing approach of postwar urban redevelopment was rarely seen in the late 20th and early 21st centuries. Instead, new development typically retained, repaired, or sensitively replaced a neighborhood's built fabric (see Figure 3.5). But developers, officials, real estate investors, and even community organizations increasingly used those buildings to attract new, affluent residents who made up ever larger percentages of gentrifying inner-city neighborhoods in New York, Chicago, Washington, DC, and San Francisco, among other cities. If a glance at Harlem's facades today suggests the accomplishment of the spatial ideal of Black Power, a deeper look reveals only a partial victory.

FIGURE 3.5 By the late 20th century, new development in Harlem typically retained, repaired, or sensitively replaced the neighborhood's built fabric, but the residents of such housing were increasingly affluent. Pictured here are two examples, both on West 131st Street: a rehabilitated building completed in 1993 (left) and Harlem Sol, a privately developed condominium involving restoration of a historic brownstone and contextual new construction, completed in 2011 (right). Photographs by author. Courtesy of Brian Goldstein

Acknowledgments

This article first appeared in the *Journal of American History*, 103, no. 2 (September 2016), 375–399. It benefited tremendously from the generous suggestions and perceptive criticism of Martha Biondi, Neil Brenner, Lizabeth Cohen, Jessica Courtier, Bill Cronon, Sarah Florini, K. Michael Hays, Laura Warren Hill, Will Jones, Edward Linenthal, Theresa McCulla, Daegan Miller, Mary Murrell, Amanda Rogers, Andrew Sandoval-Strausz, Jerome Tharaud, Komozi Woodard, Samuel Zipp, and the anonymous reviewers for the *Journal of American History*. I am also extremely grateful for the support of the A.W. Mellon Postdoctoral Fellowship Program at the University of Wisconsin–Madison and the Charles Warren Center for Studies in American History at Harvard University.

Notes

1 On Black Power's cultural implications, see Clarke 2004; Smethurst 2005; Collins and Crawford 2006; Ongiri 2010; and Widener 2010. For a brief mention of the connection between Black Power and architecture, see Wilkins 2007, 69–71. For works that cast Black Power as the end of a declension narrative or in a negative light, see Matusow 1984; Gitlin 1987; Pearson 1994; and Payne 1995. For a revision of that view of Black Power, see Woodard 1999; Joseph 2006; Biondi 2012; Self 2003; and Sugrue 2008. Histories of postmodern architecture that explore its roots in the social projects of the 1960s, in very different contexts, include Sadler 1999; Sadler 2005; Scott 2007; and Busbea 2007. On movements against modernist urbanism, see Mumford 2009; Zipp 2010; Carriere 2010; and Klemek 2011.

2 Schwartz 1993, 116, 151–159, 185–189; Ballon and Jackson 2007, 255–258, 260–261; and Carriere 2010, 182–211. For the most detailed history of public housing construction in East Harlem, see Zipp 2010, 258–260.

3 On Robert Moses, see Caro 1974; Ballon and Jackson 2007; and Schwartz 1993. On public housing and its successes and failures, see Zipp 2010; Venkatesh 2002; Bloom, 2008; Bauman 1987; and Hirsch 1983. For contemporary critiques of urban renewal, see Greer 1965; Jacobs 1961; Gans 1962; and Anderson 1964.

4 C. Richard Hatch, "Pulse of New York's Public: Architect's Views," *New York Amsterdam News,* December 5, 1964, 10; Gertrude Wilson, "A Tent in the Rain," *New York Amsterdam News,* November 14, 1964, 11.

5 C. Richard Hatch interview by Brian D. Goldstein, August 2, 2010, mp3 (in Brian D. Goldstein's possession); Andrea Lopen, "Harlem's Streetcorner Architects," *Architectural Forum,* 123 (December 1965), 50–51.

6 Economic Opportunity Act of 1964, 78 Stat. 508 (1964); Architects' Renewal Committee in Harlem, "Organizational Meeting," December 12, 1964, folder 34, box 8, Nelam L. Hill Papers (Schomburg Center for Research in Black Culture, New York Public Library, New York). Harlem's major community action agency, Harlem Youth Opportunities Unlimited–Associated Community Teams, received its first funding under the Economic Opportunity Act of 1964 in June 1965. See Lemann 1991, 169. On the War on Poverty in local contexts and on grassroots efforts by African American, Chicano, and Chicana activists seeking community control through it, see Bauman 2008; Clayson 2010; Orleck and Hazirjian 2011; Phelps 2014; and Self 2003, 198–205.

72 Brian D. Goldstein

7 Lawrence O'Kane, "Worst City Slums Due for Renewal in New Program," *New York Times,* April 14, 1964, 1; Lawrence O'Kane, "Renewal in Area around Columbia Backed by City," *ibid.*, September 30, 1964, 1; Housing and Redevelopment Board, City of New York, *Morningside General Neighborhood Renewal Plan* (New York, 1964), 25, GN-202 (C), 1–3; Ex. C, 1–3; Ex. D. The redevelopment of West Harlem formed part of the larger Morningside General Neighborhood Renewal Plan; the area of West Harlem involved was bounded by Morningside Avenue, Eighth Avenue, 111th Street, and 123rd Street. See Architects' Renewal Committee in Harlem, "A Review of the Morningside General Neighborhood Renewal Plan," March 1, 1965, folder 7, box 6, Christiane C. Collins Collection (Schomburg Center for Research in Black Culture); Architects' Renewal Committee in Harlem, "A Review of Morningside General Neighborhood Renewal Plan (draft)," January 17, 1965, Walter Thabit Private Collection (in Marci Reaven's possession); and West Harlem Community Organization and Architects' Renewal Committee in Harlem, "West Harlem Urban Renewal Area: Survey and Planning Application," January 1966, C. Richard Hatch Private Collection.

8 "East Harlem Renewal Backed to Create 'Industrial Triangle,'" *New York Times,* October 5, 1961, 30; Architects' Renewal Committee in Harlem, "Organizational Meeting"; C. Richard Hatch, "Better Cities for Whom? Panel Discussion," in *1965 Harvard Urban Design Conference,* comp. Harvard University School of Design (Cambridge, Mass., 1965), 26, 28; Davidoff 1965, 331–338.

9 Architects' Renewal Committee in Harlem, "June Newsletter," June 8, 1966, Thabit Collection; Architects' Renewal Committee in Harlem, "Urban Renewal in the East Harlem Triangle," October 1966, Hatch Collection.

10 Leonard Buder, "Showcase School Sets Off Dispute," *New York Times,* September 2, 1966, 28; "'Black Power' Moves into Harlem School Battle: Pickets Greet Stokely Carmichael with Cheers," *New York Amsterdam News,* September 24, 1966, 1; "Integration: The Sorry Struggle of I. S. 201," *Time,* September 30, 1966, 83; Podair 2002.

11 Architects' Renewal Committee in Harlem, "ARCH News," April 1967, folder 2, box 1, Metropolitan Council on Housing Records (Tamiment Library and Robert F. Wagner Labor Archives, New York University, New York); Jonathan D. Greenberg, *Staking a Claim: Jake Simmons and the Making of an African-American Oil Dynasty* (New York: Plume, 1990), 4; C. Richard Hatch to Brian D. Goldstein, February 28, 2011, email (in Goldstein's possession); Kenneth Simmons, "Thoughts on a Strategy for Urban Black Communities," February 27–29, 1967, 5–6, unpublished typescript (Environmental Design Library, University of California, Berkeley).

12 Columbia University Development Planning Workshop and Harlem Development Committee, "A Demonstration Economic Development Program for Harlem: Draft Proposal for a 12-Month Demonstration Grant under Section 207 of the Economic Opportunity Act of 1964," April 4, 1967, Hatch Collection; Preston Wilcox, "Appendix: Resident Participation in the Harlem Corporation," April 14, 1967, folder 18, box 14, Preston Wilcox Papers (Schomburg Center for Research in Black Culture); Geoffrey P. Faux, *CDCs: New Hope for the Inner City* (New York: The Twentieth Century Fund, 1971); Hill and Rabig 2012, 15–44, esp. 30–31.

13 "2 Named by ARCH," *New York Amsterdam News,* June 10, 1967, 6; Hatch interview; Architects' Renewal Committee in Harlem, *Harlem News,* October 1967, 2, folder 25, box 26, J. Max Bond Jr. Papers (Department of Drawings and Archives, Avery Architectural and Fine Arts Library, Columbia University, New York, N.Y.).

"The Search for New Forms" **73**

14 Roy Innis, "Black $$$ Power," *Harlem News,* November 1967, 1 (Research and Reference Division, Schomburg Center for Research in Black Culture); J. Max Bond Jr., "From the Publisher," *Harlem News,* October 1967, 2, folder 25, box 26, Bond Papers.

15 "Max Bond: 1935–2009, A Celebration," May 12, 2009, memorial service program (in Goldstein's possession). On J. Max Bond Sr., see Eric Pace, "J. Max Bond, Sr., 89, an American Who Headed Liberian University," *New York Times,* December 18, 1991, D23. On Ruth Clement Bond, see Margalit Fox, "Ruth C. Bond Dies at 101; Her Quilts Had a Message," *ibid.*, November 13, 2005, 43. On Horace Mann Bond, see "Biographical Note," *Five College Archives and Manuscript Collections,* http://asteria. fivecolleges.edu/findaids/umass/mums411_bioghist.html. On Rufus Clement, see Wilkerson 2010.

16 "Max Bond: 1935–2009, A Celebration"; Lynne Duke, "Blueprint of a Life," *Washington Post,* July 1, 2004, C01; James Bowe [Boone] Jr. and J. Max Bond Jr., "Fiery Cross," *Harvard Crimson,* February 21, 1952; Philip M. Cronin, "Leighton Calls Yardling 'Fiery Cross' Deplorable," *ibid.*, February 23, 1952; "Cambridge Chiefs Weigh Decision in 'Birth' Exhibition," *ibid.*, November 8, 1952; "Local Committee Backs Permit for 'Birth' Showings," *ibid.*, November 10, 1952.

17 Gaines 2006, 10, 141; J. Max Bond Jr., "A Critical Look at Tema," in *Housing and Urbanization: Report on the Postgraduate Urban Planning Course (1967–68, Term 1–2),* by S.B. Amissah (Kumasi, 1968?).

18 Duke, "Blueprint of a Life"; "East Harlem Unit to Plan Renewal," *New York Times,* June 30, 1967, 18; Architects' Renewal Committee in Harlem, *East Harlem Triangle Plan* (New York, 1968), 8–9.

19 The other new board members were Leo Rolle, Kenneth Marshall, John Killens, John Henrik Clarke, and Isaiah Robinson. See Architects' Renewal Committee in Harlem, "ARCH Review 1964/5–1966," ca. November 1966, log file L66-162 (microfilm: reel L-227), Log Files (Grant and Project Proposals), 1951–1995 Collection (Ford Foundation Archives, Rockefeller Archive Center, Sleepy Hollow, N.Y.); Max Bond to "Sir," February 13, 1968, folder 9, box 3, W. Joseph Black Papers (Schomburg Center for Research in Black Culture); Architects' Renewal Committee in Harlem, "Waiver of Notice: Meeting of the Board of Directors," January 25, 1968, Thabit Collection.

20 David Bird, "Sewage Plant Approval Delayed for Harlem; New Sites Studied," *New York Times,* April 5, 1968, 29; "Motorcade to Show Sewer Opposition," *New York Amsterdam News,* April 20, 1968, 2; Architects' Renewal Committee in Harlem, "Lindsay's New Sewage Plant to Smell Up Harlem," *Harlem News,* June 1968, 8, folder 25, box 26, Bond Papers.

21 Bond to "Sir," February 13, 1968, folder 9, box 3, Black Papers; "An Art and Architecture Training Program," n.d., folder 14, box 2, John Louis Wilson Jr. Papers (Schomburg Center for Research in Black Culture); Arthur L. Symes and Rae Banks, *Architecture in the Neighborhoods* (New York, 1968); Arthur L. Symes interview by Goldstein, July 30, 2010, mp3 (in Goldstein's possession); "Architects' Renewal Committee in Harlem– Cooper Union Training Program," 1968, folder 714, box 106, Rockefeller Brothers Fund Archives, RG 3.1 (Rockefeller Archive Center); "Negro Architects Helping Harlem Plan Its Future," *New York Times,* March 16, 1969, 57.

22 J. Max Bond Jr., "Speech to Architects and Planners against the War in Viet Nam," May 3, 1968, folder 15, box 15, Bond Papers.

74 Brian D. Goldstein

23 Neal 1971, 272–278, esp. 272–273; Gayle 1971, xxiv. Larry Neal originally published his manifesto as Larry Neal, "The Black Arts Movement," *Drama Review,* 12 (Summer 1968), 29–39.
24 Tucker 1969, 265–266; Bond, "Critical Look at Tema."
25 On the clearance-oriented approach of modernism as "the ethic of city rebuilding," see Zipp 2010. On the clearance-oriented approach of modernism as a central aspect of the "urban renewal order," see Klemek 2011; Tucker 1969, 268; "Max Bond and Carl Anthony on Afro-American Architecture: An Interview by Ishmael Reed," *Yardbird Reader,* 4 (1975), 17. Emphasis in original.
26 Architects' Renewal Committee in Harlem and West Harlem Community Organization, *West Harlem Morningside: A Community Proposal* (New York, 1968), 19; Architects' Renewal Committee in Harlem, *East Harlem Triangle Plan.*
27 Architects' Renewal Committee in Harlem and West Harlem Community Organization, *West Harlem Morningside,* 19; Architects' Renewal Committee in Harlem, *East Harlem Triangle Plan,* 37, 43.
28 Architects' Renewal Committee in Harlem, *East Harlem Triangle Plan,* 46–48.
29 *Ibid.*; Architects' Renewal Committee in Harlem and West Harlem Community Organization, *West Harlem Morningside,* 34–35.
30 Architects' Renewal Committee in Harlem and West Harlem Community Organization, *West Harlem Morningside,* 29–30; Architects' Renewal Committee in Harlem, *East Harlem Triangle Plan,* 46; "Advocacy Planning: What It Is, How It Works," *Progressive Architecture,* 49 (September 1968), 101–115, esp. 110; Tucker 1969, 267.
31 Architects' Renewal Committee in Harlem and West Harlem Community Organization, *West Harlem Morningside,* 30; Architects' Renewal Committee in Harlem, *East Harlem Triangle Plan,* 38.
32 Implementation of the plan for the East Harlem Triangle relied mostly on federal low-income housing funding. The Community Association of the East Harlem Triangle rehabilitated nine buildings with 189 apartments at East 130th Street and Lexington Avenue in 1968 and built new housing nearby, including 169 apartments in 1972 (the Jackie Robinson Houses); 246 apartments in 1975 (the 1775 Houses); 147 apartments in 1979 (the A.K. Houses); 131 apartments in 1984 (the M.S. Houses); and 39 apartments in 1990 (the Twee Mill House). See "The Community Association of the East Harlem Triangle: Improvements Developed by, Sponsored by, and Assisted by the Association," July 18, 1989, folder 7, box 18, Wilcox Papers; and "39 Units in Harlem: Housing for the Handicapped," *New York Times,* November 4, 1990, R1. Columbia University suspended the gymnasium project in the spring of 1968, after student and community protests shut down the university. Likewise, the city never redeveloped West Harlem. "Columbia to Decide Whether to Build Gym in Morningside Park on Basis of a Poll of Local Leaders," *ibid.*, February 16, 1969, 46.
33 For a list of more than 100 community design centers, see *An Architektur* (Berlin), 19 (September 2008), 11–12, 29–56. "Max Bond: 1935–2009, A Celebration"; Dutton 1991, 83–95; Laven 1984, 104–117; David Robinson, "Building for Self and Community in Harlem," *Consumer-Farmer Cooperator* 44 (January 1977), 3.
34 Black Power showed conservative tendencies in other realms as well. On the male-dominated gender politics of the movement, see Wallace 1979. For an alternative reading of the movement's gender politics through the lens of racial uplift ideology, which nonetheless emphasizes its frequently patriarchal nature, see Matlin 2006 and Matlin 2013, 123–194.

35 For the best-known critique of the fashionable appropriation of black radicalism, see Wolfe 1970. On the transformations of community development corporations and the convergence of Black Power and black capitalism, see Goldstein 2017; Hill and Rabig 2012, 25–31; Frazier 2012, 68–92; West 2012, 274–303; and Ferguson 2013, 210–254. For a parallel example in the context of the Chicano movement, see Bauman 2008, 101–108. For a description of the similar ideological malleability of the broader idea of community control, see Podair 2002, 21–47, 183–205.

36 On the historicist approaches of postmodernism, see Otero-Pailos 2010. Historians have yet to extensively examine the rise of historic preservation, reuse of existing buildings, and architectural contextualism in the late 20th century. For a study that addresses these issues up to the early 1980s, see Osman 2011. For a discussion of the frequently conflicting interests of new brownstone dwellers and existing residents, see *ibid.*, 233–269.

References

Anderson, Martin. 1964. *The Federal Bulldozer: A Critical Analysis of Urban Renewal, 1949–1962.* Cambridge, MA: MIT Press.

Ballon, Hilary, and Kenneth T. Jackson, eds. 2007. *Robert Moses and the Modern City: The Transformation of New York.* New York: W.W. Norton and Company.

Bauman, John F. 1987. *Public Housing, Race, and Renewal: Urban Planning in Philadelphia, 1920–1974.* Philadelphia: Temple University Press.

Bauman, Robert. 2008. *Race and the War on Poverty: From Watts to East L.A.* Norman, OK: University of Oklahoma Press.

Biondi, Martha. 2012. *The Black Revolution on Campus.* Berkeley: University of California Press.

Bloom, Nicholas Dagen. 2008. *Public Housing That Worked: New York in the Twentieth Century.* Philadelphia: University of Pennsylvania Press.

Busbea, Larry. 2007. *Topologies: The Urban Utopia in France, 1960–1970.* Cambridge, MA: MIT Press.

Carmichael, Stokely, and Charles V. Hamilton. 1967. *Black Power: The Politics of Liberation in America.* New York: Vintage Books.

Caro, Robert A. 1974. *The Power Broker: Robert Moses and the Fall of New York.* New York: Alfred A. Knopf.

Carriere, Michael H. 2010. "Between Being and Becoming: On Architecture, Student Protest, and the Aesthetics of Liberalism in Postwar America." PhD diss., University of Chicago.

Clarke, Cheryl. 2004. *"After Mecca": Women Poets and the Black Arts Movement.* New Brunswick: Rutgers University Press.

Clayson, William S. 2010. *Freedom Is Not Enough: The War on Poverty and the Civil Rights Movement in Texas.* Austin: University of Texas Press.

Collins, Lisa Gail, and Margo Natalie Crawford, eds., 2006. *New Thoughts on the Black Arts Movement.* New Brunswick: Rutgers University Press.

Davidoff, Paul. 1965. "Advocacy and Pluralism in Planning." *Journal of the American Planning Association,* 31 (November): 331–338. doi.org/10.1080/01944366508978187

Dutton, Thomas A. 1991. "Architectural Education and Society: An Interview with J. Max Bond Jr." In *Voices in Architectural Education: Cultural Politics and Pedagogy,* ed. Thomas A. Dutton, 83–95. New York: Bergin & Garvey.

76 Brian D. Goldstein

Ferguson, Karen. 2013. *Top Down: The Ford Foundation, Black Power, and the Reinvention of Racial Liberalism*. Philadelphia: University of Pennsylvania Press.

Frazier, Nishani. 2012. "A McDonald's That Reflects the Soul of a People: Hough Area Development Corporation and Community Development in Cleveland." In *The Business of Black Power: Community Development, Capitalism, and Corporate Responsibility in Postwar America*, edited by Laura Warren Hill and Julia Rabig, 68–92. Rochester: University of Rochester Press.

Gaines, Kevin K. 2006. *American Africans in Ghana: Black Expatriates and the Civil Rights Era*. Chapel Hill: University of North Carolina Press.

Gans, Herbert J. 1962. *The Urban Villagers: Group and Class in the Life of Italian-Americans*. New York: Free Press.

Gayle Jr, Addison. 1971. "Introduction." In *The Black Aesthetic*, edited by Gayle, xv–xxiv. New York: Doubleday.

Gitlin, Todd. 1987. *The Sixties: Years of Hope, Days of Rage*. New York: Bantam Books.

Goldstein, Brian D. 2017. *The Roots of Urban Renaissance: Gentrification and the Struggle over Harlem*. Cambridge, MA: Harvard University Press.

Greer, Scott. 1965. *Urban Renewal and American Cities: The Dilemma of Democratic Institutions*. Indianapolis: Bobbs-Merrill Company.

Hill, Laura Warren, and Julia Rabig, 2012. "Toward a History of the Business of Black Power." In *The Business of Black Power: Community Development, Capitalism, and Corporate Responsibility in Postwar America*, edited by Hill and Rabig, 15–42. Rochester: University of Rochester Press.

Hirsch, Arnold R. 1983. *Making the Second Ghetto: Race and Housing in Chicago, 1940–1960*. New York: Cambridge University Press.

Jacobs, Jane. 1961. *The Death and Life of Great American Cities*. New York: Vintage Books.

Joseph, Peniel E. 2006. *Waiting 'Til the Midnight Hour: A Narrative History of Black Power in America*. New York: Harry Holt and Company.

Klemek, Christopher. 2011. *The Transatlantic Collapse of Urban Renewal: Postwar Urbanism from New York to Berlin*. Chicago: University of Chicago Press.

Laven, Charles. 1984. "Self-Help in Neighborhood Development." In *The Scope of Social Architecture*, edited by C. Richard Hatch, 104–117. New York: Van Nostrand Reinhold.

Lemann, Nicholas. 1991. *The Promised Land: The Great Black Migration and How It Changed America*. New York: Alfred A. Knopf.

Matlin, Daniel. 2006. "'Lift up Yr Self!' Reinterpreting Amiri Baraka (LeRoi Jones), Black Power, and the Uplift Tradition." *Journal of American History*, 93 (June), 91–116. doi.org/10.2307/4486061

Matlin, Daniel. 2013. *On the Corner: African American Intellectuals and the Urban Crisis*. Cambridge, MA: Harvard University Press.

Matusow, Allen J. 1984. *The Unraveling of America: A History of Liberalism in the 1960s*. New York: Harper & Row.

Mumford, Eric. 2009. *Defining Urban Design: CIAM Architects and the Formation of a Discipline, 1937–69*. New Haven: Yale University Press.

Neal, Larry. 1971. "The Black Arts Movement." In *The Black Aesthetic*, edited by Addison Gayle Jr. 272–290. New York: Doubleday.

Ongiri, Amy Abugo. 2010. *Spectacular Blackness: The Cultural Politics of the Black Power Movement and the Search for a Black Aesthetic*. Charlottesville, VA: University of Virginia Press.

Orleck, Annalise, and Lisa Gayle Hazirjian, eds. 2011. *The War on Poverty: A New Grassroots History, 1964–1980*. Athens, GA: University of Georgia Press.

Osman, Suleiman. 2011. *The Invention of Brownstone Brooklyn: Gentrification and the Search for Authenticity in Postwar New York*. New York: Oxford University Press.

Otero-Pailos, Jorge. 2010. *Architecture's Historical Turn: Phenomenology and the Rise of the Postmodern*. Minneapolis: University of Minnesota Press.

Payne, Charles M. 1995. *I've Got the Light of Freedom: The Organizing Tradition and the Mississippi Freedom Struggle*. Berkeley: University of California Press.

Pearson, Hugh. 1994. *The Shadow of the Panther: Huey Newton and the Price of Black Power in America*. Reading, MA: Addison-Wesley.

Phelps, Wesley G. 2014. *A People's War on Poverty: Urban Politics and Grassroots Activists in Houston*. Athens, GA: University of Georgia Press.

Podair, Jerald E. 2002. *The Strike That Changed New York: Blacks, Whites, and the Ocean Hill–Brownsville Crisis*. New Haven: Yale University Press.

Sadler, Simon. 1999. *The Situationist City*. Cambridge, MA: MIT Press.

Sadler, Simon. 2005. *Archigram: Architecture without Architecture*. Cambridge, MA.: MIT Press.

Schwartz, Joel. 1993. *The New York Approach: Robert Moses, Urban Liberals, and the Redevelopment of the Inner City*. Columbus, OH: Ohio State University Press.

Scott, Felicity D. 2007. *Architecture and Techno-Utopia: Politics after Modernism*. Cambridge, MA: MIT Press.

Self, Robert O. 2003. *American Babylon: Race and the Struggle for Postwar Oakland*. Princeton: Princeton University Press.

Smethurst, James Edward. 2005. *The Black Arts Movement: Literary Nationalism in the 1960s and 1970s*. Chapel Hill: University of North Carolina Press.

Sugrue, Thomas J. 2008. *Sweet Land of Liberty: The Forgotten Struggle for Civil Rights in the North*. New York: Random House.

Tucker, Priscilla. 1969. "Poor Peoples' Plan," *Metropolitan Museum of Art Bulletin,* 27 (January), 265–269. doi.org/10.2307/3258417

Venkatesh, Sudhir Alladi. 2002. *American Project: The Rise and Fall of a Modern Ghetto*. Cambridge, MA: Harvard University Press.

Wallace, Michele. 1979. *Black Macho and the Myth of the Superwoman:* New York: Dial Press.

West, Michael O. 2012. "Whose Black Power? The Business of Black Power and Black Power's Business," In *The Business of Black Power: Community Development, Capitalism, and Corporate Responsibility in Postwar America,* edited by Laura Warren Hill and Julia Rabig, 274–303. Rochester: University of Rochester Press.

Widener, Daniel. 2010. *Black Arts West: Culture and Struggle in Postwar Los Angeles*. Durham, NC: Duke University Press.

Wilkerson, Isabel. 2010. *The Warmth of Other Suns: The Epic Story of America's Great Migration*. New York: Vintage Books.

Wilkins, Craig L. 2007. *The Aesthetics of Equity: Notes on Race, Space, Architecture, and Music*. Minneapolis: University of Minnesota Press.

Wolfe, Tom. 1970. *Radical Chic & Mau-Mauing the Flak Catchers*. New York: Bantam Books.

Woodard, Komozi. 1999. *A Nation within a Nation: Amiri Baraka (LeRoi Jones) and Black Power Politics*. Chapel Hill: University of North Carolina Press.

Zipp, Samuel. 2010. *Manhattan Projects: The Rise and Fall of Urban Renewal in Cold War New York*. New York: Oxford University Press.

4

CENTRO CULTURAL MÓVIL

Critical Service Learning and Design with Latinx Farmworkers

Silvina Lopez Barrera and Erin Sassin

Introduction

Community-based and participatory design projects offer important opportunities in architectural education. In general, architecture studio courses at the college and university level focus on the traditional relationship between the architect and the client rather than the architect or designer's role in encouraging social change. In contrast, socially engaged design presents an opportunity to immerse students in "real world" learning, encourage social change, strengthen communities, and contribute to the public good. This essay explores a participatory design project involving an architecture studio course at Middlebury College, the organization Migrant Justice, and Latinx farmworkers from rural Vermont communities. Called *Centro Cultural Móvil*, the project was a mobile hub designed to provide services to both documented and undocumented migrant farmworkers scattered across Vermont in isolated farms. While it was not built, the design process nevertheless demonstrates how young architecture students can be made fully aware of the potentially progressive role they and their work can play, even if the collaborative process undertaken also made visible some potential pitfalls of socially progressive design. The project thus presents a model of how similar integrative and collaborative projects involving multiple stakeholders and actors might proceed and succeed.

The key community involved in *Centro Cultural Móvil* is a very specific yet relatively invisible group of Latinx laborers in the largely agricultural state of Vermont. As a significant portion of today's agriculture labor force in the United States relies on migrant workers from Latin America, so too do Vermont's dairy farms, where Latinx migrants represent an important share of farmworkers. These Latinx farmworkers typically work 60 to 80 hours per week, and many of them experience extreme geographical and social isolation as well as a significant lack of access to basic resources, ranging from decent housing to health care (Migrant Justice n.d.). Informed by the many challenges faced by socioeconomically and geographically marginalized Latinx farmworkers, the goal for this participatory design project was to facilitate access to community resources.

For undergraduate students in the Architectural Studies program at Middlebury College in Middlebury, Vermont, the farmworkers' situation presented an opportunity for learning and practicing engaged design. Service learning and participatory design can offer a framework to integrate socially engaged design work into architecture studios, emphasizing both process and inclusivity to promote social change. This work requires the facilitation of relationships – not only the creation of partnerships, but also the building of trust with community partners – all of which require time and a willingness to be part of this collaboration. In this case, the shared design process between architecture students, Latinx farmworkers, and the local organization Migrant Justice allowed architecture students to expand their individual understanding of the world by carefully listening to and exchanging ideas with community members. It fostered awareness of the role of the architect and designer, not as superior technician or expert, but as partner and agent to promote social change. The planning of a mobile hub facilitating access to food, information, and community for Latinx farmworkers allowed for the introduction of social justice topics into architecture studio courses.

Paradoxically, while this project's intent was to make visible the economic, social, and environmental challenges faced by Latinx migrant farmworkers, increasing their visibility could have unintended consequences. The participatory design process can be challenging when it (as it should) recognizes the diversity of participants involved, their cultural and social diversity, and the complex power dynamics between them.

Latinx Farmworkers in Vermont

While space is produced by many parties, spatial practices and the organization of space typically embody a power relationship. As Henri Lefebvre has written, space expresses the material and political priorities of societies; each society produces its own space where some benefit from space and others are excluded from it (1991). Space is produced as a consequence of control, domination, and power. In the United States, migrant farmworkers are particularly vulnerable and disadvantaged in relation to other groups, as they experience barriers obstructing their access to both basic services and social integration.

Over the last two decades the Latinx population in the state of Vermont has increased more than 200 percent (see Table 4.1) and Latinx labor has become an essential part of the Vermont dairy industry (Baker 2013). Including both documented and undocumented migrants, these estimates show the discrepancy between Vermont's public image as a sustainable small-scale agricultural economy

TABLE 4.1 Hispanic Population by County in Vermont, 2000–2018

County in VT	2000 Hispanic population	2010 Hispanic population	2018 Hispanic population
Addison County	397	661	849
Bennigton County	344	537	675
Caledonia County	201	323	481
Chittenden County	1,561	2,731	3,685
Essex County	32	45	83
Franklin County	270	581	742
Grand Isle County	29	89	133
Lamoille County	180	316	444
Orange County	165	317	392
Orleans County	190	290	387
Rutland County	442	705	845
Washington County	732	1,019	1,111
Windham County	493	786	982
Windsor County	468	754	868
TOTAL Hispanic population	**5,504**	**9,154**	**11,677**

Source: United States Census Bureau (data: 2000–2010 US census, 2018-ACS 5-Year Estimates Data Profiles)

and a place where economically and socially marginalized Latinx migrants represent a significant portion of farmworkers on its iconic dairy farms (Radel et al. 2010; Mares 2019).

Founded in 2009, Migrant Justice is an organization that advocates for human rights and food justice for Latinx farmworkers in Vermont, as well as conducting a number of surveys and outreach programs for the Latinx migrant workers' community (Flores 2017). According to the Migrant Justice website, there are approximately 1,200 to 1,500 Latinx migrant workers on Vermont's dairy farms, many of whom are undocumented. Much of their labor is conducted in indoor environments within dairy farms, such as barns and milking parlors, where their everyday activities focus on feeding and milking cows, cleaning stalls, and other tasks (Radel et al. 2010; Baker and Chappelle 2012). In fact, the presence of Latinx farmworkers is doubly obscured: hidden indoors in remote rural areas. Migrant farmworkers in the dairy industry usually live on the farms in housing provided by the employers, often experiencing overcrowded conditions and substandard housing that often lacks clean water and heating (Radel et al. 2010; Mares 2019; Migrant Justice n.d.; Keller 2019). Additionally, in a region underserved by mass transit options, most of them lack ready access to vehicles enabling them to access basic resources, so that they are not only economically deprived, but also socially isolated and disenfranchised.[1] The great majority of farmworkers lack basic freedoms such as the ability to gather as a community, go to the hospital, or go to the market.[2] As a result of this isolation and marginalization, Latinx farmworkers struggle to gain access to essential resources, and many of them experience food insecurity and human rights and workers' rights abuses (Migrant Justice n.d.; Mares 2019).

Vermont dairy farms can be an even more hostile environment for Latina farmworkers, where they suffer different types of discrimination. The majority of Latinx farmworkers are male, and the presence of Latina farmworkers in the dairy farms is often perceived negatively by the farm owners (Radel et al. 2010). In general, male farm owners do not consider women farmworkers as appropriate labor for the dairy farms, so their employment opportunities are limited and underpaid. Additionally, housing on dairy farms is largely dependent on trailers for occupancy by male farmworkers, which further contributes to a bias against female dairy farmworkers, as well as against the establishment of family life within this community (Radel et al. 2010).

Service Learning Pedagogy in Architectural Education

With notable exceptions, the field of architecture has traditionally been presented by its practitioners and apologists as politically neutral and separate from its social and historical contexts, thus reinforcing a practice based on the valorization of the individual and "his" recognizable masterworks, even if the latter were the result of collaborative effort.[3] This approach of overvaluing the starchitect and signature building has made it difficult to maintain the permanence and presence of socially and community-engaged design in architecture studios, in part because engaged design studios and projects emphasize community collaboration and process (Rendell, Penner, and Borden 2000; Schuman 2006). Further complicating the path for engaged design efforts, traditional architectural education has also tended to overaccentuate the development of skills and technical knowledge. While this is a consequence of architectural and production practices associated with the construction industry and real estate development, such an approach gives limited value and opportunities to architectural education to focus on its humanities-based research and efforts, thus limiting the reflection on the ethical implications of architecture in society (Coleman 2010).

Service learning can bridge this gap by providing a model of social engagement – integrating socially engaged design into architecture studios and emphasizing process and inclusivity to transform unjust realities. The leading report *Building Community: A New Future for Architecture Education and Practice* advocated the following strategies for architectural education: "establish a climate for engagement, clarify the public benefits of architecture, promote the creation of new knowledge, and stress the critical importance of ethical professional behavior" (Boyer and Mitgang 1996, 133). This groundbreaking study influenced architecture education by emphasizing the ethical significance of community engagement in architecture and promoting the development of community service programs in architecture schools.

If architecture students are to become professionals whose work improves communities rather than ignores them, then service learning projects should be a key component of their training. There are a broad range of definitions and methodologies in service learning, and its benefits and significance have been extensively discussed in design fields, planning, and architecture. Service learning pedagogy emphasizes experiential learning with community partners, connecting community service and academic learning. Service learning seeks to engage students with activities that connect their learning process with human and community needs, balancing student learning and community outcomes (Jacoby 2015). The diverse approaches and methodologies can range from simple field experiences to transformative service learning. While service is an outcome of the learning process in field experiences, when using critical pedagogy service learning can be a transformative process for both students and communities – encouraging students to cultivate a critical awareness of social justice by focusing on community empowerment and agency (Schuman 2006). The use of community-based projects such as the one described here enables the combination of conventional academic learning with lessons of social justice while addressing community needs and changing the learning space from the academy to the community (Horrigan 2006).

Service learning as a pedagogy focuses on experience as a basis for learning, and it understands critical reflection to be a vital element in facilitating learning, ultimately leading to a deeper understanding of the sources of need and their complex historical, social, economic, environmental, and political underpinnings (Jacoby 2015). At its best, it integrates teaching, learning, service, scholarship, and research. The power of this integrative approach is reflected in the increasing attention to community engagement and service learning pedagogy in architecture programs and related fields, including the establishment of community design centers across the United States and around the world. However, issues of social justice, race, gender, and class, among other markers, are sometimes overlooked or superficially addressed by service learning approaches (Angotti et al. 2011). On this point it is useful to turn to Keith Morton's position that there is a distinction between "thin" and "thick" forms of service learning projects (Morton 1995, 28; Jacoby 2015, 8–9). The "thin" version of a service learning project could superficially address an immediate problem by providing a service to a community, but without engaging the community in question in solving the problem. On the other hand, a "thick" form of a service learning project involves an active collaboration between students and community to address the causes of the problem, ultimately empowering community members to advocate for change. This is the level of collaboration we sought in the project described here.

As briefly mentioned, there are a growing number of community-engaged architectural practices and organizations that are transforming the traditional relationship between architect and clients by offering design services to underserved communities (Bell 2004a). A burgeoning body of scholarship elucidates those practices: Bryan Bell emphasizes the importance of recognizing the significance of shared decision-making process in architecture education and practice, and Robert Gutman advocates for architects to engage in political action, particularly as related to low-income housing design, production, and the expansion of government programs (Bell 2004b; Gutman 2004). Community-engaged architecture presents the potential to empower communities when it encourages political engagement and pursues systemic change (Gamez and Rogers 2008). These practices recognize the essential political nature of architecture as it influences social relations and spatial power dynamics (Awan et al. 2011).

Additionally, service learning as critical pedagogy – the understanding that multiple forms of oppression occur as a consequence of power asymmetries and a culture of domination – has the potential to transform students' understanding of power dynamics and privilege and of their own place within the world (Jacoby 2015). For example, Paolo Freire's work *Pedagogy of the Oppressed* analyzes systems of oppression from multidimensional factors such as race, class, gender, culture, language, and ethnicity; in this pedagogy, the oppressed, the marginalized, and the disenfranchised reveal the dynamics of power and dominance and encourage the underprivileged to become self-empowered in order to transform unjust realities (Freire 2002). Dialogical practice is fundamental to an understanding of how oppression functions, and it is a key component in the process of learning and knowing (Freire and Macedo 1995). In this process, the experiences and identities of both groups of participants – design students and impacted community – are linked to power dynamics and history.

On the other hand, as Jacoby highlights, there is another danger: service learning without an integrated multicultural education may help to perpetuate systems of oppression by reinforcing existing hierarchies, stereotypes, and biases (Jacoby 2015). Engaging in service learning without a careful understanding of the underlying causes of social problems to be addressed may encourage privileged students to participate in systems of privilege and inequality without critically reflecting upon those systems, or their place in them. Done properly, critical service learning encourages students to become agents of social change and to use the knowledge, skills, and experiences they gained in concert with another community to address social injustice (Mitchell 2008; Mitchell 2015). As this brief discussion shows, while service learning projects are a key component of socially engaged architecture education, they require thoughtful preparation and great insight in order to be successful.

Design as a Form of Activism

In recent years, public interest design and participatory design projects have been the subject of increasing attention in the fields of architecture and design. A collaborative design process using community knowledge and encouraging authentic dialogue by embracing the diversity and interdependency of the interests of all the participants can deliver appropriate design solutions and help empower the target community (Innes and Booher 2010).

In the *Centro Cultural Móvil* project, the inclusion of critical service learning in an architecture studio challenged traditional approaches to undergraduate architectural education and de-emphasized the role of the architect as technician and expert in favor of encouraging community-engaged design work as a critical endeavor (Lopez Barrera 2018). This service learning project was developed through a participatory design process between architecture students, Latinx farmworkers, and Migrant Justice: the goal was the design of a mobile hub intended to encourage authentic dialogue and a sense of shared ownership among architecture students, Latinx farmworkers, and activists. The ultimate aim was to empower farmworkers, build access to community resources, and establish a community partnership between Migrant Justice and architecture studio courses at Middlebury College.

At its heart, this process – one centered on public interest concerns – is a form of design activism. According to Ann Thorpe, in the past decades different terms for design activism have emerged, such as social design, design for social impact, public interest design, and spatial agency (Thorpe 2012). Terms such as *public interest design* and *spatial agency* help to expand the field of architecture; in this construct architecture is understood as a social production of space that involves more than buildings and objects (Fisher 2008; Awan et al. 2011). The practice of public interest design involves critically rethinking the role of architects and architecture in contemporary issues, one increasingly embraced by many players in both professional and institutional settings as a means to encourage interdisciplinary knowledge and promote social change by working in close partnership with communities (Anderson 2014). As previously mentioned, in traditional architecture and design practices, professionals provide services to clients who can afford architectural services. This form of practice is highly inaccessible for disenfranchised individuals and communities (Fisher 2008). Community-engaged processes of respectful collaboration and long commitment are the most successful strategies of public interest design (Feldman et al. 2016). Thus, the practice of public interest design embraces participatory design processes, dialogue, and community engagement. The goal for the participatory design process is to build consensus so that disenfranchised communities – in this case Latinx farmworkers – become more empowered, adaptive, and resilient. The inclusion of participatory tools into the design process recognizes the variety of participants, their cultural diversity, their social networks, and the complex relationship of power between them (Healey 2006).

In this particular project, designing a mobile hub through a participatory process presented the opportunity to engage both farmworkers and the architecture students using critical service learning. The participatory design process took place during spring 2016 and the goal for the (as yet unbuilt) mobile hub was to provide access to community resources. The *Centro Cultural Móvil* was designed as a shared and nonhierarchical space where Latinx farmworkers could access information about their individual and collective rights and engage with other community members.

Community Partnership and Reciprocity

As stated, the process of participatory design implies both the creation of partnerships and the building of trust with community partners, a process that requires time and commitment, reciprocity and reflection. One of the complexities of service learning, particularly when dealing with an undergraduate population at a small liberal arts college, is the creation of sustainable partnerships, and coordinating student learning outcomes with the needs and expectations of the community partner. When reciprocity is embraced, student learning outcomes and the production of knowledge are attained, a community's needs are met, and social justice is advanced (Jay 2010). Thus, the first steps toward this participatory design project involved the creation of a partnership between Migrant Justice and an architecture studio course at Middlebury College (Lopez Barrera 2018). As Migrant Justice's aim is to advocate for the Latinx farmworker community and engage community partners to organize for economic justice and human rights, an important part of its work is the organization of farmworker community meetings called *asambleas* (assemblies). These *asambleas* are venues to discuss and analyze shared problems and to envision collective solutions for the farmworker community. The *asambleas* are important spaces for Latinx farmworker participation that also serve to strengthen the relationships between Latinx farmworkers and the larger community (Thompson 2020). Together, Latinx farmworkers and Migrant Justice have prioritized four areas of fundamental human rights action: the provision of dignified work and quality housing; increasing access to reliable transportation to enable freedom of movement; ensuring freedom from discrimination; and increasing access to health care (Migrant Justice n.d.). As Stewart and Alrutz (2012) suggest, university/college-community partnerships can take different configurations, with some seeking nonhierarchical configurations so decision-making and power are shared from the outset; the participatory design approach of our shared work was inspired by the way the *asambleas* are organized and the stated priorities of the farmworker community and Migrant Justice. As stated before, service learning relies on partnerships with organizations and communities, and the notion of community can be broadly defined (Stewart and Alrutz 2012). In the mobile hub participatory design project, community was defined as the Latinx farmworker community in Vermont and community partners involved both Latinx farmworkers and community organizers from Migrant Justice. Throughout the participatory design process, all participants strived to share their power where both students and community partners could benefit from the partnership.

Partnerships between academia and communities can be dynamic and evolve over time; these range from short-term collaborations focused on a particular goal to transformative partnerships whose open-ended processes allow for further collaborations (Enos and Morton 2003; Clayton et al. 2010; Thompson and Jesiek 2017). In transformative service learning, partnerships are mutually beneficial for both students and community, and partnerships are strengthened when power dynamics are acknowledged (Davis et al. 2017). At their best, transformative and reciprocal partnerships are essential to service learning pedagogy, addressing and enacting social change (Stewart and Alrtz 2012). Additionally, collaborative efforts cannot ignore the collaborators' complex dynamics influenced by relations of power (Thompson and Lopez Barrera 2019). In the mobile hub project, reciprocity was embraced by the nature of the participatory design process in which students were able to have a "real world" experience and community partners were able to develop a design vision directly addressing their needs. Throughout this participatory design, power was shared among participants in the decision-making process and its open-ended quality encouraged a transformative partnership.

Participatory Design Process: Opportunities and Challenges

The *Centro Cultural Móvil* project presented an opportunity for students to engage with community members using what the Hendler-Voss team (2008) describes as an asset-based approach; during the participatory design process, participants focused on community resources and strengths, thus identifying unrecognized assets alongside community needs. Architecture students both facilitated the process of identifying community assets and capitalized on them to develop innovative design solutions. More specifically, focusing on community assets at this point in the process allowed community members to identify existing small business initiatives, such as existing food vendor enterprises run by Latina farmworkers. These individuals cooked homemade food and drove to different farm sites where they sold their product to Latinx farmworkers who typically had little to no access to either transportation or food. This finding revealed that food access should be incorporated into the mobile hub project and that the inclusion of a food component could also provide an income opportunity for Latina farmworkers, who are otherwise underpaid and underemployed. Understanding the context and diverse values of Vermont's Latinx farmworkers and Migrant Justice community organizers presented an opportunity to connect the production of knowledge to a particular community in order to advance social justice values.

Community-engaged design with disenfranchised communities can be criticized when reciprocity is not embraced and collaborative efforts overlook the racial, ethnic, religious, and class differences between community partners and students (Lawson et al. 2011). In responding to this potential criticism, Lawson et al. (2011) recommends that multicultural education always be integrated with design instruction and that students should be given numerous opportunities to collaborate and share in the decision-making process. Thompson (2010) suggests that outreach learning opportunities involving the Latinx population need to incorporate creative inclusive elements that facilitate social networks based on trust and reciprocity that link them to the community and local institutions. In the mobile hub project, the inherently multicultural aspect allowed students to understand and reflect on different power dynamics, inequality, privilege, and their own biases. This community engagement project strove to embrace the diversity of both Middlebury students and an underrepresented community. It capitalized on the community partners' knowledge to establish a nonhierarchical relationship among all participants.

In fact, during the design process students and community partners were challenged by the paradox of increasing the visibility of Migrant Justice in remote rural areas, as this visibility might help alert immigration authorities. The unintended consequences of increasing visibility could range from immigration raids at dairy farms to the detention and deportation of Latinx farmworkers. Navigating this contested reality gave students the opportunity to understand the vulnerable situation of some farmworkers while reflecting on their own privilege.[4]

Centro Cultural Móvil: Participatory Design Meetings

During the participatory design meetings, the mobile hub was named *Centro Cultural Móvil* as a way to convey its multipurpose quality, one designed to address the different needs of the Latinx migrant farmworker community (Lopez Barrera 2018). The participatory process of designing the mobile hub involved the following phases for students and community partners: learning about daily activities of both farmworkers and community organizers from Migrant Justice; developing empathy and understanding community partners' experiences, activities, and needs; identifying community assets, needs, and visions; developing a design vision and strategies; prototyping by way of 3D physical models, sketches, diagrams, and storyboards; discussing design ideas and obtaining community partners' design feedback; and revising design ideas based on community partners' feedback (see Figure 4.1). The design process also involved the study of related projects, such as mobile health and humanitarian aid clinics, as well as migrant housing (Sinclair 2006; Bell 2004b).

Participatory design meetings included both community partners and architecture students and communication was facilitated in both English and Spanish. In addition to the largely bilingual facilitation, student volunteers from the Middlebury College student organization JUNTOS[5] offered one-on-one bilingual interpretation during the meetings. Latinx farmworkers and community organizers from Migrant Justice shared their stories, hopes, and visions for dignified labor conditions and a more just socioeconomic future (Figure 4.2). These discussions and the information shared in these sessions provided valuable insight

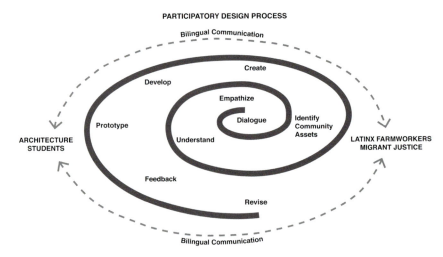

FIGURE 4.1 Participatory design process diagram. Author: Silvina Lopez Barrera. Courtesy of the author

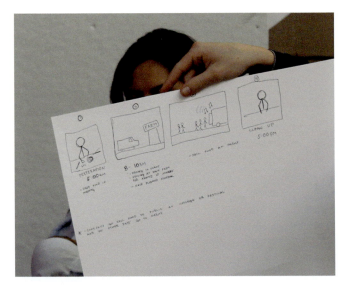

FIGURE 4.2 Storyboards produced in participatory design meetings. Photograph by Silvina Lopez Barrera and Oliver Oglesby. Courtesy of the photographers

into the community's priorities, motivated strategic design decisions, and enabled a shared design vision for the *Centro Cultural Móvil* to develop.

These participatory design meetings also enabled students and community partners to work in small teams to propose three different alternative designs for the mobile hub, all of which used sketches and storyboards as primary tools of

FIGURE 4.3 Drawing by Shan Zeng, Yihao (Lyra) Ding, and Zihan (Selena) Ling. Courtesy of the artists

representation. All three designs shared certain programmatic elements such us the inclusion of a food component (a small kitchen and a store), an information and learning center (a space promoting the mission of Migrant Justice and offering advice and information about migrant workers' rights), and an outdoor gathering space for the *asambleas*. The outdoor space for the *asambleas* was designed as a foldable and movable structure that could be used in warmer weather conditions in Vermont, generally from March to October.[6]

At the end of the design process all participants exhibited a high level of engagement with their coproduced designs (Figure 4.3). They were proud of what they were able to produce together and retained a sense of ownership of the *Centro Cultural Móvil*. More importantly, the process allowed participants to build trust and to commit to a long-term project benefiting rural Vermont's Latinx farmworker community.

Conclusion

Service learning and participatory design provide a platform for architecture students and designers to engage with social change and to have a meaningful positive impact on communities in great need. However, it is important to understand the challenges of participatory design processes where a diversity of community partners and students are involved. In order to create an inclusive decision-making process and ensure that everyone contributes equally, complex power relationships among all participants must not only be recognized, but also addressed.

In this case, the relationship of power between undergraduate architecture students and Latinx farmworkers was underscored by significant economic, educational, cultural, ethnic, and gendered differences, as well as language barriers. Considering this, it was very important in the design process to build trust, stimulate empathy, and to unpack systems of privilege. By using a participatory design process, we strove to create a positive environment where different opinions, visions, and design ideas could be expressed, ultimately resulting in a design outcome grounded in these shared visions and values.

Acknowledgments

We would like to thank everyone who participated in this design process. Specially, thank you to our Latinx farmworkers and Migrant Justice collaborators, as well as the architecture students who took part, student volunteers from JUNTOS, Oliver Oglesby, and the Middlebury College Center for Community Engagement, which generously supported this project with an Academic Outreach Endowment (2015).

Notes

1 In Addison county, as elsewhere in Vermont, bus routes are relatively expansive in town, while the routes running through rural areas provide less comprehensive coverage. The latter tend to follow major highways and primarily serve to connect towns and villages; these routes do not run directly by the vast majority of Vermont's dairy farms.

2 Certainly, Latinx migrants do not frequent the numerous farmers' markets in Addison County, the majority of which are held in town on weekday and weekend mornings, typically from 9am to 12.30pm.

3 There is a large body of scholarship on the overvaluation and undervaluation of certain types of design work along gendered lines. For a broad yet concise treatment, see Rendell, Penner, and Borden 2000.

4 Middlebury College accepts applications from undocumented and Deferred Action for Childhood Arrivals (DACA) students. As President Patton declared in 2017,

> This past year we offered assistance to help with DACA renewals, access to an immigration lawyer, and covered other emergency expenses as needed. We pledge to continue with this support and to look for ways of offering resources in case a change of immigration policy leads to a loss of status that invalidates our students' ability to work or collect financial aid.

5 JUNTOS is a Middlebury College student organization that has a long-term partnership with Migrant Justice.

6 In the design for the Centro Cultural Móvil shown in Figure 4.3 (designed by Shan Zeng, Yihao [Lyra] Ding, and Zihan [Selena] Ling), students drew on the models of a camping trailer and a food truck to propose a design that would provide flexible spaces for distributing or preparing food, for holding meetings, and for disseminating educational materials. The source of inspiration was a travel trailer that capitalized on the idea of movable expandable spaces essential in a camper, but here serving to accommodate a variety of functions geared to solving the needs of migrant workers.

References

Anderson, Nadia M. 2014. "Public Interest Design as Praxis." *Journal of Architectural Education* 68 (1): 16–27. doi.org/10.1080/10464883.2014.864896

Angotti, Tom, Cheryl Doble, and Paula Horrigan. 2011. "At the Boundaries: The Shifting Sites of Service-Learning in Design and Planning." In *Service-Learning in Design and Planning: Educating at the Boundaries,* edited by Angotti, Doble, and Horrigan, 1–17. Oakland, CA: New Village Press.

Awan, Nishat, Tatjana Schneider, and Jeremy Till. 2011. *Spatial Agency: Other Ways of Doing Architecture.* New York: Routledge.

Baker, Daniel, and David Chappelle. 2012. "Health Status and Needs of Latino Dairy Farmworkers in Vermont." *Journal of Agromedicine* (17): 277–287.

Baker, Daniel. 2013. "Latino Dairy Workers in Vermont." *2013 Series | Communities & Banking,* (Spring): 5–7. www.bostonfed.org/publications/communities-and-banking/2013/spring/latino-dairy-workers-in-vermont.aspx

Bell, Bryan. 2004a. "Designing for the Ninety-eight Percent without Architects." In *Good Deeds, Good Design: Community Service Through Architecture,* edited by Bell, 10–13. New York: Princeton Architectural Press.

Bell, Bryan. 2004b. "Finding Clients." In *Good Deeds, Good Design: Community Service Through Architecture,* edited by Bell, 22–29. New York: Princeton Architectural Press.

Boyer, Ernest L., and Lee D. Mitgang. 1996. *Building Community: A New Future for Architecture Education and Practice: A Special Report.* Princeton: The Carnegie Foundation for the Advancement of Teaching.

Clayton, Patti H., Robert G. Bringle, Bryanne Senor, Jenny Huq, and Mary Morrison. 2010. "Differentiating and Assessing Relationships in Service-Learning and Civic Engagement: Exploitative, Transactional, or Transformational." *Michigan Journal of Community Service Learning* 16 (2): 5–22.

Coleman, Nathaniel. 2010. "The Limits of Professional Architectural Education." *JADE* 29 (2): 200–212.

Davis, Katherine L., Brandon W. Kliewer, and Aliki Nicolaides. 2017. "Power and Reciprocity in Partnerships: Deliberative Civic Engagement and Transformative Learning in Community-Engaged Scholarship." *Journal of Higher Education Outreach and Engagement* 21 (1): 30–54.

Enos, Sandra, and Keith Morton. 2003. "Building Partnerships for Service-Learning." In *Developing a Theory and Practice of Campus-Community Partnerships*, edited by Barbara Jacoby, 20–41. San Francisco: Jossey-Bass.

Feldman, Roberta M., Sergio Palleroni, David Perkes, and Bryan Bell. n.d. "Wisdom from the Field: Public Interest Architecture in Practice. A Guide to Public Interest Practices in Architecture." Accessed October 16, 2016. www.publicinterestdesign.com/wp-content/uploads/2013/07/Wisdom-from-the-Field.pdf

Fisher, Thomas. 2008. "Public-Interest Architecture: A Need and Inevitable Change." In *Expanding Architecture: Design as Activism*, edited by Bryan Bell and Katie Wakeford, 8–13. New York: Metropolis Books.

Flores, Yolanda. 2017. "Latino Farmworker Activism in Vermont: Migrant Justice/Justicia Migrante." *Latino Studies* 15: 516–521. doi.org/10.1057/s41276-017-0089-4

Freire, Paulo, and Donaldo Macedo. 1995. "A Dialogue: Culture, Language, and Race." *Harvard Educational Review* 65 (3): 377–403.

Freire, Paulo. 2002. *Pedagogy of the Oppressed*. New York: Continuum.

Gamez, Jose L.S., and Susan Rogers. 2008. "An Architecture of Change." In *Expanding Architecture: Design as Activism*, edited by Bryan Bell and Katie Wakeford, 18–25. New York: Metropolis Books.

Gutman, Robert. 2004. "Two Questions for Architecture." In *Good Deeds, Good Design: Community Service Through Architecture*, edited by Bryan Bell, 14–19. New York: Princeton Architectural Press.

Healey, Patsy. 2006. *Collaborative Planning. Shaping Places in Fragmented Societies*. New York: Palgrave Macmillan.

Hendler-Voss, Amanda, and Seth Hendler-Voss. 2008. "Designing with an Asset-Based Approach." In *Expanding Architecture: Design as Activism*, edited by Bryan Bell and Katie Wakeford, 124–131. New York: Metropolis Books.

Horrigan, Paula. 2006. "Shifting Ground: Design as Civic Action and Community Building." In *From the Studio to the Streets: Service-Learning in Planning and Architecture*, edited by Mari C. Hardin, Richard Eribes, and Charles (Corky) Poster, 127–138. Sterling, VA: Stylus Publishing.

Innes, Judith, and David E. Booher. 2010. *Planning with Complexity*. New York: Routledge.

Jacoby, Barbara. 2015. *Service-Learning Essentials: Questions, Answers, and Lessons Learned*. San Francisco: Jossey-Bass.

Jay, Gregory. 2010. "The Engaged Humanities: Principles and Practices for Public Scholarship and Teaching." *Journal of Community Engagement and Scholarship* 3 (1): 51–65.

Keller, Julie C. 2019. *Milking in the Shadows: Migrants and Mobility in America's Dairyland*. New Brunswick: Rutgers University Press.

Lawson, Laura, Lisa B. Spanierman, V. Paul Poteat, and Amanda M. Beer. 2011. "Educating for Multicultural Learning: Revelations from East St. Louis Design Studio." In *Service-Learning in Design and Planning: Educating at the Boundaries*, edited by Tom Angotti, Cheryl Doble, and Paula Horrigan, 70–85. Oakland, CA: New Village Press.

Lefebvre, Henri. 1991. *The Production of Space*. Oxford; Cambridge, MA: Blackwell.

Lopez Barrera, Silvina. 2018. "Community Engagement and Community-Based Projects in Beginning Design Education." In *Proceedings of the 34th National Conference on the Beginning Design Student,* edited by Samantha Krukowski.

Mares, Teresa M. 2019. *Life on the Other Border: Farmworkers and Food Justice in Vermont*. Oakland, CA: University of California Press.

Migrant Justice. n.d. "About Migrant Justice." Accessed March 29, 2016. http://migrantjustice.net/about

Mitchell, Tania D. 2008. "Traditional vs. Critical Service-Learning: Engaging the Literature to Differentiate Two Models." *Michigan Journal of Community Service Learning* 14 (2): 50–65.

Mitchell, Tania D. 2015. "Using a Critical Service-Learning Approach to Facilitate Civic Identity Development." *Theory Into Practice* 54: 20–28. doi.org/10.1080/00405841.2015.977657

Morton, Keith. 1995. "The Irony of Service: Charity, Project and Social Change in Service-Learning." *Michigan Journal of Community Service Learning* 2 (1): 19–32.

Radel, Claudia, Birgit Schmook, and Susannah McCandless. 2010. "Environment, Transnational Labor Migration, and Gender: Case Studies from Southern Yucatán, Mexico and Vermont, USA." *Population and Environment* 32 (2/3): 177–197. doi.org/10.1007/s11111-010-0124-y

Rendell, Jane, Barbara Penner, and Iain Borden. 2000. *Gender Space Architecture: An Interdisciplinary Introduction*. London: Routledge.

Schuman, Anthony W. 2006. "The Pedagogy of Engagement." In *From the Studio to the Streets: Service-Learning in Planning and Architecture,* edited by Mari C. Hardin, Richard Eribes, and Charles (Corky) Poster, 1–15. Sterling, VA: Stylus Publishing.

Sinclair, Cameron. 2006. "I Hope It Is a Long List …" In *Design Like You Give a Damn: Architectural Responses to Humanitarian Crises*, edited by Architecture for Humanity, 11–31. New York: Metropolis Books.

Stewart, Trae, and Megan Alrutz. 2012. "Meaningful Relationships: Cruxes of University-Community Partnerships for Sustainable and Happy Engagement." *Journal of Community Engagement and Scholarship* 5 (1): 44–55.

Thompson, Diego. 2010. "'Somos del campo': Latino and Latina Gardeners and Farmers in Two Rural Communities of Iowa – a Community Capitals Framework Approach." *Journal of Agriculture, Food Systems, and Community Development* 1 (3): 3–18. doi.org/10.5304/jafscd.2011.013.001

Thompson, Diego. 2020. "Building and Transforming Collective Agency and Collective Identity to Address Latinx Farmworkers' Needs and Challenges in Rural Vermont." *Agriculture and Human Values*. https://doi/10.1007/s10460-020-10140-7.

Thompson, Diego, and Lopez Barrera, Silvina. 2019. "Building Collaborative Governance and Community Resilience under Socio-spatial Rural Disparities and Environmental Challenges." *Community Development Practice* (Fall) 2019 (23): 8–16. www.comm-dev.org/professional-development/cds-practice

Thompson, Julia D., and Brent K. Jesiek. 2017. "Transactional, Cooperative, and Communal: Relating the Structure of Engineering Engagement Programs with the Nature of Partnerships." *Michigan Journal of Community Service Learning* 23 (2): 83–99.

Thorpe, Anne. 2012. *Architecture and Design Versus Consumerism: How Design Activism Confronts Growth*. New York: Earthscan.

5
INSIDE OUT

Private Space on Public Display in Modern and Contemporary Demolition Art

Kevin D. Murphy

Capitalism has risen during the modern period, but destruction has always accompanied it in the area of urban growth and development. As capitalism became first multinational, then global, it transformed urban centers throughout the West and then around the world, remaking cities more drastically than its impact on any other environment. Urban "modernization" in the second half of the 19th century accompanied and enabled the growth of the consumer economy, particularly in North America, Europe, and Great Britain. It was also at that historical juncture that public and private spaces were increasingly differentiated from one another. The newly reconstructed cities boasted all kinds of public spaces – from squares and parks to department stores and cafés – while spaces of production (including factories and offices) were physically isolated from private, residential quarters. The difference between the public sphere and the private became a tightly controlled border between safe and unsafe, protected and vulnerable. The private became the secret, the symbol of a new kind of individual self; to expose this self to the public became an unseemly act of desecration. Only now, as capitalism morphs into something new that cannot yet be fully described, have artists addressed the violence of the public/private border – and the works they produce make this manifest through literal demolition. To understand the demolition art of Gordon Matta-Clark, Childe Hassam, Dox Thrash, Rachel Whiteread, George Shaw, and Zhang Dali, one needs to see their work as a response to the violence of urban growth and renewal.

"Home Sweet Home" was a familiar 19th-century catchphrase; cross-stitched on a pillow or embroidered on a wall hanging, it suggested the broad-based ideologies of the private sphere that grew in importance throughout the period of industrialization. The private home was so burdened with the task of safeguarding the nuclear family from the purported venality of the commercial city that it took on epic symbolic significance. The home was thought to be a sacred realm in which individual identity could be expressed and family emotional bonds could be strengthened. Whereas the individual became ever more subject to the state's disciplinary "gaze" in public, in the home she felt protected: it was arguably the only place where "privacy" could be enjoyed. Thus, when the veil is torn away from the private realm – for instance, when walls are torn down as the city is modernized – and its hidden, safeguarded private spaces are exposed, the sensation is one of violation. The provocative, disruptive effect of exposing private space is also capitalized on by artists and critics who draw away the curtain to expose the raw reality of home life which – despite its ideological construction as sacred and pure – is in fact always affected by government policies, some of them controversial. Artist David Wojnarowicz, for instance, said, "To make the private into something public is an action that has terrific ramifications" ("David Wojnarowicz" 2018). He was referring specifically to contemporary art that dared to show the domestic lives of people living – and dying – with AIDS, and in doing so exposed the failure of government action to address a public health crisis that disproportionately affected gay men and marginalized groups.

This essay looks at the small subset of modern and contemporary art that focuses on the violent exposure of private space that often results from the demolition of city buildings and neighborhoods. "Demolition art" uses the motif of destruction to address the social implications of urban development or redevelopment – of change to the built environment more generally – and to consider the contested nature of urban space. As the work makes clear, these contests are often uneven or mismatched since the domestic settings of the poor, working class, or disenfranchised are frequently eradicated by the powerful, particularly those who benefit from government support under neoliberal policies. Much demolition art is "public art" to the extent that it is produced or displayed in settings where it can be seen by a substantial audience, although it is not always directly accessible. Even if some of the projects considered here were conceived to be temporary, they live on in photographs and other media. In some instances, public projects are by artists with studio practices and thus also find expression in paintings, sculptures, prints, and other art objects that continue to document instances of spatial contestation even after those conflicts are resolved or forgotten in real time. Demolition art is no substitute for direct political action or for the claiming of actual urban space, but it does function to bring to light the complex issues surrounding access to public space and private living quarters, and has done so effectively in many cases. The artists discussed here use art to reveal the violence that lies behind the remaking of the city, a violence that destroys "home" for the already disenfranchised.

Making modern urban spaces and buildings has almost always entailed destruction, of either the "natural" environment or of earlier construction. The process is thus reciprocal, comprising both gains and losses. Development is typically justified on the grounds that the gains outweigh the losses: for example, the projected addition of residential and commercial space is considered more important than

96 Kevin D. Murphy

the loss of historic building fabric. However, the losses that urban development spins off are not just of architecture, as significant as those may be, but also of communities. This point was made by Jane Jacobs in her classic text from 1961, *The Death and Life of Great American Cities*, where she argued that modernist planning entailed the annihilation of undervalued social networks through which lower-class city residents supported one another and protected their families. The locus of such communities – the traditional city street – was all too often, Jacobs maintained, replaced by howlingly vast and vacant spaces between superblocks, the residential form preferred in the projects of modernist urban planners.[1] While Jacobs focused on New York City, her observations could be extended to anywhere modern city planning has had an impact, and by the early 21st century that means virtually the entire world.

If urban modernization is a dynamic process, entailing both construction and demolition, representations of the modern city nonetheless overwhelmingly focus on the former, to the neglect of the latter. Many are the images of skyscrapers and other modern buildings under construction; relatively few are those of old structures falling to the wrecking ball. However, when artists have focused on the loss that precedes urban modernization, they have done so to provoke a number of different responses in the viewers of their images, feelings that range from nostalgia to outrage. Such images entail critiques of the forces, be they corporate, governmental, or both, that bring about the loss of traditional spaces in favor of reconstruction.

The transformations of private life and private space were at the center of debates about modernization since the moment at which the historical process got its name, in mid-19th-century Paris. In his much-discussed essay, "The Painter of Modern Life," modeled on the real-life Constantin Guys, poet Charles Baudelaire refers to "what with our reader's permission, we have called 'modernity.'" As Jürgen Habermas comments, "[Baudelaire] puts the word 'modernity' in quotation marks; he is conscious of his novel, terminologically peculiar use of the term."[2] Baudelaire characterized the modern world as one of "constant growth and change": "Baudelaire's changing world," writes Rachel Bowlby, "is proudly urban and man-made – and woman-made: his prototype of daily change and proto-art is fashion" (Bowlby 2014, 48). That the articulation of modernity unfolded in Paris was not coincidental. During the Second Empire of Emperor Napoleon III, the city was systematically rebuilt under the direction of Prefect of the Seine Georges-Eugène Haussmann, who lent the process his name: *Haussmannization*. From the early 1850s past the Empire's collapse in 1870, the built environment of Paris was subjected to changing architectural fashions and urban intentions. Many working-class neighborhoods in the city center were replaced by newly fashionable bourgeois districts. Baudelaire invoked the confrontations of the new inhabitants and the displaced in his prose poem "Les Yeux des Pauvres" ("The Eyes of the Poor") in the volume *Paris Spleen* (1869), which centers on the visual confrontation of the bourgeoisie and the poor through the plate glass window of an opulent new café.

Visual artists of the mid to late 19th century, notably Edgar Degas, captured the sometimes awkward and uncomfortable appearances of members of the working class, such as prostitutes, in the preposterously ornate spaces of the Second Empire city. A few artists showed the process of *percement* (literally, "piercing") whereby new streets were shot through historic residential quarters as Paris's modernization continued, such as photographer Eugène Atget who depicted the construction of a new street in the city's center around 1900 (see Figure 5.1). His photograph shows a row of buildings from the 18th century or earlier, with commercial space at street level and residential quarters or offices above. The row has been propped up where what was once an internal wall has been exposed by demolition. The significant detail here, one that will often be included in later demolition pictures,

FIGURE 5.1 Eugène Atget, *Maison. Vue en perspective du percement de la rue Domat, Paris 05*, 1900. Photograph, Ministère de la Culture (France)

is the telltale indication of where a staircase had once been. Wainscots, wallpaper, painted surfaces – all of these signal private space suddenly put on public view in pictures showing urban demolitions. These finishes make the violence inherent in modernization palpable.

If Paris was the 19th-century modern city *par excellence*, American cities outpaced the European capital in the 20th century with respect to expansion outwards and upwards, especially after the development of the skyscraper in the 1880s. The sheer height of their new buildings made spectacles out of New York, Chicago, and a handful of other American cities. It would be impossible to do justice to the sheer volume of images of city-building produced in the 20th-century United States.[3] It is important, however, to point out that architectural and urban modernization in the US coincided with the advent of modernism in the visual arts. Thus, some modernist artists found compelling subjects in the new buildings of Chicago, New York, and other cities. For them, the novel architecture of steel, concrete, and glass lent itself to depiction using modernist abstract means. Perhaps the most outstanding example of an artist who used modernist abstraction and fragmentation of form to capture the unprecedented spatial experiences offered by New York City was John Marin, who depicted the Woolworth Building (1913) and other urban architectural and engineering marvels in numerous prints, paintings, and drawings (Tedeschi et al. 2011) (see Figure 5.2).

Urban development and architectural experimentation both inspired American artists at the turn of the 20th century, as the example of John Marin demonstrates. Yet there were others who lamented the loss of old New York and other cities, or whose relationship to the whole process of urban change was more ambivalent. For instance, American Impressionist Childe Hassam, a prolific painter and print-maker for whom both the contemporary streetscapes of New York and the storied villages of New England were equally compelling subjects, felt skyscrapers were "hideous" when seen individually but as a group they transformed the city's sky-line into a vision of "blended strength and mystery" that rivaled Europe's archi-tectural attractions. In his 1904 painting, *The Hovel and the Skyscraper*, Hassam foregrounded the rising metal frame of a new parish house for the Second Church of Christ, Scientist at the corner of West Sixty-eighth Street and Central Park West (see Figure 5.3). The "hovel" in the picture's title most likely referred to the Sheepfold, a brick barn seen in the picture's middle ground, or to one or another wood-frame building that was demolished to make way for new construction (Weinberg 2004, 205, 209). Hassam's skyscraper picture is unusual for his perspec-tive on the subject: unlike most other depictions of the architectural type, Hassam does not position himself in such a way that the frame of the building soars hero-ically into the skyline; instead, he takes an elevated vantage point from which he looks down on the skyscraper. Hassam is not known for trenchant social critique, but by pairing skyscrapers and hovels in his title, he does seem to suggest that towering achievements and abjection coexist in the city.

FIGURE 5.2 John Marin, Woolworth Building (The Dance), 1913, plate: 12 13/16 × 10½ in, sheet: 17 15/16 × 13 7/16 in © Estate of John Marin/Artist Rights Society (ARS), New York. Courtesy of Philadelphia Museum of Art, The Alfred Stieglitz Collection, 1949, 1949-18-28

A similarly complex point of view arises in a picture by Philadelphia artist Dox Thrash, *Demolition*, produced around 1944 (see Figure 5.4). Well known as an innovative printmaker and cultural leader in the African American community, Thrash produced images during World War II of urban and rural subjects, often focused on African Americans (Ittman 2001). This picture is divided horizontally into two sections, the top being a standard urban view of the mid-20th century that shows tall office buildings and an iconic rooftop water tower,[4] and the bottom a group of older brick rowhouses, typical of Philadelphia, in the throes of demolition, presumably to make way for new construction. Two African American workers mark the division between the picture's zones as they kick up dust from the rowhouses' floors while demolishing them. The two men are separated by a staircase that leads nowhere, the upper story of the house having already been removed. Below them, demolition has exposed the white walls of

100 Kevin D. Murphy

FIGURE 5.3 Childe Hassam, *The Hovel and the Skyscraper*, 1904. Oil on canvas, 34¾ × 31 in. Courtesy of the Pennsylvania Academy of the Fine Arts, Philadelphia. The Vivian O. and Meyer P. Potamkin Collection, Bequest of Vivian O. Potamkin. Acc. No.: 2003.1.5

what were once interior spaces but are now strangely exposed to the elements and to spectators: ourselves. Thrash's picture makes the point visually that urban growth and modernization are predicated on destruction, and he does so forcefully by dividing *Demolition* into two halves of equal visual weight.

Moreover, the artist makes clear, by including the two figures in movement, that the traditional city's transformation into a modern metropolis is only accomplished through manual labor. There is an irony here too, that the men shown at work are members of a community that is likely to be displaced as new construction replaces old. Thrash experienced racism personally during World War II when in 1942 he was denied the opportunity to apply for a job at the Philadelphia Navy Yard as an airplane insignia painter because he was African American. Thrash subsequently made an unsuccessful discrimination claim against the Navy Yard's Labor Board and was especially wounded by his treatment because he considered

Private Space on Public Display   **101**

FIGURE 5.4 Dox Thrash, Demolition, c. 1944. Oil on canvas board, 26 x 20 in. Courtesy of the Philadelphia Museum of Art, Purchased with the Katharine Levin Farrell Fund, 2002. 2002-97-1

himself a patriot and was a World War I veteran (Ittman 2001, 28–31). *Demolition* was thus painted at a moment when racism was in the forefront of Thrash's mind and therefore may reference the impact of race- and class-based discrimination on urban policy.

The painting makes its point about urban transformation very subtly. Indeed, the dilapidation of the rowhouses – signaled, for example, by the boarded-up doors of the house to the right – could suggest that Thrash welcomed the demolition of derelict buildings. Yet the skyline replacing them is not shown to be heroic as, for instance, the roofline of only one building – stepped, to the left – is included. Nothing soars. Furthermore, Thrash paints at the bottom center of the picture two blocks of white, eye-catching for their brightness that contrasts with the red brick. They are the revealed walls of lost interior spaces. Their exposure scandalizes since we do not expect the private realm to be visible at the center of the modern city. Indeed, it is this motif – the marooned interior wall – that will become a crucial element in postwar art in which the process of urban spatial transformation is clearly viewed critically.

Dox Thrash's painting of Philadelphia's modernization was produced at a moment when government policies and private development practices favored the replacement of traditional urban neighborhoods with new construction. In the 1960s, however, and emerging in the writings of Jane Jacobs and a few contemporaries, modern planning and urban "redevelopment" or "renewal" were increasingly faulted for their negative architectural and social consequences. By the mid- to late-1960s a fully "postmodern" critique of modern spatial practices, articulated by architects Robert Venturi and Denise Scott Brown among others, emerged. That was the same point at which avant-garde art, dominated by painting in the 1940s and 1950s with Abstract Expressionism, increasingly turned to other media, including photography, installations, and site-specific work. These forms of expression were frequently three-dimensional and so lent themselves to art that took as its theme the contested use of space in the postwar period, in the US, Europe, and beyond. For instance, beginning in 1967, photographer Danny Lyon documented the demolition of vast swaths of lower Manhattan in the course of the redevelopment that culminated in the construction of the World Trade Center from 1966 to 1973. Lyon published his images of demolition workers, abandoned interiors, and half-gone commercial blocks in the 1969 volume *The Destruction of Lower Manhattan* (Sussman 2016, 34–41). Postwar art that similarly concerns space and architecture occupies the remainder of this essay. More specifically, it focuses on works that deal with the loss of historic environments and the everyday habitats of people whose needs are marginalized by the institutions that control how cities are transformed.

Lonely traces of demolished spaces, of the kind Danny Lyon captured, are also the focus of a series of photographs produced by artist Gordon Matta-Clark in 1972. Entitled *Walls Paper*, the work consists of a series of black-and-white photographs taken of semidemolished housing in the South Bronx majority-minority neighborhood of New York City. They show the vestiges of private spaces exposed by demolition: bits of molding, plastered surfaces, wallpaper, and flaking paint are zoomed in on, framed in such a way as to suggest the broad areas of paint found in Abstract Expressionist color field painting. The photographs blur the distinction between painting and architecture, one that Matta-Clark was ever keen to elide, by insisting on the character of the wall as a painted surface. Eventually, the artist enhanced the color of the photographs and printed them on newsprint. Long strips of the photographs were installed floor to ceiling at the artist-run gallery space at 112 Greene Street in New York City. As Pamela Lee suggests, in that installation the photographs produced a correspondence between the depicted walls of the soon to be demolished buildings in the images and those of the gallery. She writes, "The timeliness of each building – one now 'alive,' the other now 'dead' – spoke to the virtual 'speed' of the built environment, the endlessly fluctuating historicity of its architecture."[5] Indeed, the relative rapidity of the cycle of construction-destruction-construction was the implicit theme of demolition pictures going back to the early 20th century.

Matta-Clark's visual commentary on the contest over space in New York City had a very specific historic context, however much his work can be seen as part of a continuum of image-making. He graduated from Cornell University's architecture school in 1968 and returned the following year to New York City, which he had left in 1962 to attend college. The antiwar movement and the other radical social and political movements to which it led informed the artist's early career as did the contemporary postmodern critique of modernist architectural orthodoxy. The specific postmodern movement with which Matta-Clark was affiliated was "Anarchitecture": "an explosively nihilistic proposition of highly destabilizing potential." The term came from Robin Evans, an architect and critic, and was a play on the title of Le Corbusier's classic manifesto for modernist architecture, *Vers Une Architecture*, or *Towards An Architecture* (1923, the title was often mistranslated from 1927 on as *Towards a New* [sic] *Architecture*).[6] Philip Ursprung considers Anarchitecture to have coincided with, and in some ways responded to, a moment of profound economic instability and change during the early 1970s, "characterized by the deregulation of the labor market, the end of the gold standard, the arrival of computers, huge rises in energy prices and the growth of the financial sector." This phase of industrial capitalism, Ursprung maintains, coincided with the emergence of globalization as it is now understood and "radically affected the way that time and space, private and public, individual and society, are perceived." In New York City, racial conflict and deindustrialization – among other forces – led to urban decay and the city's financial crisis (Ursprung 2011, 139–140, quoted in Bessa 2017, 8).

Walls Paper made manifest the spatial disruptions that unfolded from the chain of historical events to which Ursprung refers. Matta-Clark documents, in his own way, the widespread abandonment and eventual destruction of vast neighborhoods of housing in New York City that was part of the urban crisis of the postwar years. *Walls Paper* was only shown once, in late 1972, but the project had an afterlife in an edition of artists books containing the images printed on newsprint and bound into a small volume that was published by the Buffalo Press in Buffalo, New York. There, the photos were enhanced with color and printed on pages that were cut in half horizontally so that top and bottom could be turned separately, thereby allowing the viewer to combine the wall fragments in a variety of ways. The cutting of pages has been compared frequently to the actions in which Matta-Clark engaged in his large-scale architectural projects, such as *Splitting* (1974), wherein the artist cut in half a suburban house in Englewood, New Jersey, and tilted the rear portion

104 Kevin D. Murphy

backward on its deliberately undermined foundation. The implications of his doing so were enormous, as Jack Halberstam has observed:

> The house was not just a ruin after he split it. Rather, the act of splitting (like the splitting of a verb, say) grammatically and structurally removed the building from its place in an architectural language centered on the home – that ideological site that purports to hold family, neighborhood, market, and nation securely in place.
>
> *(Halberstam 2018)*

In both the book and the architectural project, Matta-Clark laid bare domestic spaces that had hitherto been private. By doing so he called attention to the disruptions, crises even, in the built environment that had been brought about by economic, social, and political transformations from the late 1960s onward.

Pamela Lee argues, in her discussion of the projects Matta-Clark undertook in Paris during the mid-1970s, that "the very dissipation of communities and the demolition of site served as the generating principles of much of Matta-Clark's work, and were the objects of its critique" (Lee 1998, 67). By cutting and splitting buildings, the artist evolved his own language through which to call attention to the social and spatial implications of modernization. Yet his work often relied on imagery that recalls earlier demolition art, especially where he uses exposed fragments of private space to highlight the violence of urban development. Matta-Clark also showed that the kind of disruption he responded to was truly a global phenomenon. For the Paris Biennale of 1975, Matta-Clark created *Conical Intersect* by boring a hole whose form is suggested by the title into two historic buildings adjacent to the new Centre Pompidou in Paris (see Figure 5.5). Designed by the young Renzo Piano and Richard Rogers, the Centre Pompidou was destined to become an icon of postwar architecture, but it sparked controversy because it was part of a larger urban redevelopment project that included the destruction of Les Halles. Those great iron-and-glass market buildings were planned by architect Victor Baltard, constructed under the aegis of Napoleon III and Haussmann, and had themselves been accorded a central place in the development of modern architecture. They were the subject of a heated preservation battle but eventually lost out to President Georges Pompidou's plan to construct a cultural center, underscoring how much the history of Paris's built environment centered on the relationship between destruction and construction (Co 2016, 9–12; Evenson 1973, 308–315). Lee writes of Matta-Clark's work that "More than any of his other works, the Parisian site neatly illustrated the tension between narratives of historical progress – as embodied in the construction of the Pompidou Center – and the destruction of sites that is a prerequisite to this" (Lee 1998, 70).

The conical incision into the historic buildings, visible from the street below as a hole, functioned almost like a telescope that provided a view for the present-day spectator through an obsolete structure to a futuristic monument: Piano and

FIGURE 5.5 Gordon Matta-Clark, *Conical Intersect 3 (documentation of the action 'Conical Intersect' made in 1975 in Paris, France)*, 1975, printed 1977. Gelatin silver print. Sheet: 10 × 8 in.; image: 9¾ × 6 15/16 in. Gift of Harold Berg. Inv. N.: 2017.128. New York, Whitney Museum of American Art. © Digital image Whitney Museum of Art/Licensed by Scala © Photograph SCALA, Florence

Rogers' building (Lee 1998, 73–75). Where Les Halles had announced its modernity through its materials – an iron frame stretched with a transparent glass skin – the externalized structure of the Pompidou turned monumental architecture literally inside out. With its brightly colored duct work and skeletal frame plainly visible on the exterior, the Centre Pompidou loudly proclaimed the emergence of a new aesthetic for public institutional architecture. Moreover, the externalized structure suggested the transparency or openness of the building to its community. By making his incision visible, but not accessible (as it was raised far above street level in a half-demolished building), Matta-Clark implicitly critiqued the progressive connotations that transparent architecture had had since the early 20th century. From that point forward the visual transparency of glass architecture had been equated with institutional accessibility,[7] but Matta-Clark's project undermined that association by making the ideal vantage point from which to look through the old buildings to the new one unapproachable.

At the same time, *Conical Intersect* can be understood (whether or not Matta-Clark intended it as such) as a commentary on the Haussmannian *percements*, slices through the historic fabric of Paris that were intended to restore the circulation of what some urban critics at the time considered to be the city's diseased body. Matta-Clark echoed the historic cutting open of Paris as he bored into a fragment of its past – the two historic buildings. Where Haussmann's ostensible amelioration of the city's circulatory system masked the eviction of the working-class residents of its center, so the reconstruction of the Beaubourg neighborhood to accommodate a cultural facility that was intended to demonstrate the Republic's transparency nevertheless eviscerated the heart of the city's traditional working-class core. Matta-Clark's cutting can be understood to imply that in both the 19th and 20th centuries construction and demolition were always paired operations, and that claims to urban modernization inevitably entail the loss of existing fabric and, crucially, established communities. Matta-Clark drew attention to these paradoxes, which were part of both New York City's and Paris's identities in the 20th century, by focusing on those places where – brutally – private space had been exposed to public view through the process of renewal.

Putting private space on public view is a forceful gesture when the home is valued precisely for the degree to which it holds the world at bay. As Walter Benjamin suggested, in 19th-century Paris the development of capitalism brought about the separation of places of residence and commerce, the former serving as spaces where both business concerns and social conflicts were resisted: "[The interior] represented the universe for the private citizen" (Benjamin 1968, 83). It followed then, that the interior bore its resident's imprint – or "traces," as Benjamin put it – since "Living means leaving traces" (Benjamin 1968, 84). In demolition art, those traces are all too shockingly put on view. The architectural masquerade by which the private realm maintains its distance from the commercial city is shown to be a fragile operation, one that is easily brought down by the cycle of destruction and construction.

Thus far, this essay has focused on instances in which artists represent demolition as the inevitable consequence of urban expansion or modernization in cities to which excess capital has moved. Yet demolition occurs equally in those centers from which capital has fled, cities devastated by deindustrialization and disinvestment as manufacturing has sought ever less expensive labor markets. The spatial implications of neoliberal economic policy are extreme in both instances: where intense competition to invest excess capital in "hot" real estate markets leads to the displacement of existing communities and the destruction of historic built environments, and where disinvestment and deindustrialization bring about widespread abandonment of older structures.

The outstanding example of a US city struggling with its postindustrial status is Detroit, Michigan, once the hub of the American auto industry. As its economic basis and population shrank in the postwar period, both its public and private architecture declined, precipitously so from the 1980s through the early 2000s. The ruins of Detroit's once grand public and private spaces have been the subject of a great deal of art-making and repeatedly photographed. Dora Apel demonstrates that in the wake of the 9/11 terrorist attacks, Hurricane Katrina, and subsequent disasters, "the imagery of ruination has only grown and speaks to the overarching fears and anxieties of our era: increasing poverty, declining wages and social services, inadequate health care, unemployment, homelessness, ecological disaster and degradation, and fear of the other" (Apel 2015, 3). Apel cautions that too often, however, images of Detroit's decrepit buildings collapse into "ruin porn" that highlights the paradoxical beauty to be found in depictions of the city in decline and renders the experience of looking at them "pleasurable," rather than as a provocation to consider the human consequences of global capitalism. To do so, writes Apel, "is to succumb to the profound demoralization effected by a capitalist system that has nearly suffocated the idea of an emancipated society based on equality instead of class privilege" (Apel 2015, 72).

Some of the art made in and about Detroit has dramatized the costs to its communities of the rampant demolition of its urban fabric, especially in the aftermath of the global financial crisis during the first decade of the 21st century. The targets of this deliberate destruction were often the homes of Detroit's poor and working-class populations, devastated by disinvestment in the city, predatory mortgage lending, and other factors that led to the decay of housing stock. In 2007, for example, nearly 100 houses were demolished every day in Detroit; in 2014 the federal government's Detroit Blight Removal Task Force determined that fully 30 percent of the city's building stock was either dilapidated or threatening to become so, leading to the recommendation that 40,000 buildings be demolished. As Apel points out, there was no plan for what to put in place of the lost buildings, so they became "negative ruins," not actual crumbling architecture, but rather gaps in the cityscape where structures had once stood (Apel 2015, 40).

Demolition had arisen as an issue in Detroit much earlier. In the 1980s the Urban Center for Photography had embarrassed city leaders with its project called "Demolished by Neglect." The group posted "enlarged photos of burned-out homes and decrepit theaters and other grand spaces on outdoor sites" (Rosler 2011, 12). Although Detroit lost many types of buildings, the demolition of swaths of the city's once vast neighborhoods of modest housing threatened the very survival of its diverse communities. Deindustrialization, disinvestment, and finally demolition made it nearly impossible for private life even to continue in Detroit for many of its most vulnerable residents, as "Demolished by Neglect" and some other later projects made clear.

British sculptor Rachel Whiteread brings the traces of private life into the public realm by a different means. In works dating back to the early 1990s, she has used the casting process to invert the relationship between space and its architectural container. An art student during the 1980s, first at Brighton and then at the Slade School of Art, Whiteread became known for casting domestic objects, such as mattresses, and in 1990, with *Ghost* (see Figure 5.6), an entire Victorian living room. It was made of 86 plaster panels cast from an actual building that were affixed to an armature made of standard metal shelving brackets. The effect was a positive image of the negative space formed by the architectural envelope of an unremarkable north London parlor (Sharpe 2018). As Whiteread says, "When I made *Ghost*, I was interested in relocating a room, relocating a space, from a small domestic house to a big concrete anonymous place, which is what museums have done all over the world for years and years" (quoted in Schneider 2002, 26). On view in the Chisenhale Gallery, the room's space was solid and monumental; what

FIGURE 5.6 Rachel Whiteread, *Ghost*, 1990 © Rachel Whiteread. Courtesy of the artist, Luhring Augustine, New York, Galleria Lorcan O'Neill, Rome, and Gagosian Gallery

had formerly been ineffable was now undeniably present and concrete (Mullins 2004, 24). *Ghost* and Whiteread's subsequent related works have provoked a variety of responses – positive and negative – but in any case, they have led to discussions about space: who has access to it and who is denied entrance or possession.

Even more provocative than *Ghost* was the work that gained Whiteread international recognition as well as the prestigious Turner Prize in 1993. *House* (1992, see Figure 5.7): "the internal cast of a Victorian terraced property, 193 Grove Road, in Bow, east London [was] a scaling up of the formal concerns of *Ghost* in a building scheduled for demolition" (Townsend 2004, 18). *House* engaged demolition in a number of senses. Since Whiteread knew that her casting process – in which "essentially the building became a mould" (quoted in Mullins 2004, 52) – would result in the loss of the original house, she set out to find one already slated for demolition. After a two-year search, Whiteread located the Victorian terrace house in Bow. It had been inhabited by a holdout to the planned demolition of a group of houses that were to be brought down to create a park. After the cast was produced in concrete, the "real" house was demolished, and Whiteread's sculpture was itself eventually demolished too amidst a great deal of controversy. While some considered *House* an aberration, others saw it as an effective and monumental

FIGURE 5.7 Rachel Whiteread, *House*, 1993 © Rachel Whiteread. Courtesy of the artist, Luhring Augustine, New York, Galleria Lorcan O'Neill, Rome, and Gagosian Gallery

110 Kevin D. Murphy

piece of sculpture made out of an otherwise undistinguished element of the quotidian built environment (Mullins 2004, 50–57).

Whiteread herself always considered *House* to be a temporary work, and even though potential buyers came forward near the end of its "run," the sculpture only lasted from October 25, 1993 to January 11, 1994 (Dimitrakaki 2004, 107). Whiteread's process distinguishes *House* from the work of other artists who took urban architecture and its destruction as their subjects, but the scale of her work has invited comparison with Gordon Matta-Clark, some of whose influential projects were similarly ephemeral, and with whom she shared an interest in exploring the social and political resonances of domestic buildings. Despite the distinctive method used by Whiteread, *House* deployed elements of domestic architecture that previous demolition art had also highlighted to bring the private realm to public visibility.

When Whiteread began the project on August 2, 1993, her first step was to strip the interior of the old house to prepare it to function as a form for cast concrete. The artist explains:

> The previous tenants were obviously DIY fanatics. The house was full of fitted cupboards, cocktail bars and a tremendous variety of wallpapers and floor finishes. I was fascinated by their personal environment, and documented it all before I destroyed it.
>
> *(quoted in Mullins 2004, 50, 52)*

The finishes mentioned by Whiteread are the kinds of details that were so shocking when they made their appearances in earlier images of demolished buildings. Whiteread's cast object displayed a Victorian house, but critics also frequently compared it to modernist sculpture since its mass was starkly geometric and its surface was light in color and smooth. At the same time, the surface also registered bits of the old house – "idiosyncrasies of 100 years of domestic use" – from soot to light switches (Mullins 2004, 52). *House* literally bore the imprint of its inhabitants and thus recalled a strain of thinking about the private realm that went back to the 19th century when the idea that the identity of a resident was registered in the form of her or his habitation gained currency. Demolition art frequently showed those "traces" of the subject to dramatize the violent exposure of the private realm when old houses were torn down. As Shelley Hornstein summarizes: "*House* stands alone with all its insides declared: a solid mass of inside, out" (Hornstein 2004, 67).

Exposing such palpable evidence of the previous inhabitants was one way that *House* critically addressed the practice of demolishing working-class housing ostensibly to improve a crowded neighborhood by creating a park. In this sense, *House* can be compared to earlier demolition art that similarly addressed the physical reconstruction of other cities where urban improvement and renovation were accomplished only through excision of swaths of dense lower-class neighborhoods.

Angela Dimitrakaki argues that *House* was disturbing for more than its unconventional form:

> The controversy that broke around this particular piece of sculpture, a structure turned inside out, suggested that *House* was relevant to a wider realm of intersecting debates, ranging from the meaning of public space in art (and vice versa), to the meaning of democracy, with the relationship between the two clearly being the most unsettling.
>
> *(Dimitrakaki 2004, 109)*

Dimitrakaki borrows the term "political unconscious" from Fredric Jameson to describe the way that *House* engaged contemporary issues: "It is a hidden sign of the times, an umbilical cord connecting reality and representation" (Dimitrakaki 2004, 110). Although this distinction between art (or representation) and "reality" might be challenged, the general point is well taken. *House*, like other demolition art, was powerful precisely because it spoke to something outside of itself, and also like earlier works that featured city clearance, it sparked debate over the consequences of urban decay, architectural obsolescence, and renovation. Like earlier demolition art, *House* bore the traces of displaced inhabitants, but Whiteread's process went further: by solidifying the space of a domestic interior, the artist made a house that could not be entered even imaginatively. Wallpaper, flaking paint, and other ghosts of residences in previous demolition art were powerful precisely because they spurred the viewer to picture the vanished homes that once were. *House*, on the other hand, was an "uncanny" home that offered up an absence of space where a domestic interior had previously stood, and thereby forced the viewer into the space around the work. It was a piece of public art that repelled its public.[8]

Anthony Vidler has written of *House* that

> even the illusion of return "home" is refused, the uncanny itself is banished. No longer can the fundamental terrors of exclusion and banishment, of homelessness and alienation, be ameliorated by their aestheticization in horror stories and psychoanalytic family romances; with all doors to the *unheimlich* firmly closed, the domestic subject is finally out in the cold forever.
>
> *(Vidler 2000, 147)*

In this passage, it is all viewers of the work who are refused a home, even an uncanny one, who experience "homelessness," and are "out in the cold." But of course the "homeless" for contemporary viewers and readers represent a specific category of people, those who lack a permanent place of residence. For them, the absence of a home is not only a psychological problem but also, and perhaps more importantly, a material one, and *House* inevitably spurs a consideration of

112 Kevin D. Murphy

this marginalized group. A hulking block of impenetrable concrete, Whiteread's work recalls an abandoned modernist housing project just before its demolition, and suggests the failures of Western democracies to adequately accommodate all their citizens. Further, the sculpture draws attention to urban policy in London and elsewhere that relied upon the familiar cycle of demolition and construction to address the need for housing, with mixed (and sometimes disastrous) results.

One failed effort was captured in a work that Whiteread executed around the time that *House* was being completed. Perhaps thinking of the notorious photographs documenting the implosion of the derelict Pruitt-Igoe public housing complex in St. Louis in the mid-1970s,[9] Whiteread set out to capture visually the failure of modern housing projects in London's East End. The result was *Demolished*, "a series of twelve screenprints of three suites of photographs [… that] captured the moment when a high-rise block of flats was blown up, leaving a mushroom cloud of dust and smoke where people's homes once were" (Mullins 2004, 67). The series was explicitly demolition art and the object of its critique was unambiguously a housing policy that had promised improvement through the construction of massive blocks of modern apartments, but in the end collapsed (literally) back into the same cycle of destruction-construction-destruction that had characterized modern urban development for a century or more.

Whiteread's *Demolished* series has been compared with more recent work by British painter George Shaw. Most of Shaw's practice, which includes many monumentally scaled paintings, has focused on the housing estate in the English Midlands, outside the city of Coventry, where he grew up and where his family still lives: Tile Hill. In some 200 paintings, Shaw depicts the housing development constructed just after World War II, in which much of Coventry's core was destroyed, and assesses the long-term fate of a complex that was initially admired as a preeminent example of modern architecture in Britain (Hallett 2018, 1–3). Where Whiteread's uncanny *House* denied the homeless viewer access to domestic space, thereby pointing to the failures of postwar housing policy, Shaw's perspective on Tile Hill, where he grew up in the 1970s and 1980s, is more nuanced. Shaw foregrounds in many of his paintings the dereliction of the low-cost housing at Tile Hill, but he also shows woods, open greenspaces, and nature; he has said that it was a good place to spend his childhood. In fact, the greenery was an important aspect of Tile Hill's design by Coventry City architect Donald Gibson, whose approach was informed by that of the American urban critic and theorist Lewis Mumford, who advocated for an "ecological" approach to planning (Schinkle 2018, 45–46). Mumford, a founding member of the Regional Planning Association of America, called for development that would remedy both environmental destruction and the decline of civic life: in short, he viewed "the city as polis in relation to the organic complexities of the regional ecosystem" (Luccarelli 1995, 3).

Despite the progressive aspects of Tile Hill's design, it suffered physical deterioration, in part due to extrinsic factors such as deindustrialization in Great Britain during the last quarter of the 20th century. In capturing the decaying fabric of the housing estate, Shaw takes up some motifs that appear and reappear in demolition art. For instance, much as Dox Thrash focused on the exposed plaster walls of a partly demolished rowhouse interior, or in the way that Matta-Clark sequenced battered and peeling tenement walls in *Walls Paper*, Shaw depicts the "found monochromes" he encounters in Tile Hill, including the boarded-up walls of the local library and temporary enclosures erected around demolition sites. In these works, the flat surfaces are likened to those of a stretched canvas.[10] Shaw's visual rumination on Tile Hill is thus both formal and thematic; his concern with the flatness of the canvas has been one of the core problematics of modernist painting from its inception but at the same time his exploration of the formal concerns of easel painting opens onto a sober consideration of the complexities of urban and regional planning. Shaw's found monochromes are not just any blank surfaces but those that precisely mark the former locations of defunct institutions and abandoned housing.

Like Rachel Whiteread, who chronicled the implosion of a modern housing project in *Demolished*, George Shaw registered in his work the controlled explosions in July 2012 of the 16-story Massey Ferguson tower in Tile Hill.[11] What followed were a series of large-scale paintings depicting the sites of demolished buildings. Among them is *The End of Care* (2013), which shows the former site of an elder care facility at Tile Hill called Hawthorn Lodge (see Figure 5.8). In a 2018 exhibition, the painting was described as "a flattened landscape" in which "The only trace left of [Hawthorn Lodge] is in the ghostly outlines of individual rooms that pattern the ground. A melancholy group of trees gathers around the site like mourners at a funeral" (Hallett 2018).[12]

A comparison of Shaw's painting with other works of demolition art is illuminating. Most significantly, in *The End of Care*, as the exhibition label observes, the traces of private space are on the ground. In earlier demolition art, the telltale signs of vanished private space were left stranded on bits of standing verticals walls, but in Shaw's work they are found on the horizontal. The traces of domestic settings thus become archaeological, almost like the shin-high walls of Pompeiian ruins. At the same time, the outlines of former walls trace the receding orthogonals of the painting's perspectival system on the ground, akin to what some Renaissance painters did with the geometric patterns of floor tiles. Shaw also marks the vanishing point of the perspective system with a gabled building, reddish in color, that stands out behind a row of shrubs and trees along the horizon line. That boundary between land and sky is itself something out of earlier landscape art: it is relatively low and flat as in the much admired and often emulated landscape style of the Dutch 17th century. In adopting a two-part composition, with a deep greenspace in the lower half and an open sky above, Shaw also builds on the romantic tradition in British landscape painting. Like his forebears, Shaw attends to the particularities of light and sky, but where an 18th- or 19th-century English landscapist would have introduced a ruined church or abbey to suggest the passage

114 Kevin D. Murphy

FIGURE 5.8 George Shaw, *The End of Care*, 2013. Humbrol enamel on board 36 × 47 in. Courtesy of the artist and Anthony Wilkinson Gallery, London

of time, the contemporary artist lays the tracks of an elder care facility on the ground to carry our eye into the middle distance and background.

In the 18th and 19th centuries, a classical or medieval monument in a landscape painting served to remind the viewer of the cyclical nature of human culture and history. Here, the architectural motif has a more immediate and less lofty function. It indicates the postwar history of publicly supported building and the pattern of destruction, construction, and ultimate demolition that has characterized it. The multidimensional history of demolition and its national significance is invoked by the very scale of Shaw's paintings, which absorbs the viewer and demands that she consider the complexities involved in the processes of building and destruction.

As economic globalization accelerated dramatically in the mid-20th century, Western forms of urbanism and capitalist development spread around the globe and had a particular impact on developing nations. Sometimes operating under political conditions that afforded them far less freedom than what Western artists enjoyed, Chinese avant-garde artists nonetheless also used demolition art to critique the social and environmental impact of urban modernization. One important figure in this movement is Zhang Dali, who graduated from the Central Academy of Fine Arts and Design in Beijing and subsequently spent several years living in

Bologna, Italy, in self-imposed exile following the 1989 Tiananmen Square pro-democracy protests. While living in Italy, Zhang was inspired by the graffiti he found on Bologna's walls and went on to make art that was comparable to that of New York graffiti artist Keith Haring and others. On his return to China after six years in the West, Zhang used his own brand of graffiti art tactics to critique offi-cially sanctioned urban "modernization" and "beautification."[13]

As in the West, rebuilding cities in China, and particularly Beijing, also entailed massive destruction: "Although large-scale demolition is a regular feature of any metropolis, the enormity and duration of the demolition in Beijing was unusual" (Hung 2002, 200). The city's "Old and Dilapidated Housing Renewal" program, initiated in 1990, led to extensive losses of Beijing's historic fabric (Auyeung 2008, 217). Zhang perceived that this massive demolition program spelled the destruction not just of buildings – including thousands of traditional houses – and streetscapes, but also of communities. Zhang says that "Human beings leave signs in the cities" (quoted in Marinelli 2009, 35), much as Benjamin discussed the traces left on interiors by their inhabitants. Demolishing old buildings meant dispersing groups of people who were accustomed to living in close proximity to one another, and it expunged material evidence of their communities from the built environment. By 2000, 4.2 million square meters of historic housing had been demolished in Beijing, which had an impact, including relocation in some instances, on a half million residents. While many had welcomed the move to more modern living quarters, they had not anticipated removal from Beijing's center, which was largely transformed from a residential district to a commercial and entertainment zone.[14]

Zhang's method of criticizing modernization was conceived of as a "dialogue" he hoped would be spurred by the caricatural images of his own bald head which he painted and incised on the walls of Beijing starting in the mid-1990s. His work was treated as controversial in the press, which reported and probably exaggerated the responses of the public that was sometimes either mystified or repulsed by his imagery. Still, he persevered, and in 1998–1999 focused particularly on the issue of demolition by spray painting his silhouette on the walls of houses in the throes of demolition, "thus 'reclaiming' an abandoned site, however temporarily" (Hung 2002, 200). These works, such as *Demolition: Forbidden City, Beijing* from the series *Dialogue with Demolition* (1998, see Figure 5.9), were documented in photographs that preserve Zhang's ephemeral interventions.[15]

Zhang's work draws on the same elements of the modernizing city that attracted artists from the turn of the 20th century, in particular the partially demolished house whose remaining walls bear the traces of earlier private spaces. But his image-making goes a step further: his pictures actually occupy the contested spaces of modernization, they intervene in urban environments. Zhang takes the language of demolition art and mobilizes it in real space, however much the actual impact he has on urban policy may be circumscribed by the Chinese political and

116 Kevin D. Murphy

FIGURE 5.9 Zhang Dali, *Demolition, Forbidden City*, 1998. Chromogenic color print. Denver Art Museum, Gift from Vicki and Kent Logan to the Collection of the Denver Art Museum, 2015.659. © Zhang Dali. Photography courtesy Denver Art Museum

economic systems. *Demolition: Forbidden City* can thus be compared to Matta-Clark's *Conical Intersect* as both works are enacted in the built environment itself while it is in the throes of demolition. Both works also create, although in different ways, vantage points from which the new city is viewed through the lens of the old one that is on the brink of eradication. Matta-Clark's surgery on two old houses created a viewpoint on the Centre Pompidou, albeit one that was inaccessible to the public. Zhang, in contrast, established a more approachable prospect through a hole in a crumbling wall to the restored architecture of the Forbidden City, one of the attractions that was then being prioritized in the rebuilding of Beijing. Both artists intervene in the transforming modern city in ways that highlight the violence of the changes to the built environments, both to its architecture and its communities.

Zhang's graffiti art is a fragile gesture of resistance to what was by the first decade of the 21st century a much larger campaign, described by David Harvey, who writes that

> China is only the epicenter for an urbanization process that has now become genuinely global in part through the astonishing global integration of financial markets that use their flexibility to debt-finance urban mega-projects from Dubai to Sao Paulo and from Mumbai to Hong Kong and London.
>
> *(Harvey 2008, 7)*

Reflecting on the history of urban modernization from Haussmann's Paris to contemporary Beijing and beyond, Harvey observes that "Violence is required to achieve the new urban world on the wreckage of the old" (Harvey 2008, 9). Effective demolition art makes that violence palpable. Such art cannot replace a "right to the city" movement that would insist upon the claims of all citizens to occupy urban space and to be considered when development policies are made – as opposed to simply the desires and profits of the rich and powerful. Nevertheless, as the work of some modern and contemporary artists has already shown, cultural production can make visible in powerful ways the ongoing contestations over urban space. Some of these projects are interventions in the actual spaces of transforming cities; they use the same violent means as do the demolishers – cutting, incising, opening up holes in the urban fabric – but put them to progressive ends. Other demolition art provokes its audience from the pages of a book, the wall of a gallery, or more dramatically, as a massive and unexpected sculpted form in a public space. These works have jarringly exposed private space to the public's gaze in efforts to shock viewers into recognizing the violence that goes along with urban development – even with projects that ostensibly result in "renewal" or "rehabilitation" – inflicted most often on the very constituents least able to resist modernization.

Notes

1 Jacobs 1961. Criticism of "urban renewal" also came from the communities disproportionately affected by it, such as the African American community, as Brian Goldstein argues in his essay in this volume.
2 Habermas 1987. Here, Habermas is quoting Charles Baudelaire, "The Painter of Modern Life," written around 1859–1860, first published in 1863, and subsequently reprinted and translated frequently, especially after the revival in the 1980s of interest in the writings of Walter Benjamin, who was an influential critical writer on Baudelaire.
3 For one attempt to do so, see Schleier 1986.
4 The water tower features in many 20th-century urban images as well as in contemporary art. Some well-known photographs of dancer Trisha Brown's *Roof Piece* (1974) show performers on Manhattan rooftops where scattered water towers punctuate the cityscape. The form is also the centerpiece of a work, *Water Tower* (1998–1999) by Rachel Whiteread, some of whose other works are discussed below. On *Water Tower* see Lee 2004, 128–148.

118 Kevin D. Murphy

5 Lee 2001, 81. On the series also see Tate n.d., "Gordon Matta-Clark, Walls Paper 1972."
6 Bessa 2017. On the relationship between the architectural concepts of Matta-Clark and Le Corbusier see Attlee 2007.
7 There is a substantial bibliography on architectural transparency as a metaphor. See for instance Hagg-Bletter 2001, 350–358, and Hagg-Bletter 1978.
8 Dimitrakaki's discussion of *House* as uncanny is indebted to Anthony Vidler's discussion of Whiteread's work in *Warped Space* (2000). See also Vidler 1992.
9 Joseph Heathcott provides a brief review of the many places where the destruction of Pruitt-Igoe was taken as a symptom of the larger failure of liberal housing policy and the modernist architecture it employed, but concludes that

> Pruitt-Igoe was in fact a canary in the coal mine, but for something much larger than the decline of one federal housing program. Rather, the failure of the project registered the massive seismic shifts already underway in Northeastern and Midwestern cities through capital flight, disinvestment, suburbanization, and population decline.
>
> *(Heathcott 2012, 450)*

10 The "found monochromes" by photographer David Batchelor, taken from blank surfaces of boarded windows, doors, and so on, and exhibited at the Ikon Gallery in Birmingham in 2004, have been considered an influence on Shaw (Hallet 2018, 206).
11 Hallett 2018, 249. A similar concern with documenting the process of change in a postindustrial British city motivated the project of photographers Liz Lock and Mishka Henner who exhibited their work under the title *Raw Material* at the AirSpace Gallery in Stoke-on-Trent in June, 2008. Their photographs taken in Stoke-on-Trent included images of rowhouses, originally constructed in the 19th century as workers' housing, being demolished. Similar to other examples of demolition art, many of their photographs showed partially demolished rooms where wallpaper, paint, and other interior finishes were still visible.
12 *George Shaw: A Corner of a Foreign Field*, Yale Center for British Art, New Haven, 4 October–30 December, 2018.
13 Cornell University Archive of Chinese Avant-garde Art, biography of Zhang Dali, www.chinesecontemporary.com/artist.php?artistID=9&cv=0, consulted December 12, 2018; my introduction to the work of Zhang Dali and his Chinese contemporaries who engaged with the built environment was as a member of the dissertation committee of the late Poyin Auyeung, PhD. See Auyeung 2008.
14 Auyeung 2008, 221–227. David Harvey puts the figure of affected residents much higher, at three million, in his article "The Right to the City."
15 Sally O'Driscoll and I use this term to characterize short-lived political and artistic projects that employ a variety of media and take place in public space. See Murphy and O'Driscoll 2015.

References

Apel, Dora. 2015. *Beautiful Terrible Ruins: Detroit and the Anxiety of Decline.* New Brunswick, NJ: Rutgers University Press.
Attlee, James. 2007. "Towards Anarchitecture: Gordon Matta-Clark and Le Corbusier." *Tate Papers* (7). Accessed November 10, 2018. www.tate.org.uk/research/publications/tate-papers/07/towards-anarchitecture-gordon-matta-clark-and-le-corbusier

Auyeung, Poyin. 2008. *Art, Urbanism, and Public Space: Critical Spatial Responses to Urban Redevelopment in Beijing (1976–2000)*. PhD diss. CUNY Graduate Center.

Benjamin, Walter. 1968. "Louis-Philippe or the Interior" in "Paris – Capital of the Nineteenth Century." *New Left Review* 1 (48): 77–88.

Bessa, Antonio Sergio. 2017. "Nothing Works: Gordon Matta-Clark." In *Gordon Matta-Clark Anarchitect*, edited by Bessa and Jessamyn Fiore, 1–20. New York: Bronx Museum of the Arts with Yale University Press.

Bowlby, Rachel. 2014. "'Half Art': Baudelaire's *Le Peintre de la Vie Moderne*," *Daedalus* 143 (1): 46–53.

Co, Francesco dal. 2016. *Centre Pompidou: Renzo Piano, Richard Rogers, and the Making of a Modern Monument*. New Haven: Yale University Press.

"David Wojnarowicz: History Keeps Me Awake at Night." 2018. Whitney Museum of American Art, New York, July 13–September 30, 2018.

Dimitrakaki, Angela. 2004. "Gothic Public Art and the Failures of Democracy: Reflections on *House*, Interpretation and the 'Political Unconscious.'" In *The Art of Rachel Whiteread*, edited by Chris Townsend, 107–127. London: Thames & Hudson.

Evenson, Norma. 1973. "The Assassination of Les Halles." *Journal of the Society of Architectural Historians* 32 (4): 308–315.

"George Shaw: A Corner of a Foreign Field," Yale Center for British Art, New Haven, 4 October–30 December, 2018.

Habermas, Jürgen. 1987. *The Philosophical Discourse of Modernity: Twelve Lectures*. Translated by Frederick Lawrence. Cambridge: Polity Press.

Hagg-Bletter, Rosemary. 2001. "Mies and Dark Transparency." In *Mies in Berlin*, edited by Barry Bergdoll and Terence Riley, 350–358. New York: Museum of Modern Art.

Hagg-Bletter, Rosemary. 1978. "Opaque Transparency." *Oppositions* 13: 121–130.

Halberstam, Jack. 2018. "Unbuilding Gender," *Places Journal*, October 2018. Accessed 20 November 2018. doi.org/10.22269/18100.

Hallett, Mark. 2018. "A Corner of a Foreign Field." In *George Shaw, A Corner of a Foreign Field*, edited by Hallett. New Haven: Yale University Press. Exhibition catalogue.

Harvey, David. 2008. "The Right to the City." *New Left Review* 53 (September–October). Accessed December 12, 2018. https://newleftreview.org/II/53/david-harvey-the-right-to-the-city

Heathcott, Joseph. 2012. "Planning Note: Pruitt-Igoe and the Critique of Public Housing." *Journal of the American Planning Association* 78 (Autumn): 450–451.

Hornstein, Shelley. 2004. "Matters Immaterial: On the Meaning of Houses and the Things Inside Them." In *The Art of Rachel Whiteread*, edited by Chris Townsend, 51–67. London: Thames & Hudson.

Hung, Wu. 2002. "Zhang Dali's *Dialogue*: Conversation with a City." In *Cosmopolitanism*, edited by Carol A. Breckenridge, Sheldon Pollock, Homi K. Bhabha, and Dipesh Chakrabarty, 189–208. Durham: Duke University Press.

Ittman, John. 2001. "Dox Thrash: 'I Always Wanted to be an Artist.'" In *Dox Thrash: An African American Master Printmaker Rediscovered*, edited by Ittman, 20–35. Philadelphia: Philadelphia Museum of Art and University of Washington Press. Exhibition catalogue.

Jacobs, Jane. 1961. *The Death and Life of Great American Cities*. New York: Random House.

Lee, Pamela M. 2004. "As the Weather." In *The Art of Rachel Whiteread*, edited by Chris Townsend, 128–148. London: Thames & Hudson.

Lee, Pamela M. 2001. *Object to be Destroyed: The Work of Gordon Matta-Clark*. Cambridge, MA: MIT Press.

Lee, Pamela M. 1998. "On the Holes of History: Gordon Matta-Clark's Work in Paris." *October* 85 (Summer): 65–89.

Luccarelli, Mark. 1995. *Lewis Mumford and the Ecological Region: The Politics of Planning.* New York: Guilford Press.

Marinelli, Maurizio. 2009. "Negotiating Beijing's Identity at the Turn of the Twentieth Century." In *Dissent and Cultural Resistance in Asia's Cities,* edited by Melissa Butcher and Selvaraj Velayutham, 33–52. New York: Routledge.

Mullins, Charlotte. 2004. *Rachel Whiteread.* London: Tate Publishing.

Murphy, Kevin D., and Sally O'Driscoll. 2015. "The Art/History of Resistance: Visual Ephemera in Public Space." *Space and Culture* 18 (4): 328–357.

Rosler, Martha. 2011. "Culture Class: Art, Creativity, Urbanism, Part III." *E-flux journal* 25 (May). Accessed February 25, 2019. www.e-flux.com/journal/25/67898/culture-class-art-creativity-urbanism-part-iii

Schleier, Merrill. 1986. *The Skyscraper in American Art: 1890–1931.* Cambridge, MA: DaCapo Press.

Schneider, Christiane. 2002. "The Body and the City." In *Rachel Whiteread, Haunch of Venison,* edited by Christiane Schneider, 15–35. London: Haunch of Venison.

Sharpe, Emily. 2018. "Rachel Whiteread's Breakthrough Work *Ghost* Gets Complex Conservation Treatment," *Art Newspaper* 306, November 16, 2018. Accessed December 10, 2018. www.theartnewspaper.com/news/rachel-whiteread-s-ghost-given-new-lease-of-life-by-cross-discipline-team

Schinkle, Eugenie. 2018. "Painting, Photography, Photographs: George Shaw's Landscapes." In *George Shaw, A Corner of a Foreign Field,* edited by Mark Hallett, 45–61. New Haven: Yale University Press. Exhibition catalogue.

Sussman, Elisabeth. 2016. "'The Story was the Destruction.'" In *Danny Lyon: Message to the Future,* edited by Julian Cox et al., 33–41. San Francisco: Fine Arts Museums of San Francisco in association with Yale University Press.

Tate. n.d. "Gordon Matta-Clark, Walls Paper 1972." Accessed November 28, 2018. www.tate.org.uk/art/artworks/matta-clark-walls-paper-t14658

Tedeschi, Martha, Kristi Dahm, Ruth Fine, Charles Pietraszewski, and Christine Conniff-O'Shea. 2011. *John Marin's Watercolors: A Medium for Modernism.* Chicago: Art Institute of Chicago.

Townsend, Chris. 2004. "When We Collide: History and Aesthetics, Space and Signs in the Art of Rachel Whiteread." In *The Art of Rachel Whiteread,* edited by Chris Townsend, 6–33. London: Thames & Hudson.

Ursprung, Philip. 2011. "Architecture: Gordon Matta-Clark and the Legacy of the 1970s." In *Laurie Anderson, Trisha Brown, Gordon Matta-Clark: Pioneers of the Downtown Scene, New York, 1970s,* edited by Lydia Yee, 133–141. London: Prestel.

Vidler, Anthony. 2000. *Warped Space: Art, Architecture, and Anxiety in Modern Culture.* Cambridge, MA: MIT Press.

Vidler, Anthony. 1992. *The Architectural Uncanny, Essays in the Modern Unhomely.* Cambridge, MA: MIT Press, 1992.

Weinberg, H. Barbara. 2004. "Hassam in New York, 1897–1919." In *Childe Hassam: American Impressionist,* edited by Weinberg, 203–230. New York: Metropolitan Museum of Art.

SECTION 2

Artists and Public Space

Kevin D. Murphy's essay on demolition art in Section 1 acts as a transition between the concept of the built environment as purely architectural, and the methods artists use to reframe it in order to make visible that which powerful entities might wish to hide. Laura Anderson Barbata provides a dynamic discussion of how community engagement, artistic practice, and a respect for cultural tradition can be combined to create an artistic intervention that reclaims space while creating and educating a community in the contested streets of Brooklyn's Bedford-Stuyvesant neighborhood. Her photo essay, "Intervention: Indigo," weaves together traditions from Mexico and the African diaspora, melding them into wearable sculptures to be worn by stilt-walkers and dancers who process down the street and challenge police brutality. Jerome Reyes works on the opposite coast, but with a similar theoretical bent: his essay, co-written with collaborator tammy ko Robinson, describes his career's work of creating art with and within communities of immigrant people of color who are being displaced by gentrification in San Francisco. His artwork reclaims the spaces of the community's history, using everything from billboards to archives, and the process of making that art brings the community together to articulate its significance and foster resistance. Joanna Gardner-Huggett's essay reminds us of the forces that obstruct artists' attempts to use public space in the way that Anderson Barbata and Reyes were able to do: she documents the plans of a feminist art collective in Chicago in 1985 to display their work on the public transportation system. Gardner-Huggett details the work and the objections raised against it, in a discussion that makes visible the challenges feminist art posed to mainstream culture. In the final essay of this section, Sheila Pepe introduces us to the work of Tanya Aguiñiga, an artist who uses the contested space of the US/Mexico border to remind travelers what the border really means, and encourages them to participate in her attempts to make meaning of the divide. All of these essays tease out the significant role that community involvement plays in even the failed attempts to use art to publicly intervene and change the discourse; they demonstrate how community is essential to the work of reframing the public discussion around what public space means and how it can be used.

6

INTERVENTION

Indigo

Laura Anderson Barbata

An intervention is an act that reclaims public space, modifies the way we interact in it, and invites spectators to respond. My interventions combine procession, dance, sculpture, textile arts, costuming, music, ritual, and protest. They are imbued with intention: each calls attention to a specific instance of social injustice. The process begins with the need to externalize – and materialize – a response to an injustice, which develops as I am working. It's like facing a blank canvas: I can't visualize the end result, it takes its shape as I am working.

In 2015, the Brooklyn Jumbies, Chris Walker, Jarana Beat, Rene Cervantes, and I worked together to present *Intervention: Indigo* in Brooklyn, New York: a public takeover of the streets of Brooklyn. It began at the Bushwick Police Precinct where Rolling Calf, a solitary character portrayed by Chris Walker, performed a ritualistic dance in honor of all people of color who have been victims of police violence, after which he was joined by all of the characters: Indigo Queen (portrayed by Augusta Brulla, see Figure 6.1), Little Jaguar (which I portrayed), and the Brooklyn Jumbies (portraying Indigo King, Indigo Angel, Trinidad Jumbie, and Rogue Cop), followed by Jarana Beat musicians inspired by the music and dance of Los Diablos de la Costa Chica, Los Rebeldes de El Capricho from the African-Mexican Coast of Guerrero. We made our way through the neighborhood, stopping at significant landmarks that have witnessed violence, and ended in an area inhabited predominantly by artists. We performed it again in February, 2020, in Mexico City. This time, we were joined by Los Diablos de la Costa Chica, Los Rebeldes de El Capricho who traveled from their community of Ometepec in the state of Guerrero to take part in *Intervención: Indigo*. We started at the center plaza of the Glorieta de los Insurgentes, facing two significant buildings: Secretaría de Seguridad Ciudadana CDMX (Ministry of Public Security of Mexico City) and Fiscalía General de la República (the Attorney General of Mexico). Little Jaguar and Rolling Calf

FIGURE 6.1 Indigo Queen, Intervention: Indigo, Bushwick, New York, 2015. Photograph courtesy of Rene Cervantes

initiated the intervention at the center of the roundabout, and were joined by Los Diablos in a choreographed symbolic call for justice and protection directed toward the institutions we were facing, and to all citizens. As we made our way through informal street vendors, traffic, residential areas, we were joined by the rest of the performing artists and by onlookers who not only followed us but became an integral part of the unfolding narrative. *Intervención: Índigo* ended at muca-Roma, a museum space that is part of UNAM and is situated in the Roma neighborhood, where many artists reside. In both cases, the spectacle was massive, not in size but in impact: it was led by towering stilt-walkers accompanied by masked dancers, and traditional musicians dressed in indigo-dyed regalia, dancing down the streets while interacting with onlookers who encountered us unexpectedly. As we moved through the streets, we transformed them and our relationship with public space, and offered a new narrative that demands visibility, recognition, and justice for all Afro-descendant communities and BIPOC.

Being There

First come the sounds of the drums beating and the music playing. Then the vision: huge, tall stilt-dancers striding down the streets of Bushwick and Mexico

FIGURE 6.2 The Brooklyn Jumbies, *Intervention: Indigo*, Bushwick, New York, 2015. Photograph courtesy of Rene Cervantes

City (see Figure 6.2). The garments they wear are indigo-colored, they are regal, striking: the performers are larger than life, more than human – they channel rituals and traditions that they carry with them, and through this act they are simultaneously in dialogue with the past and the present. The figures embody power and they tell a story – the story of police oppression toward people of color, and the need to challenge that oppression (see Figure 6.3). As the performers stride onward, their presence demands that they be recognized and acknowledged.

As curator Ixchel Ledesma says,

> *Intervention: Indigo* is a call to action, for the reoccupation of public spaces and to acknowledge the violence which African American communities have suffered, not only in the USA, but all over the world. This work … seeks to remind us … of the original public intervention, which creates a living memory, a poetic space where bodies can move freely to occupy a protected, magical and transformative space.[1]

Through the act of the intervention we exercise our right to occupy public space, and in doing so it becomes an act of defiance. For me, it is important that the intervention take place without permits, so it must be well orchestrated in advance with all details carefully planned (for example, where to put garments and stilts on and off, and being accompanied at all times by "handlers" to protect the stilt-dancers from danger). You could say that it is a form of guerrilla tactic.

FIGURE 6.3 Little Jaguar, portrayed by Laura Anderson Barbata. *Intervention: Indigo*, Bushwick, New York, 2015. Photograph courtesy of Rene Cervantes

Having this work unfold in the street, in a public space (Figure 6.4), is important because it is my intention to place the narrative in an area that does not expect it and isn't prepared for it. It's also a provocation. First I want to grab the attention of bystanders, and then have them feel drawn to engage with the work in whatever way they feel comfortable. There are different points of entry into the work – they can feel drawn in by the spectacle of the beautiful characters, or think about the traditions that each one of the characters represents; they can explore the narrative, unpack the critique embedded in the work, or respond to the participatory nature of the work. I try to incorporate as much as possible in terms of complexity so that people have the opportunity to experience it on many levels. Because of that, the intervention operates on different levels for each one, and that's okay.

Indigo

Indigo is one of the oldest natural plant-based dyes; it has been used all over the world and is culturally imbued with symbolism and spirituality, power, and nobility. The color historically represents absolute truth, wisdom, justice, protection, and responsibility. Indigo is best known for its use in denim, but in this intervention I mostly used textiles hand-woven and dyed in Burkina Faso, Guatemala, Japan, and the United States to create characters that are deeply saturated with layers of meaning.

FIGURE 6.4 *Intervención: Índigo*, Mexico City, 2020. Photograph courtesy of Erik Tlaseca

As Ledesma says:

> Currently, the color indigo is used by almost all police forces in the world, thus, the color can be associated with protection, but also with repression. In this sense, the processional route of *Intervention: Indigo* from the police precinct to the artists' area refers not only to physical displacement, but also to new ways of understanding. Through the unfolding of an artistic ritual, the protective and spiritual functions of indigo are returned to the creative world. This twist of meaning in ritual dimension incorporates in [sic] a magical moment for all people in society while at the same time, empowering people of color as they symbolically appropriate public space, while wearing the color that has repressed them to protect them.[2]

It's not a coincidence that the police and the army wear blue – this shade of blue carries with it a long history; indigo blue is a powerful color, it reverberates inside of us, we subconsciously respond to it with respect. So I reclaim this color and utilize textiles hand-dyed with indigo to create all of the characters' regalia, headpieces, and masks. What the performers wear are not costumes – rather, they are wearable sculptures that have been activated in space and time – they will live on their own after the intervention as sculptures, and will continue to carry the message of the original intervention as they are exhibited in galleries and museums.

FIGURE 6.5 Indigo King portrayed by Najja Codrington, and Los Diablos de la Costa de Guerrero portrayed by Jarana Beat. *Intervention: Indigo*, Bushwick, New York, 2015. Photograph courtesy of Rene Cervantes

Stilt-Dancers and Ritual: Procession/Tradition

The traditional function of the Moko Jumbie stilt-dancers is to serve and protect their communities. In Western Africa, Moko Jumbie is a spirit who watches over a village, and due to its towering height, is able to foresee danger and evil. The Moko Jumbie is traditionally called in to cleanse and ward off evil spirits that have brought disease and misfortune to a village. On the other side of the Atlantic, in Oaxaca, Mexico, the Zancudos (stilt-dancers in the town of Zaachila) perform annually to call upon the power of their saints to give them protection, blessings, and miracles.

The characters I created for *Intervention: Indigo* were informed by my work in Trinidad and Tobago with Moko Jumbies (who traditionally perform annually during carnival celebrations), the Brooklyn Jumbies (stilt-dancers who follow the Chakaba stilt-dancing traditions of West Africa and the Caribbean), the Danza de los Zancudos (traditional stilt-dancers from Zaachila, Oaxaca), and the Dance of the Devils (Danza de los Diablos) from the African-Mexican coast of Guerrero (see Figures 6.5 and 6.6). In Mexico, the tradition of stilt-walking can be traced to pre-Columbian Mesoamerica with representations found in pottery and the *Popol Vuh*. The Danza de los Zancudos takes place annually to honor the patron saints of Zaachila and to request protection, blessings, and miracles; the Danza de los Diablos is performed by people of African descent

FIGURE 6.6 Indigo Angel portrayed by Ali Sylvester, and Indigo King portrayed by Najja Codrington. *Intervention: Indigo*, Bushwick, New York, 2015. Photograph courtesy of Rene Cervantes

in Guerrero to remember all African descendants and to reaffirm their place in society.

Each of the characters in *Intervention: Indigo* calls on traditions from the African-Caribbean diaspora and Mexico. Traditionally, horned masquerade figures, for example, are afforded strength, power, status, and superiority; the mask opens up the possibilities of identity beyond the performer. The Rolling Calf (developed with and performed by Chris Walker, Figure 6.7), is a mythical character only represented in Jamaican duppy 'tory (ghost stories). Its power, however, permeates the Jamaican cultural landscape in relation to when and how space is accessed. In *Intervention: Indigo,* Chris Walker introduces Rolling Calf as a *mas* (carnival masquerade) character. He aligns Rolling Calf with the devils and the cow characters, digging deep into their shared history while reimagining the mythical as a purposeful contemporary *mas* performance. Rolling Calf is typically presented as an oversized or large ghost with the physical characteristics of a cow with red eyes and wide nostrils from which smoke flows constantly, and its commanding presence can be felt as soon as one hears the chains dragging along the ground with a clunking sound.

As Chris Walker says:

> The portrayal of the *Rolling Calf* character presents the mythical as purposeful … the character affords a space to reimagine what is possible for

130 Laura Anderson Barbata

FIGURE 6.7 Rolling Calf portrayed by Chris Walker. Photograph courtesy of Rene Cervantes

this black body attempting to find liberation, to find a better space, in this place, another way to make and claim space, anchored in the vitality, power, superiority, and the supernatural potentials the mask affords … It is a way to make and claim space, empowered by the collective and shared moment of the intervention.[3]

Transcommunality

I work *with* people to build bridges of collaboration and exchange of knowledge between communities and geographies. The *Transcommunality* project was initiated in 2002 when I began working with Dragon Keylemanjahro School of Arts and Culture in Trinidad and Tobago, and since 2007 I have been working consistently with the Brooklyn Jumbies. Both groups provide, free of charge, extracurricular activities to youth in low-income urban areas, as well as reviving the art and tradition of West African stilt-dancing. My artistic interventions with them include thematic development and costuming for street performances, created with volunteers and/or residents of the neighborhood. Through artistic interventions during special events, carnival competitions, workshops, and outreach programs, the groups reinforce social ideals such as healthy life choices and respect for cultural heritage. In 2009, *Transcommunality* expanded to Mexico to include Los Zancudos de Zaachila, a traditional stilt-dancing group that honors the patron saints of Zaachila, Oaxaca. From this project stem my series of "interventions" that have been performed in different locations in response to specific social and environmental topics.

In 2011 during the Occupy Wall Street movement, the Brooklyn Jumbies and I presented a public performance in New York's Financial District. The work – titled *Intervention: Wall Street* – responded to the global impact of the financial crisis and the urgent need to inspire change in the values and practices of the financial sector. Wearing giant business suits, the Brooklyn Jumbies and I walked and danced in the financial district of New York while handing out gold foil-covered chocolate coins to onlookers (Figure 6.8).

As artists we can unite to name the forces that are oppressing our societies and identify a common purpose by using all forms of creativity we have available – dance, music, stilt-dancing, spoken word, the creation of ritual space through interventions, and the creation of wearable art from textiles (see Figure 6.9). These expressions have the capacity to cross boundaries and invite us to honor traditions. Through the process we recognize ourselves in the work and build art-based social practice projects that result in long-term exercises of reciprocity and collaboration. This is the foundation of my artistic practice.

The Artists

Laura Anderson Barbata, born in Mexico City, is a transdisciplinary artist best known for her collaborative social art projects, including *Transcommunality*. This project has been performed in numerous venues internationally since 2002. In 2007, Barbata presented *Jumbie Camp*, closing down 24th Street in the gallery district of Chelsea in New York City for a street performance by 70 costumed children and members of the Brooklyn Jumbies. In 2015 Barbata was the Interdisciplinary Artist in Residence at the University of Wisconsin, Madison, where she created a community project involving more than 500 people from 50 local community groups that included a street procession titled *STRUT!* Her work has received numerous awards and is included in collections and museums internationally.

The Brooklyn Jumbies is an organization whose sole purpose is to heighten the community's cultural awareness of African and African-Caribbean culture.

FIGURE 6.8 The Brooklyn Jumbies and Laura Anderson Barbata. *Intervention: Wall Street, New York*. Photograph courtesy of Frank Veronsky

Brooklyn Jumbies perform stilt-dancing, which is one of the numerous cultural elements of the African and Caribbean diaspora.

Jarana Beat is a world music band that incorporates dance and activism. With Afro-Amerindian Mexican sounds, it offers a new interpretation that blends the origins of Mexican music with contemporary elements and draws from other cultures in the New York scene that share the same roots.

Chris Walker is Professor of Dance at the University of Wisconsin, Madison, who creates contemporary dance, theatre, and performance artwork based on the visual and performance cultures of the African diaspora. He is the founding artistic director of the First Wave program in the Office of Multicultural Arts Initiatives at UW-Madison, choreographer with the National Dance Theatre Company of

FIGURE 6.9 Rolling Calf portrayed by Chris Walker, and Los Diablos de la Costa Chica, Los Rebeldes de El Capricho. Intervención: Índigo, Mexico City, 2020. Photograph courtesy of Erik Tlaseca

Jamaica and Braata Productions NYC, director/facilitator of #barsworkshop at The Public Theatre. His work has received numerous international and national awards.

Notes

1 Ixchel Ledesma, curator's statement for *Intervención: Índigo* (Oaxaca: Museo Textil de Oaxaca, 2018), n.p. Exhibition catalogue.
2 Ixchel Ledesma, curator's statement for *Intervención: Índigo* (Mexico City: MUCA Roma, 2020), 4. Exhibition catalogue.
3 Chris Walker, artist's statement. September 10, 2015.

7

"NO MATTER WHERE WE MOVE, WE LOOK AT THE SAME MOON"

A Half-Century Between the Pacific and Stars

Jerome Reyes and tammy ko Robinson

In this essay I review my two decades (2001–2020) of work in the areas of contemporary art practice and arts education. These 20 years, and the larger half-century of activist movements cited here, serve as a provocation to cultural practitioners. My collaborators Daniel Phil Gonzales and tammy ko Robinson and I present strategies simultaneously retrospective and prospective, humorous and tactical, hopeful and as pliable as needed moving into uncertain futures. I ask cultural practitioners now who and what they must become as artists, researchers, and global citizens.

Over two decades, I have come to see projects that consider public space as an opportunity to expand artistic practice and to ask new questions, and as a way to broaden dialogue in the larger civic sphere. This essay describes my artistic work through intergenerational, transdisciplinary, and cross-institutional collaborative relationships at a time of shifting civic identity in San Francisco.

Through each of the long-term projects described here, I cultivated previously marginalized voices and initiated conversations that unfolded through works of visual art and took place in multiple forums, including higher education and arts institutions, senior housing, and social justice nonprofit organizations. This strategy of intertextual and intercultural analysis also prioritizes years-long working relationships with elder scholar-activists, student leaders, and arts professionals. These projects engage participants with objects, images, and shifting social situations and environments to produce the means for exhaustive research and emotionally charged textures.

In my work, I employ conceptual territories of architecture and alterity to examine fluid notions of space and time. I shape projects to ponder the instability of contemporary life. My practice straddles installation, text, and time-based media, along with public events and long-term pedagogical initiatives. Many projects

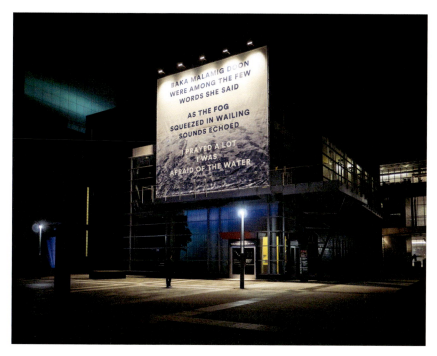

FIGURE 7.1 Jerome Reyes, *Abeyance (Draves y Robles y Vargas)*, 2017. Yerba Buena Center for the Arts. Photograph courtesy of Jeremy Keith Villaluz

have become multiplatform endeavors taking several years to complete. My work also employs a range of both institutionally supported and unsanctioned tactics. These projects realize (among other things) archive-centric and site-responsive exhibitions that go from sleek sculptures to gritty ephemeral materials, temporary public interventions, art pedagogy, large-scale billboards, and architectural drawings (see Figure 7.1).

The projects act as portals: I focus on collapsing time and space through these meeting sites, entry gates and, importantly, those lives that have created and continue to circulate freedom-seeking material culture. My art-making practice works in tandem with social engagement and arts pedagogy. However, I am not convinced that socially engaged art practices are necessarily the best option for creating change. It's a critical field, still in a period of thrilling progress compared with older art-making traditions. In this dynamic context, I pull from other knowledge fields and sociocultural legacies, providing more conceptual options and differing notions of success. A measure of my work ultimately comes back to relationships. During collaborations with many former activists-turned-scholars and artists from various 1968 movements, and locally from the Third World paradigm and International Hotel anti-eviction saga, I've witnessed relentless change in the everyday concerns of individuals: students, families, co-educators, and various audiences. Working alongside locals has informed my intuitive approach when shaping projects and art education frameworks with people; I have learned when to push hard, listen, shut up, or just play.[1]

In this essay, I describe four complex ongoing projects that illustrate my approach to working with collaborators: Contact Points (2006–present), the South of Market Community Action Network (2011–present), the Abeyance billboard/public art commission (2017–present), and public square drawings (2018–present).

Contact Points (2006–Present)

The starting point of this project was a series of curricular and archival explorations conceptually influenced by the 1960s student movements that led to the strike at San Francisco State College (now San Francisco State University) in 1968. Contact Points pays constant homage to the activist spirit of 1968, but at the same time recognizes that the contemporary situation is always understood in relation to local conditions (Palumbo-Liu 2011). For myself, it stems from working as an informal archivist since 2001 with Daniel Phil Gonzales, JD, native-born Filipino American San Franciscan, original 1968 student striker, cofounder of the nation's first School (now College) of Ethnic Studies in 1969, Professor of Asian American Studies, and codirector of the current All Power to the People object and audio archive at San Francisco State University (Figure 7.2). My collaboration

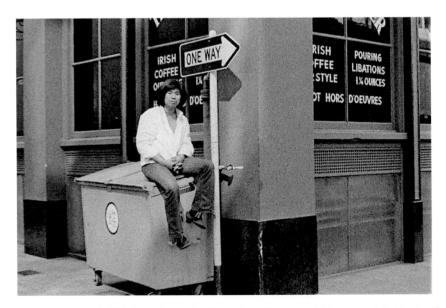

FIGURE 7.2 Daniel Phil Gonzales in San Francisco, Commercial Street and Leidesdorff Alley. 1971. Photograph courtesy of Linda Palaby Gonzales

FIGURE 7.3 Protesters linking arms in front of the International Hotel at 848 Kearny Street near Jackson Street in San Francisco, California on August 4, 1977. Photograph by Nancy Wong. Courtesy of Creative Commons

on the Contact Points/CP project serves to honor his life's work and conceptual guidance throughout these decades.

The Contact Points project started at the site of First International Hotel (see Figure 7.3), located at the pivot of Chinatown, North Beach, and Financial District in San Francisco, and occupied by many long-term elderly immigrant workers (Tani 2011, 4). On the early morning of August 4, 1977, the largest cross-alliance coalition to date organized around the corner of Jackson and Kearny streets in solidarity to prevent the eviction of the elderly tenants from the building (Carlson 2010). The allied groups – who brought together a human chain of more than 3,000 activists – included Yellow Power, the Black Panther Party, the American Indian Movement, and the Third World Liberation Front, all working with the anti-eviction movement.

tammy ko Robinson relates the Contact Points project (Figure 7.4) to a long history of occupation and resistance. She writes:

> Our training prompts us to take on both art and sociohistorical lenses, and then consider what portraits come to the foreground, what landscapes emerge and are being contested, and what prior dreams are we obligated to that have brought us into relation with one another now?
>
> So beginning with dates, these are unforgettable: March 1968: SF State College's Third World Liberation Front forms among students of color.

FIGURE 7.4 Installation image of exhibition *Contact Points: Field Notes Towards Freedom*, 2006–2016. Courtesy of tammy ko Robinson and Jerome Reyes

October 28th, 1968: First eviction notice served on 196 International Hotel tenants given until the first of January 1969 to leave. January 21, 1969: UC Berkeley Third World Strike begins. Among the many portraits, and among our many connections, are relationships with first-generation college students and artists enrolled at San Francisco State College and UC Berkeley, who took part in both the strikes between March and October of 1968 and the struggle to save or rebuild the I-Hotel, and later became faculty and our mentors. Moreover, artists, filmmakers and photographers that include Curtis Choy, Malcolm Collier, Nancy Hom, artists who have worked with Kearny Street Workshop and Galeria de la Raza, including Julio Morales who served as an anchor for a number of years in this project, have instilled in us the significance of a meaningful curriculum connecting colleges and communities. They also serve as a bridge in what is now a multigenerational dialogue that takes place through an art practice where the city is a studio and various spatial politics serve as material. As Hou Hanru and the late Okwui Enwezor who helped us in the incubating stages of this project might suggest, this matters both wherever we go and as the cities we live in undergo contested changes.

Considering a historical and landscape view captured in films like "The Fall of The I-Hotel" or Bob Hsiang's photographs, what seems significant about this multisited but place-specific practice is how the San Francisco Bay Area was a testing ground in architectural design and urban planning, as it aimed to secure its place as one of three finance cities each of which sought to stabilize itself in a period of crisis for US capitalism post World War II. Our interviews with two UC Berkeley architects, Sarah Ishikawa and John Liu,[2] involved with advancing the value of community living, senior immigrant residential rights, and the "right to stay put" for the inhabitants in the Chinatown and Manilatown through SRO redesign, offer this picture: if after World War II we see bombed out cities throughout Europe and Asia recovering by researching experiments in community housing and living, we see in the United States two decades later, as the country starts to achieve global hegemony, an emerging culture of evictions, and waves of redevelopment that by the 1970s include community participation in its own relocation. San Francisco, Chicago, and New York would become key in the armature of capitalism in regards to banking services, futures, and the stock exchange, and the struggle of the I-Hotel was not only a test case for the financialization of housing in the US, but also an example of how to keep struggling in the face of the violent evictions of the elderly to eventually secure a precedent where the city realized its responsibility to protect its residents. In other words, this was a localized fight within a neighborhood, informed by a vision of decolonization and Third World Internationalism where the conception of both the city and public responsibility was a part of the wager taken up throughout the world.[3]

This project, Contact Points, was named after the phone tree and security guidelines developed for mobilizing supporters of the International Hotel tenants to stop evictions following the rally around the hotel, and also the strikes. The phone tree worked this way: one person had five phone numbers to call when they discovered the eviction was happening; those five people had their own five people to call, and so on. This tactic mobilized thousands with only a few hours' notice on numerous occasions, and we felt the effects of its pull on us.

When we began the project in 2006, we committed ourselves to work in the same way, to ask, "Who do you know and trust?" With the concept of a network of allies in mind, I formulated research questions in this multiphase project (as in my larger body of work) that are site-responsive and work across generations, with Gonzales a key advisor and a respected peer observer of the original anti-eviction leadership. This project asked what conditioned such an unprecedented response of solidarity for the I-Hotel situation across these allied formations that had not been seen before in the United States, and ponders its global pertinence as a model today. How can a current art project recapture the excitement of the I-Hotel mobilization in order to address the contemporary situation with that same sense of urgency, along with grace and rage?

140   Jerome Reyes and tammy ko Robinson

The tenants of the First International Hotel (the I-Hotel) were evicted in 1977, and the hotel was demolished in 1981; in 2005, there was a euphoric reopening of a newly built hotel that offered senior legal services and other social services. That was the start of the Contact Points project: the activities of archiving and indexing, interviewing, and observing would honor the history of the anti-eviction struggle. Combining the intergenerational synergy of young student activists with older immigrant laborers in the 1970s I-Hotel, students from Stanford, San Francisco Art Institute, and the San Francisco Unified School District collaborated with earlier activists who had become scholars, artists, professors, and professionals working in many forms of civic equity in the Bay Area. The proposed new multiplatform framework would probe the legacy of the I-Hotel, but for the first time through the simultaneous lenses of contemporary art, social practice, and the community-trusted methods of talk-story and potluck gatherings.

Platform 1: Exhibition

Inside the first floor of the current I-Hotel we began renovations of a gallery space, opening our first exhibition there in 2010. Art historian and curator Ellen Tani asks: "How do you negotiate the currency of bodily affect when bodily presence isn't a possibility?" She describes the exhibition as a "combination of perceptual intimacy" using "video, performance, drawing, sculpture and installations of ephemera to carve an affective social architecture out of the already highly charged site" (Tani 2011, 3).

The installation *Routes and Seasons (After Carlos Villa's quilt of hope)* (Figure 7.5) used the original I-Hotel bricks recovered early in the research process. Here a fedora and 2,005 feathers made from brick dust simulate the scale of a single-person room, made from detritus accumulated in the act of protecting the bricks. Mostly single male transients who often sported the said headwear arrived, to leave immediately or remain for years and even decades, and this installation considers their displacement and travel in modest personal spaces.

There was also a video projection, *Analgesia (and Armament)*, on a raised platform at the back of the space (see Figure 7.6). It tells a compelling story: right before the police broke in during the eviction, tenant leader and elder Wahat Tampao pulled out a butterfly knife and walked out of the room; while everyone was screaming and crying, he returned to serve slices of cantaloupe to calm the last activists down. Then the police broke in. The video is a reenactment of that scene, with original anti-eviction leader and historian Dr. Estella Habal (Habal 2007) cutting the fruit (see Figure 7.7). In that crowded activist room, the sound of her knife is determined and irreversible, heard throughout the first floor – blending with street noise – in current senior housing offices, and wherever the viewer looks.

ko Robinson also notes that this piece is indicative of what is at the heart of our shared methodology. In light of the struggle against multiple forms of violence, there are so many things that are forgotten or made memorable out of necessity or

"We Look at the Same Moon" **141**

FIGURE 7.5 *Routes and Seasons (After Carlos Villa's quilt of hope)*, 2010. Cast fedora made of International Hotel brick debris, fedora bird feather made with brick dust (accumulated from transporting and protecting the last remaining ton of I-Hotel bricks, as a promise to the activists not to break any of them), raw wood table designed from tenant interviews, 2,005 bird feathers covered in brick dust. 8 × 8 ft (floor), 30 × 20 × 24 in (table) 9 × 7 × 7 in (hat). Courtesy of Jerome Reyes

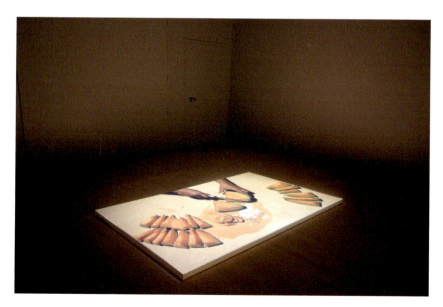

FIGURE 7.6 *Analgesia (and Armament)*, 2009. High definition video 8 × 6 ft floor projection, 4 min. 45 sec. Courtesy of Jerome Reyes

FIGURE 7.7 Dr. Estella Habal during video shoot. Courtesy of Jerome Reyes

resilience. So many of the conversations and interviews we conducted shifted the conceptual frame depending on whether the individual was inside the I-Hotel, outside as a person serving as a barrier against police, or across the street as safety observers or even further distanced, residing in another country but mailing in annotated reading lists or writing news stories about the I-Hotel in their local papers – we refer to these as *adjacencies*. However, one memory that was shared by those inside on the night of the eviction was made accessible by the reenactment of Wahat Tampao's gesture: instead of taking his own life when he pulls the blade, he imparts a final memory of living in community.

Platform 2: Program

With the contemporary art exhibition anchoring the first floor, the larger Contact Points project explored the question of how to operate the space's regular legal senior services in harmony with, and even amplified by the new interior environment. The project progressed with the notion that architecture is not just about buildings, but also about people. A recurring image in our research showed Penelope Houston of the Avengers playing at the nearby Mabuhay Gardens punk rock club in the 1970s. This project platform asked: how does one place this adjacent musical history in an already contextually rich project? The physical exhibition embodied this with a gritty and sturdily built senior karaoke punk-rock stage: it encouraged multipurpose functions, regular playful senior programs, and artist talks.[4]

Platform 3: Pedagogy

The Contact Points framework also comprised classes held in venues across the Bay Area that ran parallel to the programming, senior services, and art exhibitions, and supported the steady, behind-the-scenes collection of archives.

Inspired by the pedagogy of the early School of Ethnic Studies, I engaged longtime Bay Area artist-activists with a coordinated framework of courses taught by faculty from the San Francisco Art Institute (SFAI) and Stanford University. These courses even included high school studio art classes led by SFAI's City Studio program and accredited by the San Francisco Unified School District.

In an appropriate environment, local high school, undergraduate, and graduate students would together learn a dynamic San Francisco history that was rarely taught: a history of underserved ethnic communities focused on the I-Hotel. Energized elder organizers found willing ears among excited younger students, now in educational spaces such as the I-Hotel itself, and physically interacting with the same historic downtown neighborhood. Students often sang with tenants, served snacks in senior programming, and worked with scholars to help archive documents.

The spread and success of three dynamic, participant-driven, interdependent platforms created a momentum that led to more objects and documents being unearthed by activists and added to the archives.

Contact Points: Field Notes Toward Freedom

This Contact Points praxis led to platforms 4 and 5. ko Robinson's work moved to Korea while mine stayed in San Francisco. ko Robinson and I created an ongoing archive exhibition in Gwangju, Korea, at the new Asia Culture Center/ ACC. Gwangju is politically known for the 1980 May Uprising for Democracy in Korea. In an unprecedented stadium-sized building situated in the contested grounds of downtown Gwangju, the ACC serves to commemorate the uprising by archiving and commissioning new art projects initiated within Asia or by Asians that contribute to expanding freedom and democracy. If the Contact Points project in San Francisco focused on localized audiences and intentional art-making, this next step would vastly alter its anticipated reception, halfway across the world.

Platform 4: Archive

The Korean archive, now solidified in its title as *Contact Points: Field Notes toward Freedom*, was positioned among a larger set of dynamic, idiosyncratic conceptual frameworks for a "Library Park" as part of the larger ACC institution. Contact Points featured a multimedia immersive installation that employed many strategies to address a wide range of viewers, both local and international.

Visitors to the Korean archive are invited to contemplate the international connections the Contact Points project makes possible:

> Contact Points: Field Notes towards Freedom are staged here as both decades-old and recently realized adjacencies comprised of: the community center (1), third world college (2), community housing (3), Asian arts complex (4), solidarity bookstore (5), sanctuary and clinic (6), and the lending library (7).

The soccer-field scale of this citizen-funded institution, with its extraordinary array of researchers across Asia, allowed the Contact Points display to be a resource and in conversation with Asian diasporic materials to which it otherwise would never have had physical proximity. Student identification cards of a college-age Daniel Phil Gonzales were placed on the same shelves as UC Berkeley curricula that had influenced architectural thought in Taiwan. Children's books highlighting life in San Francisco sat mere feet away from Philippine activist-scholar Walden Bello's books on land and food rights in multiple languages. The nature of the Korean archive-installation allowed the Contact Points project work back in San Francisco to now adopt a global perspective on contemporaneity.

Platform 5

Back in San Francisco, the same coalition of anti-eviction activists from decades past and willing younger generations came together again. Platform 5, in progress, is a collection of texts and conversations that bring together more than a decade of this research.

South of Market Community Action Network (2011–Present)

In keeping with the relationship-based mode of art-making and art education addressing justice and equity I had already established with Contact Points, I turned to the nearby urban area south of central Market Street known as the South of Market/SOMA neighborhood.

Moving an artist practice across my hometown here mimics the pattern where tenants and similar immigrants left the North of Market during the I-Hotel eviction to go to the South of Market, fraught with its own decades-long history of rapid redevelopment in the midst of both recent dot-com booms. My prime organizational collaborator since 2011 has been the South of Market Community Action Network, also known as SOMCAN, which is a multiracial, community-based organization that serves low-income immigrant youth and families in South of Market and greater San Francisco.

Long before I started collaborating with SOMCAN, a multi-issue, multi-strategy organization, they had envisioned and realized a playfully versatile and diverse range of free programs for local residents. These include bike repairs, housing-rights workshops, school uniforms, a computer lab, weekly food drives, and even an in-house recording studio. This variety of programming they continue to offer shows how SOMCAN relentlessly asks, what does SOMA need and how should it be done ethically with style and fun? I worked to add to this already established momentum across their organization.

My partnership with SOMCAN continues to produce a range of projects and services co-led by their immigrant family member base: community-led art exhibitions, media workshops, contemporary art courses, and cross-institutional neighborhood campaigns. The success of these efforts derives from the underlying joy and urgency in all my projects carried out with their staff and boisterous youth, whom I taught in art classes made specifically for this partnership. This focus on social justice through contemporary art resulted in various workshops and a 2014 multimedia exhibition.[5] This art/activism mentorship happened with 15 SOMCAN youth organizers resulting in campaign materials. Project sites included contested urban spaces and key locations ranged from public parks to senior centers and civic offices.

I subsequently expanded the SOMCAN partnership with more public interventions throughout the neighborhood. These projects have focused on playful storytelling based on the daily lives of SOMCAN members and staff in tandem with existing programs.

A public projected text, *Pharos (still a nice neighborhood)*, comes from the poetry and spirit of San Francisco native, I-Hotel activist, and writer Al Robles (1930–2009). Fragmented in Spanish and Tagalog and placed on the storefronts of various organizations that work in the South of Market area, these projections alternate and appear at given times throughout the day.

Lighting equipment outside the SOMCAN headquarters storefront projects versions in multiple languages. Emerging from searchlights used for stage portraiture and scenography, this setup offers a statement that is simultaneously paradoxical, troubling, yet enduring. The project is part of a larger system of artworks presented simultaneously in different locations. This framework also conceptually operates through SOMCAN to represent its members and the area through multiple lenses.

At this point I wanted to engage in a much wider spectrum of interactions and conversations with a multigenerational group who were all invested in making San Francisco more equitable in various ways. Over the years, the youth I taught in art workshops became staff and led their own art projects, while leveraging the trust they had built with the neighborhood. They would show me accessible ways to work with people they had known longer, and more deeply, than I.

One project has former SOMCAN staff member Mary Claire Amable distribute a takeaway flyer in both Spanish and Tagalog, catering to SOMCAN's local family community: the flyer notes how her mother immigrated to San Francisco to work at a fast-food restaurant. Her mother mostly ate hash browns when

FIGURE 7.8 Jerome Reyes in collaboration with Alexa Drapiza. Russ Street, 2016 (excerpt). Audio file and sound installation on front steps of 50 Russ Street, South of Market San Francisco. Courtesy of Jerome Reyes

pregnant with Claire, while trying to maintain residence in the city. This flyer is circulated to working-class families and seniors during regular free-food drives in the neighborhood, and is often given to people who have working relationships with Claire's mother and have seen Claire grow up in the SOMA.

Another is a public art sound project that amplifies former SOMCAN staff member Alexa Drapiza's post-eviction recollection of her former home. It is written as a love note directly to the alley where she lived: a loudspeaker replays her memories of the people who used this public space in the South of Market. It is placed in public spaces in front of buildings mentioned in her monologue and near several cultural landmarks, where the nearby pedestrians/listeners include people she grew up around and professionals working in organizations she has frequented (Figure 7.8).

SOMCAN and I are currently working on a multiplatform political campaign that generates and circulates artwork throughout the SOMA neighborhood. Created materials focus on local issues of importance to SOMCAN's Filipino and Latin American immigrant membership. These include the South of Market Filipino Cultural Heritage District, pedestrian and bicycle safety, food rights, and housing. Recent activities range from workshops for button-making, graphic design, banner and printmaking, and creating the first youth-authored SOMA historical audio tours. A 2017 iteration of the partnership presented an exhibition at the City College of San Francisco, in tandem with programming and courses offered in the city's largest community college.

Most SOMA issues are addressed in singular effective forms of policy-making, stand-alone workshops, street-level dialogue, and parent organizing. This multi-year progression of art projects amplifies these successful tactics and combines them in a self-reflexive, referential, larger dynamic partnership that encourages people to notice public texts, listen to voices, and enjoy receiving and distributing flyers, buttons, and other ephemera that circulate downtown. Older students now visit and help, or have become SOMCAN staff themselves. The neighborhood has always been a convenient laboratory to attempt these art projects for me as a native San Franciscan, and for those who grew up in the vibrant alleys and streets where these interventions are tested.

SOMCAN can extend their often slogan-heavy campaigns into more powerful public, or separated, intimate-sized, phrases to lead people directly to their range of services while permeating the neighborhood; from the other direction, SOMCAN can introduce people to artwork. Over recent years, with the participation of public office holders, organizers, and families, and with support from local social justice and arts foundations, they have expanded their programs and built a robust public mission of social justice and immigrant-focused activities in the context of rapid urban development.

In this programmatic versatility and chaos, SOMCAN embodies a Bay Area tradition. The storied, continuous decades of social justice in the Bay Area have actually taken place mostly during the weekday, during the after-school period from roughly 4pm to 6pm. This potentially charged time of the day became the prime slot for SOMCAN's experimental arts programs. That's the proving ground for many educators, unregulated by state standards, where the most fearless curricula are being tested. It is the after-school programs and services many families rely on that create necessary and often introductory spaces for sociopolitical discussion. This is also the time when college student activists and groups gather to plan and to even be so ambitious as to reshape the infrastructure and pedagogy of their respective institutions, such as the Nine-Unit Block at San Francisco State University.[6]

SOMCAN are still key contributors and are highlighted in my current art projects, especially in separate public art commissions in nearby contested grounds. Three blocks away is the highly visible Yerba Buena Center for the Arts (YBCA). SOMCAN would inspire the lyricism in artworks made for YBCA moving forward, even participating in public ceremonies (see Figure 7.9).

Abeyance (Draves y Robles y Vargas)

When I received the Yerba Buena Center for the Arts 2016 Artist in Residence Award, YBCA offered me multiple spaces and possibilities for public engagement. However, an unused billboard scaffolding became the most promising in a 2017 YBCA public art commission invitation. I already knew about the heavily contested Yerba Buena development, and an unrealized and storied 1992 public art project by Los Angeles artist Daniel Joseph Martinez, titled *This Is A Nice Neighborhood*, gave the impetus for a new billboard directly resulting from its

148 Jerome Reyes and tammy ko Robinson

FIGURE 7.9 2017 Formal ribbon cutting ceremony with (left to right) Jerold Yu, Mary Claire Amable, Alexa A. Drapiza, Philip Maverick Rostrata Ruiz, Raymond Castillo, Tony Robles, Dr. Estella Habal, Daniel Phil Gonzales JD and project curator Katya Min at Yerba Buena Center for the Arts. Courtesy of Jerome Reyes

phantom presence (Snow 1991). Martinez's lifelong practice of presenting provocative and incisive language, and his use of billboards and banners, serve as direct art-historical lineage to the tone and complexity of this downtown San Francisco public art project, *Abeyance (Draves y Robles y Vargas)*.

Designed as a potentially endless rearrangement of words among the daily shifting demographic of Yerba Buena Gardens, *Abeyance* relies on three cited authors (and four voices in particular) against a photographic backdrop of a ubiquitous ocean: here, it is the edge of San Francisco, but ultimately it is the edge of the United States, and, for some, the edge of the world, shifting by the second from land to sea. Meant to be in spatial dialogue with the nearby Dr. Martin Luther King Jr. memorial waterfall, the billowing billboard welcomes a multitude of parkgoers, from local residents to international visitors (see Figure 7.1).

The descriptive text is printed on a large plaque underneath the suspended 30 × 30 foot billboard:

> YBCA has commissioned Bay Area–born artist Jerome Reyes to create the site-specific billboard project Abeyance (Draves y Robles y Vargas) (2017),

installed on the facade of YBCA's Theater facing Yerba Buena Gardens. Featuring both texts and altered photographic imagery from San Francisco's Ocean Beach, Abeyance honors three Bay Area natives by sharing their stories of migration, displacement, and resilience. The billboard is located in the SOMA neighborhood, a site that during the 1980s and 1990s underwent dramatic redevelopment, still in process today.

The panel continues:

> The billboard's texts, which can be read as a single statement or in fragments, weave together the voices of three prominent Bay Area Filipino/a Americans: the Pulitzer Prize–winning journalist and filmmaker Jose Antonio Vargas (b. 1981), the celebrated poet and activist Al Robles (1930–2009), and the Olympic gold medal diver Victoria Manalo Draves (1924–2010). Simultaneously collapsing and expanding time and space, Reyes's project places these individuals in dialogue with Yerba Buena Gardens' daily visitors. It blends the voices of the past and the present through a tapestry that alludes equally to care, despair, endurance, fear, and hope.
>
> One of Abeyance's quotes is from a *New York Times* article written in 2011 by Jose Antonio Vargas, where he remembers the parting words of his mother, Emilie Salinas, uttered in Tagalog, as he left the Philippines at age twelve to begin a life in the United States – an undocumented immigrant in search of what his mother hoped would be a better life. Al Robles was an integral figure in the fight to save San Francisco's International Hotel, demolished in 1981. Also known as the I Hotel, it was an epicenter of activist resistance to redevelopment and the displacement of its elderly immigrant tenants. Reyes honors Robles's advocacy in remembrance of the fortieth anniversary of the International Hotel evictions on August 4, 1977. Lastly, a quote by Vicki Manalo Draves, who grew up in this South of Market district, recalls the famed athlete's memories of the night before her historic double gold medal victory at the 1948 Summer Olympics, held in London. Draves was the first-ever Asian American Olympic champion, breaking both race and gender barriers for athletes to come. She is also honored with a park nearby in her name.
>
> *(Reyes et al. 2017)*

Abeyance:

1: A state of temporary disuse or suspension
   1.1 Law: the position of being without, or of waiting for, a claimant

Billboard texts:

> "'Baka malamig doon' were among the few words she said ('It might be cold there')."
>
> *— Jose Antonio Vargas (b. 1981), journalist and filmmaker*[7]

> "As the fog squeezed in wailing sounds echoed."
>
> *— Al Robles (1930–2009), poet and activist*[8]

> "I prayed a lot." "I was afraid of the water."
>
> *— Vicki Manalo Draves (1924–2010), Olympic gold medal diver*[9]

I designed the public art billboard's opening ceremony to feature many past collaborators, including many scholar-organizers and artists. I surprised some of them, notably all previous young people and former SOMCAN staff I had worked with in similarly motivated art education projects in the SOMA, by announcing that they would cut the ribbon. On the other side were four older people: senior staff at SOMCAN and the Robles family/Manilatown Heritage Foundation, and 1960s activist scholars Estella Habal and Daniel Phil Gonzales. With key agents having their own impact on various communities pertinent to this essay, this image exemplifies the intergenerational, interdisciplinary, cross-sector nature of the billboard's intended audiences and my art practice more generally.

In an interview with Dr. Leslie Rabine ("Jerome Reyes" 2017), Professor Emeritus of Women's Studies at University of California at Davis and board member of SOMCAN, we discussed these dynamics.[10] I remarked at that time that:

> The quality work of projects I did with the I-Hotel, for instance, and with the older people who were at the ribbon-cutting ceremony, is built over time. Often, the best archival materials are never in museums. They're in houses of people who have lived through this history and have materials getting dusty in their attics or garages.
>
> And the way to get to this material is through the trusted relationships, where you remind them who they were. They haven't completely abandoned the selves who once participated in those justice movements, but you're reminding them of the amazing intellectuals and on-the-fly activists that they were, often as students, who also played music, also were artists, who then started families. They are all still those same people.
>
> So when I say it's about those relationships, this is the way I build that type of synergy, through trust, which is fun, and which becomes serious research. And it's the same way I interact with those four younger people who cut the ribbon. It's the same relationship-building when I tell them: "Oh, go to this professor or this organizer, they helped raise me …"

This momentum led to the featured (2018) public program of the billboard commission, which brought Jose Antonio Vargas into spirited conversation with me onstage at YBCA.[11] Current students and participants in the art practice and art education projects described above filled the capacity crowd. Also on hand were 1968 student strike leaders, who sat next to San Francisco housing and South of Market artist-activists, and some skeptics of YBCA as an institution, who were brought by SOMCAN staff and youth. Vargas and I discussed such topics as migration, race, documentation, and ultimately, the need for a new, hopeful language in America. The idea of discussing the potential of art in public space led to the actual gathering of various publics into this contested space for the first time.

The Horizon Toward Which We Move Always Recedes Before Us

Building on the momentum of previous long-term projects, this ongoing series of galaxial, architectural renderings takes the practice of student organizing in public squares to be of global significance (Figure 7.10). The project honors these locations, which can be obscure or internationally iconic. This method leans on long-term working relationships across the world with organizers, scholars, curators, and locals helping to identify each location. The project title ("the horizon toward …") comes from colleague and cultural critic Jeff Chang's

FIGURE 7.10 *The horizon toward which we move always recedes before us*, 2018–ongoing. Drafting ink, corrective fluid, sprayed housepaint, painter's tape on vellum, 21.5 × 34 in. Courtesy of Jerome Reyes

152 Jerome Reyes and tammy ko Robinson

culminating passage in his book *We Gon' Be Alright* (2016). Sites are individually selected, composited and the time of day noted by an organic network of people who identify important, contested locales, which are often anchored in legacies linked to 1968 student movements. These studies inform a suite of drawings that draft escape routes, key locations, and storied congregation sites that include Delhi, Paris, Gwangju, and Seoul in tandem with sites from other continents.

This process alters an overall architectural and research method influenced by activist allies, public records, and intimate artifacts to make drawings that present a vacancy for viewers to enter these various public places. With figures removed from each location, each vellum sheet is pre-treated with house paint, then rigorously worked with layers of painter's tape, corrective fluid, and fluorescent and drafting inks. These drawings use only architecture and construction materials to fabricate luminous documents focused on affective spaces and tonalities. This method combines precision with an atmospheric quality, a specific portal with a welcoming sense of absence. Like all the projects in this essay, these works implicate other complicated sites, and ultimately foster the exchange of ideas to create the more expansive and inclusive world that is necessary for tomorrow.

"No Matter Where We Move, We Look at the Same Moon"

This extended artist statement presents a constellation of projects anchored by the gravity of recurring social and political concerns. Positioned as an homage to the 1968 movements at San Francisco State University, through a range of more established political, archival, and contemporary art specific modalities, these works aim to index and shift forms of public knowledge in public space. They show how to work with and for people, to keep collaborative work equally joyous and pragmatic. This practice relies on the global venues and localities that inform and steer new conversations about who gets to live, play, and author multiple civic futures.

This love letter to 20 years of work shows the possibilities of projects achieved through a potent chemistry of contemporary art and collaboration. This tapestry of families – associated by blood, politics, pedagogy, poetics – all live through these fraught, globally historical moments to build robust lives. So, what are the possibilities and rigors of friendship in a time when human beings need it the most, in this regional worldview? To sing at the edge of the world with each other. To mine one's home while mining the sky. To continuously reach across decades, hand in hand together toward many magnificent horizons.

Acknowledgments

This chapter was supported by the Hanyang University Global Research Fund.

Notes

1 My website, www.jeromereyes.net, documents my pedagogical projects (at Stanford University and elsewhere), activism, and transnational art practice.
2 John K.C. Liu is one of the earliest architects who conducted the rehabilitation plan for senior housing in collaboration with Chinatown Community Development Center in San Francisco, and engaged in serial spatial practices aimed at realizing the right to stay put for the inhabitants in Chinatown/Manilatown. Liu moved to Taiwan in 1997 and worked at the Graduate Institute of Building and Planning, National Taiwan University, until 2009, where he taught principles of community living and architecture. The conversations between John, tammy and Hung-Ying Chen, one of his former students and Convenor of East Asian Regional Tribunal on Eviction in 2015, are archived in the Contact Points collection together with his landmark 1980 study for the National Science Foundation on everyday living patterns of Asian immigrant elderly which served as a basis for federal protection and economic investment.
3 tammy ko Robinson and Jerome Reyes, "I-Hotel: Exchanges on Urbanism, Spectacular Fictions, Archives" (presentation/lecture at Open Engagement Conference, Pittsburgh, Pennsylvania, April, 2015).
4 The stage is built to California ADA code, so that seniors can easily walk up the ramp to get onstage.
5 Supported by the Art Matters Foundation, New York, and two San Francisco Arts Commission Artist Communities and Innovative Partnerships Grants.
6 The Nine-Unit Block project at San Francisco State University's School of Ethnic Studies was an interdisciplinary approach to identifying, investigating, and applying social service theory to the real-world circumstances of underserved Third World communities in San Francisco. Though the project was short-lived because of its cost, it informed and supported the attainment of BA and MSW degrees by several participants, spawned several funded studies of local community needs, and contributed to the formation of direct-service nonprofits, particularly in the South of Market area.
7 Vargas 2011.
8 Al Robles 1996 (courtesy of the Robles family and UCLA Asian American Studies Center Press).
9 Vicki Draves, "An Olympian's Oral History: Vicki Draves, 1948 Olympic Games, Diving" (Los Angeles: Amateur Athletic Foundation of Los Angeles, 1999), 2, 13.
10 "Jerome Reyes, Part 1." *South of Market Community Action Network (SOMCAN)*, 2017. Accessed August 27, 2018. www.somcan.org/jerome-reyes-interview-1.
11 The full conversation was recorded and is available online at www.youtube.com/watch?v=HVo3UswULnY.

References

Carlson, Michele. 2010. "Jerome Reyes." *Art in America*, 2010. Accessed August 27, 2018. www.artinamericamagazine.com/reviews/jerome-reyes
Chang, Jeff. 2016. *We Gon' Be Alright*. New York: Picador Press.
Habal, Estella. 2007. *San Francisco's International Hotel: Mobilizing the Filipino American Community in the Anti-Eviction Movement*. Philadelphia: Temple University Press.
Palumbo-Liu, David. 2011. "Embedded Lives: The House of Fiction, the House of History." *Profession*, 13–22.

Reyes, Jerome, Lucia Sanroman, and Susie Kantor. 2017. "Wall text, *Abeyance (Draves y Robles y Vargas)*." San Francisco: Yerba Buena Center for the Arts.

Robles, Al. 1996. *Rappin' with Ten Thousand Carabaos in the Dark: Poems*. Los Angeles: UCLA Asian American Studies Center.

Snow, Shanua. 1991. "A 'Neighborhood' Tiff: S.F. Officials Put Moscone Art Project on Hold." *Los Angeles Times*, Los Angeles Times, August 9, 1991. Accessed August 27, 2018. articles.latimes.com/1991-08-09/entertainment/ca-284_1_public-art-project

Tani, Ellen. 2011. "Spectral Frameworks: Jerome Reyes' Passages of Affect." *Academia.edu*, 2011. www.academia.edu/10456634/Spectral_Frameworks_Jerome_Reyes_Passages_of_Affect

Vargas, Jose Antonio. 2011. "My Life as an Undocumented Immigrant." *New York Times*, June 22, 2011. www.nytimes.com/2011/06/26/magazine/my-life-as-an-undocumented-immigrant.html?

"Jerome Reyes, Part 1." South of Market Community Action Network (SOMCAN), 2017, accessed August 27, 2018. www.somcan.org/reyes-1.

"Jose Antonio Vargas in Conversation with Jerome Reyes at YBCA." 2018. www.youtube.com/watch?v=HVo3UswULnY

8

SILENCED SUBVERSIONS

Critical Messages Exhibition at Artemisia Gallery, Chicago (1985)

Joanna Gardner-Huggett

Artemisia Gallery's exhibition *Critical Messages: The Use of Public Media Art for Women* highlighted the work of 57 women artists in three different venues in Chicago. Artists created posters for the Chicago Transit Authority's (CTA) elevated trains and buses, the Cultural Center mounted an artists' book exhibition, and public television's "Image Union" (WTTW) screened video works.[1] The principal curators – Artemisia members Anita David and Nicole Ferentz and *Whitewalls* editor Buzz Spector – envisioned an exhibition that engaged the public and circulated well beyond the confines of the gallery. Timed to coincide with the International Art Expo held each May in Chicago, *Critical Messages* also intended to demonstrate that alternative spaces could effectively support political art without being compromised by the consumer market.

What the curators did not anticipate were the major obstacles in bringing art into dialogue with a city audience. Just prior to the opening of the show, the CTA rejected ten out of the 18 posters created for the project and Artemisia could not find a radio station willing to air a set of planned Public Service Announcements that would complement the public transit images.[2] Focusing specifically on the censoring of the CTA placards, this reconstruction and reevaluation of *Critical Messages* will not only expand the history of political art and activism in Chicago, but also illuminate the challenges facing women artists' collectives who wished to implement activist agendas that insisted on both a collaboration between art and politics and a dynamic engagement with the public sphere. Tracing this history of *Critical Messages* also reveals that this exhibition was just one casualty of arts and political censorship in Chicago during the 1980s and exposes a significant pattern of opposition to politically charged public art and activism during the height of the Reagan-Bush era in the United States.

156 Joanna Gardner-Huggett

A Brief History of Artemisia

Founded in 1973, Artemisia was part of a nationwide eruption of organizations committed to creating agency and visibility for women artists in the early 1970s. Taking their name from the 17th-century Italian Baroque painter Artemisia Gentileschi (1597–c.1651) "whose best work had been credited to her father," the founding members were determined to create a forum for their art in Chicago and beyond. The collective's adoption of Gentileschi's violent and graphic *Judith and Holofernes* (1611–1612) in the gallery's advertising is evidence of Artemisia taking a strong feminist stance in its early years (Holbert 1983; Schulze 1975, 71). Like many feminist organizations formed in the early 1970s, Artemisia rejected the hierarchical structure of patriarchal governance and distributed authority among all the members, implemented a rotating leadership, made all decisions a participatory process, conceptualized power as empowerment rather than domination, and argued that the process was as valuable as the outcome (Bordt 1997, 11).

Artemisians believed they needed to create a safe space outside traditional institutions in order to counter patriarchal bias in the art world that rejected the work of women. Members were committed also to creating a community where feminist art ideology could be debated through exhibitions, workshops, panel discussions, public talks, and performances with an exclusively female membership supported by its educational branch, the Artemisia Fund. For example, in 1979 feminist critic Lucy Lippard curated *Both Sides Now: An International Exhibition Integrating Feminism and Leftist Politics,* which she organized "to reconcile cultural and socialist feminisms" (Lippard 1989, 266). It featured a who's who of feminist art, including Mary Kelly, Suzanne Lacy, Adrian Piper, and Martha Rosler, and is one of many examples of national and international female artists being introduced to Chicago through the gallery. In 1980 Artemisia hosted the exhibition *The Art of the Woman's Building*, highlighting both the history of the 1893 Woman's Building at the World's Columbian Exposition in Chicago and graphic, performance, and video art from the gallery's feminist peer the Woman's Building in Los Angeles.[3] Anita David, along with David Faulkner and Michelle Fire, coordinated two invitational shows, *Looking at Women* in 1983 and *Looking at Men* in 1985, exploring how contemporary artists approached representations of women and men in a post-ERA moment and the conservative realm of a Reagan presidency.[4] *Critical Messages*, however, evinced a shift in programming, as it became the gallery's first major foray into public art. Like the precedents for *Critical Messages* discussed below, Artemisia's membership sought to counter a broader critique of alternative spaces as too insular and talking largely to each other by expanding its engagement with the city of Chicago.[5] Equally important, as a public art project *Critical Messages* promoted women artists and feminist agendas at a moment when they were largely absent from the streets of Chicago.[6]

Precedents for *Critical Messages*

The inspiration for *Critical Messages* came from a trip David made to Buffalo, where she encountered the public art program coordinated by the Center for Exploratory and Perpetual Arts (CEPA). Its first iteration in November 1973 featured the work of Ellen Carey and Cindy Sherman on a city bus without a designated route that would serve as a public exhibition moving through Buffalo for one month (Mitchell 1984, 14). It would soon expand to bus shelters and billboards and inspired David to do the same in Chicago.[7] In the early 1980s, projects like CEPA flourished across the country and frequently were funded by city and state arts councils.[8] Group Material's public transit projects *M5* (1981–1982) and *Subculture* (1983) – staged in New York City on bus routes running along Fifth Avenue from Harlem to SoHo and on subways across the city – are also important precedents.[9] The collective emphasized public and wide dissemination of their artwork, asserting,

> We've learned that the notion of alternative space isn't only politically phony and aesthetically naïve – it can also be diabolical. It is impossible to create a radical and innovative art if this work is anchored in one specific gallery location. Art can have the most political content and right-on form, but the stuff just hangs there silent unless its means of distribution makes political sense as well.
>
> *(Avgikos 1995, 99)*

Group Material's statement effectively describes Artemisia's new interest in moving feminist discourse from the periphery of the alternative arts scene into the day-to-day lives of commuting Chicagoans.

Closer to home and less than a year before *Critical Messages* opened, *Streetfare Journal, The Magazine of the Rider* debuted on the CTA in October 1984; it was a combination of poetry, art, maxims, and health tips, and was paid for by CTA's advertising arm, the Winston Network. Another model for *Critical Messages* was the exhibit *Window Shopping*, which consisted of 15 artists' installations in shop windows on the corners of Hubbard and State and Hubbard and Wells, right at the heart of alternative spaces in Chicago, including Artemisia. Curated by Margo Rush and Kay Rosen (the latter's work would be censored in *Critical Messages*), they negotiated with Howard Ecker, owner of the buildings, not only to provide space, but also to pay for publicity and insurance; this forged a productive alliance between arts and the private sector.[10] As a contributor to the exhibition, David undoubtedly agreed with reviewer Christopher English's assessment: "Window Shopping showed that even in Chicago it is possible to produce radical art and to present it to channels other than of traditional art institutions" (English 1983, 13).

By May 1984, David and Ferentz had secured permission from the CTA to install *Critical Messages* on buses and trains along with funding from the National

158 Joanna Gardner-Huggett

Endowment for the Arts, the Illinois Arts Council, and City Arts II Challenge Grant Program.[11] The curators began recruiting artists, and the list boasted now canonical figures engaged in media-based art from the early 1980s, such as Ilona Granet and Rosen, as well as Jenny Holzer and Babara Kruger who contributed to Group Material's *M5* and *Subculture* respectively.[12] These artists not only shared an understanding of how media represented gender, but also hijacked its modes of circulation to broadcast their own messages and subvert what Spector described as "the cultural homogenization engendered in this era of centralized and syndicated communication" (Fryd 2007, 34; Spector 1985). Serving as a cultural intervention, the art made by these women functioned best in public space where they potentially disrupted the everyday commute and forced passersby to question their own values, rather than be seduced by advertising's proclamations of a better life through consumption. Here Grant Kester's phrase "rant" art, which he uses to describe Kruger's work, equally applies to all of the artists in *Critical Messages*. He observes, "The excess of affective language in the rant, for example, seems designed to overcome the indifference of the dominant culture to the issues of exploitation and oppression being explored by sheer rhetorical force" (Kester 1998, 122). Yet, it also "gained most of the attention in the arts funding controversy" (Kester 1998). The contributions to *Critical Messages* were no exception.

An Exhibition Seen and Unseen

David and Ferentz agreed to submit a mock-up of each placard to the CTA for final approval.[13] According to correspondence between the curators and the CTA, the only types of content deemed not acceptable were "nudity, profanity or support of a political candidate."[14] On March 20, 1985, David sent the CTA a detailed description of the visuals and text for each work and slowly began to receive phone calls from the CTA informing Artemisia that a particular piece would not run. David and Ferentz petitioned the CTA stating that none of the artists violated CTA guidelines, but the agency simply responded that their "contract reserved the right to reject any ads" (Maschinot 1985, 12). On May 6, Artemisia's lawyer Jonah J. Orlofsky received a letter from the CTA outlining the agency's objections to ten of the placards only after several weeks of persistent requests for documentation and only two weeks before *Critical Messages* was to open. The CTA lawyer Tom W. Stonecipher writes that the agency's

> primary function is to move large numbers of captive riders quickly and inexpensively in an environment which will not disturb or disrupt them and which respects them and which respects the fact they are already a captive audience. To accomplish this objective, the CTA has consistently not accepted advertisements which are, or which experience shows would be vulgar, shocking, misleading, controversial or otherwise dis[ru]ptive [sic] of the CTA ridership.[15]

Nowhere were "nudity, profanity or support of a political candidate" mentioned as criteria for refusal. With the public art component of *Critical Messages* now more than cut in half, the curators decided to exhibit the rejected placards at Artemisia in conjunction with the correspondence between the gallery and CTA.

The rejected images that did not ride rails or buses took on questions of misogyny, race, war, the military industrial complex, nuclear proliferation, and President Ronald Reagan. Barbara Jo Revelle's photographs of four different white men juxtaposed with four panels of text with responses to the question "How do you look at women?," such as "I look at them from the bottom up," was rejected "because it is vulgar, immoral and demeaning to women" (see Figure 8.1).[16] Photographs of rabbits in a science lab with an inset photograph of soldiers in the field created by Rebecca Michaels was rejected "because the photographs of rabbits confined in containers in a testing lab would be disturbing and offensive" (see Figure 8.2).[17] Kay Rosen's poster simply states, "I have a synching feeling that a lynching is occurring" in black block print on a bright red background (see Figure 8.3). It was "Rejected … in large part because of the role lynchings have played in racial conflict in America."[18] Although Chicago elected its first black mayor, Harold Washington, in 1983, the city remained sharply divided in terms of race – as it does today – so the elimination of this poster is not surprising.[19]

Also utilizing text, but in a bold white font set against a black background, Holzer's piece read "OUTER SPACE IS WHERE YOU DISCOVER WONDER. WHERE YOU FIGHT AND NEVER HURT EARTH. IF YOU STOP BELIEVING THIS YOUR MOOD TURNS UGLY," rejected because it "could reasonably be construed as being prowar" (see Figure 8.4).[20] It "raises controversial public issues, which would subject its captive ridership to that controversy while riding the CTA."[21] Former Artemisian Esther Parada contributed a poster depicting Smedley Butler under the title "Who was Smedley Butler?" A United States Marine Corps General, he is flanked by two questions: on the left "One of the really great generals in American history?" and on the right "A racketeer for capitalism?" Viewers then evaluate General Douglas MacArthur's glowing evaluation of Butler versus his own assertion that he prepared Latin America for US corporate investment in the early 1900s.[22] According to the CTA, it was "Rejected because it raises controversial public issues concerning Central America and the possible use of American military forces in that area" (Jacobsen 1991, 51).

California-based artist Sheila Pinkel's image of two hands with text, "Fear is our Gross National Product," was rejected "because it is disruptive, unsettling, misleading" (Maschinot 1985, 12) (see Figure 8.5). Kruger's poster with a close-up black-and-white photograph of a tooth being extracted with accompanying text, "You are a captive audience," was rejected by the CTA because an "extreme close-up photograph of a tooth being extracted is vulgar and offensive" (Lifton 1985, 61). Susan Schulson's photomontage of Asian, black, and white children and

160 Joanna Gardner-Huggett

FIGURE 8.1 Barbara Jo Revelle, *How to Look at Women, Critical Messages* exhibition, Artemisia Gallery, 1985. Elevated train platform billboard, 46 x 30 in. Courtesy of Barbara Jo Revelle

adults, entitled an "American Portrait," was rejected due to its text, "American apart hide" – a play on *apartheid* – "which raises the issue of racism in America."[23]

Artemisia member Silvia Malagrino's photograph of a horse seen through a car window with text, "An impenetrable cloud of dust and smoke masked the area.

Silenced Subversions **161**

FIGURE 8.2 Rebecca Michaels, Untitled, *Critical Messages* exhibition, Artemisia Gallery, 1985. Bus ad placard, 11 × 28 in. Courtesy of Rebecca Michaels

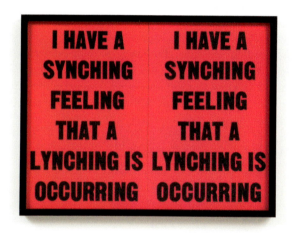

FIGURE 8.3 Kay Rosen, Untitled, *Critical Messages* exhibition, Artemisia Gallery, 1985. Bus ad placard, 11 × 28 in. Courtesy of Kay Rosen

The immense steel tower was vaporized …" was rejected "because it's war-related and deals with nuclear weapons, controversial and disturbing"[24] (see Figure 8.6). Lastly, Jan Ballard's poster was the only one to reference a politician directly. It features a television still of President Reagan on the left framed by two smaller images: two people cast in shadow talking and a woman consuming food, perhaps from the TV dinner featured on the right, and text reading "One result of advertising is the neutralization of critical consciousness"; rejected because "it is misleading and demeaning to a national public office, to the present holder of that office and to the advertising industry."[25]

Clearly, the lawyers read the images literally and dismissed the artists' intent to critique sexism, racism, military might, and nuclear power, and their desire for

FIGURE 8.4 Jenny Holzer, *Survival: UNEX sign*, 1984. Electronic sign. 30.5 × 113.5 × 12 in.; 77.5 × 288.3 × 30.5 cm. Text: *Survival*, 1983–1985 © 2020 Jenny Holzer, member Artists Rights Society (ARS), New York

viewers to interrogate their own ideologies. Nancy Bless comments in correspondence with David, for example, that Kruger's tooth extraction "didn't look so controversial," but that jolted lawyers more than the artist's interest in confronting constructs of the media's political and economic power. As Norma Lifton suggests, Kruger's poster ironically reaffirmed the CTA's own message regarding passengers as a captive audience.[26]

For a number of contributors, censorship was nothing new.[27] For example, Pinkel's "Fear Is Our Gross National Product," which is part of a larger series entitled *Thermonuclear Gardens* that explored the rapid growth of the military industrial complex, already was suppressed in 1981. Exhibited in an antinuclear show with the California-based feminist collective Mother Art in the Federal Building in downtown Los Angeles, the artwork was removed after 24 hours due to numerous complaints. As Pinkel explains in a talk she gave on art and censorship in 1986, "It appears that public space is really private space and artists have no ability to enter into the forum of the larger culture."[28] One year later, Kruger's media-based work also was censored. The Public Art Fund (PAF) in conjunction with Collaborative Artists Inc. (better known as Colab) artists negotiated with George Stombly, the owner of the Spectracolor board in Times Square, to purchase ad time at a reduced rate. After being granted funding from the NEA, each artist was given one minute every 20 minutes for two weeks. Kruger's message "equated the size of a man's penis with the size of a country's weapon arsenal" (Dixon 1985, 66). Like the CTA, Stombly demanded a review of each piece before being screened. At the time, he did not reject Kruger's submission, but did so only after receiving complaints. Press coverage prompted Stombly to back down, but he started to monitor subsequent proposals more carefully (Dixon 1985, 66). The NEA rejected the Washington Project for the Arts' grant application to sponsor

FIGURE 8.5 Sheila Pinkel, "Fear is Our Gross National Product" from the *Thermonuclear Garden* series (1982–1991). Elevated train platform billboard, 46 × 30 in. *Critical Messages* exhibition, Artemisia Gallery, 1985. Courtesy of Sheila Pinkel

Jenny Holzer's *Sign on a Truck*, which was designed as a New Age soapbox for people to send their own campaign messages just prior to the 1984 presidential election. Holzer only found financial support through New York City and New York State arts organizations after promising to resist identifying with any one political opinion and maintain a balanced set of responses.[29] Unfortunately, David and Ferentz had no access to an individual or major organization with whom to negotiate and were only met by a wall of lawyers and their memos when they requested dialogue.

FIGURE 8.6 Silvia Malagrino, "A Rain of Ruins" from the series *A Bomb Desert*, 1982. Silver print photograph, 20 × 24 in. Elevated train platform billboard, 46 × 30 in., *Critical Messages* exhibition, Artemisia Gallery, 1985. Courtesy of Silvia Malagrino

The posters that did receive a "ticket to ride" were displayed with the artist's name and Artemisia's phone number, leaving potential for feedback. The images accepted by the CTA tackled the controversial issues addressed above, but they are much less confrontational in appearance and content. Four posters rode major local and express bus routes traversing the north and south sides of the city of Chicago.[30] First, Sally Alatalo's placard juxtaposes a text comparing Greco-Roman and American style wrestling superimposed with "US" with a collage of men wrestling. What most observers would miss is the first line, "The history of Wrestling is so closely interwoven with the history of men and nations," creating a link with Parada's depiction of Smedley Butler and US imperialism. A very playful triptych, yet a less confrontational take on sexism than Revelle's, was Illona Granet's *Dear Men, While on the streets …, Maintain 8 feet distance. Thanks* (see Figure 8.7).[31] Irene Seaglove's image featured the phrase "Don't Forget You're Human Today," framed by a man's forehead exploding while he eats; two shocked 1920s-styled women look on with their mouths wide open. Lastly, Anne Turyn's poster read, "Life Story" "Funny. Something significant happens. Time keeps passing" (see Figure 8.8). Below the text are six black-and-white photographs that trace significant moments in one's life, such as birth, marriage, and having children.

Platform billboards were located in several elevated train stations in the Loop in the heart of the city and one on the north side.[32] Leslie Bellavance contributed

Silenced Subversions **165**

FIGURE 8.7 Ilona Granet, Untitled (Dear Men, While on the streets ... Maintain 5 feet of distance), 1985. Hand-painted sign, collection of Barry Holden. Photograph by Barry Holden. Courtesy of Ilona Granet

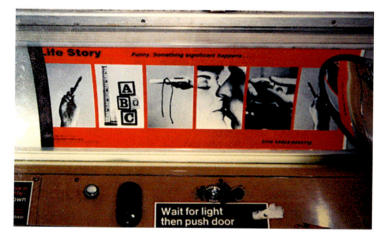

FIGURE 8.8 Installation photograph of Anne Turyn, *Critical Messages: Life Story*, 1985. Bus placard, 11 × 28 in., *Critical Messages* exhibition, Artemisia Gallery, 1985. © Anne Turyn. Photograph courtesy of Artemisia Gallery Fund. Courtesy of Anne Turyn

a photo-collage of ocean water with seven rows of white silhouettes of fish. Under each fish a particular emotion is inscribed from "chagrin" to "worry." Nancy Bless's billboard was drawn from a photograph of a painted mural and simply features two ancient Greek images: on the left a woman in profile on a black background unaware of the male warrior wielding a sword behind her, who is rendered in black and set against a white background (see Figure 8.9). Linda Nishio's poster, like Kay Rosen's, just offers text: "Hōōz Responsible." Interrogating the viewer without referencing a specific subject, such as racism, probably saved it from censure. Lastly, Alexis Smith's "Watch Your Step" features a ballerina teetering on an industrial stairway unaware of the warning just behind her. The banana peel in the lower foreground humorously suggests the dancer's impending fall. Unfortunately, there is only one photograph of the works in situ

166 Joanna Gardner-Huggett

FIGURE 8.9 Nancy Bless, *Manifestation at 12th and Vine,* c. 1982. Elevated train platform billboard, 46 × 30 in., *Critical Messages* exhibition, Artemisia Gallery, 1985. *Critical Messages* Exhibition, Artemisia Gallery, 1985. Courtesy of Nancy Bless

and there is no existing documentation of the audience's reaction to the images that were approved (see Figure 8.8).[33]

More on Censorship

Although many cities during the 1980s sponsored public art projects like *Critical Messages* with state and federal agency support and without incident, Artemisia certainly was not the first to face censorship by a mass transit authority. In 1965 antiwar activists Lee Baxandall and Fred Gardner wanted to buy space on the New York Transit Authority trains for an anti-Vietnam war poster featuring a ten-year-old Vietnamese girl in profile with the text "Why Are We Burning,

Torturing, Killing the People of Vietnam? … To Prevent Free Elections" and then encourages viewers to write Lyndon Johnson in protest with the tagline "Students for a Democratic Society." The transit authority immediately rejected the proposal. Twenty years later the artist Michael Lebron tackled Reaganomics on the DC metro with his poster "Tired of the Jellybean Republic?" featuring President Reagan mocking unemployed workers; that was also denied advertising space (Maschinot 1985, 13). Closer to Chicago, the Milwaukee-based group Mobilization for Survival attempted to purchase advertising space for a poster of a gun-toting President Reagan accompanied by the text, "In this nuclear age can we afford leaders who shoot from the hip?" Milwaukee Public Transit first demanded that the peace group supply a $10,000 bond to protect the agency should any lawsuits be filed (Maschinot 1985, 13).

With the exception of Ballard's representation of Reagan and Rosen's provocative text, the majority of the banned images in "*Critical Messages*" were mild mannered compared to the cases in New York City, Washington, DC, and Milwaukee, despite raising similar issues, such as US imperialism and nuclear threats. Rather, the images occupied a space between political agitation and the more pleasurable and easier posters offered by the *Streetfare Journal*. Yet once these political posters entered the public sphere, they quickly became associated with propaganda and no longer were protected by the white cube of the art gallery. Returning to Kester's categorization of this media- and text-based work often produced by women as "rant" art, it can easily be associated with female hysteria and something to be suppressed from the public domain.[34]

Carol Jacobsen reminds us that arts censorship cases often fail to acknowledge that gender is critical to these public responses (Jacobsen 1991, 54). She defines censorship as "the suppression, the removal or alteration of artists' works or the conditions of their display *after the fact* – when those works have already been accepted or installed for public exposition." Further, she argues that censorship aligns with conservative ideology based on the natural entitlement of the dominant white, heterosexist Western male to public expression. Given these conditions, Jacobsen draws a direct parallel between the omission of white women and people of color from the art world and their systematic historical erasure in public space, concluding that in this political climate it is no surprise that the Guerrilla Girls formed in 1985 as the conscience of the art world (Jacobsen 1991, 42, 51; Guerrilla Girls 2012).

David and Ferentz did not have the benefit of Jacobsen's hindsight and would soon discover that the CTA lawyers' insistence on censoring ten of the artists was not just a reaction to *Critical Messages*, but part of a much longer history of suppressing feminist agendas. In the midst of negotiating the exhibition details with Winston Network, the curators were unaware that the CTA was appealing a recent Illinois court ruling in August 1984 that declared its refusal to grant Planned Parenthood advertising space unconstitutional, arguing further that the CTA's decision was based on a policy "contrived" for rejection.[35] For this reason, the curators contended that the CTA lawyers were scrutinizing any advertising that might jeopardize their case against Planned Parenthood by exposing another example of the CTA using feigned criteria. The ACLU, already supporting Planned Parenthood's case, began to investigate Artemisia's claims and initially sounded hopeful. Spokesman Jane Whicher states,

> The CTA has created a public forum with its advertising space and the Supreme Court says that once a public forum is created, you cannot discriminate in terms of content … We ought to be seeing an era of increased freedom on the CTA.[36]

In July 1985, the court ruled in favor of Planned Parenthood, but as David explains, she found it difficult to move forward with any suit after the challenges of simply mounting *Critical Messages*.[37] The commitment required to pursue a freedom of speech case clearly could be daunting to curators working on a volunteer basis and already holding jobs, not to mention trying to sustain their own artistic careers. Baxandall, Gardner, Lebron, and Mobilization for Survival spent years in litigation in order to secure the right to buy advertising space on their respective transit authorities. Taking on the CTA may well have resulted in changing its policies, but also possibly at the expense of Artemisia's larger intent to support its members and immediate community. Jenny Dixon adds, "If Artemisia wins its case, the CTA will more likely be reluctant to allow future artists to exhibit … a renegade artform [sic] deserves to thrive with the non-legitimatized energy that created it" (Dixon 1985, 67). In the end, the CTA retained its power to control advertising imagery on Chicago's trains and buses and Artemisia remained on the margins, much less likely to engage in public projects in the future.

Evaluating Impact

Lifton observes,

> While some of their goals may have been frustrated, the curators of *Critical Messages* should feel satisfied in having once again pointed up the difficulties that outsiders have, and always have had, in getting past the insiders to reach a wide public audience.
>
> *(Lifton 1985, 61)*

Nevertheless, the curators and artists succeeded in generating pockets of dialogue. First, Spector moderated a panel on public art with Kay Rosen, as well as the artist Bob Peters, codirector of the Video Databank Kate Horsfield, advertising executive Maureen Moore, and sociologist Howard Becker, which was originally part of the exhibit, but took on greater importance after the CTA's decision. Rejected artists were given a small stipend by Artemisia as a way to compensate for the costs of their work. Michaels, for example, used the money to print a larger run of her poster and distributed it anonymously, pasting it on walls in Philadelphia and New York City, as well as slipping it into newspapers and mailing it to a list culled from a phone book.[38] Only months after *Critical Messages* closed, Esther Parada's Smedley Butler poster won the artist first prize and $1,000 in a political art contest sponsored by the *Village Voice*.[39] In addition, it was reproduced and sold in a variety of independent bookstores in Chicago and as part of the exhibition *Expanding Commitment: Diverse Approaches to Socially Concerned Photography*, held at the Maryland Institute College of Art in 1986.

Parada created another version of the poster for the Newsletter of the Smedley D. Butler Brigade, published by the Massachusetts Chapter of Veterans for Peace, which was juxtaposed with an editorial calling for vets to challenge US intervention in Central America.[40] The newsletter generated a number of written responses, with one 70-year-old ex-Marine writing to Parada, "I am bit curious – I recall Smedley Butler, but I have never heard of his frank sentiments about his role in using his military position to further certain business interests." He signs off by asking Parada to explain if this information came directly from her research.[41] The civil rights and peace activist Norman C. Jimerson told Parada, it "was one of the most effective messages in a poster that I have seen."[42] A year later Jimerson requested free copies of the poster to distribute to every House and Senate office in Washington, DC.[43]

The correspondence between the CTA and the *Critical Messages* curators became its own artwork. Pinkel wrote to Ferentz from Santa Monica in July 1985:

> The display about the show is in the window of my neighborhood radical bookstore … they xeroxed the attorney's letter and circled all the juicy statements and put it above the exhibition description published by Artemisia. They have done a whole display devoted to censorship and your exhibition is featured so there!!![44]

After *Critical Messages* closed, the curators also contributed documentation of the exhibit and its censorship to a few shows, including *Uncensored*, held at Spaces Gallery in Cleveland in 1987, and *Inalienable Rights/Alienable Wrongs*, sponsored by the Committee for Artists' Rights, Chicago Artists Coalition, and the New Art Examiner in 1989. Yet, because they lost the collective experience of viewing these placards in public dialogue as David, Ferentz, and Spector originally sought, the show remained an internal discussion, limited primarily to artists, critics, and curators in Chicago.

Censorship on the CTA Continues

Although the ACLU believed there would be increased freedom on the CTA, the censorship of *Critical Messages* by the transit authority would not be the last of its controversial decisions as activist organizations sought opportunities to create campaigns in the manner of consumer advertising, which would not be limited to the "bounds of any one community or subculture."[45] In September 1989, the ACLU would again file suit against the CTA for barring an AIDS awareness advertisement paid for by the Kupona Network, a nonprofit promoting AIDS prevention in the African American community. The ad depicts a pair of eyes reflecting two different images. The left pupil shows a naked couple with the man's arm around the woman sitting next to him; she holds a condom package. In the right pupil there is a man warning another man to avoid used drug needles, and lastly a man ingesting drugs. The text below reads "Sex without condoms + drug abuse = AIDS, AIDS in the black community is very real." The CTA rejected the poster for being "inappropriate and too black oriented."[46] The CTA finally ran the posters over a year later after the Kupona Network took the transit authority to court (Burris 1983, 102).

Nearly simultaneously, the ACLU would find itself in another battle with the CTA and the city of Chicago. Alderman Robert Shaw proposed a city-wide ban on Gran Fury's poster entitled *Kissing Doesn't Kill*, which was part of the "Art Against AIDS on the Road" tour to Chicago, Washington, DC, and San Francisco (to which *Critical Messages* participant Kay Rosen also contributed). Shaw viewed *Kissing Doesn't Kill* as a recruiting tool for a gay lifestyle, stating, "These posters have nothing to do with AIDS … They are sending out the wrong message to the children of our city, and the CTA should not be involved in helping to send out that message."[47] As Richard Meyer explains, the poster faced challenges even before it reached Chicago and Shaw's eyes. It was sponsored by the American Foundation for AIDS Research (AmFAR), and the organization demanded that Gran Fury remove the rejoinder text from *Kissing Doesn't Kill* ("Corporate Greed, Government Inaction, and Public Indifference Makes AIDS a Political Crisis"), fearing that it would alienate its many corporate donors. Instead of dropping out of the project altogether, Gran Fury decided to remain on tour, believing that the poster stood on its own merit. The Illinois State Senate responded by approving a measure that prevented the CTA from displaying any poster featuring physical contact or embrace within a homosexual or lesbian context in any space where individuals under age of 21 could see it, which would make it impossible for Gran Fury's work to be shown. The Illinois House of Representatives later voted down the bill and eventually *Kissing Doesn't Kill* was installed on CTA buses and train stations only to be defaced after two days. In contrast to *Critical Messages*, however, the furor surrounding the poster's installation led to increased circulation of Gran Fury's original message (Meyer 2002, 237–239).

The Private Is Now Public

In the late 1980s, it was not just alternative spaces like Artemisia and activist organizations that clashed with the city government; the private sphere of the art school also became a site of scrutiny. In May 1987 David K. Nelson, a white painter, contributed the crudely rendered painting *Mirth and Girth* – portraying Mayor Harold Washington dressed merely in a pink bra, panties, garters, and stockings – to a student exhibition in a nonpublic space of the School of the Art Institute (SAIC). Many deemed it racist and offensive, and it caused a national uproar. It was painted just after the mayor's sudden death, and a group of aldermen concerned about Washington's legacy arranged for the painting to be "arrested" because they considered it to be so inflammatory and feared riots would ensue. Nelson explained that he was inspired by an image of Washington transformed into a deity, floating above Chicago with Jesus Christ on his side, but the feminized representation of the mayor fueled speculation regarding Washington's sexual identity due to his long-standing bachelor status. In addition, the title was far too close to the name of an organization for overweight men, "Girth and Mirth." The Black community – still in mourning for Washington, as well as worried about their political future in Chicago – did not want a young white man speaking for them, and viewed the incident as part of a pattern of assaults rather than an isolated incident.[48] Escalating the public's anger was the suggestion that Nelson executed the piece as a publicity stunt, with a fellow student acting as Nelson while he circulated the building in disguise as the controversy unfolded. After significant public pressure, SAIC issued an apology in major Chicago newspapers and agreed to intensify its efforts to recruit faculty of color. The painting eventually was returned to Nelson with a gash and he sued the city of Chicago with the support of the ACLU, arguing that his rights as an artist were violated under the First, Fourth, and Fourteenth amendments.[49]

Only two years later, one of Silvia Malagrino's former School of the Art Institute students, Dread Scott, became the target of media and protests for his installation *What Is the Proper Way to Display a U.S. Flag*; this was included in the exhibition *A/Part of the Whole*, which was staged to strengthen relationships with students of color after the *Mirth and Girth* controversy.[50] Although Scott's case is often discussed in connection with Nelson's, the artist dismissed the *Mirth and Girth* painter as shallow and offensive. A middle-class black student from Hyde Park on the south side of Chicago, he attended elite white schools, but was regularly subjected to racist taunts and started interrogating the history of slavery and racism in the United States while at SAIC. His adopted name, "Dread Scott," first references the 1857 Supreme Court case Dred Scott v. Sandford, which affirmed Scott as a slave and property, fostered divisions between abolitionists and pro-slavery advocates, and contributed to the start of the Civil War. In addition, "Dread Scott" alludes to the dreads of Rastafarians and inspiring dread. Scott does not

172 Joanna Gardner-Huggett

identify as a Rastafarian, but is committed to opposition movements and is a self-proclaimed revolutionary (Dubin 1992, 104–105).

Scott's controversial installation consisted of a photomontage of South Korean students burning the US flag, flag-draped coffins in a troop transport, and printed text, "What Is the Proper Way to Display a U.S. Flag"; there was a shelf just below with a notebook for visitors to write comments and below it a US flag stretched across the floor, which means that the viewer has to step on the flag in order to write anything in the notebook. Although it was displayed without incident in a local alternative space, there was a national uproar when it was shown at SAIC. Veterans were particularly incensed, coming in each day to pick up the flag, fold it, and place it on the shelf; the group Windy City Vets filed an injunction with the Cook County court for its removal, but Judge Kenneth L. Gillis ruled that *What Is the Proper Way to Display a U.S. Flag* did not violate state or federal laws regarding the appropriate treatment of the flag.[51] Instead Judge Gillis argued, "this exhibit is as much an invitation to think about the flag as it is an invitation to step on the flag." The Chicago Park District, however, threatened to cut 28 million dollars of funding from eight museums, individuals canceled their memberships to SAIC's sister institution the Art Institute of Chicago, and the Illinois state legislature moved to reduce the school's funding from $130,000 to $1 as retribution (Dubin 1992, 116; Scott 2018).

Therefore, 1989 in Chicago and beyond marked a juncture where policing culture in United States rapidly moved from the public domain to the internal networks of the art world and would soon explode on the congressional floor. Senator Jesse Helms authored legislation that would bar the NEA and NEH from funding "obscene art" and requiring grant recipients to sign an anti-obscenity oath. Individual artists and organizations awarded grants would refuse to sign and lawsuits against the NEA were filed (Atkins 1991, 37). As Grant Kester argues, by the end of that decade the art world needed to reformulate the relationship between publicly funded artists and the publics they hoped to represent (Kester 1998, 131). For Chicago, it means that public art now remains primarily under the jurisdiction of the Department of Cultural Affairs and Special Events, which coordinates art commissions for the Chicago Transit Authority funded by the federal government's Art in Transit program. Although Artemisia faced serious obstacles in bringing *Critical Messages* to CTA platforms, women artists are now well represented and have completed nearly half of these CTA station commissions since 2011.[52] Each public art project enhances passengers' experiences of individual stations, but unlike *Critical Messages*, the images do not take on the role of Kester's "rant art"; instead they highlight histories and affirm identities of the wide-ranging neighborhoods in Chicago and are much less likely to engender any controversies.

Epilogue: A Return to the Streets

Spector contends in his catalogue essay for *Critical Messages* that because of the show's "… existence outside (literally) of the usual spaces for exhibition, this art is free, logically and financially, from subservience to commercial inhibitions of the art support system"; yet the promise of the public domain proved to be a site of silencing subversions, rather than freedom of speech. By the early 1990s the incident had been largely forgotten and *Critical Messages* only garners an occasional mention in the literature on the visual arts and censorship. However, the history of this exhibition exposes a critical moment in the history of both alternative spaces and public art. Artemisia's entry into the realm of public art came just too late: it missed the experimental freedom of the 1970s and early 1980s, before Reagan conservatism became entrenched and filtered into the policies of arts funding, and then it landed right in the midst of the emerging culture wars. After *Critical Messages* closed, the Artemisia Fund remained committed to feminism and social justice, but shied away from major public art projects, thus illustrating how the political and economic forces of the city of Chicago could widen, rather than close, the gap between artists and the public. By the end of the 1980s, feminist artists with activist agendas who were committed to working in the public sphere individually or collectively in Chicago returned to Dixon's earlier assertion that "a renegade artform [sic] deserves to thrive with the non-legitimatized energy that created it" (Dixon 1985, 67).

The Chicago-based radical feminist collective SisterSerpents, for instance, formed in 1989 to engage in "idea warfare," countering the physical and emotional violence women faced on a day-to-day basis.[53] Inspired by the campaigns of Berlin Dadaists during World War I and operating anonymously, like the Guerrilla Girls (founded four years earlier), SisterSerpents wheat-pasted provocative Xeroxed posters and stickers across the city of Chicago, including one that read, "The modern individual family is founded on the open or concealed slavery of the wife," and another stating "Misogyny: Look it up, Stamp it out."[54] Similar to the contributors to *Critical Messages*, they appropriated mass media images and combined them with language exposing numerous examples of the exploitation and oppression of women. Founder Jeramy Turner explains that the posters were especially powerful because people did not expect to encounter them in the street, so they functioned very differently from social media where individuals can curate what they follow on Facebook, Instagram, and Twitter – potentially never reading any information that counters their own worldview.[55] Unlike Artemisia, the SisterSerpents refused to operate collaboratively with public agencies that were complicit in suppressing feminist agendas. As they state in their manifesto, "SisterSerpents is fierce, uncompromising, refusing to plead or gently persuade," aiming to engender hostility in the street, at public meetings and events, and in the media, concluding, "keeping up appearances are totally irrelevant."[56]

While they were broadly committed to overthrowing patriarchy, the erosion of reproductive rights was a decisive issue in creating the SisterSerpents. After learning of the Supreme Court's decision to uphold Webster v. Reproductive Services, a Missouri law that imposed restrictions on the use of state funds for the provision of abortions, artist Jeramy Turner placed an advertisement in a Chicago

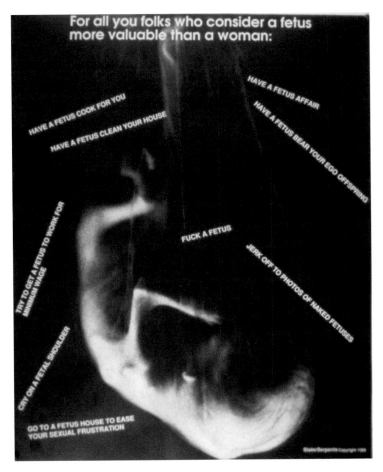

FIGURE 8.10 *SisterSerpents, For All You Folks Who Consider a Fetus*, 1989. Poster, 23⅙ × 18⅞ in. Courtesy of Loyola University Chicago, Women and Leadership Archives, SisterSerpents Records

newspaper inviting political artists to join her in forging a feminist movement. Membership in the group required a pro-abortion philosophy and willingness to poster the streets.[57] Four artists answered Turner's call and one of the first posters they created, *For All You Folks Who Consider a Fetus*, garnered international notoriety after being plastered across the city and sent to activists and publications across the globe (Brandhuber 2018, 3–5; Shrage 2003, 160 n. 91) (see Figure 8.10). The poster features a black-and-white photograph of a jarred fetus taken at the Museum of Science and Industry and then overlaid with the text,

> For all of you folks who consider a fetus more valuable than a woman: have a fetus cook for you, have a fetus clean your house, jerk off to photos of

naked fetuses, cry on a fetal shoulder, try to get a fetus to work for minimum wage, fuck a fetus.

(Shrage 2003, 117; Brandhuber 2018, 5)

Because SisterSerpents were much more confrontational than artists Barbara Kruger and Ilona Granet, who produced works for the reproductive rights movement such as *Untitled (Your Body is a Battle Ground)* and *State Womb* in 1989, respectively, it is not surprising that they immediately faced opposition. Turner explains that it was extremely difficult to find a printer and eventually it was a women's print workshop that created 5,000 copies for the group.[58]

Once *For All You Folks Who Consider a Fetus* went public, the SisterSerpents quickly became targets of conservative political groups along with Gran Fury and Dread Scott. Talk radio condemned their radically delivered pro-choice messages and Senator Jesse Helms labeled them a hate group.[59] Outraged by NEA funding for the SisterSerpents' first exhibition *Rattle Your Rage* held at Filmmakers Gallery in Chicago in 1990, which included a wall plastered with the *For All You Folks* posters, the Heritage foundation circulated a copy of John Stevenson's review, "Group efforts: women who hate men who have penises," published in the *Chicago Reader*; at the top they added, "The National Endowment for the Arts gave $18,000 of tax money to help fund the exhibit described in the following article."[60] Physical threats also ensued. The day before the show opened someone broke the gallery window with an iron pipe and the director of Filmmakers Gallery discovered a bomb set off at her home, leading one SisterSerpent to wear a bulletproof vest to the gallery reception (Laskow 2018).

Although the SisterSerpents rattled their opponents and faced serious threats, simultaneously women in Chicago and beyond rushed to support their work (Brandhuber 2018, 6). Just as Artemisia included the gallery's phone number in their *Critical Messages* placards, SistersSerpents added a PO Box number so viewers could reply to their imagery, generating a significant and positive response.[61] Turner observes that SisterSerpents' guerrilla art work and exhibitions "gave women a sense of clarity, an escape valve, which was and is, vitally needed … It gave women a glimmer of the strength of camaraderie." Fellow SisterSerpent Mary Ellen Croteau, who was recruited by Artemisia members to join the gallery after the *Rattle Your Rage* exhibition, adds, "I saw women thrilled that their feelings and reactions were being validated and put forward by this group that was expressing women's anger in a very public and confrontational way" (Brandhuber 2018, 7).[62] Continuing to produce posters and exhibitions through 1998 in Chicago, as well as in Denver, Hamburg, and New York, Croteau argues that the work of SisterSerpents remains as relevant and necessary today, especially with the election of President Trump.[63] Famously recorded saying of women, "Grab `em by the pussy. You can do anything," Trump further demonstrated his disregard for women by rescinding Obama-era protections for women in the workplace within months of taking office; in particular "a ban on forced arbitration clauses

176 Joanna Gardner-Huggett

for sexual harassment, sexual assault or discrimination claims."[64] In addition, the confirmation of Supreme Court Justices Neil M. Gorsuch and Brett Kavanaugh, along with the soon to be decided (at the time of writing) replacement for late Justice Ruth Bader Ginsburg, will most likely result in a majority conservative court that could overturn Roe v. Wade.[65] It is striking that the CTA's refusal to show Planned Parenthood advertisements and its censorship of *Critical Messages* in 1985 does not seem any less out of the realm of possibility in 2020.

The media-savvy visual models established by the *Critical Messages* exhibition and the SisterSerpents resonate with the resurgence of women's activist protests since Trump's inauguration in January 2017. On January 21, 2017, women in more than 600 cities across the country flooded streets with pink pussy hats as a symbol of reclaiming their bodies; in Chicago, crowds reached 250,000 and 300,000 for the second Women's March in January 2018. The first march established a broad feminist platform demanding civil rights, disability rights, environmental justice, the end of violence against women, reproductive rights, and rights for immigrant and LGBTQIA communities; several of these key issues had already been addressed by *Critical Messages* artists and the SisterSerpents.[66] While not designated as art in commercial terms, banners witnessed at the 2018 march, such as *Unleash the Fury of Women as a Mighty Force for Revolution*, not only confront a wider public, but accompanied by mass numbers of women chanting through the streets these banners take the feminist rant to a new political level; they reflect the spirit of Nishio's *Hōōz Responsible* and the SisterSerpents' banners, such as *Piss on Passivity, Piss on Patriarchy* (see Figures 8.11 and 8.12). Judith Butler contends that collective bodies in protest forge new alliances and by animating these public spaces resignify their embedded ideologies (Butler 2012, 125). It is also important to acknowledge the role of the messages conveyed by protesters' visually enticing posters, echoing the feminist media-based art of the 1980s discussed in this essay, and establishing the foundation for negotiating new political platforms for the future.

Recognizing the tremendous range of visual ephemera produced by protests and how it distills the evolving landscape of social action, the Newberry Library in Chicago announced that it is building an archive of "modern protest." Martha Briggs, the Newberry's Lloyd Lewis Curator of Modern Manuscripts, explains,

> We also wanted to encourage everyone to think of their protest signs as worth saving for future generations interested in looking back on how citizens of our time framed pressing political issues and organized themselves for the causes they cared about.[67]

Critical Messages may have failed to be viewed in its intended manner, but the spirit of feminist disruption it sought to engender on the CTA is now a legitimized cultural intervention in Chicago and does not require collaboration with its public agencies to find visibility and dialogue.

Silenced Subversions 177

FIGURE 8.11 Unleash the Fury of Women as a Mighty Force for Revolution, Women's March, Chicago, January 20, 2018. Banner. Photograph courtesy of Joanna Gardner-Huggett

FIGURE 8.12 *SisterSerpents, Piss on Passivity, Piss on Patriarchy*, 1992. Banner. Courtesy of Loyola University Chicago, Women and Leadership Archives, SisterSerpents Records

178 Joanna Gardner-Huggett

Acknowledgments

This book chapter would not be possible without the generous assistance of Artemisia Gallery members and *Critical Messages* co-curators Anita David and Nicole Ferentz, as well as many of the contributors to the exhibition, who kindly shared important information and documentation. I am also grateful to Mary Ellen Croteau who sadly passed away in March 2019. I dedicate this chapter to Croteau's radical feminist practice. This research is supported by a DePaul University Research Council Competitive Research Grant.

Notes

1 *The Artists' Book* exhibition was curated by Janice Snyder and the video program on WTTW by Chris Straayer. Unfortunately, little documentation of the book exhibition exists. However, the following artists were included: Jacki Apple, Babette Baker, Jan Ballard, Nan Becker, Leslie Bellavance, June Blum, Barbara Cushman, Ann Fessler, Susan Hiller, Jenny Holzer, Susan King, Barbara Kruger, Elizabeth Kulas, Nancy Lambert, Judy Levy, Jennifer Ley, Lucy Lippard, Joan Lyons, Rebecca Michaels, Rose Parisi, Martha Rosler, Kristine Stiles, May Stevens, Barb Van Tuyle, and Janet Zweig. *Bikini Girl* magazines and *Little Girl Games* magazines also were featured. The video program featured the following artists: Max Almy, Mindy Faber, Liz Graves, Lynn Hershman Leeson, Martha Rosler, and Lynne Smilow. The list of book artists and the video program is preserved in the Artemisia Gallery Records, Ryerson and Burnham Archives, The Art Institute of Chicago, Chicago, Illinois.

2 The curators were informed that the artists' statements did not meet Public Service Announcement broadcast rules. Anita David, interviewed by the author in Chicago, Illinois, January 13, 2014. The proposed public service announcements were created by Laurie Anderson, Catherine High, Jenny Holzer, Barbara Kruger, Suzanne Lacy, Louise Lawler, Adrian Piper, and Yvonne Rainer. See Artemisia Gallery Records.

3 *The Art of the Woman's Building* included graphics curated by Arlene Raven and selected by Sheila de Bretville and Sue Mayberry. It featured performances selected by Cheri Gaulke and video works selected by Nancy Angelo; Arlene Raven and Ruth Iskin curated the exhibition historicizing the 1893 Woman's Building. See documentation of the exhibition and its accompanying events in Artemisia Gallery Records.

4 Exhibition catalogs for *Looking at Men* and *Looking at Women* are available in the Artemisia Gallery Records.

5 See, for example, Mitchell's critique of alternative spaces as failing to engage the public (1984, 28).

6 Women's contributions to large-scale outdoor public art projects remain limited in Chicago. See for example, Doss 2012. The CTA implemented a city-wide public art program for the transit authority after 2011, and there women artists find parity. See "CTA Public Art," www.transitchicago.com/assets/1/6/2016_CTA_Public_Art_Catalog_-_FINAL.pdf. Women artists are also well represented in commissions for public libraries and police stations in Chicago. See *The Chicago Public Art Guide*, www.cityofchicago.org/content/dam/city/depts/dca/Public%20Art/publicartguide1.pdf.

7 Anita David, interviewed by the author in Chicago, Illinois, January 13, 2014.

8 See Mitchell 1984, 12–28, for an extended discussion of public art projects like CEPA in other US cities, including *Critical Messages* artist Nancy Bless who completed *Public Transit* in 1978 in collaboration with the city of Columbus, Ohio. Bless interviewed approximately 50 commuters on Columbus buses about their thought patterns while riding and then combined the text with photographic portraits by collaborator Stephanie Bart that traveled on two public Columbus buses for two months (Mitchell, 27).

9 Documentation of Group Material's *M5* and *Subculture* exhibitions can be found in the Group Material Archive 1976–2009, Fales Library and Special Collections, New York University, New York, New York.

10 The other artists included in the exhibition were: Ida Applebroog, Roxanne Ault, Jenny Holzer, Mike Love, Gary Allen Justis, Heather McAdams, Bob Peters, Bill Rowe, Duncan Smith, Margaret Wharton, Charles Wilson, and Karl Wirsum. See English 1983, 13.

11 See Peggy Constantine, "Poetry, Art Are Going for A Ride-On CTA buses," *Chicago Sun-Times*, January 18, 1985, and "A 'Magazine' On Wheels. Streetfare Journal Brings Art, Poetry to City Buses," *Christian Science Monitor*, March 31, 1986. Accessed December 12, 2013, www.csmonitor.com/1986/0331/dbus.html/(page)/2.

12 For a list of artists featured in Group Material's *M5* and *Subculture*, see the press releases found in the Group Material 1976–2009 archive held in the Fales Library and Special Collections.

13 Anita David, letter to Silvia Malagrino, January 20, 1985.

14 Neil Tesser, "HOT TYPE, Art Police: CTA Takes Gallery for a Ride," *Chicago Reader*, July 5, 1985.

15 Tom W. Stonecipher to Jonah J. Orlofsky, May 6, 1985. Artemisia Gallery Records.

16 Tesser, "HOT TYPE, Art Police."

17 Maschinot 1985, 12. Full text superimposed on the far left side of the placard,

> Worry is a feeling of fear, but it is never of the present. It is always about something that may happen or that has happened. It is generally in the future, sometimes in the past, but never in the present. An animal that knows neither future nor past cannot worry. All creatures, excepting the human beings live only in the present and therefore do not remember what happened in the past or goes what is going to happen. A human being is given such powers that the mind can go back into the future as one thinks it will be because we have imagination. As a matter of fact, we live less in the present than in the past or in the future.

18 Tom W. Stonecipher to Jonah J. Orlofsky, May 6, 1985. Artemisia Gallery Records.

19 For a more detailed discussion of Chicago and Mayor Harold Washington in the 1980s, as well as an assessment of David K. Nelson's controversial representation of the mayor after his death in 1987, which will be discussed later in the essay, see Dubin 1992, 26–43.

20 The lightbox version of Jenny Holzer's *Survival: UNEX sign*, 1984 shown in Figure 8.4 has the same text as the placard featured in *Critical Messages*.

21 Tom W. Stonecipher to Jonah Orolofsky, attorney for Artemisia Gallery, May 6, 1985. Artemisia Gallery Records.

22 The image and full text of Parada's "Who Was Smedley Butler" poster is available on the Art Institute of Chicago's collection website at www.artic.edu/artworks/187514/who-was-smedley-butler.

180 Joanna Gardner-Huggett

23 Tom W. Stonecipher to Jonah Orolofsky, attorney for Artemisia Gallery, May 6, 1985. Artemisia Gallery Records. The full text reads,

> Mammy pappy's new faced nuclear family, fashioned from whitewalled double brimmed American apart hide, all fit up in dressy kid's wear, longlegged silksocked armwrapped loudly-laughing close-joy singing beyond the was and the now so the will-be won't be a prism-cast prison-life.

24 Tom W. Stonecipher to Jonah Orolofsky, attorney for Artemisia Gallery, May 6, 1985. Artemisia Gallery Records. Full text reads,

> An impenetrable cloud of dust and smoke masked the area. The immense steel tower was vaporized. Two observers were knocked down and more; when a rain of ruins from the air, a rain of ruins never seen before on earth, oh a rain of ruins …

25 Tom W. Stonecipher to Jonah Orolofsky, attorney for Artemisia Gallery, May 6, 1985. Artemisia Gallery Records.

26 Undated letter from Nancy Bless to Anita David, c. Summer 1985; Lifton 1985, 61.

27 Barbara Jo Revelle's work was censored many times, even when featured in a show devoted to the question of censorship. Email correspondence with the author, June 20, 2020. See "Doubly Forbidden," *New York Times Magazine*, February 1, 1998, 15.

28 Sheila Pinkel manuscript, "Art and Censorship," presented at the Midnight Special Bookstore in October 1986. Copy of the text found in Esther Parada Papers, box 22, folder 6, Special Collections and University Archives, University of Illinois of Chicago, Chicago, Illinois.

29 For a general description of Holzer's *Sign on a Truck* see https://publicartfund.org/view/exhibitions/5960_sign_on_a_truck. Jacobsen 1991, 52, explores the difficulty in securing funding for Holzer's project. Also see Buchloh (1985) for further discussion of the content and audience interaction with *Sign on a Truck*.

30 The bus placards were featured on the Chicago Transit Authority routes 8, 11, 22, 82, 147, and 151. Artemisia Gallery Records.

31 Granet's *Untitled (Dear Men, While on the streets … Maintain 5 feet of distance.)*, 1985 shown in Figure 8.7 is from the same series and visually very similar to Ilona Granet's contribution to *Critical Messages, Dear Men, While on the street, Maintain 8 feet Distance, Thanks!*

32 The train placards were featured at the following stops: Randoph/State, Jackson/State, Jackson/Dearborn, Clark/State, and Ravenswood (Artemisia Gallery Records).

33 David does not recall anyone phoning Artemisia to praise or critique the placards shown, and gallery comment notebooks held in the Artemisia Gallery Records do not reveal any specific commentary on the exhibition.

34 While Kester does not solely apply the phrase "rant" art to work made by women and offers an important critique of how this work functions and circulates, as well as acknowledges issues of gender, he does not fully address how this phrase might contribute to gendered categorization outside of the art world (Kester 1998, 122–129).

35 See Maurice Possley, "Pro-choice ads on CTA win ruling," *Chicago Tribune*, July 16, 1985, A3.

36 Maschinot 1985, 13. Unfortunately, the ACLU office in Chicago does not currently hold any files on the *Critical Messages* case.

37 Anita David, interviewed by the author in Chicago, Illinois, January 13, 2014.

38 Rebecca Michaels, email to the author, December 13, 2013.

39 "Political Contest Results," *Village Voice*, October 15, 1985, 76.

40 *Newsletter of the Smedley D. Butler Brigade,* Massachusetts Chapter of Veterans for Peace, Inc., 1 (Winter 1987). n.p. Esther Parada Papers, box 18, folder 1, Special Collections and University Archives, University of Illinois Chicago, Chicago, Illinois.

41 A.Z. Waltzer to Esther Parada, February 22, c. 1987. Esther Parada Papers, box 18, folder 1, Special Collections and University Archives, University of Illinois Chicago, Chicago, Illinois.

42 Norman C. Jimerson to Esther Parada, March 16, 1987. Esther Parada Papers, box 18, folder 1, Special Collections and University Archives, University of Illinois Chicago, Chicago, Illinois.

43 It is not clear whether the posters were actually distributed. Norman C. Jimerson to Esther Parada, January 9, 1988. Esther Parada Papers, box 18, folder 1, Special Collections and University Archives, University of Illinois Chicago, Chicago, Illinois.

44 Sheila Pinkel to Nicole Ferentz, undated. Personal papers of Anita David.

45 See Meyer 2002, 236. Here Meyer is referring specifically to Gran Fury's *Kissing Doesn't Kill*, which will be discussed below. However, it is equally applicable to the aims of the Kupona Network.

46 Jack Houston, "Suit Challenges CTA for Barring AIDS Ad," *Chicago Tribune*, September 14, 1989.

47 Robert Davis, "Most Aldermen just Kiss Off Special Meeting on AIDS Posters," *Chicago Tribune*, August 23, 1990, pg. N_A5; Meyer 2002, 237.

48 See Chinta Strausberg, "Racism Cited at Art School," *Chicago Defender*, May 16, 1988, for black SAIC students' response to Nelson's painting.

49 Dubin, 28, 30–38. Bob Greene also indicated that he received a call from someone before the controversy became public, explaining,

> I have no way of knowing whether he actually was [Nelson]. But he described the painting for me, and said that the city's political forces were trying to get it removed from the School of the Art Institute. He said I should write about it.
> ("*Editors Choose Just To Say 'No',*" Chicago Tribune*, May 18, 1988, D1)*

Nelson eventually reached a settlement with the city of Chicago. See "Paying the Bill for a Tantrum," *Chicago Tribune*, September 28, 1994, D 24.

50 Silvia Malagrino, email message to the author, December 8, 2013.

51 "Flag Exhibit Upheld in Chicago by Judge," *New York Times,* March 3, 1989, A00016; Dubin 1992, 103–111.

52 For descriptions of Art in Transit projects, see CTA Public Art.

53 SisterSerpents, "SisterSerpents Manifesto," *SisterSerpents: Art as a Weapon*. Accessed August 7, 2018, https://ssfeministart.omeka.net/items/show/1.

54 Although there are similarities between the Guerrilla Girls and the SisterSerpents, the latter emerged independently. A majority of the group remains anonymous, but artists Jeramy Turner and Mary Ellen Croteau are two members who have openly discussed the history of their participation in the group. See Brandhuber 2018.

55 Interview with Jeramy Turner, Audio Interference 52: SisterSerpents, June 14, 2018. Accessed August 9, 2018. http://interferencearchive.org/audio–interference-52-sisterserpents.

56 SisterSerpents Manifesto.

57 Interview with Jeramy Turner, Audio Interference 52: SisterSerpents, 14 June, 2018.

58 Interview with Jeramy Turner, Audio Interference 52: SisterSerpents.
59 See Shrage, 111–112 and 118 for discussion of Kruger and Granet's pro-choice artwork.
60 SisterSerpents, "Anti-SisterSerpents Flyer," *SisterSerpents: Art as a Weapon*. Accessed August 7, 2018. https://ssfeministart.omeka.net/items/show/2.
61 Interview with Jeramy Turner, Audio Interference 52: SisterSerpents.
62 Mary Ellen Croteau was a member of Artemisia Gallery from 1990–1996. Mary Ellen Croteau, correspondence with the author, July 24, 2018.
63 Mary Ellen Croteau, correspondence with the author, July 24, 2018.
64 "Transcript: Donald Trump's Taped Comments About Women," *New York Times*, October 8, 2016. www.nytimes.com/2016/10/08/us/donald-trump-tape-transcript.html. Mary Emily O'Hara, "Trump Pulls Back Obama-Era Protections for Women Workers," April 3, 2017. www.nbcnews.com/news/us-news/trump-pulls-back-obama-era-protections-women-workers-n741041.
65 Adam Liptak and Matt Flegenheimer, "Neil Gorsuch Confirmed by Senate as Supreme Court Justice," *New York Times*, April 7, 2017. Accessed August 9, 2018. www.nytimes.com/2017/04/07/us/politics/neil-gorsuch-supreme-court.html; David Grewal Singh, Amy Kapczynski, and Issa Kohler-Hausmann, "Commentary: There Is Absolutely No Liberal Case to be Made for Brett Cavanaugh," *Chicago Tribune*, August 5, 2018. www.chicagotribune.com/news/opinion/commentary/ct-perspec-scotus-brett-kavanaugh-hostile-liberal-causes-lawyers-0806-story.html#.
66 "Mission," Women's March. Accessed July 19, 2018. www.womensmarch.com/mission.
67 "Building a Living Archive of Modern Protest," January 2017. Accessed July 17, 2018. www.newberry.org/building-living-archive-modern-protest.

References

Atkins, Robert. 1991. "A Censorship Time Line," *Art Journal* 50 (3) (Autumn): 33–37. doi.org/10.1080/00043249.1991.10791456

Avgikos, Jan. 1995. "Group Material Timeline: Activism as a Work of Art." In *But is it Art? The Spirit of Art as Activism*, edited by Nina Felshin, 85–116. Seattle: Bay Press.

Bordt, Rebecca. 1997. *The Structure of Women's Non-Profit Organizations*. Bloomington, IN: Indiana University Press.

Brandhuber, Steph. 2018. "The Controversial Pro-Choice Collective Republicans Labeled a 'Hate Group.'" *Vice.com*, July 4, 2018. www.vice.com/en_us/article/3k4xyn/sisterserpents-pro-choice-art-collective-history

Buchloh, Benjamin. 1985. "From Gadget Video to Agit Video: Some Notes on Four Recent Video Works." *Art Journal* 45 (3): 217–227. doi.org/10.2307/776856

Burris, Scott. 1993. *AIDS Law: A New Guide for the Public*. New Haven: Yale University Press.

Butler, Judith. 2012. "Bodies in Alliance and the Politics of the Street." In *Sensible Politics, The Visual Culture of Nongovernmental Activism*, edited by Meg McLagan and Yates McKee, 117–137. New York: Zone Books.

Dixon, Jenny. 1985. "A Politic to Public Art." *Heresies* 20 (4): 66–67.

Doss, Erika. 2012. "Public Chronicles: Louise Bourgeois' *Helping Hands* and Chicago's Identity Issues." *Public Art Dialogue* 2 (1): 94–102. doi.org/10.1080/21502552.2012.653237

Dubin, Steven C. 1992. *Arresting Images, Impolitic Art and Uncivil Actions*. New York: Routledge.

English, Christopher. 1983. "De-Merchandising Art: Shopping for an Alternative." *New Art Examiner* 10 (10) (Summer): 13.

Fryd, Vivien Green. 2007. "Suzanne Lacy's *Three Weeks in May*: Feminist Activist Performance Art as `Expanded Public Pedagogy.'" *NWSA Journal* 19 (1): 23–38. doi. org/10.2979/nws.2007.19.1.23

Guerrilla Girls. 2012. *Not Ready to Make Nice: Guerrilla Girls in the Art World and Beyond.* Chicago: Columbia College. Exhibition catalogue.

Holbert, Virginia. 1983. *Artemisia X: Ten Years.* Chicago: Artemisia Gallery.

Jacobsen, Carol J. 1991. "Redefining Censorship: A Feminist View." *Art Journal* 4 (Winter): 42–55. doi.org/10.2307/777322

Kester, Grant H. 1998. "Rhetorical Questions: The Alternative Arts Sector and the Imaginary Public." In *Art, Activism & Oppositionality, Essays from* Afterimage, edited by Grant H. Kester 103–135. Durham, NC: Duke University Press.

Laskow, Sarah. 2018. "The Forgotten History of the Controversial SisterSerpents." *Atlasobscura,* March 14, 2018. www.atlasobscura.com/articles/feminist-art-sister-serpents

Lifton, Norma. 1985. "Exhibition Review: Critical Messages, Artemisia Gallery." *New Art Examiner* 12 (10) (Summer): 61.

Lippard, Lucy. 1989. "Both Sides Now: A Reprise." In *The Pink Glass Swan, Selected Feminist Essays on Art*, 266–277. New York: W.W. Norton.

Maschinot, Beth. 1985. "Political Images No Ticket to Ride." *In These Times*, September 4–10, 1985.

Meyer, Richard. 2002. *Outlaw Representation, Censorship and Homosexuality in Twentieth-Century American Art.* Boston: Beacon Press.

Mitchell, Michael. 1984. "Gallery-in-Transit, Photography Rides the Transit System," *Photo Communique* (Summer): 12–28.

Schulze, Franz. 1975. "Women's Art, Beyond Chauvinism," *ARTnews.* 74 (March): 70–73.

Scott, Dread. 2018. TED Talk, *How Art Can Shape America's Conversation About Freedom.* www.ted.com/talks/dread_scott_how_art_can_shape_america_s_conversation_about_freedom

Shrage, Laurie. 2003. *Abortion and Social Responsibility: Depolarizing the Debate.* Oxford: Oxford University Press.

Spector, Buzz. 1985. *Critical Messages.* Chicago: Artemisia Gallery. Exhibition catalogue.

9

INTERNATIONAL REVOLUTION BY DESIGN

The Art of Tanya Aguiñiga

Sheila Pepe

Few places in today's American landscape are as hotly contested as the Mexican/ US border. Most Americans have never crossed it, and if they have, then they have done so in the air. It exists for many as an imagined space made emotional through political rhetoric and the depiction of salesmen's samples of enormous walls.

On the ground, however, the boundary between the two nations is very real. It runs 1,954 miles from the Pacific Ocean to the Gulf of Mexico. It crosses urban, rural, and desert lands. According to the *Guinness Book of World Records*, it's the most frequently crossed border in the world (Glenday 2009, 457). The United States–Mexico Border Health Commission reported in 2012 that 350 million legal crossings take place annually.[1] From afar, these facts might seem astounding, even frightening. At the border, on the contrary, most understand that the crossing points are filled with commuters, people going to work and coming home at night, kids going to school, folks going to see relatives.

This contested borderland is the conceptual center of the work of Tanya Aguiñiga (b. 1978), who grew up in Tijuana and knows what the borderlands and the crossing itself are like: "I crossed the border every day for years and my parents did it for 40," recalls Aguiñiga. "The best way to describe it is like waiting in the DMV for three to six hours. Every day." The border, and all it means in this political climate, is the source of her art, design, and activism. Aguiñiga's work is not only focused on this particular border, but it is this one that has made her sensitive to borders in all their forms: as physical obstacles, as easily traversed boundaries between one artistic category and another, between activism and the aesthetic.

Aguiñiga is currently based in Los Angeles. She holds a BA from San Diego State University and an MFA in furniture design from Rhode Island School of Design (RISD). In her formative years, she created various collaborative installations with

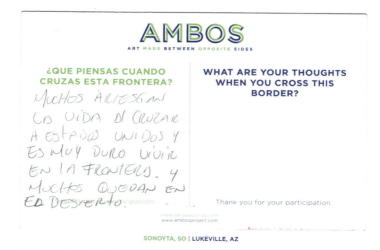

FIGURE 9.1 *Border Quipu/Quipu Fronterizo* (AMBOS Project). Commuter participant postcard. Courtesy of AMBOS Project

the Border Arts Workshop, an artists' group that engages the languages of activism and community-based public art. Her current work uses craft as a performative medium to generate dialogues about identity, culture, and gender while creating community.

Take, for example, the AMBOS Project (Art Made Between Opposite Sides), which was launched in 2016. The project was originally intended to engage car-bound commuters to help illuminate daily life between San Ysidro, California, and Tijuana, Mexico. Since its inception, the project has been expanded to chronicle the barriers and landscape across the entire border between Mexico and the US.

The interactive base of the AMBOS project involves the artist and her team handing out postcards (see Figure 9.1) printed with a bilingual question: "What are your thoughts when you cross this border?"

Yet it is something much more – and much less – than the typical border control interrogations (Figure 9.2). Attached to each card is a colorful string (Figure 9.3). As cards are collected, strings are knotted into the *quipu*, the Inkan knotted cord system of accounting. Thus, the volume and cultural origins of the responses are made visible. I say *origins* because the Inka predate any English-speaking immigrants to the Americas, and given that the US border states were part of Mexico first, one assumes, as Aguiñiga does, the primacy of the quipu as a mathematical tool.

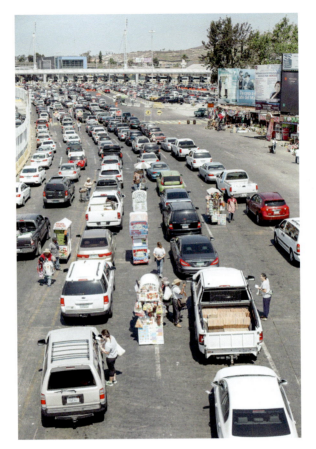

FIGURE 9.2 *Border Quipu/Quipu Fronterizo* (AMBOS Project), 2016. Commuter participation documentation at the San Ysidro Port of Entry. Photograph by Gina Clyne. Courtesy of AMBOS Project

Aguiñiga herself describes the mission and significance of AMBOS as an expression of the emotion connected to the border:

> AMBOS seeks to express and document border emotion through art made on opposite sides by providing a platform to binational artists along the border.
>
> This project was born out of the need to use [Aguiñiga's] skills to address the ongoing issues that her family and community face where she grew up. Aguiñiga was raised in Tijuana, México, where the border fence cuts into the ocean. She crossed the border every day for 14 years to get an education in the US. Additionally, her formative years as an artist were spent as part of the Border Arts Workshop, a community of artists that addressed border

FIGURE 9.3 *Border Quipu/Quipu Fronterizo* (AMBOS Project), 2016. Commuter participation documentation at the San Ysidro Port of Entry. Photograph by Gina Clyne. Courtesy of AMBOS Project

issues. There she helped found a community center in an autonomous land-squat run by indigenous women in the outskirts of Tijuana.

After leaving the Border Arts workshop, Tanya connected with communities in need that were different from her own. She worked with indigenous communities in Chiapas and Oaxaca, native peoples in Alaska and underserved urban communities in Los Angeles. Yet, the experience of growing up as a binational citizen kept coming back to her work. This experience is not unique to her, and she wanted to give a voice to the community that continues to cross daily despite stigma and discrimination. Thus, AMBOS was born.[2]

This description of the AMBOS project, however, hints at only one layer of art that Aguiñiga's work makes visible to viewers. This is not only art but is also a site for mentoring: the project was labor intensive and required her to bring in many Mexican and Mexican–American women to work with her on, for example, handing out and collecting the cards. It served as a way to bring a core team of arts and social justice workers together, and draw a small army of volunteers together, exposing them to an alternative way of looking at things and paying them; some of the women lent their voices to a panel held in conjunction with her 2018 exhibition, *Care & Craft*, at the Museum of Arts and Design in New York City.[3]

The AMBOS project is also political. As Aguiñiga stresses, the work is an act of *re*humanizing the borderlands and those who live there, those who have been *de*humanized: "It is part documentation of the border, part collaboration with artists, part community activism, part exploration of identities influenced by the liminal zone of the borderlands."

And finally, this collaborative border-centered work has had an effect on museums and nonprofits in the United States and Mexico; these institutions have

188 Sheila Pepe

diversified their audiences by connecting marginalized communities through collaboration.

One of the most interesting elements of Aguiñiga's work is the way it explores the borders and tensions between art and craft. When the AMBOS project was exhibited as part of the *Care & Craft* exhibition, it was shown alongside some of the innovative, craft-bending furniture she also designed: before her foray into socially engaged public art, Aguiñiga had been known for furniture, drawing on her early training at RISD. Artists and craftspeople/designers tend to approach the creative process from very different assumptions: to simplify the difference, designers are given a problem or address a standing problem (a ubiquitous utilitarian object) and solve it, while artists come up with their own problems, and then solve them. There's a level of utility in design, and often in craft, that art doesn't have to address. And some might argue that the work has to lose utility to become art. Aguiñiga is sensitive to the places where those differences occur, using each location as necessary. However, she crosses boundaries with little concern. She locates each work through seamless execution of an idea, expanding on each work physically. And in doing so, she continues to expand the kinds of work she makes.

There is, of course, great prestige and market value associated with Art, and Aguiñiga has been successful at making work that sits well within this territory. Despite her additions to her training roots at RISD, her early craft and design practice and the attendant organizational skills made the AMBOS Project not just a critical art success,[4] but also a model enterprise for nothing less than local/international revolution – something that has a vibrant life both in and out of the white box of a gallery.

As Gloria Anzaldua has described it, the US/Mexico border is an open wound:

> The U.S.–Mexican border *es una herida abierta* where the Third World grates against the first and bleeds. And before a scab forms it hemorrhages again, the lifeblood of two worlds merging to form a third country – a border culture. Borders are set up to define the places that are safe and unsafe, to distinguish us from them. A border is a dividing line, a narrow strip along a steep edge. A borderland is a vague and undetermined place created by the emotional residue of an unnatural boundary. It is in a constant state of transition ... The only "legitimate" inhabitants are those in power, the whites and those who align themselves with whites. Tension grips the inhabitants of the borderland like a virus. Ambivalence and unrest reside there and death is no stranger.
>
> *(Anzaldua 1987, 25–26)*

We could think of it as a festering, suppurating slash across a land that was once whole, registering the insult of US border policies as infection and pain. Aguiñiga's work invites us to acknowledge the pain of the wound, and to repopulate the borderland that the US sees as empty with real people who try to carry on their work and lives there every day – people who recognize that there are multiple connections of all kinds that reach across the walls and customs posts. Those connections make the border itself recognizable as a temporary but violent super-imposition on a human landscape that by itself would nurture relationship rather than foreignness.

That image of the festering wound is picked up in Julia Bryan-Wilson's description of Aguiñiga's work as a process of *suturing*: "Aguiñiga's practice argues that while dividing populations and landscapes, this seam [the border] also irrevocably sutures the two countries together." Her work, that is, refuses to accept the border as a permanent reality, refuses the meanings that US policy attaches to it.

Bryan-Wilson also points out the other ways that Aguiñiga connects, joins, and sutures in all her work – in this case, rendering the distinctions between all the different kinds of work she does "porous," and eradicating disciplinary differences between art/craft/performance/community:

> For the artist, furniture is not only tied to familial domesticity, but can suggest or even actively create alternative social relations; she often converts typically hard industrial chairs and tables made of wood or metal into softer, more accommodating fabric structures. A small selection of such work is featured in the show; for instance, in *Felted/Woven Low Rod Chair* (2015), Aguiñiga adds texture, warmth, and a touch of gendered perversion in the form of crotch-shaped woolen embellishments to an iconic Eames mid-century modernist design. In *Support* (2014), a low-lying modular config-uration of sewn denim and leather brick-like units filled with rice and salt can be infinitely rearranged to produce seating, bedding, or, in emergencies, can be split open and eaten.
>
> *(Bryan-Wilson 2018)*

As this suggests, what at first seem to be disparate, unconnected modes of art-making are in fact connected aspects of Aguiñiga's complex yet internally unified vision.

Lorissa Rinehart also draws attention to this significance of Aguiñiga's work, pointing out that "she has become like a loom's shuttle, weaving together either side of a rent land [see Figure 9.4]. The Museum of Arts and Design [exhibit] features the work that results from a lifetime of creating a tapestry from broken threads" (Rinehart 2018).

And so, two sides of the same experience: the fundamental oneness of the land, the pain produced by the unnatural and violent division. The interrogation of those who wish to cross: "Has anyone in your family been convicted of a crime?" and "Have you ever been part of a political or social group?" As Rinehart puts it, the AMBOS Project "is an effort to document and express the emotions and trauma elicited from the repeated act of having one's person searched and identity questioned while crossing national borders."

FIGURE 9.4 *Border Quipu/Quipu Fronterizo* (AMBOS Project), 2016. Installation of quipu on billboard at the San Ysidro Port of Entry market. Photograph by Gina Clyne. Courtesy of AMBOS Project

The rupture and woundedness of the borderland are reproduced in the physical human body in one of Aguiñiga's performance pieces:

> The pain of rupture is also explored in Aguiñiga's performance piece *Grapple*, (2018) documented on video. Wearing a raw linen shirt, Aguiñiga wraps her body around the iron pillars of the border that emerge from the sand at the ocean's edge and stretch beyond the frame of the camera, signaling that even the sky is divided. The tide rolls in and out, the sun sets. Aguiñiga shivers as she continues to cling to the boundary. Displayed alongside the video, the shirt she wears throughout the performance is split in two by a dull orange rust stain, a mark that implies the body that wore it is divided as well.
>
> *(Rinehart 2018)*

Aguiñiga's work on the borderlands – her exploration of the human attempts to redress the artificial dividedness of the border and the pain that effort produces – could not have emerged in a more timely political moment. As we are besieged by images of children in cages, migrants dying in rivers and deserts, ICE arrests – a litany of dehumanization – Aguiñiga's work recalls us to the underlying connectedness that she strives to make visible.

Now, in the time of the pandemic, Aguiñiga's home town of Tijuana is a Covid-19 epicenter: her response has been to make care packages for kids with

International Revolution by Design   191

FIGURE 9.5 *Tension* (AMBOS Project), 2017. Performed by Tanya Aguiniga and Jackie Amezquita at the Douglas, Arizona/Agua Prieta, Sonora in constant view of the US Border Patrol. Photograph by Gina Clyne. Courtesy of AMBOS Project

paper and paints and crayons so that they can draw what they experience. Artist, activist, organizer – she operates on many platforms at once.

Borders are a form of policing public space: the US/Mexican border, for example, defines who can use the space in which way, who can be "legal" in it, and who is marked as unwelcome and without rights. Yet these borderlands have a history: they were a space that has been used very differently in various past periods. A border is presented to us as a thin line, but Aguiñiga pushes us to expand it, to see it not just as a slender tracing on a map but as a fully dimensional place. With the AMBOS Project, she makes visible the traces of the peoples who lived there before. She politicizes our view of the space and fills it with people who are rendered invisible in the current discourse (Figure 9.5). The politics of her work is urgent; in the wake of it she leaves us with the categorical differences (of art, design, and craft) as she pushes us to consider what is at stake in the policing of those boundaries. Her work invites us to consider the occupation of space in all its possible meanings.

Notes

1 US Border Health Commission, www.hhs.gov/about/agencies/oga/about-oga/what-we-do/international-relations-division/americas/border-health-commission/index.html.
2 Aguiñiga, www.tanyaaguiniga.com.
3 "In Conversation: Tanya Aguiñiga and Art Made Between Opposite Sides," Museum of Arts and Design, New York, May 12, 2018. Participating AMBOS members include Jackie Amezquita, Cecilia Brawley, Gina Clyne, Natalie Godinez, Diana Ryoo.
4 See: www.architecturaldigest.com/story/tanya-aguiniga-us-mexico-border-museum-art-and-designandwww.theguardian.com/artanddesign/2018/aug/07/artists-speaking-out-on-us-mexico-border-relations-immigration.

References

Anzaldua, Gloria. 1987. *Borderlands/La Frontera: The New Mestiza*. San Francisco: Aunt Lute Books.
Bryan-Wilson, Julia. 2018. "Tanya Aguiñiga: The textile artist and activist traces the seam between the US and Mexico." *4 Columns,* June 29, 2018. www.4columns.org
Glenday, Craig. 2009. *Guinness World Records 2009*. Random House Digital. Accessed March 9, 2011.
Rinehart, Lorissa. 2018. "Tapestries that Mend the Divides Between Mexico and the US." *Hyperallergic,* September 11, 2018. https://hyperallergic.com/458532/tapestries-that-mend-the-divides-between-mexico-and-the-us

SECTION 3

Activists and Urban Space

The role that activists play in reclaiming public space for use by all is not necessarily as visible as the colorful, dynamic act of creating stunning but ephemeral visual interventions created by artists. The work of documenting activism functions on a different timeline: it requires the painstaking organization of legal and political strategies to allow bodies to be, act, and remain in public space. Susan Fraiman begins this discussion with a consideration of how even the most idealistic of urban protests, Occupy Wall Street, still was unable to perceive its own allegiance to a visible marker of inequality: gender. The very nature of the experiment of Occupy required the creation of public domesticity, and unfortunately produced the same blindness and inequality that marks private domesticity. Marlisa Wise then addresses and expands on Fraiman's investigation by visualizing it: she creates maps that enable viewers to see and experience the hidden labor that sustained Occupy even when Occupy refused to acknowledge or value it. The issue of private living being made public arises again, and on a different scale, with the essay by Maria Foscarinis and Eric Tars, which documents the increasing crackdown by local governments on the homeless. As local governments enact laws and actively enforce them, they chivvy the homeless out of their jurisdictions, trying to make them invisible to the mainstream and thus to deny their needs. Finally, L.A. Kauffman closes the discussion with a thoughtful review of her 35 years as an activist and organizer of public protests: does it still matter, she asks, whether activists do the work of keeping public space open for protest? The answer, a fitting closing to the work of this volume, is a resounding yes.

10

OCCUPYING DOMESTICITY

Reproductive Labor in Zuccotti Park

Susan Fraiman

On September 17, 2011, some 300 people bedded down in the open air of Zuccotti Park. For mattresses, they had pieces of cardboard, for walls the loom of tall buildings, for a roof the light-polluted sky of downtown Manhattan. In the coming weeks, what began as a makeshift campsite would grow to the density and complexity of a small village. Large-scale marches and mass arrests would coincide with sleeping, eating, and cleaning – hundreds of bodies needing daily care, both physically and emotionally. My project in this essay is to consider Occupy Wall Street as a political movement bound up with an experiment in domesticity. For two months, OWS was a reinvention of home with the roof torn off. Situated in a public space, an object of media fascination around the world, Occupy generated riveting images of domestic life deprivatized, collectivized, and shaped by a commitment to social justice. Offering to reorganize "housework" and reconfigure "family," the practices elaborated by OWS resonated with long-standing feminist critiques identifying the kitchen and bedroom as fundamental sites of oppression and resistance.[1] As a feminist scholar intrigued by alternative domesticities, I came to Occupy Wall Street with the following question: in what ways and to what extent did it succeed in remaking domestic life along feminist lines?

In Search of Radical Equality

Building on a three-week occupation by New Yorkers Against Budget Cuts, inspired by the Arab Spring and European Summer, Occupy Wall Street gave the US its own spectacle of dissenting bodies massed in public spaces. Three days after that first night in Zuccotti Park, an occupation in San Francisco began to swell; by October, the nation would be criss-crossed by a network of Occupy encampments. The criticism that occupiers had no specific demands was always disingenuous.

196 Susan Fraiman

The movement was (and still is) transparently an outraged demand for radical inclusion and equity, especially in economic terms. Whether by scrawling on pizza boxes, posting on social media, or occupying a new locale, tens of thousands of OWS supporters rallied behind such basic progressive measures as regulating banks, reining in corporate influence, strengthening unions, paying a living wage, tackling the housing crisis, providing universal healthcare, curbing state violence, and forgiving student debt.

As many have noted, however, OWS was more than a set of demands and blueprint for the future. It was also a real-time model of daily living reimagined from the ground up – an effort to show as well as tell the world what democratic governance and social equality might look like.[2] Most visibly and self-consciously, Occupy Wall Street offered a model of direct democracy and leaderlessness ("horizontality," in movement parlance). At the heart of this model were nightly General Assemblies (GAs), where shoulder-to-shoulder crowds made decisions by consensus about matters large and small. (How to stave off eviction? How much to budget for garbage bags?) Led by rotating facilitators, the GA's reliance on the "human mic" (waves of voices repeating each phrase), their repertoire of hand signals, and their use of the "progressive stack" (giving priority to marginalized voices) made for a process that, however time-consuming, was impressive and moving in its commitment to inclusivity.[3]

If Occupy Wall Street exemplified a collective political process, it also sought to model a society in which – addressing the inequities so glaring and pervasive today – such necessities as medical care, books, and food were freely and equally available to all. Alongside an ever-growing number of working groups – Media, Direct Action, Security, Sanitation, People of Color, among many others – OWS boasted a Medical working group staffed by experienced street medics, a Library working group with a collection topping out at 4,000 volumes, and a Food working group (commonly known as Kitchen) that would come to serve around 1,200 nourishing meals per day, and more on weekends. A number of the working groups had designated locations within the park, effecting divisions in space as well as labor, and together they constituted a highly efficient infrastructure. Working group meetings were also opportunities to practice horizontality. As in GAs, echoing the logic of the progressive stack, more elite members were encouraged to "step up/step back," the better to hear less privileged voices. In recognition of those with trans or nonbinary gender identities, meetings typically began with "pronoun rounds."[4] While the movement's public critique was directed primarily at Wall Street and other root causes of class inequality, the rituals and protocols within Zuccotti Park also took aim at daily habits of domination based on race, sexuality, and gender.

Needless to say, where gender is concerned, these habits involve not only a binary view of male and female but also a hierarchical one. Placing men over women, its further effect is to subordinate a host of categories and qualities perceived to be "feminine." In the pages to come, I will consider the internal politics of OWS with an eye to its success at challenging this particular hierarchy, keeping in mind that gender always interacts with multiple other identity categories.[5] My feminist perspective on Occupy Wall Street is not without precedent. Comments on the movement's gender politics emerged almost immediately from within its own ranks. On October 11, Angi Becker Stevens wrote a piece for the *Ms. Blog* calling on women to join OWS, while also urging some benighted occupiers to recognize gender concerns as intrinsic to – rather than a distraction from – its campaign for economic justice (Stevens 2011). On October 15, a blog by CodePink coordinator Melanie Butler noted that the voices of female occupiers were vastly underrepresented in the media, adding that women were also having trouble speaking up at GAs. She went on to report that a Safer Spaces working group had been formed to address the issue of sexual harassment (Butler 2011, 71–75). Just days earlier, Ashwini Hardikar had blogged about confronting an obtuse male protester over his unwelcome "hug" (Hardikar 2011).

On the one-month anniversary of OWS, Stephanie Rogers of *Bitch Flicks* described similar feelings of solidarity mixed with disappointment. Likening Occupy's emphasis on dialogue to Second Wave consciousness-raising, she praised the movement for trying to call out white male privilege, despite its uneven success in doing so. But Rogers also shared her disgust at a popular video posted on Facebook by the OWS administrator. Riddled with misogyny, the video's stab at humor included ridiculing mothers with strollers as enemies of the revolution.[6] The piece closed by citing Stevens, underlining her point that women, especially women of color, cluster at the bottom of the 99%. Toward the end of October, Sarah Seltzer's article for *The Nation* asserted the centrality of OWS women and their demands. To illustrate the progressive stack and other anti-oppression measures, Seltzer told of two South Asian women objecting to a GA resolution on the grounds that it glossed over racism. Overcoming their nervousness, Hena Ashraf and Manissa Maharawal addressed the crowd and succeeded in blocking it. It was Seltzer's sense that women in OWS were speaking out, and her view of sexual harassment in the movement was likewise cautiously upbeat, emphasizing the feminist response to incidents like that reported by Hardikar.[7]

Four years after the birth of Occupy, sociologist Heather McKee Hurwitz completed a doctoral dissertation entitled "The 51%: Gender, Feminism, and Culture in the Occupy Wall Street Movement." Based on participant-observer research at multiple sites and interviews with 73 participants, it was the first full-length study of the movement's gender politics. Like the activist and journalistic accounts cited above, the study gave Occupy mixed marks. On the one hand, OWS endorsed and inspired feminist tactics; on the other, many of these tactics were a response to sexism within the movement. While touching on the gendered division of domestic labor, Hurwitz focused primarily on evidence of women's subjection to sexual harassment and men's de facto predominance in leadership roles, topics on which she would proceed to elaborate in two articles drawn from the dissertation (Hurwitz and Taylor 2018; Hurwitz 2019).

198 Susan Fraiman

I take my cue from all of the above-mentioned sources and am especially grateful for Hurwitz's in-depth sociological research. Drawing on her analysis, I will begin by offering some further thoughts about gender and leadership in a "leaderless" movement. The context for these is my own central concern with the organization, working conditions, and status of domestic labor. Based on interviews with seven full-time members of the Kitchen working group (see note 3), my remarks will probe the experiences of female leaders in preparing and serving food for OWS. Comments by Kitchen members are the basis for observations not only about the subgroup's internal workings but also about the status of Kitchen relative to other working groups and OWS as a whole. The last section of my essay will branch off from kitchen work to explore another significant category of domestic labor: childcare in particular and emotional/physical care work more generally.

Before I turn to these topics, a few words about my theoretical orientation and methodological approach. This essay builds on my recent book examining unorthodox and precarious versions of home, including the domestic practices of those lacking secure shelter. My goals in that project were several. First, I wanted to sever domesticity from a necessary tie to conservative values. Second, in keeping with the views of Silvia Federici and other Marxist feminists, I wanted to make housework – the unpaid or underpaid labor long shouldered primarily by women – visible *as work*.[8] Third, I wanted to appreciate the competencies and modes of knowledge involved in cooking, cleaning, and care work. Fourth, I wanted to denaturalize these activities as women's work and urge their equal distribution between women and men. Finally, I wanted to question the coding and stigmatizing of domestic labor as "feminine" and low in status, whether performed by males or females. All of these notions will come into play in my analysis of Occupy Wall Street.

As a cultural critic trained in literary studies, I take a qualitative approach, with the goal of capturing tensions and ambiguities while also indicating what appear to be consistent patterns. The interviews I conducted were informal but rich in impressions and mutually informing. While few in number, my participants represented a significant proportion of those at the core of New York Kitchen operations for the greater part of two months. Supplementing information gleaned from textual sources, their comments enabled me to make some connections and draw some conclusions with a reasonable degree of confidence.

While the rhetoric, rituals, and landscape of daily life in Zuccotti Park have all been documented at some length, little attention has been paid to the organization of its reproductive labor. Even feminist critics, while shedding valuable light on the issues of governance and safety, have not paused long over such matters as planning meals, chopping vegetables, washing dishes, or holding hands. Turning my attention to these conventionally female activities, I will be fleshing out the following broad observations. Breaking with tradition (and with the practices of many a progressive movement), food preparation within OWS fell to men as well as women.[9] It was also apparently the case that, among the men and women in the Kitchen working group, female leaders predominated. At the same time, as in conventional domestic settings, the labor performed by Kitchen, though grueling and relentless in the extreme, was scarcely acknowledged by those being fed. Lastly, it appears that the bulk of OWS care work – by which I mean the physical and emotional labor of caring for other people regardless of their age – more often fell to women. As with food preparation, much of this work took place outside Zuccotti Park and was, if anything, even less acknowledged as an aspect of OWS domestic life. The relative invisibility of both kitchen and care work has been, as I've mentioned, replicated at the level of commentary on the movement. One goal of this essay is to counter that invisibility by naming and giving credit to seven activists from the Kitchen working group – Anj, Marlisa, Joshua, Amy, Heather, Benedict, and Samantha – whose competence, creativity, and tireless labor fueled the Occupation.[10]

The Status of Female Leaders in Kitchen

As we have seen, OWS took numerous steps to institutionalize horizontality and foster equality among its participants. Seltzer quotes longtime activist Jackie DiSalvo on the "macho leadership" and "aggressive sectarian fighting" she witnessed in the 1960s. The less sexist climate of OWS may be due in part, DiSalvo suggested, to the intervening women's movement. Yet even within a "leaderless" movement, some are inevitably more visible and influential than others.[11] To what extent, we might ask, did the reality of leadership within OWS align with its egalitarian ideals? How, moreover, did the ethic of "leaderlessness" affect those who emerged as de facto leaders? Accounts by observers and participants suggest that women did play leading roles both at GAs and in working groups. Yet some women struggled with self-doubt as well as external resistance when attempting to lead (see narratives by Ashraf and Maharawal), and others were thwarted in their efforts to do so.

Seltzer reported that women were well represented and no less vocal than men in the working groups she visited. Yet willingness to lead is not always enough. Hurwitz's research highlights the part played by followers in validating or disavowing leaders. In social movements as in business settings, she explains, women must win over followers by seeming strong enough to lead, but also "nice" enough to pass as properly feminine. In addition to facing this familiar "double bind," women leading public meetings may be undercut by male followers who compete with, harass, or intimidate them – whether directly or by dramatizing their power over women in the audience. Studying these dynamics within OWS, Hurwitz found numerous cases in which "followers opposed women and genderqueer persons' leadership and rewarded men's leadership."[12]

The occupiers I spoke to expressed a range of views on this issue. Marlisa felt that outsiders overstated the degree to which OWS women were silenced and harassed. In keeping with this view, Sam described a number of women who were "really strong" and readily identifiable as leaders. There were definitely, she said,

200 Susan Fraiman

some "exceptional women who had a lot of respect and could speak." But she went on to characterize the OWS leadership overall as "heavily male from my point of view," perhaps in part because men outnumbered women in the park. The gender dynamics of leadership also varied depending on the specific context. At the working group level, women's ability to lead seems to have differed from group to group. By all accounts, Media was dominated by tech-oriented white males who were, on the whole, highly educated and well resourced.[13] As Marlisa noted, Media was marked by its class as well as gender privilege. In addition to Media, my interviewees named Facilitation, Security, and Sanitation as conspicuously male-dominated.[14] Sam also singled out the "male mentality" of Infrastructure. She recalled showing up in her van with a load of donated pallets: "The men were, like, wait, who are you? We can handle this. And they just kind of took – and I was like, *it's my van.*"

In Sam's experience, "Kitchen was much easier to deal with." In contrast to other working groups, in Kitchen she felt empowered to make business decisions and apply her years of managerial experience to coordinating meal production on a massive scale. The other interviewees were in agreement that, within Kitchen, female leadership was recognized and generally respected. All five of the women identified themselves and were spoken of by the others as leaders. Women led, moreover, in a group that had, to my initial surprise, a gender split of approximately 50/50. Such a ratio seemed, in and of itself, to suggest a more equitable sharing of kitchen work. As I soon realized, however, with food production dramatically scaled up, the OWS model was less the family home than the commercial kitchen. Many of the Kitchen volunteers had experience in professional food service, an area in which not just male presence but male leadership is the rule.[15] But if the simple participation of men in Kitchen turned out to be neither surprising nor necessarily progressive, the predominance of women at the helm of such a mixed and monumental operation was both. Overseeing a fluid staff of male and female volunteers; securing off-site kitchen facilities; coordinating with donors, wholesalers, organic farmers, cooks, and drivers; budgeting for, planning, and producing thousands of vegetarian meals and ferrying them to the park several times a day; serving and washing up and serving again – all this on little sleep in unstable, makeshift, and partly outdoor conditions, surrounded by armed police and with the world watching – the indefatigable women who led Kitchen defied the gender norms of home and restaurant alike.[16]

It is clear they were able to do so in part because of the movement's strong, explicit commitment to step up/step back. Though Joshua was referred to by others as a leader, both he and Benedict were very aware of and concerned to check their cis male privilege. Joshua described being grateful for critical feedback: "It's always good to have yourself caught in a check. I mean, I did try to work on the ego." While all the occupiers I spoke to were hesitant about generalizing or appearing to speak for others, Joshua struck me as especially so. Asked about whether the overall tenor of OWS was feminist, he wondered if he was qualified to answer: "Moving through this world as a man, I'm just not even aware of all the micro-oppressions that I wouldn't experience on a day-to-day basis." Benedict was similarly committed to acknowledging and resisting the gender status quo. Despite credentials suggesting a fit with Media, he had chosen for that very reason to go against the grain by getting involved with Kitchen.[17]

While men made an effort to step back, women did indeed step up to lead. According to Anj, leadership in Kitchen was based primarily on "who had been there the longest, or who had been spending the most consecutive hours there, because then you had a better grasp of what was going on." As one of the earliest volunteers, Anj held what she described as "a slight leadership position for a little while." In fact, along with Amy, Anj was responsible for establishing the Kitchen site in Zuccotti Park. Since the actual cooking was done elsewhere, the park site served as "donation hub" and "food distribution zone." As Anj explained, given the "constant struggle to stay on top of feeding everyone," working there meant being confined to a "ten by 15 area that I just didn't leave for some weeks basically." Yet despite the stressful conditions, Anj appreciated being recognized as a leader. In her early twenties at the time, she was surprised and pleased to find that men looked to her for direction: "They would come up and say, hey, what can I do, can I wash dishes, can I take the trash out, like, where can I go, what can I do. That felt really cool as a young woman, that felt good." As for sexual harassment, Anj found Kitchen "a pretty safe working environment." Overall, the men she encountered weren't predatory, nor did they assume that women need special protection. Anj recalled occupiers marching in the streets "almost like soldiers. It was men and women on an equal footing, and women got arrested and pepper sprayed just as much."

If Anj's account of leadership was largely positive, the other women I spoke to had more complicated feelings about their time with Kitchen. Certainly all were effective leaders and proud of what they had achieved in two short months: improvising from scratch one of the largest soup kitchens in the country. (The quality of meals was so healthful and high, it was mocked by the media; in the greatest of ironies, even one percenters and police were known to take advantage.) Yet as Amy summed up this period in her life, "It was a very traumatic time and it was an incredible time." Based on my analysis of both oral and written accounts, I suggest that one source of trauma was a version of the "double bind" documented by Hurwitz.

Heather, for example, ran up against classic resistance to and demonizing of female authority. With many years of professional restaurant experience, Heather immediately saw the need for a sanitary commercial kitchen, for cold and dry storage, for the ability to rotate and inventory food. Unlike my other interviewees, she was trained in food safety procedures and acutely aware of their importance. As she emphasized to me, "Food safety was probably the thing I was most concerned with. Knowing the conditions of the park, if we didn't take it seriously, we could potentially poison thousands of people." Despite her clear expertise, Heather's efforts to implement basic sanitation measures and to ensure that necessary tasks were done (if only by doing them herself when others slacked off), prompted complaints that she was "bossy." By no coincidence, the same structure of feeling crops up in Michael Taussig's "exuberant" participant-observer account of OWS. As we read of his intoxication by the "strange" magic of the Occupation, we suddenly encounter something not strange at all: his derisive description of a woman who dares to address the crowd. Replicating the effects of the human mic – "Hello Hello I am the sanitation group I am the sanitation group" – Taussig sees fit to add, "Her voice is shrill, authoritative, nagging."[18] What strikes me here is how the misogynist descriptors "shrill" and "nagging" surround "authoritative," as if to contain the woman who would lead. Evidently, even in such a radical, self-conscious context as OWS, women may still be policed by language ("bossy," "shrill," "nagging") that attacks them personally and serves to vilify their leadership.

According to the logic of the double bind, the other option for female leaders is to finesse their authority and play to gender expectations. In that case, though approved as "likeable," they are apt to be disregarded as leaders. Amy had no interest in being properly feminine. Having just read Deepak Chopra's *The Soul of Leadership*, she saw herself as ready and qualified to lead. Inspired by Chopra, however, Amy was committed to leading through empathy rather than domination. Her goal, she explained, was to create a "community of care" by "listening to people, making them feel like part of the group." But while Amy focused on hearing others, she herself was left feeling unheard. As she told me, "I felt like I was doing all the work and then there was a way that the decision-making power was kind of … that my voice wasn't as loud and that it wasn't that respected." Amy's principled example of alternative leadership seems to have been, at least by some, mistaken for and collapsed back into conventional femininity, thereby diminishing her voice – such is the co-opting power of gender stereotypes.

Disparaged as "masculine" or ignored as "feminine," female leaders everywhere must deal with this double bind. In the context of OWS, women faced the additional dilemma of reconciling their leadership with the emphatically "leaderless" ethic of the Occupy movement. For Amy this compounded her sense of being "disempowered and disrespected." As she put it, "You were leading but you can't say you are leading. I was putting in so much energy and so much care, but there is almost this shame around taking credit for it." (Recall Anj's self-diminishing reference to her *slight* leadership for a *little* while.) Urging women to "step up" while enforcing a general ethic of "stepping back," OWS was effectively telling women to lead and shaming them for doing so. As my conversation with Benedict helped me to realize, the OWS taboo against leading played out asymmetrically. As he pointed out, it was genuinely subversive for white males to find, perhaps for the first time, that taking charge was shameful. For women, on the other hand, the mandate to *not lead* coincided with and reinforced their schooling in deferential femininity. If members of the dominant group were chastened, for anyone already burdened by shame at leading, Occupy Wall Street doubled the dose.

I will be returning in my next section to the issue of Kitchen not getting credit. First, however, I am struck by the fact that both Heather and Amy, in describing their vexed leadership, invoked the figure of the mother. Heather did so when speaking of volunteers resistant to instruction in safe, large-quantity cooking:

> They resented me, telling them what to do. They were there to contribute and do something, but it was only on their terms, and that made me feel like such a mom. Like a mom with teenagers, you know what I mean?

Amy, by contrast, identified positively with the role of nurturing mother. Indeed, she saw her position in Kitchen as "being everybody's mother," adding, "I think the boys in Kitchen felt like I was their mother too in a way." As we have seen, however, as an effect of persistent gender norms, Amy's "maternal" style of leadership seems to have landed her back in the role of the endlessly self-sacrificing woman. In Amy's words, she found it hard "to say no and to have boundaries," and the result was getting utterly burned out. Looking back, she felt that Kitchen as a whole suffered from always giving people what they wanted, "trying to always accommodate." And if Kitchen gave and gave to the point of exhaustion, others took for granted and benefitted from their willingness to do so. As Amy explained, "We tried to put up boundaries and to, like, take care of ourselves, and there was a backlash."

It makes sense that both Heather and Amy would liken themselves to mothers, since our culture offers few other images of female authority. Yet given our distorted view of them, mothers make for problematic role models: if our teenaged selves resent their control, our infantile selves expect unconditional catering to our needs. True that the raised consciousness of OWS put men in the kitchen while also voicing support for female leadership. True as well that gender relations within Kitchen itself were pretty equitable. But while Occupy's communal social structures might have seemed a far cry from the nuclear family, the problematic experiences of women in Kitchen suggest that at least some traditional dynamics continued to hold sway.

The Status of Kitchen in Occupy Wall Street

The OWS Kitchen, I was soon to learn, had its life in multiple spaces spread out across the city, including the vehicles (like those driven by Sam and Benedict) carrying people and food between them. For most occupiers, however, Kitchen was the site at the center of Zuccotti Park where people lined up by the hundreds to fill their plates with vegetarian fare. Although the actual "hearth" was elsewhere, it is clear that this location in the park was central to OWS in a symbolic as well as literal sense. For Anj, who grew up in a large, conservative family, the evident importance of Kitchen was a welcome change. While her mother "worked 18 hours a day in the home" with little recognition or appreciation, Anj found that

204 Susan Fraiman

"people were mostly extremely grateful" for meals served in the park. Joshua, too, described Kitchen as "the heart of the park." If and when an eviction began, "people were going to circle around the kitchen," he told me. As it turned out, when police in riot gear stormed Zuccotti Park on November 15, 2011, Heather and Sam decided to dig in and were among the very last arrested. In Sam's words, "Kitchen was the hold-out."

Occupying Wall Street: The Inside Story ends its discussion of Kitchen, centered on Heather, by describing her arrest. She and others who spent the occupation "cooking, serving, and washing dishes, then cooking, serving, and washing some more" were, it concludes, "heroes of the kitchen" (Writers for the 99% 2012, 72). This congratulatory account does a good job of giving Heather's perspective on such behind-the-scenes Kitchen achievements as its collaboration with upstate organic farmers. By contrast, this volume's closing chapter, "Day in the Life of the Square," bears out the complaint voiced by my interviewees that not everyone recognized the existence, much less credited the heroism, of the movement's most overworked members.[19] It offers support as well for Amy's wry observation that, all too often, men did the *talking*, while women did the *work*. Taking us from morning to night, the narrative opens with a view of coordinators from various working groups who "delivered reports on ongoing initiatives, discussed proposals, and brainstormed solutions" (197). It goes on to introduce a cast of characters, including Dan who staffs the Information Desk and Bill who oversees the Library. There's also Dicey Troop, the GA Twitter reporter who participates in Direct Action, Facilitation, and Structure. Hermes spends his days handing out leaflets and speaking with passersby. Rich works Security. Patricia of Direct Action is the only woman who warrants a mention.

Meanwhile, throughout the day, meals appear as if by magic. The mind-boggling logistics, professional expertise, and nonstop labor described by my interviewees is nowhere to be found. Indeed, until the last three weeks, occupiers are said to rely largely on donations from local restaurants supplemented by "food from OWS supporters who had, on their own initiative, prepared dishes in their homes." In this breezy account, "Lunch, like breakfast, was a free-form affair, with volunteers whisking vegetarian food on trays around the camp to members of working groups." Information Dan sometimes "availed himself of this service" (198). Dinner, we are told, was normally served at 6pm. But on November 8, there was a glitch: "6pm had passed, the food the kitchen had been expecting had not arrived yet (no one knew why), and occupiers waiting in the food line were growing impatient" (200). I'm guessing that at least some Kitchen workers knew exactly why dinner was delayed, but our narrative pivots at this point from the line of "testy" diners to Security worker Rich, who posted himself "at the entrance to the kitchen, where he felt he needed to be if he was to prevent anyone unauthorized from entering. However, this meant he could not avoid also obstructing kitchen volunteers." As reported here, Rich refused to budge, resulting in a "tense standoff" with "an anonymous kitchen worker" (200). Moving on, we hear of Dicey Troop tweeting about the nightly GA, after which he might join a discussion at a local spot where, in his words, "the real work gets done." Finally, "On many nights, an OWS supporter came around at 11pm with vegan food for anyone who wanted it" (201).

I cite this narrative at length because its angle on OWS illustrates so well the centrality of the "People's Kitchen" coexisting with the anonymity of Kitchen workers and the failure to register their labor as "real work." There are, I would say, several reasons for this failure. One is that the actual OWS kitchen – where crates of raw materials came under the knife of industrious prep workers led by experienced chefs – was literally miles away (sometimes at multiple locations). As Anj pointed out, the space in Zuccotti Park was less kitchen than cafeteria, "distribution zone" for meals produced elsewhere. If the kitchen is always a kind of backstage, the spatial arrangements of OWS placed it still further out of sight. Other factors, however, are less peculiar to Occupy. As feminists have long argued, the unpaid or poorly paid status of women's housework is both cause and effect of its invisibility as labor. Within traditional families, the mother's care for the bodies of others is seen not as work but as a natural, effortless expression of her love. At least some of this sentiment seems to have carried over to OWS. Having first visited the park with her son, Sam was directed to Kitchen, as if it were the obvious place for an activist mom. Heather's experience was also telling. The message from other occupiers seemed to be: "You're here because you love cooking. So your labor doesn't really count. You get to do the fun cooking thing while the rest of us are busy, you know, talking about what we're going to occupy next." "Day in the Life of the Square" paints a similar picture of meal production as non-work: cooks acting "on their own initiative," meals as "free-form," and light-footed volunteers "whisking" around apparently weightless trays.

The language of "Day in the Life" points further to a view of OWS cooks as mere "supporters" of the occupation rather than core participants in their own right. Even the person serving vegan food at 11pm is deemed "an OWS supporter," while those being fed or gabbing at a café are presumably the real thing. The same narrative tells of unnamed lunch workers providing a "service" to knowledge workers like "Dan." Stressing the relevance of class as well as gender biases, Marlisa felt there was indeed "sometimes an attitude from other working groups that Kitchen was there to serve." Assumed to require no particular credentials and always in need of more hands, Kitchen's bar for entry was low. As Marlisa explained, while college kids with laptops self-selected into groups doing "intellectual" work, occupiers with backgrounds in food service tended to slot themselves or were slotted by others into Kitchen, with the effect of replicating normative class hierarchies.

As I have noted, the Kitchen working group was split quite evenly between men and women. Even so, my research suggests that OWS kitchen duty did not escape being subtly feminized as somehow less serious, less demanding, and less valuable than the "real" work of planning actions and communicating with the public. Like the conventional mother, Kitchen's role was construed as helping others to achieve their goals, as being supportive rather than central, handmaid to the movement proper. Performing the low-status "maternal" work of nurturing was one reason Kitchen had less cachet than the talky, public-facing working groups. Its low rank was informed as well by the (actual and stereotypical) association of food service not only with women but also with working-class people, people of color, and immigrants. Describing to me the tacit hierarchy among working groups, Benedict spoke of some occupiers who initially "landed in Kitchen and then sort of graduated to roles that, within the movement, could be seen as more glamorous."

The effects of Kitchen's subordinate position within OWS were significant, and not unlike those felt by subordinate groups in the "outside world." The experiences described by my interviewees suggest, among other things, that their political voice was muted, their competence discredited, and their need for resources ignored. "Kitchen people weren't the cool ones," Sam commented. "People would forget to inform us of things." Yet because the GA coincided with dinner, Kitchen was, by definition, unable to get information directly or share in the general discussion. Benedict spelled out the ironic result: "Because our labor was required for the reproduction of the camp, we couldn't participate in the deliberative democracy." There was, however, a memorable occasion on which Marlisa and Heather attended a GA on behalf of Kitchen. As Marlisa explained, weary of relying on a "crazy assortment of apartment kitchens," they went seeking money for a proper commercial space. The answer was a flat refusal of funds that felt like a slap in the face. Denying the scale and complexity of Kitchen operations, the assembly also discounted the women's knowledge of what was needed. "We were shut down in a way that was really frustrating for us," Marlisa told me. "Both of us got kind of burned by the experience."

If Kitchen was disenfranchised politically, it was also abused as a workforce. The difficulty of its job and enormity of its achievement was, as we have seen, continually underestimated. As the occupation grew in size, Kitchen struggled to keep up with a punishing pace and workload that were rapidly becoming unbearable. Between people clamoring and produce threatening to spoil, Kitchen workers never had a day off or even a moment's rest; in between meals they would be prepping for the next one. All occupiers were committed to putting their bodies on the line, but for those in Kitchen the cost to physical and mental health seems to have been especially high. Joshua described Kitchen as "working in emergency mode. It was almost like we were trying to deal with trauma." Heather recalled "being at meetings and crying. Towards the end, I was so burned out."[20] At one point she actually collapsed and was rushed to the ER. Marlisa described "people working 12 to 16 hours a day every day. We were feeling unsupported, under-resourced, and yelled at a lot." The problem, she recalled, was that "we were stretched so thin, and it was just exhausting. We were spread out around the city and we couldn't be in the same place to have a conversation about how to fix

Occupying Domesticity **207**

things." By the end of October, things had reached a breaking point. Feeling desperate, Kitchen made the decision to "simplify" meals for a few days, serving just peanut butter and jelly. The idea was a short "retreat" to talk about scaling up in a way that would be sustainable. The truth was they simply couldn't go on.

The nature of domestic work is to be most visible when left undone – when a child is left crying or the dishes go unwashed.[21] With the brief absence of hot meals, Kitchen's contribution, previously taken for granted, was suddenly thrown into high relief. The response from other occupiers was not, however, appreciation or understanding but, on the contrary, an outpouring of righteous anger. Benedict told of a guy named Haywood, a union organizer and member of Finance, who stood up at a meeting shouting, "You're fucking with people's food. You're fucking with my food!" Nor did he stop at that. Heather took up the story there, reporting that Haywood actually proceeded to organize a protest against Kitchen. Inverting the real power relations at stake, he led a march to confront Kitchen in the manner of beleaguered workers "marching on the boss" – only here it was effectively the "boss" marching on beleaguered workers. Hearing about this sequence of events, what appalled me the most was the way a language of class resistance was mobilized to attack an exhausted workforce and to disguise the transparently gendered source of Haywood's rage: his masculine sense of entitlement (apparently shared by other marchers) to have his dinner on demand.[22] Benedict had some advice for him, which I thought was well taken: "If you care about it, you know, step out of the Finance office and cook some food for yourself."

Caring for the Revolution

There's an anecdote in *Occupying Wall Street: The Inside Story of an Action that Changed America* that caught my eye for a couple of reasons. It comes at the end of reporting on an OWS solidarity protest held in Times Square on October 15. The diverse crowd included students, workers, those with and without jobs, "undead" protesters in town for a zombie convention, and families with children. About 80 people were arrested that day. A mother and her young daughters, regular visitors to Zuccotti Park, were nearly among them, but ducked out just as police nets were dropping. The narrative concludes on a light note: for most families, however, the "protest ended with nothing more dramatic than hunger" – witness the five-year-old chanting at his parents, "The people! United! Will now have dinner!" (Writers for the 99% 2012, 142–143).

This story interests and amuses me for several reasons. For one thing, the child's demand, fitting primal hunger and infantile entitlement to the rhythms of protest, can't help but recall hungry Haywood and his march against Kitchen. To me, the anecdote exposes the underlying emotional drama of that high-minded protest: a child crying out to a maternal figure ("You're fucking with my food!"). (Come to think of it, my own first protest was an elementary school "strike" over the lunch menu.) As I have suggested, the inevitable association of Kitchen with the parent

208 Susan Fraiman

who fed you as a child – a person likely for cultural reasons to have been female – helps to explain both why its work was commonly taken for granted and why the "retreat" evoked such panic and fury. As Seltzer put it, citing the views of occupier Suzahn Ebrahimian, those OWS groups handling "feminine" care work got "more complaints than they deserve, due, she thinks, to stealth sexism" (Seltzer 2011). In psychological terms, echoing normative family dynamics, the women and men of Kitchen collapsing from exhaustion were simply being bad mothers.

Another reason I invoke the chanting boy and almost-netted girls is that they are among the very few children to appear in accounts of Occupy Wall Street. Even here, they are mentioned alongside zombies as evidence of an unusually colorful crowd. Elsewhere in this volume, again suggesting their rarity, children and parents are described as "unexpected visitors to Zuccotti and its sister encampments nation-wide." There were, in fact, at least a few encampments that expected and provided for the presence of children. One mother proudly reported that, after consider-able debate, Occupy Dallas had established an "Occuplay" child center. Occupy Oakland – more inclusive than most in terms of race, ability, and age – actually had a free school as well as a designated children's area.[23] These provisions seem, however, to have been the exception. As far as Zuccotti Park was concerned, those parents who chose to bring children (like the mother referenced above) were pretty much on their own. Anj observed that the 2016 Standing Rock Protest Camp had organized childcare. By contrast, she said, in Zuccotti Park, "it was like, yeah, you can bring your kids here but you better keep an eye on them." Others noted that the park, under siege as it was by police, was seen as unsafe for children. Heather pointed to the absence of toilets as an added factor and agreed that the movement in general was geared to the "young, able-bodied, and childless."

Among feminist organizers, providing childcare is axiomatic – understood as essential to the full participation of women with children, especially those who are single mothers. Given Occupy's commitment to equity, I expected there to be an OWS working group devoted to childcare and was therefore surprised at how little attention seems to have been paid to this issue. It appears that childcare was not a felt need among those in the park. Perhaps, however, in the absence of childcare, this reflected a demographic already skewed toward non-parents. And if conditions in the park were not ideal for young kids, all the more reason, in my opinion, for the movement to have established childcare off-site. To me the neglect of this issue, as with the low status of Kitchen, has everything to do with continuing assumptions about labor marked as "maternal." Naturalized and individualized as a female responsibility, the tending of children is work that is crucial but rarely credited, all around us but easily overlooked, at the core of our personal histories and homes, yet displaced from the stage of public life. In the context of Occupy Wall Street, the failure to make childcare a priority – to reinvent it, in keeping with its egalitarian vision, as accessible, collective, and gender-neutral – marked a political blind spot. The result was to prevent or limit the equal involvement of many parents, especially those who happened to be women.[24]

Occupiers with childcare needs were thus on their own to figure something out. Hoping to find someone who had done so, I was told to get in touch with Sam, who had quickly assumed a leadership role in Kitchen despite being a single parent. Asked how she had managed, Sam's first reaction was to exclaim, "When you sent me that email I was, like, holy moly! That's the first time anybody's ever asked me how I did it with a child!" Readers will recall Sam's proprietary relation to a certain loaded van. Dubbed "Kitchen Sam," she told me her actual role was navigating the streets of New York, ferrying food in the white cargo van she had found for 600 bucks. Seeing Kitchen's need not only for a vehicle but for access to food at wholesale prices, she had gotten a restaurant friend to hook them up. Busy driving and coordinating by day, most nights she went home to tuck in her son and see him off to school the next morning. It helped that Aidan was 12 at the time and starting to be more independent. Sam's other secret was a large support team consisting of her mother, her sister, her roommate, and assorted friends. "I'm lucky," she explained, "I have really solid girlfriends that helped me with him." Even so, much depended on Aidan's age. "If he would have been younger," she told me, "I would not have been able to do it." Among OWS parents, Sam was clearly exceptional in the intensity of her participation. As she recalled, "Nobody was full-time in OWS with a child. People would come on the weekends with their kids to walk through the park, but nobody was full-time with children because there was no childcare."

Sam's story is revealing as to how, where, and by whom the labor of OWS childcare was handled. In the absence of formal structures, activist parents relied on the largely invisible, informal, off-site labor of people like Sam's "really solid girlfriends." Before concluding this essay, I want to glance at a related form of care work that was similarly dispersed in space and easily forgotten: the work of "reproducing" weary activists by offering them shelter, showers, and emotional support. Like cooking and childcare, the comforting of other adults is another example of maternalized labor, typically though not necessarily performed by women. It seems, indeed, that the majority of trained street medics and social workers who responded to conspicuous freak-outs and disputes in Zuccotti Park were male. At the same time, it was apparently female occupiers, like women in general, who took the lead in meeting the emotional needs of others on an everyday basis.

While some of this affective labor presumably happened on park benches, under tarps, and in police stations, Sam's experience points once again to the role played by off-site domestic spaces. As she put it, the word among occupiers was "if you're cold one night and you need a break, you go to Sam's house. If you're sick you go to Sam's house. I literally had floor-to-floor bodies sleeping in the apartment because they wanted to have some comfort." The fact that Sam had a child and that so many occupiers were of college-age heightened what was already a mother-child dynamic. And while Sam's door was always open, her complaint was a mother's complaint: the "kids" treated her place "like a hotel and just kind of took it for granted." They flocked to her house when needing some care, but

210 Susan Fraiman

did not help with cleaning, could not do laundry, and were not good at saying thank you. Like a parent, the care Sam provided was psychological as well as physical. She told me her place felt "like a therapist's office and I'd have to listen to all this stuff. So it was emotionally exhausting for me." Eventually Sam's care work extended beyond occupiers to their worried parents. Surrogate mother to their children, she ended up "mothering" the parents in turn – reassuring them, when they phoned in a panic, that she was keeping an eye out. Even the emotional end game resonated with the maternal. As Sam lamented, the kids bonded a bit, got what they needed, and returned to the park. Years later, she still has friends from Kitchen, but it saddens her a little that the floor-to-floor kids did not bother to stay in touch.[25]

The Occupy Wall Street "Principles of Solidarity," approved by a consensus of the GA on September 23, 2011, included the goals of "Empowering one another against all forms of oppression" and "Redefining how labor is valued." (Writers for the 99% 2012, 22). My concern in this essay has been to ask the following questions: to what extent did Occupy Wall Street succeed in redefining how domestic labor is valued? To what extent did it counter the oppression of domestic workers on the basis of both gender and class? We recall that OWS set out not only to demand a more equal society but also to model one. In the day-to-day life of the camp, everyone would be heard, everyone would be fed, hierarchies would be leveled, and even leadership would be evenly distributed. Taking a page from the women's movement, OWS addressed both the global flow of capital and the politics of everyday life – the way structures of domination and subordination are manifest in who gets to speak, whose body feels vulnerable, whose identity is validated, whose authority and competence are credited. And if part of the goal is to reorganize the social relations lived by occupiers, then reproductive labor is no longer just the means to a higher end. Instead of supporting the "real work" of political protest, cooking and caring are themselves political projects – sites where the revolution can be won or lost.

Did OWS succeed in occupying domesticity? Echoing the feminist commentators before me, my answer is yes and no. As we have seen, Kitchen's 50/50 gender split, however varied the reasons behind it, represented a significant improvement over past progressive movements in which, for the most part, cooking fell to women. Stepping back from fronting the movement, men like Benedict and Joshua also consciously stepped into the less glamorous role of Kitchen worker. Just as encouraging, despite the large cohort of men, it was women like Anj, Marlisa, Amy, Heather, and Sam who predominated as Kitchen leaders. Generally, though not uniformly, their leadership was well respected, especially by those within the group. Overall, Kitchen's internal gender politics were seen as positive – all the more so in comparison to male-dominated areas like Media and Infrastructure. At the same time, both Heather and Amy reported some frustration with responses to their leadership. These responses, I have suggested, bespeak our readiness as a culture to conflate authoritative women with authoritative mothers – figures we regard with deep-seated ambivalence. This conflation is all the more likely when the kind of work overseen already has a maternal cast.

From a feminist perspective, the most negative finding of my research was the lack of equality among OWS working groups. As my interviewees agreed, those groups concerned with intellectual, theoretical, and technological matters were seen as more important than those dealing with care for bodies and emotions. Accordingly, Media and Facilitation were toward the top of the heap and Kitchen (along with Sanitation and Comfort) was somewhere toward the bottom. Needless to say, in addition to valuing mind over body and reason over emotion, such a ranking reflected and reinforced a host of related preferences: for professional over service workers; for highly educated activists over those from working-class backgrounds; for public-facing activities over those hidden offstage; for waged over unwaged categories of work; for practices associated with men over those identified with women. Tied to the negative pole of these classed and gendered binaries, Kitchen work could be, and was, easily dismissed as repetitive and unskilled. Replicating the norms of society at large, OWS too often failed to acknowledge the actual culinary and managerial demands of this work; the knowledge, competence, and creativity of Kitchen workers; the wide range of experiences and various forms of expertise they brought to the job. It was thus for ideological as well as logistical reasons that Kitchen's needs and perspective were, as we have seen, largely ignored by the General Assembly and even, at one point, denounced by other activists.

As I heard repeatedly in the course of my interviews, Kitchen workers were at the mercy of an especially cruel combination: a brutalizing workload shouldered from love of the work and loyalty to the cause and, at the same, a failure by many other occupiers to acknowledge, credit, or sometimes even see it. As Heather blogged at the time, from a hopeful, determined activist, "wanting to materially nourish the most important social movement of our lives," she had been changed by the thanklessness of her never-ending labor into "an indignant housewife for the revolution" (Squire 2011). Kitchen's position was, indeed, precisely that of the housewife, the invisibility of whose labor feminists have long decried. Sam, as we know, was similarly dismayed that her OWS care work – whether for Aidan or other occupiers – was simply taken for granted. Like Haywood's outrage, the movement's inattention to childcare along with the careless ingratitude of Sam's young guests point to a view of domestic labor as something women naturally do for children and men. Crucial to our survival, it is labor whose value is recognized only at the moment someone refuses to do it.

The occupation of Zuccotti Park was a hopeful experiment in reconfiguring domestic practices along more collective lines. With its People's Kitchen providing free food to all, it offered to level class disparities while razing the walls of the private home and severing housework from traditional notions of family. In reality, as we have seen, kitchen and care work tended to be imaginatively as well as literally walled off from the movement's public sphere. Generally speaking, domestic labor

212 Susan Fraiman

for Occupy Wall Street, though no longer exclusively female, was nevertheless feminized as well as subordinated in class terms. It continued, moreover, to be mired in the emotional dynamics of the patriarchal family. My goal in sharing these conclusions is not, I should stress, to question the movement's integrity or minimize its success in holding capitalism accountable. It is simply, in solidarity, to remark that the occupation seems to have stopped short at the threshold of the kitchen.

Notes

1 The many, diverse contributions to this tradition, beginning in the late 19th century and exploding with the Second Wave Women's Movement, include those by Charlotte Perkins Gilman, Simone de Beauvoir, Betty Friedan, Shulamith Firestone, Angela Davis, Arlie Hochschild, Heidi Hartmann and Silvia Federici, among many others. On Federici as an example of Marxist feminism, see note 8.

2 In W.J.T. Mitchell's elegant formulation, "It was not that the occupiers needed a place to sleep, but that they were saying something by doing something, a neat reversal of speech act theory that focuses on saying as doing in performative utterances" (Mitchell, Harcourt, and Taussig 2013, xi). I would only add that some occupiers *did* actually need a place to sleep; for them, political expression came together with practical exigency. Given my concern with Zuccotti Park as a domestic formation, I am interested in its status as, among other things, *a place to sleep*.

3 In addition to assorted articles and blogs in the popular media, my sources on the daily workings of OWS included the following volumes: Writers for the 99% 2012; Taylor and Gessen, et al. 2011; Hazen, Lohan, and Parramore 2011; van Gelder et al. 2011; Mitchell, Harcourt, and Taussig 2013. In June 2018, I also conducted phone interviews (lasting an average of one hour) with seven OWS protesters, all full-time members of the Kitchen working group, who agreed to be identified by their first names. I am grateful to Anj, Marlisa, Joshua, Amy, Heather, Benedict, and Samantha for their activism as well as their invaluable contributions to this essay.

4 Discussing pronoun rounds, Benedict noted that trainings by Facilitation provided a common language across working groups. He also mentioned that, since OWS, he finds himself surprised by meetings at which white males routinely feel free to dominate the conversation.

5 My primary focus below will be on the interaction of gender with constructions of class. Of paramount interest to OWS, class issues were also raised by most of the participants I spoke to. And while US class relations are typically racialized, with minorities clustered at the bottom, from what I can tell, that particular pattern seems to have been less prevalent in Zuccotti Park – perhaps because the New York City encampment was, overall, whiter than the surrounding population. It appears the most visible majority were "white college kids," while the majority of those actually sleeping in the park were poorer white males (see note 14). Nor did racial minorities appear to cluster in the lower-status working groups. (Of the Kitchen members I interviewed, six were white and one was biracial.) For remarks on OWS racial politics by a South Asian woman see Ashraf 2011, 33–35. For the suggestion that black women's support for OWS was expressed primarily through longstanding work "behind the scenes in their own communities," see Brunner 2011, 76–77.

Occupying Domesticity **213**

6   As this example begins to suggest, the importance of childcare was largely overlooked by the New York occupation, on which more below. Unlike such sites as Occupy Oakland, neither stroller nor wheelchair access seems to have been a high priority in Zuccotti Park.

7   Rogers 2011a, "Occupy"; see also Rogers' follow-up piece, "What Occupy Wall Street" 2011b; Seltzer 2011, "Where Are the Women." For Ashraf's own account of the GA block, see Ashraf 2011, 33–35; for Maharawal's account, see Maharawal 2011, 34–40. In keeping with a familiar pattern, the period following the November eviction saw a rise in OWS subgroups and offshoots dedicated specifically to women's rights – Women Occupying Wall Street or WOW, Feminist Direct Action, Occupy Patriarchy, and Women Occupy, among others. See Seltzer's report on the first New York feminist GA, which took place in the spring of 2012 (Seltzer 2012a, "Can Occupy"); see also a later update by Seltzer (Seltzer 2012b, "We Are the Many").

8   Fraiman 2017. For a Marxist-feminist analysis of housework, see especially Silvia Federici 2012. As Federici (2012) explains,

> Marx's analysis of capitalism has been hampered by his inability to conceive of value-producing work other than in the form of commodity production and his consequent blindness to the significance of women's unpaid reproductive work in the process of capitalist accumulation.
>
> *(92)*

For Marx, she continues, "all that is needed to (re)produce labor power is commodity production and the market. No other work intervenes to prepare the goods the workers consume or to restore physically and emotionally their capacity to work" (93). Housework thus "remained invisible and unvalued until a movement of women emerged [in the 1960s] who refused to accept the work of reproduction as their natural destiny" (96).

9   Hurwitz notes that women were more often relegated to kitchen and other domestic duties during such progressive campaigns as the Freedom Summer voter registration drive and the 1985 Wheeling-Pittsburgh Steel strike (Hurwitz 2015, 51).

10 Since open flames were prohibited and electricity scarce, all of the actual cooking was done off-site. Initially, meals were either purchased or prepared in the homes of Kitchen workers. (Marlisa and Benedict began by offering theirs; Sam and others soon followed.) When OWS denied funding for a commercial kitchen, a church in East New York saved the day by offering use of its soup kitchen facilities. Care work was similarly dispersed. OWS participants and supporters with apartments opened them to those needing showers and a night indoors. As we will see, Sam made her place in Red Hook available in this way. It was Marlisa who first underlined the significance of these various off-site domestic spaces. Her drawings of these, a companion piece to this essay, is included in this volume.

11 Schooled by Jo Freeman's "The Tyranny of Structurelessness" (1972), OWS was well aware that official "leaderlessness" may disguise actual consolidations of power – thus its array of structures designed to check this tendency.

12 Hurwitz 2019, 157. For examples of the "double bind" and "leadership labyrinth" (maze of obstacles to female leadership) in the context of OWS, see Hurwitz 2019. For another article attesting to such difficulties, see McVeigh 2011.

13 Senia Barragán, an early member of Media along with her partner, Mark Bray, recalled the group's initial white maleness and subsequent efforts to diversify. She also reported

214   Susan Fraiman

being taken less seriously by journalists reporting on OWS. *Occupying Wall Street: The Inside Story of an Action that Changed America*, describing Senia's role in OWS, notes in passing what I take to be an added gender constraint: her visits to Zuccotti Park (but not Mark's?) were limited "due to family obligations" (Writers for the 99% 2012, 80–83).

14 Sanitation is perhaps the only surprise here, given women's traditional responsibility for cleaning up. But as with many forms of domestic labor, once scaled up to "commercial" levels and situated within public spaces, cleaning house becomes the masculinized labor of janitorial work and trash collection. As Marlisa added, a further factor was that most of those actually sleeping in the park were "poor white dudes"; unlike occupiers who went home to apartments, these men were necessarily more concerned with sanitation in the park. The effect was to give Sanitation both a class and gender skew, and to group it with "service" working groups like Kitchen and Comfort, rather than with those male-dominated groups tied to more "intellectual" activities.

15 Marlisa commented that the Kitchen working group also attracted "more typically masculine, ego-driven types," who saw it as a form of direct action and "liked the physical work." Some of these men shifted from Kitchen over to Direct Action, once that working group was formed. In other words, within an activist context, kitchen labor may be (at least temporarily) recoded to coincide with traditionally male, action-oriented qualities.

16 Needless to say, cooking food in one borough and serving it in another added one more layer of difficulty to an already formidable task. In addition, as the occupation grew, so did the number of people to feed – including those lining up for reasons of poverty as well as politics. On the Occupy movement and homelessness, see note 22.

17 Choosing the Kitchen working group, Benedict sought to challenge class as well as gender norms. He and Marlisa, who participated in OWS as a couple, are both architects; given her similar training, for Marlisa, too, joining Kitchen was a conscious repudiation of class/tech privilege.

18 Taussig 2013, 19–20. Outnumbered in Sanitation (see note 14), this woman's grasp on authority was, we might guess, rather loose in any case. The lines following Taussig's interjection anticipate my discussion below of OWS women encouraged at once to claim and disavow leadership: "I am not *the* leader I am not *the* leader (long pause) I am *a* leader I am *a* leader" (20).

19 Writers for the 99% 2012, "Living in the Square," 67–72, and "Day in the Life of the Square," 197–202. The discrepancy in perspective between these two chapters is most likely a result of the book's collaborative authorship. (The many contributors, "writers for the 99%," are listed in the back but, in the spirit of leaderlessness, their particular contributions are not identified.)

20 For a powerful blog post capturing her exhaustion and frustration at the time, see Squire 2011.

21 As Federici comments, "It seems to be a social law that the value of labor is proven and perhaps created by its refusal" (Federici 2012, 96). As with Kitchen's slowdown, it was the refusal of domestic labor by second wavers that served, Federici says, to reveal its value (see note 8).

22 As part of the effort to spin the march as an act of class resistance, Haywood et al. accused Kitchen of attempting to shut out the homeless population. Occupy encampments everywhere struggled to define their relationship to the very poorest of the 99%. While some occupiers saw them as "freeloaders," others pointed to

the hypocrisy of a justice movement excluding those most in need. Sites such as Occupy Philadelphia actively embraced the role of feeding all-comers, but others questioned shifting from away from political protest to an emphasis on providing social services. A vexed issue for the movement as a whole, the involvement of homeless people was one of many stressors operating on OWS at the time, and not Kitchen's particular cross to bear; as we have seen, its slowdown was fundamentally about self-preservation and not directed at a specific demographic. Indeed, Sam told me Kitchen actively supported feeding the homeless community, many of whom were in their teens: "We were, like, food has to be free, has to be free for everybody." For an account of this controversy asserting that "kitchen's difficulties got mixed with other problems," see Writers for the 99% 2012, 71. For an overview of the movement's varied responses to homelessness, see Herring and Glück 2011, 163–169.

23 Writers for the 99% 2012, 193; Jaffe 2011, 67; Taylor 2011, 136.

24 In "The 51%," Hurwitz (2015) describes interviews with several female activists for whom parenting responsibilities conflicted with OWS activities. Many important roles, such as facilitating a GA, were off-limits for those unable to spare three or more hours in the evening (61–62). See also note 13 on Senia Barragán.

25 In "The 51%," Hurwitz (2015) offers similar evidence that "women participated more heavily in the devalued traditionally female jobs such as women's care work and food preparation" (86). Her examples include Dee, whose "motherly care work" involved, as Sam's did, taking home "kids" who were sick or needed their laundry done. Unlike Sam however, and despite spending days in the camp, Dee echoed the conventional view of such work as positioning her on the sidelines, offering "support" to the movement, rather than making her an actual member (87).

References

Ashraf, Hena. 2011. "Claiming Space for Diversity at Occupy Wall Street." In *This Changes Everything: Occupy Wall Street and the 99% Movement*, edited by Sarah van Gelder et al., 33–35. San Francisco: Berrett-Koehler Publishers.

Brunner, Mikki. 2011. "Who Are the Black Women Occupying Wall Street?" In *The 99%: How the Occupy Wall Street Movement Is Changing America*, edited by Don Hazen, Tara Lohan, and Lynn Parramore, 76–77. San Francisco: AlterNet Books.

Butler, Melanie. 2011. "Finding Our Voices and Creating Safe Spaces at Occupy Wall Street." In *The 99%: How the Occupy Wall Street Movement is Changing America,* edited by Don Hazen, Tara Lohan, and Lynn Parramore, 71–73. San Francisco: AlterNet Books.

Federici, Silvia. 2012. *Revolution at Point Zero: Housework, Reproduction, and Feminist Struggle.* Oakland, CA: PM Press.

Fraiman, Susan. 2017. *Extreme Domesticity: A View from the Margins.* New York: Columbia University Press.

Hardikar, Ashwini. 2011. "The Value of a Safe Space: One WOC's experience with harassment at Occupy Wall Street." In *front and center: critical voices in the 99%*, October 13, 2011. https://infrontandcenter.wordpress.com

Hazen, Don, Tara Lohan, and Lynn Parramore, eds. 2011. *The 99%: How the Occupy Wall Street Movement is Changing America.* San Francisco: AlterNet Books.

Herring, Christopher, and Zoltán Glück. 2011. "The Homeless Question." In *Occupy! Scenes from Occupied America*, edited by Astra Taylor and Keith Gessen, et al., 163–169. New York: Verso.

Hurwitz, Heather McKee. 2015. "The 51%: Gender, Feminism, and Culture in the Occupy Wall Street Movement." PhD diss., University of California, Santa Barbara.

Hurwitz, Heather McKee, and Verta Taylor. 2018. "Women Occupying Wall Street: Gender Conflict and Feminist Mobilization." In *100 Years of the Nineteenth Amendment: An Appraisal of Women's Political Activism*, edited by Lee Ann Banasak and Holly J. McCammon. New York: Oxford University Press.

Hurwitz, Heather McKee. 2019. "Gender and Race in the Occupy Movement: Relational Leadership and Discriminatory Resistance." *Mobilization: An International Quarterly* 24 (2): 157–176.

Jaffe, Sarah. 2011. "The Radical Infrastructure of Occupy Wall Street." In *The 99%: How the Occupy Wall Street Movement is Changing America,* edited by Don Hazen, Tara Lohan, and Lynn Parramore, 65–67. San Francisco: AlterNet Books.

Maharawal, Manissa. 2011. "Standing Up." In *Occupy! Scenes from Occupied America,* edited by Astra Taylor and Keith Gessen, et al., 34–40. New York: Verso.

McVeigh, Karen. 2011. "Occupy Wall Street's Women Struggle to Make Their Voices Heard," *The Guardian*, November 30, 2011.

Mitchell, W.J.T., Bernard E. Harcourt, and Michael Taussig. 2013. *Occupy: Three Inquiries in Disobedience*. Chicago: University of Chicago Press.

Rogers, Stephanie. 2011a. "Occupy Wall Street and Feminism and Misogyny (Oh My?)," *Bitch Flicks*, October 17, 2011.

Rogers, Stephanie. 2011b. "What Occupy Wall Street Owes to Feminist Consciousness-Raising," *Ms. Blog*, December 13, 2011.

Seltzer, Sarah. 2011. "Where Are the Women at Occupy Wall Street? Everywhere – and They're Not Going Away," *The Nation*, October 26, 2011.

Seltzer, Sarah. 2012a. "Can Occupy Fight Back Against the War on Women?" *The Nation*, May 18, 2012.

Seltzer, Sarah. 2012b. "We Are the Many, Not the Few." *Ms. Magazine*, Winter 2012, 32–35.

Squire, Heather E. 2011. "Tunnel Vision and the Harsh Realm of Everyday Occupation." *Recovering Hipster*, November 14, 2011.

Stevens, Angi Becker. 2011. "We Are the 99%, Too: Creating a Feminist Space Within Occupy Wall Street," *Ms. Blog*, October 11, 2011.

Taussig, Michael. 2013. "I'm So Angry I Made a Sign." In *Occupy: Three Inquiries in Disobedience*, edited by W.J.T. Mitchell, Bernard E. Harcourt, and Michael Taussig, 3–43. Chicago: University of Chicago Press.

Taylor, Astra, and Keith Gessen, et al., eds. 2011. *Occupy! Scenes from Occupied America.* New York: Verso.

Taylor, Sunaura. 2011. "Scenes from Occupied Oakland." In *Occupy! Scenes from Occupied America*, edited by Astra Taylor and Keith Gessen, et al., 134–145. New York: Verso.

van Gelder, Sarah, and the staff of *Yes!*, eds. 2011. *This Changes Everything: Occupy Wall Street and the 99% Movement*. San Francisco: Berrett-Koehler Publishers.

Writers for the 99%. 2012. *Occupying Wall Street: The Inside Story of an Action that Changed America*. Chicago: Haymarket Books.

11

OCCUPY WALL STREET

Mapping a Movement

Marlisa Wise

In the fall of 2011, the "movement of the squares" – which had spread from Athens' Syntagma Square in 2010, to Cairo's Tahrir Square in the spring, to Madrid's Puerta del Sol in May – came to New York City, with the occupation of Zuccotti Park in Lower Manhattan under the banner of Occupy Wall Street. While Occupy actions extended to several American cities over the course of the fall, the park remained the site most prominently identified with the movement, where, from September 17 to their eviction from the park on November 15, thousands of people participated in General Assemblies, joined working groups, ate food together, and learned from each other. But the park was only the most visible site in a network of spaces that supported OWS. In the following maps, the larger landscape of OWS is described through the many locations that were involved in the operations of the OWS Food Working Group, also known as the Kitchen.

From its inception, the Occupy Wall Street movement used a spatial strategy to resituate politics as an embodied, physically contested practice. The occupation of Zuccotti Park, a privately owned public space (POPS), while seemingly spontaneous, followed a summer of initial organizing meetings, many held in Tompkins Square Park, and a predecessor protest, Bloombergville, during which activists camped out from June 14 to July 5, 2011, on the sidewalk in front of City Hall. Siting the occupation in a privately owned public space underscored the activists' aims of wresting political power from corporations, not (only) through messaging and statements but through a direct reappropriation of urban space. The occupation staged a conflict between the corporate ownership of "public" land and practices of commoning that attempted to reclaim space through actions: sharing food, clothes, and books, and caring for each other and for the park.

218 Marlisa Wise

The project of retroactively charting the geography of the Occupy Wall Street Kitchen makes visible this practice of politics through mapping the ephemeral network that sprang up to support the occupiers in the fall and winter of 2011. The maps show the spatial extents of the sites that assembled around and through the Kitchen to support its daily work.

As an architect and urbanist, I use conventions of architectural imaging, such as the drawing of plans or maps, as both a means of research and as a way to construct narratives that render visible spatial relationships that would otherwise remain imperceptible. In documenting the spatial range of the Kitchen, these drawings show that Occupy Wall Street was never only about the encampment in Lower Manhattan, but about the creation of an interconnected and polycentric political arena that extended well beyond the bounds of the park. Visualizing the distribution of this network as a layer over the familiar street grid of the city allows a re-reading of the occupation as more than just a narrowly cordoned encampment in a single downtown Manhattan location. In drawing the sites of production, storage, and free distribution of food by the Kitchen, it is evident that the occupation of Zuccotti Park was not only embedded in the networks of the city, but that the work of the Kitchen was constitutive of a larger field of actors and operations – the volunteers, cooking sites, food co-ops, farms, churches, and businesses that became part of Occupy Wall Street by helping to feed the movement. The maps that follow trace a series of relationships between the most visually concentrated center of OWS – the occupation of Zuccotti Park – and this more geographically extensive network of support, in an attempt to visualize the social and material co-constitution of these spaces.

OWS in Lower Manhattan

While "Wall Street" is today largely a shorthand for the machinations of the global financial systems, many OWS actions were, in fact, also geographically situated in the blocks surrounding its rhetorical target (see Figure 11.1).

The main location at which the Kitchen served meals was Zuccotti Park (location 1 on Figure 1), where during the height of the movement it was estimated that around 1,200 meals were provided daily, making it the largest provider of free meals in the city during that period.[1] Other locations where the Kitchen frequently served food in the neighborhood of the park included the large interior atrium at 60 Wall Street (2), a privately owned public space that was a popular location for meetings during inclement weather, and at "The Office" (3), the workspace donated by the United Federation of Teachers that was the administrative center of OWS. The Kitchen also provided meals for meetings of OWS working groups at Charlotte's Place (4), a community center run by Trinity Church. After a raid by the NYPD ended the occupation of Zuccotti Park, food was served outside Trinity Church (5) and at the steps of Federal Hall on Wall Street (6). The support offered by the Kitchen to these organizing spaces adjacent to the park helped to sustain occupiers who met, collaborated, and worked long hours together. The Kitchen also brought meals to large rallies at Foley Square (7),

FIGURE 11.1 Benedict Clouette and Marlisa Wise. Map 1: OWS in Lower Manhattan

and to the plaza outside 100 Centre Street (8), the jail of the New York Courts, as part of "jail support" for people being released after protest-related arrests. In jail support, Kitchen members offered a comforting meal to protesters who were being released after having been arrested and detained, working alongside legal volunteers who offered guidance on navigating the court system and street medics who tended to injuries sustained during arrests. To offer food to those being released was a political act of refusing the misery imposed by jail.

To prepare the volume of meals that were served at these various locations, the Kitchen cooked in a variety of spaces over the course of the occupation. Many of these spaces were in Brooklyn or Queens (see Figure 11.2), but in Lower Manhattan, the Kitchen operated for a few weeks from a commercial kitchen at 56 Walker Street (9), and also served food during meetings of the OWS Spokescouncil held at that location. The Spokescouncil, a model for consensus decision-making in larger groups, was an effort to adapt the organization of OWS to the increasingly large crowds that assembled every evening in Zuccotti Park for the General Assembly meetings. The Spokescouncil was initiated as a means of scaling and distributing the consensus process through a formalized system of delegates of the working groups, allowing decisions to be reached through discussions happening indoors, among a group of people that could be accommodated inside a building, which was necessarily smaller than the group that filled the plaza for the General Assemblies. Perhaps predictably, moving the decision-making body of OWS out

220 Marlisa Wise

MAP 2: OWS in New York City
┄┄┄ Area shown in MAP 1
(13) Washington Square Park
(14) Union Square
(15) Tompkins Square Park
(16) Duarte Square
(17) Bryant Park
(18) Riverside Church
(19) Judson Memorial Church
(20) 702 Vermont Ave
(21) 477 W 142nd St
(22) DeKalb Farm
(23) Red Hook Community Farm
(24) Amy's Bread
(25) Park Slope Food Coop
(26) 4th Street Food Coop
(27) Leticia's Apartment
(28) Lisa's Apartment
(29) Marlisa's & Ben's Apartment
(30) Bill's Apartment
(31) Samantha's Apartment
(32) Maura's Apartment
(33) 33 Flatbush Ave
(34) Liberty Cafe
(35) The Catholic Worker
(36) In Our Hearts House
(37) Two Boots Pizza
(38) Lucky Strike
(39) Jetro
(40) Park Slope United Methodist Church
(41) West Park Presbyterian Church
(42) Middle Collegiate Church
(43) Colors Restaurant

FIGURE 11.2 Benedict Clouette and Marlisa Wise. Map 2: OWS in New York City

of the park and into an interior space was controversial; the most materially consequential decisions became separated from the space of the park, and now took place at an indoor location where access could be controlled, at least by implication, and where decisions were made by a group that, for some, too closely resembled the forms of representative democracy and leadership by elites that the movement had supposedly rendered obsolete. The Kitchen similarly weighed the implications, both political and logistical, of serving food at the proliferating spaces of the occupation and the increasingly specialized roles those sites performed: how many meals should go to the park, to the Spokescouncil, to working groups and

Occupy Wall Street: Mapping a Movement **221**

organizers at "The Office," or to actions initiated by working groups in faraway neighborhoods? If the Kitchen was offering bodily nourishment to the political project of the Occupy movement, whose bodies were part of that project?

In addition to the sites where the Kitchen served and prepared food, the working group's operations in the neighborhood of the park were supported by a handful of local organizations and businesses. Throughout the occupation, the Kitchen stored food and supplies at the OWS storage facility known as SIS (10), or Supply/Inventory/Storage, located in a space donated by Amalgamated Bank, the country's largest union-owned bank. Each morning, hot water for coffee, tea, and oatmeal was given by a neighborhood deli, TAZ Café (11), and carried to the park by Kitchen volunteers. At times, the Kitchen had trouble keeping up with demand, and as a stopgap measure, the phone number for Liberato's Pizza (12) would be tweeted, and stacks of pizzas would arrive for dinner, donated by the occupation's Twitter followers.

OWS in Greater New York

While the area around Zuccotti Park was certainly a major nexus of OWS's activities, the Kitchen drew resources from a larger geographical area and supplied regular meals far beyond the park (see Figure 11.2). The Kitchen served food at General Assemblies and marches in Washington Square Park (13), Union Square (14), Tompkins Square Park (15), Duarte Square (16), and Bryant Park (17), as well as at events at Riverside Church (18) and Judson Memorial Church (19). The Kitchen also provided meals to ongoing occupations of homes in East New York (20) and in Harlem (21) that were under foreclosure or where residents were under threat of eviction, which represented an important shift in the tactics of Occupy and led to the formation of the group Occupy Homes.

The food served by the Kitchen was prepared using groceries and supplies either received as in-kind donations or bought with donated money, which was distributed daily to the Kitchen from the central accounts of OWS. The DeKalb Farm (22) and the Red Hook Community Farm (23) gave fresh, Brooklyn-grown vegetables; Amy's Bread (24) provided a seemingly endless supply of bread; and the Park Slope Food Coop (25) and 4th Street Food Coop (26) regularly donated a range of produce. The Kitchen also received in-kind donations from a network of upstate farmers, who drove pickup trucks filled with crates of vegetables from their rural farms to the park to support the occupation.

The Kitchen prepared meals at various locations throughout the city, initially by bringing volunteers from Zuccotti Park to cook at the apartments of individual Kitchen members (27–32). In those early days, the use of residential spaces as the occupation's first off-site kitchens enabled hot meals to be served, and for larger quantities of food donations to be stored than was possible in the park alone. These apartment kitchens allowed the Kitchen to increase its production at a crucial moment when the occupation was growing rapidly, and provided food for increasingly large dinnertime crowds during lengthy General Assemblies. Later, the Kitchen moved to other off-site cooking facilities, using commercial-style kitchens at 33 Flatbush Avenue, a cooperatively run workplace called the Metropolitan Exchange (33), and Liberty Café, a restaurant and soup kitchen run by Pastor Leo Karl (34), during the off-hours when the equipment was not needed by the soup kitchen. In both locations, the Kitchen shared space with sympathetic organizations and businesses, and recruited new allies in the process.

Other locations where members of the Kitchen cooked meals included the headquarters of the Catholic Worker (35) and a house associated with the anarchist collective In Our Hearts (36). These communitarian groups, one dating from the 1930s and one formed in the early 2000s, both use the serving of free food as a form of prefigurative politics in line with the work of the Kitchen. Along with the anarchists and radical Catholics, a few businesses lent their support to the occupation through donations of prepared food; the restaurants Two Boots Pizza (37) and Lucky Strike (38) donated prepared food to events organized by OWS. In addition to receiving donated food and prepared meals from businesses, the Kitchen purchased supplies from vendors using donated funds, particularly after the group began preparing meals in commercial-grade kitchens on a large scale. Ingredients and supplies were often purchased in bulk at the restaurant wholesale market Jetro (39), as well as from the co-ops who had previously donated food.

Other organizations provided shelter to members of the Kitchen who had moved to the city to participate in the movement or who were already without stable housing. Kitchen members were accommodated at the Park Slope Methodist Church (40) and West Park Methodist Church (41), and the apartments of fellow Kitchen workers and OWS participants. Middle Collegiate Church (42) and Colors (43), a worker-co-op restaurant, generously hosted gatherings of the Kitchen, allowing the group to spend an evening together while someone else cooked dinner.

Taken together, the maps show the heterogeneity of the spaces that were assembled to support the activities of the occupation in Zuccotti Park: churches, businesses, union headquarters, farms, food co-ops, activist spaces, and houses. These maps are a form of visual research that hopefully contributes to a better understanding of the sociospatial organization of a recent movement and the networks of support that it built. But, perhaps more importantly, the research is also an exercise in mapping potentialities for a future insurgent politics. To document how, during two short months in 2011, such a complex network of mutual aid was formed with elegance and speed may help future movements to learn from, and improve upon, the tactics used by Occupy. Furthermore, the maps suggest the myriad ways in which the strategies employed by Occupy were first and foremost a form of embodied politics in which the spaces gathered around the occupation were as important as the movement's declarations and ideas.

Author's note: The sites shown on the maps were compiled with the assistance of former members of the Kitchen: Amy, Benedict, Bill, Emery, Ethan, Heather, Joshua, Maura, Samantha, Stina, Thomas, Vevlyn, and Will.

Note

1 This point was raised during the occupation when members of the Kitchen met with representatives of Coalition for the Homeless (CFH), a New York nonprofit organization whose headquarters are located near the park. The meeting was requested by CFH because the creation of a relatively safe and comfortable space with free food and medical services in Zuccotti Park had resulted in many homeless New Yorkers relocating to the park and the surrounding area during the period of the occupation, which had temporarily affected the operations of the established shelter system and outreach programs. The participation of many people in the occupation who were formerly or currently homeless, along with others who had been previously diagnosed with mental disorders or suffered from drug addiction, prompted questions that were intensely debated throughout the course of the occupation: whether practices of radical care, which were often resource- and labor-intensive, were a key part of the embodied politics of the Occupy movement, and a repudiation of the financialization of housing and the institutions that pathologize and ultimately criminalize neurodiversity and poverty, or, conversely, were taking resources away from effective political organizing and offering the city administration an excuse to forcibly end the occupation.

12

TENT CITY, USA

The Growth of America's Homeless Encampments and How Communities are Responding

Maria Foscarinis and Eric Tars

Homelessness has been an urgent and widespread problem in the United States since the early 1980s, and it is increasingly visible (Foscarinis 2018). Spurred by a decades-long failure to ensure the availability of affordable housing, it ranges from the stereotype of highly visible street homelessness (also known as unsheltered homelessness) to more hidden homelessness: families living doubled up with friends or family, having lost their own homes; youth "couch surfing" after being pushed or thrown out of their homes; working people who, no longer able to afford the rent, have moved into their cars.

Available data vary widely, as do the methods used to compile it. But even the most recent estimate from the US Department of Housing and Urban Development – which by its own admission is likely to significantly undercount unsheltered homeless people – found that from 2017 to 2018 unsheltered homelessness increased by 2 percent,[1] on top of a 9 percent increase from 2016 to 2017.[2] People experiencing homelessness without formal shelter often devise makeshift ways to shelter themselves – cardboard boxes, tarps, or tents, for example – and may come together in informal communities, sometimes referred to as homeless encampments or tent cities. A 2017 report by the National Law Center on Homelessness and Poverty (the Law Center), *Tent City, USA: The Growth of America's Homeless Encampments and How Communities are Responding*, estimated that over the prior ten years such encampments increased by over 1,300 percent (see Figure 12.1).[3]

Unlike protest movements such as Occupy, much of this public presence is born of dire necessity, rather than political strategy; it is a very visible consequence of the crisis in affordable housing gripping the nation, as well as the increasingly torn social safety net. But inevitably, because they make visible the extreme poverty and need that coexist, often side by side, with extreme wealth,

Tent City, USA **225**

FIGURE 12.1 Tent City, USA: The Growth of America's Homeless Encampments and How Communities are Responding. Report by National Law Center on Homelessness and Poverty, 2017. Image courtesy of the National Law Center on Homelessness and Poverty

in a country typically viewed as advanced and affluent, these encampments also make a political statement simply in their existence, with some more actively embracing a dual role of survival and protest. Whether it is generally seen (or legible) as such is an open question: a contrary, and common, narrative, tracing back at least to the Reagan era, is that homeless people simply "choose" to live outside. And whether it is seen at all is now at the center of battles going on in cities across the country.

Currently, cities across the country are enacting and enforcing laws aimed at removing homeless people from public view, making all manner of otherwise innocent and necessary human activities – from sleeping, eating, and sitting to urinating and defecating – criminal acts when performed in public, even in the absence of private alternative places to perform them. Nationally, data make clear the dearth of affordable housing: following drastic funding cuts beginning in the early 1980s – cuts that have never been restored – currently only one in four of those poor enough to qualify for low-income housing assistance actually receives it. Emergency shelter is also in short supply, and people seeking it are regularly turned away. Even when it is available, it may not be a realistic option for many people, and certainly not a long-term one.

226 Maria Foscarinis and Eric Tars

Eugene Stroman, a homeless man living in Houston, TX, explains:

> There are … reasons to say no when officers offer to bring you to shelter. Agreeing to go to a shelter in that moment means losing many of your possessions. You have to pack what you can into a bag and leave the rest behind, to be stolen or thrown away by city workers. For me, I would have lost my bulky winter clothes, my tent, my nonperishable food, and the bike parts I used to make repairs for money. You give up all this property just for the guarantee – if you trust the police – of a spot on the floor *for one night*. It's not really a "choice" for me to give up all those resources. I needed to make smart survival decisions.
>
> *(National Law Center 2017, 8)*

Challenges to efforts to criminalize homelessness are now going on in cities across the country, as homeless people and their advocates – including, prominently, our organization – fight *against* city laws that make this public presence criminal and *for* housing and supportive services so that people need not live in public in the first place. These battles are, first and foremost, a fight for survival. But in broader perspective, they also pose fundamental questions about community response to extreme poverty and need. As cities increasingly gentrify, developing luxury housing and displacing lower income communities, criminalization seeks to remove the "blight" of homeless people – who, not coincidentally, are also disproportionately people of color, more so even than the larger poverty population. Advocates are not only fighting criminalization, we are also fighting for housing and inclusion. Advocacy campaigns such as Housing Not Handcuffs seek to frame that larger issue. This essay introduces a summary of the Law Center report and contextualizes it in the framework of this volume.

The Rapid Growth of Tent Cities

The Law Center's report documented the apparent rapid growth of encampments of people experiencing homelessness (or "tent cities") across the United States from 2007 to 2017, and the legal and policy responses to that growth (see Figure 12.2). Documenting encampments is a challenge: many are deliberately hidden to avoid legal problems or evictions, and some are forced to move frequently. The report relied on media reports as a proxy, using only those referencing the state in which the encampment occurred. Only one report was counted for each encampment. While this is an imperfect proxy, the trends within that limited data set are useful and confirm anecdotal reports from across the country. Between 2007 and 2017:

- **The number of encampments reported grew rapidly**: the Law Center's research showed a 1,342 percent increase in the number of unique homeless encampments reported in the media, from 19 reported encampments in 2007 to a high of 274 reported encampments in 2016 (the last full year for data); by

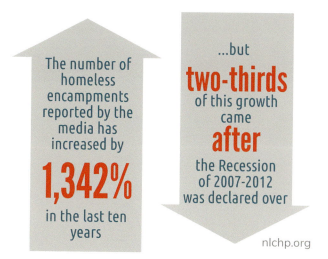

FIGURE 12.2 "The number of homeless encampments reported by the media has increased by 1,342% in the last ten years ... but two-thirds of this growth came after the Recession of 2007–2012 was declared over." Graphic included in the "Tent City, USA" report by the National Law Center on Homelessness and Poverty, 2017. Image courtesy of the National Law Center on Homelessness and Poverty

mid-2017, 255 were reported, indicating continued rapid growth. Two-thirds of this growth came *after* the Great Recession of 2007–2012 was declared over, suggesting that many are still feeling the long-term effects.

- **Encampments are everywhere:** a total of 1,302 unique homeless encampments were reported over ten years, located in every state and the District of Columbia. California had the highest number of reported encampments by far (569), but states as diverse as Iowa, Indiana, Louisiana, Michigan, Oregon, and Virginia each tallied more than 50 reported encampments.
- **Many encampments are medium to large**: half the reports that recorded the size of the encampments showed a size of 11 to 50 residents, and 17 percent of encampments had more than 100 residents. Larger encampments are obviously likely to garner more coverage, but these figures suggest that there are high numbers of both medium and large encampments across the country.
- **Encampments are becoming semipermanent features of cities:** close to two-thirds of reports that recorded the time in existence of the encampments showed they had been there for more than one year, and more than one-quarter had been there for more than five years.
- **But most are not sanctioned and are under constant threat of eviction:** three-quarters of reports which recorded the legal status of the encampments showed they were illegal; 4 percent were reported to be legal; 20 percent were reported to be semilegal – that is, tacitly sanctioned (see Figure 12.3).

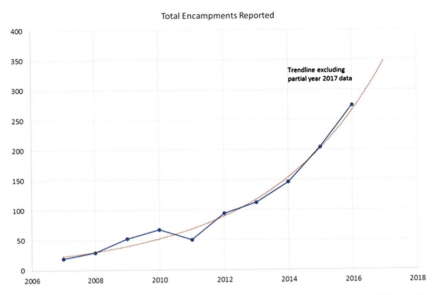

FIGURE 12.3 "Total Encampments Reported" graph published in the "Tent City, USA" report by the National Law Center on Homelessness and Poverty, 2017. Image courtesy of the National Law Center on Homelessness and Poverty

This increase in encampments reflects the growth in homelessness overall, as well as the inadequacy of the US shelter system. The growth of homelessness is largely explained by rising housing costs and stagnant wages. A report by Freddie Mac (2018) documents a 60 percent drop in market-rate apartments affordable to very low-income families over just the past six years. Zillow recently documented a strong relationship between rising rents and the growth of homelessness, particularly in high-growth cities like Los Angeles, where a 5 percent rent increase equates to 2,000 additional homeless persons on the streets.

In the United States, the wealthiest country on earth, encampments of homeless people are unacceptable. They are the predictable result of policy choices made by elected officials. Because the growth of encampments is primarily due to these structural factors rather than individual character flaws or choices, the most effective responses will be systemic and avoid involving individuals in the criminal justice system unnecessarily. But city responses vary widely (see Figure 12.4).

Many Communities are Responding with Punitive Law Enforcement Approaches

Municipalities often face pressure to "do something" about the problem of visible homelessness. For many cities, the response has been an increase in laws prohibiting encampments and an increase in enforcement. When a city evicts residents of an

Tent City, USA   229

FIGURE 12.4 "Many Cities are Failing to Protect Encampment Residents" info-graphic published in the "Tent City, USA" report by the National Law Center on Homelessness and Poverty, 2017. Image courtesy of the National Law Center on Homelessness and Poverty

encampment and clears their belongings, it is often called a "sweep." The Law Center surveyed the laws and policies in 187 cities across the country and found:

- 33 percent of cities prohibit camping city-wide, and 50 percent prohibit camping in particular public places, increases of 69 percent and 48 percent from 2006 to 2016, respectively.
- 50 percent have either a formal or informal procedure for clearing or allowing encampments. (Many more use trespass or disorderly conduct statutes in order to evict residents of encampments).
- Only five cities (2.7 percent) have some requirement that alternative housing or shelter be offered when a sweep of an encampment is conducted.
- Only 20 (11 percent) had ordinances or formal policies requiring notice prior to clearing encampments. Of those, five can require as little as 24 hours' notice before encampments are evicted, though five require at least a week, and three provide for two weeks or more.

230 Maria Foscarinis and Eric Tars

- Only 20 cities (11 percent) require storage be provided for possessions of persons residing in encampments if the encampment is evicted.
- Regional analysis found western cities have more formal policies than any other region of the country, and are more likely to provide notice and storage.

Some law enforcement officials agree that criminalizing homelessness is not good policy. Andy Mills, Santa Cruz Police Chief, stated:

> I honestly believe that people need to sleep and that people are healthier when they get sleep, they can make better decisions when they get sleep. If at some point in the future, we can have a place where people can go and sleep lawfully, I think that makes great sense. At the same time, [our decision not to enforce the anticamping ordinance] gives us the opportunity to say, we can't enforce this [ordinance] rigorously when there aren't enough beds or even close to it for people to sleep.
>
> *(National Law Center 2017, 9)*

Encampment Evictions are Expensive

Using the criminal justice system to move people who have nowhere else to go is costly and counterproductive, for both communities and individuals (see Figure 12.5). Honolulu, HI, spends $15,000 per week – three-quarters of a million dollars a year – sweeping people living in homeless encampments, many of whom simply move around the corner during the sweep and then return a day later. Washington, DC, spent more than $172,000 in just three months on sweeps. Research shows that housing is the most effective approach to end homelessness, with a larger return on investment. Beyond this misuse of resources, sweeping encampments too often harms individuals by destroying their belongings, including their shelter, ID, and other important documents, medications, and mementos. More often than not, this leaves the homeless person in a worse position than before, with a more difficult path to exit homelessness.

Moreover, sweeps frequently destroy the relationships that outreach workers have built with residents, and that residents have built with each other, again putting further barriers between residents and permanent housing. As Milton Harris, who had been homeless in Sacramento, CA, explained:

> Did I get arrested? Sure. I had nowhere else to go. They took me to jail, and took away my stuff … I was chased and cited by the city, but I was determined to sleep somewhere … Arrests delayed me getting stabilized for six months.
>
> *(National Law Center 2017, 9)*

Some cities also spend thousands of dollars on fences, bars, rocks, spikes, and other "hostile" or "aggressive" architecture, deliberately making certain areas of

FIGURE 12.5 Homeless encampment by the Arroyo Seco, South Pasadena CA, almost entirely abandoned following a sweep by police. Photograph by Levi Clancy, September 25, 2012. Image courtesy of the photographer

their community inaccessible to homeless persons without shelter. San Diego, CA, recently spent $57,000 to install jagged rocks set in concrete underneath an overpass in advance of the Major League Baseball All-Star game. Other cities, like Chicago, IL, simply fence off areas under bridges to prevent homeless persons from sheltering there. In either case, the money did not reduce the need for people to find shelter but potentially put people at greater vulnerability to exposure and hazards.

Some of the Law Center's local partners offer these examples of how the criminalization of encampments is felt on the ground:

- **Denver, CO**: law enforcement removed blankets from sleeping people in the middle of the night while the temperatures were below freezing.
- **San Diego, CA**: the city uses a law intended to keep trash cans off the sidewalk to arrest and jail people who are living outside.
- **Olympia, WA:** the city uses trespass laws to charge people who are sleeping in the woods, despite the fact that there are only 250 shelter beds for at least 800 homeless people.
- **Titusville, FL:** the city dismantled an encampment in 2011 that was mostly home to veterans, destroying irreplaceable items including the ashes of one man's father and the World War II flag that another man's father earned for service in the military.

Law Enforcement Threats Do Not Decrease the Number of People on the Streets

Many communities state that they need criminalization ordinances to provide law enforcement with a "tool" to push people to accept services, such as shelter. Conducting outreach backed with resources for real alternatives, however, is the approach that has shown the best, evidence-based results. The 100,000 Homes Campaign found permanent housing for more than 100,000 of the most "service-resistant" chronically homeless individuals across America by listening to their needs and providing appropriate alternatives that actually meet those needs.

Most cities in the United States have insufficient shelter beds for the number of people experiencing homelessness; in some cities, the shortage is stark (Figure 12.6). Even where shelter beds are open, they are not always appropriate, or even adequate, for all people. Some are available only to men or only to women; some require children, others do not allow children. Some do not ensure more than one night's stay, requiring daily long waits in line – sometimes far from other alternatives. Others do not allow people to bring in personal belongings, much less store them during the day. These restrictions can make it very difficult to hold

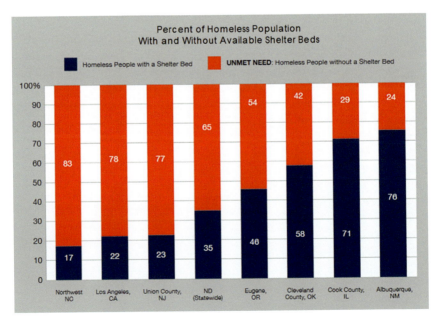

FIGURE 12.6 "Percent of Homeless Population With and Without Available Shelter Beds," graph published in the "Tent City, USA" report by the National Law Center on Homelessness and Poverty, 2017. Image courtesy of the National Law Center on Homelessness and Poverty

a job, whether in daytime or nighttime. And some shelters require residents to participate in religious activities, while others have time limits, charge money, or have other rules or restrictions that bar groups of people. Very few shelters allow pets. All of these factors may mean that even if a shelter has an empty bed, it may not be actually accessible to an individual living in an encampment. Tammy Kohr, a formerly homeless woman in Houston, TX, explains:

> I learned from other homeless people that the shelters were usually full, and it wasn't worth the effort to constantly wait in line … Going and seeking out shelter would have meant losing many of my things. I would have to pack a bag and leave everything else behind, trying to hide it in the bushes. I'd be risking a lot of my property just to try to get a shelter space for one night. Plus, with my cancer diagnosis, it felt like it was a health risk for me to go inside. It was cleaner on the street than it was in any of those shelters. In a tent, I could keep my area as clean as I wanted … Rather than sacrificing my health and my dignity, I focused on moving on and making do with what was stable: a tent.
>
> *(National Law Center 2017, 11)*

Encampment Evictions are Not the Best Way to Protect Health and Safety

City officials frequently cite concerns for public health and safety as reasons for sweeps of encampments, but again the cost is high and the impact is either minor or counterproductive (see Figure 12.7). At the extreme are cities like Denver, where law enforcement officers were caught on video pulling blankets off homeless persons in subzero temperatures. The Denver mayor claimed his concern was for the homeless persons: "Urban camping – especially during cold, wet weather – is dangerous and we don't want to see any lives lost on the streets when there are safe, warm places available for people to sleep at night" (National Law Center 2017, 11). But Denver has far fewer available shelter beds than homeless people, meaning that the city increased exposure and health risks for vulnerable people instead of decreasing them.

City officials will often highlight the hazards of open fires, litter attracting rodents, and open urination and defecation as threatening the homeless individuals living in encampments. While those concerns are valid, sweeps rarely result in improved health or safety. What works is providing access to sanitation facilities and water, regular trash removal, and safe cooking facilities – all things that a city can do that improve the health and safety of all its residents.

Tammy Kohr from Houston again explains:

> I know the city is also saying they need to ban tents because our encampment is so dirty. The only reason it's dirty is that people are getting overwhelmed

FIGURE 12.7 Notice of Violation at the Arroyo Seco Homeless Encampment. Photograph by Levi Clancy, September 25, 2012. Image courtesy of the photographer

and they don't know what to do with their trash. If the city would give them a solution, they'd use it … It's not like we can pay for a trash man. The tents themselves are clean. People have their own areas that they generally keep tidy. It's the areas where we leave trash to be picked up that are not clean. It's where we have to go to the bathroom that is not clean. Those problems have nothing to do with the tents, and they can be fixed with solutions other than jail.

(National Law Center 2017, 12)

Case Studies of Non-Enforcement Approaches Show Promising Lessons

A number of cities have adopted approaches other than arbitrary evictions or criminalization, or at least approaches to lessen the number and negative consequences of evictions. These are not all of the possible alternatives, nor are they perfect. But these examples illustrate how some cities are addressing concerns about homeless encampments more effectively, more humanely, and at lower cost.

Cities Ending Encampments Through Housing

In 2015, the US Interagency Council on Homelessness published guidance for cities entitled *Ending Homelessness for People Living in Encampments*. As the title implies, it emphasizes that the best approach to ending encampments is to end homelessness for the people living in them.[4] It sets out four basic principles for effectively dealing with encampments:

1. Preparation and Adequate Time for Planning and Implementation
2. Collaboration across Sectors and Systems
3. Performance of Intensive and Persistent Outreach and Engagement
4. Provision of Low-Barrier Pathways to Permanent Housing

Examples of cities implementing this approach, at least in part, include:

- **Charleston, SC**, ensured adequate time for planning, outreach, housing and services to close a 100-person encampment through housing most of its residents, without a single arrest.
- **Indianapolis, IN**, adopted an ordinance requiring residents be provided with adequate alternative housing before an encampment can be evicted, and mandates at least 15 days' notice of planned evictions to encampment residents and service providers.
- **Charleston, WV**, settled litigation by adopting an ordinance requiring that encampment evictions cannot proceed unless residents are provided with adequate alternative housing or shelter, and providing 14 days' notice to encampment residents and service providers of planned evictions, and that storage facilities will be made available for homeless individuals.
- **Seattle, WA, and San Francisco, CA**: both cities proposed, but did not pass, ordinances that would improve upon Indianapolis's and Charleston's by ensuring adequate provision for sanitation and hygiene needs in existing encampments, as well as clear notice and provision of adequate housing alternatives and storage in the event of displacement. In 2016, the US Department of Justice analyzed the Seattle proposal and found it to be a constitutional approach that is consistent with federal policy against criminalization.

Cities Integrating Encampments as a Step toward Addressing Homelessness

Encampments are not an appropriate long-term solution to homelessness or the nation's affordable housing crisis. However, while we advocate for long-term solutions – primarily increased affordable housing – homeless people need a place to sleep, shelter themselves, and store belongings. A few cities have responded to this need by explicitly permitting some form of legalized camping.[5]

In order to be successful, legalized encampments require a tremendous amount of planning, consultation, and collaboration with all stakeholders, most especially the homeless residents of the encampment; in many cases, this time and effort may be better spent developing other interim or permanent housing solutions. However, the following cities, which allow some forms of temporary encampments, may have lessons for others on how to effectively use them to get people closer to adequate housing and avoid subjecting them unnecessarily to the criminal justice system:

- **Las Cruces, NM**, hosts a permanent encampment with a colocated service center.
- **Washington State** permits religious organizations to temporarily host encampments on their property.
- **Vancouver, WA**, permits limited overnight self-sheltering encampments on city property.

Some additional approaches that may merit further study: Eugene, OR, Los Angeles, CA, San Luis Obispo, CA, Santa Barbara, CA, and San Diego, CA, permit local nonprofits to sponsor safe parking areas with sanitation facilities for those who are living out of their cars. Seattle, WA, and Multnomah County, OR, have pilot programs that permit, or even pay for, residents to host tiny homes in back yards to house persons experiencing homelessness.

Courts are Increasingly Affirming the Rights of Homeless Persons

Courts are increasingly weighing in on the side of homeless people, and in some important cases the message conveyed by that public presence is key to the rulings (Figure 12.8).

At the federal level, an increasing number of courts are ruling that the US Constitution protects the rights of homeless individuals to perform survival activities in public spaces where adequate alternatives do not exist, and the rights of homeless individuals not to be deprived of their liberty or property without due process of law. At the state level, the record is more mixed, but lawyers have created some important precedents. Settlements have generally resulted in minimum notice periods before "sweeps" can take place and requirements for cities to store belongs that are seized, in addition to compensation for the victims of the sweeps At least one settlement, in Charleston, WV, led to a requirement of providing alternative housing for encampment residents before they can be evicted.

In a recent landmark decision, Martin v. Boise, the federal court of appeals for the Ninth Circuit, which covers nine states, struck down a Boise ordinance criminalizing camping in public. Filed by a group of homeless plaintiffs represented by Idaho Legal Services and our organization, the National Law Center on Homelessness and Poverty, which brought in crucial pro bono support from the law firm of Latham & Watkins, this case has a long history.[6] Originally filed in 2009, the case drew support from the Obama Administration's Department of Justice, which filed a brief supporting homeless plaintiffs' challenge to the law.

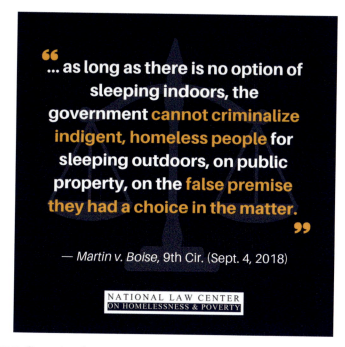

FIGURE 12.8 Quotation from Martin v. Boise, 9th Cir. (September 4, 2018) Decision. Image courtesy of the National Law Center on Homelessness and Poverty

The case was nevertheless dismissed by the trial court, but the administration's support helped galvanize public attention. On appeal, the court reversed the lower court. Rejecting the city's claim that sufficient shelter was available, the court ruled that criminally punishing people for sleeping in public in the absence of private alternatives is "cruel and unusual" punishment in violation of the Eighth Amendment to the US Constitution – and amounts to punishing homeless people for their status. In the absence of other shelter, sleeping in public space is constitutionally protected as a place of last resort for survival.

Another form of limiting the use of public space by homeless and poor people involves restrictions on begging or "panhandling." Laws banning panhandling are prevalent across the country: in a 2016 report, the National Law Center on Homelessness and Poverty found that of 187 cities surveyed, 27 percent had laws prohibiting begging citywide; 61 percent had laws prohibiting begging in particular parts of the city (these are usually downtown areas). Such laws have been challenged, and a 2015 Supreme Court ruling, Reed v. Gilbert, clarified the First Amendment protections for public place solicitations generally. In Norton v. Springfield, the federal Court of Appeals for the Seventh Circuit applied that ruling in the begging context, striking down that city's ban and noting that the Supreme Court ruling had "[r]eject[ed] the idea that the government may remove controversial speech from the marketplace of ideas by drafting a regulation to eliminate the topic." Since then, virtually every panhandling law that has been challenged has been struck down or voluntarily repealed. These cases make clear that begging – asking a fellow human being for help – is constitutionally protected speech entitled to protection. It conveys a message that cannot simply be silenced.

Finally, in another recent, groundbreaking case, the federal Court of Appeals for the Eleventh Circuit ruled in favor of Fort Lauderdale Food Not Bombs (FLFNB), whose members were arrested for serving food to homeless and poor people in a public park, in violation of a local law. The court held that the First Amendment protects outdoor food sharing as "expressive conduct" under the First Amendment to the US Constitution: "Food sharing in a visible public space, according to FLFNB, is 'meant to convey that all persons are equal, regardless of socioeconomic status, and that everyone should have access to food as a human right.'" In contrast to Martin v. Boise, and other cases involving living in public, this ruling recognized the public space rights of people offering help – not of those they were helping. And, unlike Martin and similar cases, it involved, at least in part, the intentional use of public space for expressive purposes. Thanks to the activists who challenged the city's attempt to prevent this use, and the resulting court ruling, the effort to make extreme poverty "legible" through this particular form of expression in a public arena, and to take a stand for equality and human rights, is constitutionally protected.

Ending Encampments: Successful Approaches

Ultimately, ending encampments is a common goal for advocates, cities, and homeless people themselves: no one wants to live outside, if viable indoor options are truly available. This is a goal that advocates as well as cities can agree on; the point of contention is how to reach it. In researching the Tent Cities report, the Law Center found that certain key principles and corresponding practices underlie successful interventions to end encampments. The key principles are:

> Principle 1: all people need safe, accessible, legal places to be, both at night and during the day, and a place to securely store belongings, until permanent housing is found.
> Principle 2: delivery of services must respect the experience, human dignity, and human rights of those receiving them.
> Principle 3: any move or removal of an encampment must follow clear procedures that protect residents.
> Principle 4: where new temporary legalized encampments are used as part of a continuum of shelter and housing, ensure it is as close as possible to fully adequate housing.
> Principle 5: adequate alternative housing must be a decent alternative.

Principle 6: law enforcement should serve and protect all members of the community.

Specific recommendations, elaborated in the report, operationalize these principles. But beyond these recommendations for responding to encampments, it is critical to create the long-term housing solutions communities need to permanently end encampments. This is the work of the Housing Not Handcuffs Campaign. The campaign, launched in 2016 by the Law Center together with over 100 allied organizations, and now endorsed by almost 900 organizations and individuals, including many public officials and law enforcement, provides models for local, state, and federal legislation to shorten homelessness by stopping its criminalization, preventing people from becoming homeless through increased renter protections, and ending homelessness through increasing access to deeply affordable housing.[7]

In the meantime, the growing presence of visibly poor people living in public spaces serves as a reminder of extreme need amidst wealth – for those who are able or choose to read it as such. At the same time, and perhaps because of this, efforts to erase or make invisible this reminder continue to grow, as criminalization of homelessness and poverty continues and deepens. As activists fight back, courts are drawing a line: at least in the nine states covered by Martin v. Boise, simply criminalizing sleeping in public – in the absence of alternatives – is not a constitutionally acceptable option. This opens up a tremendous opportunity for positive change. And in the case of homelessness, the ultimate in positive change is less visibility: a place to call home.

Notes

1 US Department of Housing and Urban Development (HUD), "2018 Annual Homeless Assessment Report (AHAR) to Congress." https://files.hudexchange.info/resources/documents/2018-AHAR-Part-1.pdf.

2 US Department of Housing and Urban Development (HUD), "2017 Annual Homeless Assessment Report (AHAR) to Congress." https://files.hudexchange.info/resources/documents/2017-AHAR-Part-1.pdf.

3 The report was researched and drafted with the generous assistance of the Law Center's pro bono partners, in particular Sullivan & Cromwell LLP, Blank Rome LLP, Nixon Peabody LLP, O'Melveny & Myers LLP, Ballard Spahr LLP, and Hunton & Williams LLP, without which the Law Center's report would not have been possible. Many others, including staff and interns, contributed. A full list of acknowledgments is in the report.

4 US Interagency Council on Homelessness 2015.

5 Our survey of 187 cities found only ten of these cities had done so.

6 The case was then known as Bell v. Boise; it was later renamed Martin v. Bell, reflecting a shift in the makeup of the plaintiff class.

7 Readers may view these policies and endorse the Housing Not Handcuffs Campaign at housingnothandcuffs.org.

References

Foscarinis, Maria. 2018. "Strategies to Address Homelessness in the Trump Era: Lessons from the Reagan Years." *Journal of Affordable Housing* 27 (1): 161–181. www.americanbar.org/groups/affordable_housing/publications/journal_of_affordable_housing_home/volume_27_1

Freddie Mac. 2018. *The Major Challenge of Inadequate U.S. Housing Supply.* www.freddiemac.com/research/insight/20181205_major_challenge_to_u.s._housing_supply.page

National Law Center on Homelessness and Poverty. 2017. *Tent City, USA: The Growth of America's Homeless Encampments and How Communities are Responding.* https://nlchp.org/wp-content/uploads/2018/10/Tent_City_USA_2017.pdfUnited States Interagency Council on Homelessness. 2015. *Ending Homelessness for People Living in Encampments.* www.usich.gov/resources/uploads/asset_library/Ending_Homelessness_for_People_Living_in_Encampments_Aug2015.pdf

13

BODIES IN SPACE

A Conversation with L.A. Kauffman

L.A. Kauffman with Sally O'Driscoll

Introduction

The art of effective protest is a topic that has been on many minds during the Trump presidency: on both sides of the political spectrum, the desire to mobilize protesters and bring them into public space continues to be considered one of the primary ways to make a political position known, and to sway public opinion (Figure 13.1). Yet the efficacy of putting bodies in space – of having protesters occupy streets – is now also being questioned: is it still an effective tactic, and what made it effective in the past?

Few are in as good a position to answer those questions, and consider their implications, as L.A. Kauffman. Kauffman has been an activist for more than 35 years, and has been involved in organizing some of the largest public protests ever held in the US, such as the New York protest against the Iraq War in 2003 and the 2004 protest at the Republican Convention in New York, one of the ten largest marches in US history. Her two recent books offer detailed historical accounts of protests in the US: *Direct Action: Protest and the Reinvention of American Radicalism* (2017) and *How to Read a Protest: The Art of Organizing and Resistance* (2018). Based on exhaustive archival research, *Direct Action* analyzes the organization and effect of a handful of important protest marches and smaller actions. *How to Read a Protest* continues that work by focusing on the issue of long-term effectiveness, answering the question of why mass direct action still matters in the larger world, rather than just in terms of the personal satisfaction of the protester.

The question of what it means to put bodies in space is articulated by Judith Butler:

> So when we think about what it means to assemble in a crowd, a growing crowd, and what it means to move through public space in a way that

FIGURE 13.1 Panoramic view of the January 2017 Women's March in Washington, DC, one of the largest demonstrations in US history. Photograph by L.A. Kauffman. Courtesy of L.A. Kauffman

contests the distinction between public and private, we see some way that bodies in their plurality lay claim to the public, find and produce the public through seizing and reconfiguring the matter of material environments; at the same time, those material environments are part of the action, and they themselves act when they become the support for action.

(Butler 2012, 125)

The power of being physically together in space, participating together in an organized protest, has its own energizing effects: as Brad Will puts it, direct action "is like a conduit, like electricity. It moves through you, not just into you. You're a battery, not a wire" (Kauffman 2017, xiii). In this conversation with Kauffman, we explore the issues raised in the two books, considering particularly what can be learned about the physical occupation of public space for political purposes.

In *Direct Action*, Kauffman considers the political movements of the last few decades that have used both mass public protest and smaller radical actions as tactics: as she reminds us, the fundamental rationale for such protests is found in Dr. Martin Luther King Jr's *Letter from a Birmingham Jail*:

Nonviolent direct action seeks to create such a crisis and foster such a tension that a community which has constantly refused to negotiate is forced to confront the issue.[1]

The book explores methods of organizing after the Civil Rights movement, and considers why some protests were more effective than others. As Kauffman points out:

Some of the movements chronicled in this account have had enormous impact: ACT UP saved millions of lives by hastening the development of key AIDS medications and expanding access to their use. Others, though, only added a modicum of friction as policies they opposed moved forward: though they had a variety of important impacts, the global justice movement and Occupy Wall Street no more stopped the forward march of neoliberalism than the antiwar movement stopped the 2003 invasion of Iraq. Protest actions that felt important and empowering to participants sometimes had few repercussions outside the small world of activism, while others that seemed futile at the time had far-reaching effects that weren't felt for years.

(xii)

Kauffman also carefully traces the effect feminist and radical queer organizers had on the shape of direct actions, and on the structures of leftist organizations in general. As she points out, after the 1971 Mayday action,

244 L.A. Kauffman with Sally O'Driscoll

while neither activists or anyone else would remember this unpopular protest for the outsized impact that it had, the political innovations of Mayday would quietly and steadily influence grassroots activism for decades to come, laying the groundwork for a new kind of radicalism: decentralized, multivocal, ideologically diverse, and propelled by direct action.

(33)

In *Direct Action*, Kauffman (2017) focuses on a handful of specific actions – not necessarily the ones that are remembered today, but ones that nevertheless had a profound effect:

- The 1971 Mayday antiwar protest in Washington, DC, which included an encampment and attempted to stop the government from functioning that day, blocking street space, until the National Guard closed the protest down.
- The 1976 Seabrook antinuclear protest.
- The 1980 Women's Pentagon action.
- Anti-apartheid actions in the 1980s.
- The changing style of "in your face" street protests of the 1980s, from punk anarchist action to ACT UP.
- Increasing police repression of protests, for example with the 1999 WTO in Seattle, the 2003 antiwar protest in New York City, Occupy Wall Street, and Ferguson.

Kauffman's analysis, much of which is based on her new research and documentation, shows which methods worked – either for their immediate political goal, or because they were used in future protests.

In *How to Read a Protest*, Kauffman (2018) zeroes in on the question of the effectiveness of direct action in the form of mass protests and marches (difficult to measure as it may be), and the complex impacts large marches can have on resistance and organizing. Are protests merely gestures, the "weapons of the weak" used only when the protesters are powerless? To answer this question, Kauffman develops a taxonomy of protests, categorized according to the kind of signs being carried, the level of coordination with authorities, the control over speakers and participants, and the organizing structure (top-down or nonhierarchical). Her nuanced discussion of iconic marches provides the most detailed consideration available of the larger meaning of protest marches as a form of direct action. For example, the 1963 March on Washington may have been misunderstood by most as the single reason the Civil Rights Act was passed, but it did (despite, not because of, its authoritarian organizing structure) open "up both literal and metaphorical space for political action, in ways that constitute one of its most enduring contributions" (45). The Women's March on Washington in 2017 (see Figure 13.2), with its coordinated sister marches, provided impetus for resistance to the Trump presidency:

Bodies in Space   **245**

FIGURE 13.2 The most important impact of the Women's Marches of 2017 was how they inspired participants to take up other kinds of organizing work afterwards. Photograph by L.A. Kauffman. Courtesy of L.A. Kauffman

> When women and allies emerged from their stunned state [immediately after Trump's 2016 election] to march all around the country on January 21, they were reclaiming their voices and the public and political space for action in the very act of marching. The low-tech medium of the do-it-yourself sign proved to be a deeply satisfying and powerful part of that process, but it was the larger tactic of the mass protest march – the direct, bodily experience of assembling in large numbers and acting in concert – that broke the nationwide spell of fear and silence.
>
> *(75–76)*

Kauffman considers the concrete and practical effectiveness of major marches: their impact is almost impossible to measure. She concludes that when the government is sympathetic, marches may help, but they have a different role against a hostile government:

> Mass marches targeting hostile administrations – whether the antiwar marches of the late 1960s or the pro-choice marches of the Reagan and Bush years – set a larger political tone and kept dissent alive and visible, but in policy terms, they could feel like shouting into the void.
>
> *(80)*

Yet how can one know what might have happened without the protests? And how can one measure the effect of constraining the scope of direct action by acquiescing to the application for police permits? Permitted actions do not represent a threat to the established order. As Kauffman concludes, "Big marches might feel like a form of collective direct action, when you're there in the midst of a huge crowd with shared purpose – a scaling-up of tactics like sit-ins and blockades. But that's mostly not how they function. They're less about wielding power than about gathering it" (84) – that is, their effectiveness is about building long-term movements and broadening recognition of issues, and about opening up political and discursive space. In the case of the 2017 Women's March, with its peculiarly spontaneous grassroots and viral development, it was also about creating space for new leaders to step forward unexpectedly and grow into their role. As Kauffman concludes, organizing mass direct actions is an art rather than a science, a gamble and an act of faith with no guaranteed results: "sometimes, the most consequential way a mass protest can work is by changing the protesters themselves, giving them the taste of collective power they need to stay in the fight" (95).

Kauffman's analysis ends with a consideration of what happens when small actions arise spontaneously. For example, the immediate gathering of people at JFK airport on the announcement of the Muslim travel ban in January 2017 could not have been foreseen or contained, and yet was extremely effective. But what might have happened if, during the 2017 Women's March on Washington, small groups had sparked an impromptu nonviolent blockade of the White House that continued after the March was over? These are the questions that need to be pondered by those who wonder now how to use public space effectively to cause political change. In this conversation, we move away from direct discussion of Kauffman's books, and into a broader discussion of the use of public space for dissent.

The interview, conducted in January 2019, has been edited and corrected for clarity.

The Effect of a Protest on the Protesters

SO: In *Direct Action* you talk about particular ways that being in a protest physically has an effect on protesters themselves. You also discuss the effect on the object of the protest, and then finally the effect on longer-term organizing. Those are three really separate things that you pull out, so could we just go through them – let's start with the effect on the protesters themselves. What happens when people actually get themselves into a public space and become part of a protest?

LAK: I want to preface any of these comments by saying that there are limits to how much you can generalize about protests, because so much of what happens in a protest and what a protest means either for the people who organize it or the people they are trying to affect is dependent on context.

The context of history, the context of unfolding events, the context of policing, the context of weather – there are all of these outside factors. So it's hard to generalize about the effect on protesters. There are times when the effect on the protesters of taking part in a protest is dispiriting: there are times when you go and you're hoping to make a change and it ends up being five of you out in the freezing rain feeling like you're making your noble stance, but you're pretty sure it's not going to change the course of events. And then there are times when the effect on the protesters is profound and transformative and sometimes even life-changing. There are a great many people who went to the women's marches all around the country in 2017 for whom it was their very first time protesting, and the fact of being out in space – their bodies in space with all these other women and allies – changed their sense of what was possible to do with the world, and changed their sense of who they were in the world. They went on from that experience to join or form groups and dig into all kinds of organizing work that they had never done before – and many of them I know to this very minute continue to be active in organizing.

The effects can vary really greatly. What you're always hoping to do when you organize a protest is, at the very least, to have people come out feeling solid about that use of their time and energy. You can't count on any given protest creating the change you want. You don't want people to necessarily come out with illusions that standing together once is going to win what-ever it is you're fighting for, particularly when you're fighting for some-thing big like stopping a war, or to drive an unfit president out of office. But you want people not to just feel like they were wasting their time, and that there's no point in coming back and doing it again.

Those are reasons why so many movements put a lot of thought into weaving art and culture and music and creativity into protests. Those are partly about how you communicate to the larger world, and they're powerful in that regard. But they are also important ways of sustaining the resolve that you need to go to a protest without having immediate evidence of what effect it's going to have, and feel good enough about that contribution to come back again, since we know that repetition and persistence are how we win.

SO: You're talking about the ways in which you want to involve people politically by putting them in the middle of a protest that feels satisfying to them and that they want to continue doing. But there are other ways that people talk about it – in fact, there's actually a bodily effect on the nervous system from being in space with people with a joint purpose; it functions physically on people. Is that something you've thought about?

LAK: It's something I've *felt*, absolutely, and I always return to the idea in this era of social media, and when people want to talk about the power of digital organizing, I always return to the idea that there's something different and special about the physicality of a protest – the being together with others in the space. I'm not knowledgeable about the actual physiological effects, but I have felt them. And I have felt in particular the way in which you can, deep in your bones, you can really feel the difference between being in a crowd of a hundred, being in a crowd of 1,000, being in a crowd of 10,000, being in a crowd of a 100,000, and being in a crowd of a million. That's rare. There have only been a few times that we've assembled crowds of a million or close to, and that's a very different feeling.

The Effect of Protests on Their Object

SO: Even though it's not generalizable, could you talk a little bit about the ways in which protests can have an effect on their object?

LAK: Well, I'll start with a paradox that relates back to what we were just discussing, which is that we think intuitively that the larger a protest is in size, the greater effect it's going to have on its target – and my experience is that that is not true. That may be true at moments, but that is not a rule of thumb; the power of a protest as a pressure tactic is not proportionate to its size. Now, the other effect that we were just talking about – the effect on the participants – I think does scale up with size. But that's a different kind of effect.

This is partly because the conditions under which we are able to mobilize huge crowds in the United States are conditions of constraint, where we have negotiated agreements with the police – they are permitted gatherings that are designed so that anyone can participate with small kids or with elders or folks with disabilities. So they're prenegotiated and contained in a way that makes them a great on-ramp for people who want to get involved. That means that they send a weak threat signal to those in power. They are not unnerving to those in power. So that cycles us back to the original question, because I think part of the impact on a target of a protest is when it doesn't have to do so much with the absolute size as with maybe the transgressiveness or unexpectedness of it – the sense of pattern disruption that it triggers. A sense that protest energy is surging around a particular question has more of a pressure effect on a target, in the sense that the fact that the numbers are growing matters more than the absolute numbers. If you start out the first time you mobilize on a campaign and you've got 10,000 people, and then the next time you have 9,000, or 5,000, that's going to have a different effect than if you purposely start small, you start with 5,000 and then the next time you have 10,000, then it seems like, oh my gosh, interest and anger around this injustice is growing. The effect – particularly in an era where there are many protests unfolding all the time – it's oftentimes again not the absolute size of a protest but whether it pops up where it's really not expected and leaves bodies where they really don't belong. For instance, some of the really powerful Black Lives Matter protests that I was involved in a few years back, after the police murder of Eric Garner, were during the holiday shopping season when we would go into Macy's and H&M and an Apple store, into these retail spaces where protest is almost never experienced, and we weren't blockading, we were doing roving protests. We would come in and we would chant, we would do a die-in and maybe somebody would speak a little bit, and then we would leave. It wasn't like we were shutting down the stores permanently, but our presence was so surprising and so unexpected that it had – inside the stores, going up and down the escalators with Black Lives Matter signs and lying down, or in the clothes racks, or in the – oh my God, we went into Saks and we were all in the perfume and jewelry section, and we all lay down. It was such an interruption of the normal decorum of commerce in the holiday season that it felt like it had a power for bystanders that no marching on the sidewalk or picketing in front of the stores ever would have. So instead we were bringing these bodies into a place where they weren't officially prohibited but by the normal rules of public behavior – people expect to see protesters on the sidewalk, they don't expect to see protesters in the perfume section at Saks.

SO: Now that is really interesting, because those small mobile, incongruous protests that you're talking about – in the books you talk about the effect of the 1963 Civil Rights march on Washington and that huge 2003 anti-Iraq war protest, and you talk about those as not necessarily being immediately effective on their object. The kind of comparison that you're making there indicates that obviously, historically speaking, the Civil Rights march and the Iraq war protest are in the history books and are somehow extremely important in the memory of people who are thinking about social change. But for you, they didn't have a direct effect on what they were trying to achieve. They didn't stop the Iraq war, they didn't – and that's an interesting argument you make [in your books], that the march was not the real reason why the Civil Rights legislation moved through – that that march was not necessarily the thing that caused that [legislative success].

LAK: I want to pause there, because my argument about the 1963 march has a bit more complexity than that. I argue that it was not the single most instrumental step; I think it's been given outsized credit. Yes, it was a step along the way, but it was a movement-building step, not a pressure-building step.

SO: Right, and I don't want to oversimplify your argument, what you said in the book. But it's interesting to me that you dissect its effect in a much less hagiographic way than most people do when they talk about it.

LAK: Yes. One of the things that I uncovered when I went into the archives and dug around in the records of the organizations that co-sponsored it was the fact that it didn't actually build the membership of any of the sponsoring organizations in the way that we might assume it did. On the contrary, it drained quite a few. And that doesn't mean it's not an inspiring and historically important event, but it's important for us – it gets used so much as this hallowed example that no subsequent movement could ever hope to replicate that I think it's important to have a more realistic taking-stock of what it did and didn't contribute; otherwise it makes us feel like we're just doomed never to repeat the mythic accomplishment of the admittedly extraordinary organizers of 1963.

They were extraordinary and they pulled off something historic that still has deep meaning, but that doesn't mean it was the perfect mobilization that did everything and that can be credited in some simplistic way as having led to the passage of that legislation. Or to have the false understanding that it built the movement in terms of organizational goals, because it didn't.

SO: Which leads us directly to the third part of the effects of a protest, which is what is the effect of a protest on building a movement? And precisely what you're talking about there is that not all historic, wonderful protests help, practically speaking, to build a movement.

LAK: And not all protests that build movements have measurable short-term effects as pressure tactics, is the inverse of that.

SO: One question I have is, how aware are organizers of what they're trying to achieve? You've talked about how, for example, the first Women's March in 2017 was an on-ramp for a lot of people; it was an on-ramp because it created an incredibly welcoming space for a vast number of people who had not been activists at all, so in the sense of making people active it was extraordinarily successful. And I don't know if you would agree with this, but doesn't it seem as if the larger number of women coming into Congress, and the people who worked for them, we might say that that was certainly energized by that march where people began to see that they could intervene in the process in a different way and support people for Congress who weren't even running before? But how much do organizers talk or think about that? Or, do organizers say sometimes, "no, what we need now is a much more hit-and-run kind of protest, incongruous, transgressive, to achieve something different"? How conscious is that on the part of the organizers? I don't think I've ever heard anyone say that.

LAK: That's a great question; I have to think about that. That's going to be really hard to generalize, because I think there was a mix – a lot of people who threw down to make those women's marches happen in January 2017 (and I always underscore that it was women's marches in the plural; there were more than 650 of them, which in itself was record-breaking in terms of the number of coordinated protests happening on one day – that hadn't happened on that scale before); the women who threw down – some men, too – to make those events happen were a mix. Some were women who had been active in Planned Parenthood or the National Organization for

Women or queer issues or who had been with Black Lives Matter – there were longtime activists who stepped up to apply their experience to that moment. And a lot were brand-new, people who had maybe organized meetings or events of a nonactivist nature but who had never done anything of this sort.

And so what intentions they brought to that moment, when those events were organized in such a scramble, it's really hard to say. I don't think anybody – maybe some people dreamed of really kick-starting an entire mass of women-led movements – but I don't know that anybody could have foreseen that.

There's so many times with protests where there's an alchemy, where when something really happens it's like when something goes viral – when something hits the right spot and inspires so many people, there's something about that that outstrips any planning you could ever do.

But I have to say, having been deeply enmeshed in the organizing around the antiwar protests in 2003 and 2004, we hoped that we were – when we marched on February 15, 2003, we hoped that we were kicking off a strong and growing movement. And that that was part of what those actions were going to do.

And I don't know how to say this, but we were kicking off a relatively strong movement that steadily dwindled for years. That was not our plan. We did the best we could to try to have it be otherwise. But we started so big, and then once Bush invaded Iraq it was hard for people to feel that it was worth coming out again. And we had many, many protests – and our protest outside the Republican convention in 2004 was huge, one of the biggest protests ever in US history. But there still was a sense of losing ground, or at least not gaining ground through that whole fight. I don't know if this answers your question.

SO: It leads us actually to the next question I was going to ask, because one thing I am curious about, what is in the organizers' minds when they try to shape a particular protest? How much are people thinking, this is going to be an on-ramp, this is going to be inclusive, or this is going to be – like the Black Lives Matter protest in Saks – something else; surely you know from the beginning that it's something else that you're thinking about doing. But I was just curious about how conscious or consciously discussed that might be among organizers.

LAK: I think it's a mix. I see lots of times where people organize protests just because this bad thing happened and we need there to be a visible response. And that's about as far as the thinking goes. The thinking isn't, this bad thing happened, and we need to have a visible response, and, while we're having our visible response, let's see if we can reach out to some of the people who see our response and pull them in to build our movement further.

In many campaigns I'm involved in they always have this insistence that we should always have a piece of paper we hand out that says who we are, what we're doing, and one action step you can take today to support what we're doing – because if you get people to take an action step they're more likely to actually take multiple action steps. It's not so much because that action step is going to create change, it's because it creates connection to the issue. And then how to get involved, how they come to the next meeting or get on your email list or join your Facebook group or what have you. And it's remarkable how few groups actually do that. Which suggests to me that they're thinking about the response and not about the larger trajectory of the movement. But then there are plenty of people who do think all those things through in their actions and do incorporate all of that.

One of the striking things about this moment in time since Trump took office is that we're seeing historically unprecedented levels of protest in terms of the numbers of actions and numbers of groups, the numbers of participants. And yet from the perspective of someone who's been around for a long time, I feel like there are fewer trainings, conferences, and the like where people are learning and discussing these organizing skills than there used to be. There are webinars and there are a lot of phone calls, there are a lot of conference calls that are sort of trainings, but I come back to the bodies in space. I don't think people get the same thing from a training call that they get from an in-person training. This is a thing to flag: there are some ways in which organizing is – I always make the analogy to cooking because I think organizing is an art, but it's a popular art – where there are many ways that it can be done well and it's often conveyed through oral tradition. And there are many different ingredients that could make for a delicious dish. And it's also something that at the most rudimentary level pretty much anybody can do with hardly any training at all, but learning from others how to do it well in most cases matters and helps you to be a better cook. So there is a way in which I feel we haven't – I feel like that infrastructure is atrophied relative to the scale of mobilizations. There are a lot of these lessons about how you can be designing any given protest to operate on multiple levels that aren't as widely known as they could be.

SO: That seems interesting and really important, and also problematic. And do you have any suggestions for how that might be addressed? Because surely at this point, building a functional long-term movement to address the things that have arisen most clearly with Trump – and certainly not only with Trump, and not first with Trump – if that's what we need to do, you're saying we're not doing something that we should be doing.

LAK: I don't have any brand-new ideas. I guess what I have as a response is really a call for more. Again, the analogy is cooking: there are lots of people with skills out there. There are a lot of people. And we used to have this idea for these trainings where it wasn't necessarily "experts" teaching non-experts. It was skill-sharing: that was always the language we used, and framed it as the training session for social skills share. The idea was that everybody had things to teach each other, and some people had a lot of skills to share. But it was framed in this way that it was inviting people's talents as opposed to setting up experts and those receiving instruction. I would just love to see that become more of our culture. I would love to see afternoons and evenings and weekends set aside for those kinds of skill-sharing training sessions all around the country. Then they also become, if you do them well, they become opportunities for dialogue and cross-fertilization outside of the pressure of direct coalition work. If you're working together to organize an action together you do collaborate and learn from each other in the process. But there's a lot of external pressure, and having this kind of training is a nice way to bring people together and have dialogue in a more open-ended way.

SO: Now, I want to take a different aspect of predictability that you talk about in *How to Read a Protest*, which is, what if that surge of energy in the Washington, DC, Women's March, what if a few people had decided to harness that energy at the end of the march and, in tactical groups, surround the White House? It didn't happen, because there weren't people who knew how to do that, or think that through in the right places or there wasn't –

LAK: Or felt that it wasn't their place to do that, right? Because there are always these questions about ownership and decision-making, and it's not cool to just step in and totally change the nature of a protest that you didn't organize, right?

And yet it was a moment that I fantasized about. It wouldn't have taken many people. People were looking for a next thing – people were itchy, they would have liked to have done a little more. And if there had been people that they felt they had confidence in saying, "Hey, why don't you do this?" My fantasy was more or less a noise protest – a *cacerolazo*, where you surround the space and you make a bunch of noise and you just stick around for a while, I don't know, just longer than you were supposed to, not days, but maybe just into that night – that would've invoked the idea of threat signaling. That would've been a warning shot across the bow that was even stronger than the mobilization. It didn't happen, and it's impossible to imagine how it could've happened, really. It was a fantasy.

Acts of Faith

SO: I want to go back because one thread we've been talking about is the ways in which protests can be understood. I think that that's incredibly important, but they can't be controlled, which is another thing that you've been talking about. Also the question of unpredictability, when you talk about context and when you talk about the multiple factors that shape an intervention, as I would call it, a protest that you cannot control and that has enormous effects. So I want to come back to this question of unpredictability and unmanageability, and how you experience that as both a protester and an organizer.

LAK: Well, when you say that they can't be predicted or managed, that doesn't necessarily mean that the way that the action unfolds is always unpredictable. Usually, you've got people who are with you, you feel solid about them in many cases and know that – you don't always know this, but you could feel pretty confident – everybody is going to behave in a nonviolent fashion and pay attention to the safety and security of fellow protesters. But in terms of how it's going to land on your target, how it's going to land on the world at large, whether it's going to inspire people, you totally don't know. Which is why I use the phrase "act of faith," even though I'm not a religious person; when I talk about protests, I talk about protesting as an act of faith. It's a little like the distinction that Rebecca Solnit makes in her work between optimism and hope, where optimism is the sunny belief that everything is going to turn out okay. Hope can be much more clear-eyed about how dire things can be, but it's the belief that we make it better than it otherwise would be if we didn't intervene. Now, that belief may not always come true, but hope is holding on to that and so continuing to intervene because you have the sense that we can make it better than it would be if we didn't take action. But again, that's in the aggregate. It's not necessarily – you don't go in knowing that any single protest or action is going to have that effect. It's in the aggregate.

SO: So I should have been more clear in my question when talking about the effect of protests. You can't predict or have control over the effect of protests. In your long experience of protesting – and there are very few people who are really going to have that kind of vision that you have of a vast number of protests and a vast number of years of doing it – are there any conclusions you could draw, or any lessons to be learned about how to make something land differently, as you put it?

LAK: A few. When I look back, a lot of times, the protests or the protest campaigns that I feel had the most power were the ones where those of us who organized the protest had the least to do with what happened afterwards – where we unleashed or catalyzed something else, which you can never be absolutely sure that you were the one who did, right? But it feels very real. And another that is related, which is that often with protests, one of the best ways to win is to not seek any credit for winning, and to essentially open up the space in which somebody else can win and claim it. When I think back over a lifetime of protesting, there are a handful of times where I can point to, "We won this concrete specific thing, thanks to our campaign" – like when we saved the community gardens in New York

City from being bulldozed. On that occasion, the front-page story about the gardens being saved did not mention (except maybe as protesters generically) the groups that started the campaign and did all the work – it mentioned the land trusts that bought the properties in the end and the politicians who brokered that deal. They were the ones who got the credit for saving the gardens. They would not have made that deal, that deal would not have been thinkable or imaginable or conceivable had it not been for the protests that put the issue on the map and steadily built pressure around it …

SO: And you were okay with that? The story on the front page ignored you totally and all of what you had done and yet you had won. But you accepted that as, that's life?

LAK: Oh, totally. I never expected we would get credit for any of it. There's so much power in being willing for other people to take the credit. Because change is complex, and other people need to step up and make things happen. And being okay with playing some kind of uncredited catalyst role has real power. The problem though is that it then contributes to the sense that protest doesn't change anything and protest doesn't accomplish anything. That's the downside – a story like that reinforces the idea that essentially it's elite actors who make things happen, and it's not scruffy grassroots protest movements. But what you're often trying to do with protest is force decision-makers to make different decisions than they would have otherwise – to change their sense of what's wise, or practical, or expedient. So I think it only helps if you're comfortable with that role, which is simultaneously instrumental and kind of invisible.

Digital Organizing versus Bodies in Space

SO: So, digital organizing versus bodies in space. How effective can digital organizing be? Can it take the place in any way of physical participation protests? When is it good? And one of the examples you used in the Q&A after your reading at Greenlight Books [in Brooklyn] was getting the news out about the Muslim ban really quickly in order to produce bodies in space very quickly.

LAK: Well, that is a specific example: most people probably would assume that word got out through social media, but what happened was it first got out through text loops of people who knew each other and organizers who had connections through texting, which is digital but different – it's a little closer to the old phone trees that old-timers like me can remember. And it wasn't just that word got out on social media: there was a certain critical mass that was created by people who had offline relationships. The power of social media in organizing is indisputable, and if I often strike a cautionary note, it's because so much of the talk about it can be celebratory without complexity. It's also because I feel like so many of our other tools are at risk of atrophying: social media and the Internet (as methods of outreach and mobilizing) have in too many cases completely replaced other methods rather than supplementing and being layered upon them, or being in relationship to them.

I'm a big believer in paper. I'm a big believer in handing out leaflets to people and getting people involved that way. And that happens very little anymore. I'm a big believer in things like stickering, these kind of guerrilla interventions in public space – I think they have a real power. And that happens some, but not as much as it used to. People are much likelier to make a meme and spread that through social media. And there are so many proclamations like, people can reach out on a scale that we never could before through social media. That's true, but people mobilized huge numbers of people before computers even existed. And there are things to learn from those methods that we could be using now.

The most famous story about this is about the Montgomery bus boycott and the network of women's clubs that had a plan in place. They were waiting – there had been a couple of instances of people arrested for not going to the back of the bus and violating the rules of segregation, but they hadn't found the right person to be the test case legally until Rosa Parks came along. So they had this entire plan in place and managed in, I believe, about 24 hours to mimeograph off notices saying that there was going to be a bus boycott and have them secretly distributed to pretty much every black household in Montgomery. Again, within 24 hours there was a network of couriers distributing all of these leaflets. That was a vast outreach effort that happened lightning quick and that we'd be hard-pressed to replicate today. We don't have any way to do that kind of thing anymore.

I guess my perspective on the rise of digital organizing is to simultaneously appreciate it and to always be wondering about ways to supplement it, complement it, do other kinds of work in parallel to it, and remember that connections of different kinds have different significance. There's a difference between seeing a meme that somebody posted online and responding to it, and taking a leaflet that somebody hands you and then engaging with them about the reasons they're handing it out. I still think those offline interactions have greater force in staying power and significance than the online ones do. Even though I'm well aware that we would not have had – that part of the reason why there were 650 coordinated women's marches instead of the roughly 200 coordinated protests that we had seen in the past is because of the Internet. Because it made it possible for people in all kinds of tiny places to reach out across a geographic range and assemble people on short notice in a way that they would not have been able to do.

Bodies in Space **257**

Taking Back Public Space

LAK: One thing that always strikes me is that the rise of the Internet as part of the rise of neoliberal capitalism happened simultaneously with the scrubbing of public spaces of all but corporate messages. In New York City, if you just walked around the city before there were the Business Improvement Districts [BIDs] … businesses and corporations are paying for people to scrub the streets of anything that weren't ads. That's what those BIDs are doing – they're cleaning up. We used to wheat-paste all the time – that was one of the major ways that we got messages out, and yes, in some ways they reached smaller numbers than you can reach by posting something on the Internet, but think about, for instance, the way that ACT UP's wheat-pasting campaigns transformed the sense of momentum and possibility around AIDS activism. I know from my own experience with the community garden fight [on the Lower East Side of New York], the wheat-pasting that we did – I want to find this wonderful line. Here it is: from Avram Finkelstein (2018) in his book *After Silence: The History of AIDS in Its Images*, he has this wonderful line about postering, about the ACT UP posters that they did; he says that they were designed both to "stimulate organizing and create the illusion that the community was already fully mobilized," which I love. It was both mobilizing people and creating the sense that people were already mobilized in a greater scale and force than they actually were. I thought about that a lot, that there really was this cleansing of public spaces in New York – I refer to it as the evolution from TAZ to DAZ. The TAZ, the Temporary Autonomous Zone, this idea by Hakim Bey that was very much part of an anarchist direct-action culture in the 1990s – I associated that with movements like Reclaim the Streets and Earth First. This idea that instead of imagining that you're part of a revolution that's going to topple the state and replace it, you're opening up these spaces for intervention that are simultaneously pressure tactics to create change in the here and now, and are spaces for visionary enactment of the ideal world you'd like to create.

Our wheat-pasting campaigns were part of that – we were constantly trying to turn the streetscape into our own Temporary Autonomous Zone. We now have in Times Square the DAZ, Designated Activity Zones, where the Time Square Alliance, which keeps all the streets clean, says who can have access and for what reasons. There was a moment where they allowed people to do a poster-making thing for the Women's March; they'll have these moments where there is a Designated Activity Zone for dissent circumscribed by their rules. It's a form of erasure and containment in public spaces. As I say, this coincided in time with the rise of the Internet, which people think of as this very powerful space for political expression, and it is, but it too is within the bounds – where we're posting these

258 L.A. Kauffman with Sally O'Driscoll

messages and memes, we're doing them on platforms that are designed to yield profit for corporations. They're not platforms that are designed to create a robust and functioning democracy.

SO: And they are also platforms that will remove any message without warning that they do not feel is appropriate. The discussion of censorship on the Internet, I don't hear much about it in relation to political organizing. That seems problematic.

What to Do Now?

SO: I want to move on to the question of shame – the implicit assumption that when a mass of people gather to protest an issue, they are taking the moral high ground and causing shame to the establishment that opposes them. In other words, it seems that the effectiveness of direct action depends on a social consensus around certain behavioral or value norms, a consensus that has been ripped apart in the Trump presidency. You suggest that the effectiveness of a protest depends on a social consensus that is open to the possibility of shame, and that does not wish to be shamed, that can be told that its current position is shameful and that it will respond to that. That does seem to be something that we have lost or that is diminishing.

LAK: Well, there are always going to be forms of power that are impervious to shaming, and I think there always have been, and so, for all the power of awakening the moral conscience there are those in power who simply don't have one, and Trump is not unique in that respect of being a figure who is not susceptible to shaming. But I think what that points to is that Trump shouldn't really be the target of that protest.

The "Bye-Bye 45" action guide that I edited as part of the "UnPresidented" *Washington Post* – a fake, future-dated edition of the paper I published with a group of people in January 2019 that had Trump fleeing the White House after a women-led popular uprising – leads with saying that the way to dislodge Trump from office or a way to pressure Trump may be to not focus on him. Instead of focusing on Trump, we should be focusing on all the politicians and institutions that enable Trump, that legitimize him and provide support for him, that treat him as a normal leader, including – most emphatically –the Democratic Party. The story we tell in the newspaper is that this revolt kicks off with protests against Chuck Schumer, not against Donald Trump. Chuck Schumer is a politician who can theoretically be shamed by his base; we're saying you've been approving all these Trump-appointed judges, you've been cooperating with his administration in all these ways, you say you'll work against Trump, but actually you have a variety of means at your disposal to withdraw your consent to cooperation more fully, and that's what we want to demand.

In the case of Trump, I think we can go stand outside Trump Tower saying, "You're a bad man doing bad things" endlessly, without it affecting him one bit, except perhaps to energize him and make him feel like the center of attention. So, I think he's not the best target for protests, it's all those figures in the Republican party who have gone along with his presidency, some of whom can't feel shame, some of whom can. And it's all the ways in which the Democratic Party has colluded, and all the other institutions and news media, who will broadcast his speeches that are nothing but a bundle of lies, rather than just denying him a platform to spread those lies. It's Twitter who continues to allow him to have access to their platform even though he's violating the terms of service over and over again, and they're constantly kicking people off who violate the terms in less egregious ways. So, I think the way that protest could weaken Trump is certainly not by appealing to his conscience, and not really by focusing on him at all, but focusing on all the people and institutions who are enabling him to continue doing the harm that he's doing. It's a theory of change that came from Otpor, the movement that brought down Slobodan Milosevic, this idea that you go after pillars of support for your opponent rather than taking him on directly — it's like, if you're knocking down a table, instead of pounding on the table you pull out the legs.

It Still Matters ...

SO: Is there anything you feel that we should have talked about and we didn't? Understanding that obviously, we're not going to get to everything that's in the two books, and hoping that people will – if they haven't already – move on to read those if they want more details.

LAK: Yeah, I want to cycle back to that dispiriting 2003 protest, to get another look at one of these longer-term effects, and because I think having bodies together in space matters – defending the right to do that matters deeply; defending the right to be able to protest. Part of what happened in that moment in time, this is hard to remember but after the lead-up to 9/11, already, in reaction to the global justice movement, the public space for protest in many cities around the US was closing down alarmingly. It was *before* 9/11 that we started seeing the surge of police in riot gear at protests, the use of pepper spray – a lot of these very openly repressive paramilitary responses to protest preceded 9/11, and then 9/11 accelerated that trend, and a lot of people were afraid to come out into the streets at all. It was difficult to get permission at all to protest on February 15, 2003. And so there's a way in which even though I still think we should have marched instead of having the stationary rally, that was all the police would permit, and people got hurt because of the pens and the police horses, and it was dispiriting to be part of, it did hold open and push open some of that space to be able to protest in a way that I think was important. Sometimes, what we are doing when we are protesting, we are pushing for whatever we're pushing for, but we're also holding space for dissent now and in the future, and that's just another layer of the effect to look for and look at.

Note

1 *Letter from a Birmingham Jail*, www.africa.upenn.edu/Articles_Gen/Letter_Birmingham. html.

References

Butler, Judith. 2012. "Bodies in Alliance and the Politics of the Street." In *Sensible Politics, The Visual Culture of Nongovernmental Activism*, edited by Meg McLagan and Yates McKee, 117–137. New York: Zone Books.

Finkelstein, Avram. 2018. *After Silence: The History of AIDS Through Its Images*. Berkeley: University of California Press.

Kauffman, L.A. 2017. *Direct Action: Protest and the Reinvention of American Radicalism*. London and New York: Verso Books.

Kauffman, L.A. 2018. *How to Read a Protest: The Art of Organizing and Resistance*. Berkeley: University of California Press.

INDEX

Note: Page numbers in *italics* indicate figures and in **bold** indicate tables on the corresponding pages.

Abeyance (Draves y Robles y Vargas), *135*, 147–151, *148*
Abstract Expressionism, 102
activism, design as a form of, 83–85
activists, 193
acts of faith, 253–255
ACT UP, 243
After Silence: The History of AIDS in Its Images, 257
Aguiñiga, Tanya, 121; activism through art of, 184–185; AMBOS Project and, *185–187*, 185–191, *190–191*; on the borderlands, 184; *Care & Craft* exhibition of, 187–188; on emotion connected to the border, 186–187; pain of rupture in pieces by, 190
Alatalo, S., 164
Alberti, L. B., 21
Amable, M. C., 145–146
AMBOS Project, *185–187*, 185–191, *190–191*
American Institute of Architects (AIA), 21, 49
Amezquita, J., *191*
Analgesia (and Armament), 140, *141*
Anderson, B., 8
Anderson Barbata, L., 121, *126*, 131–133, *132*
Angelou, M., 54

anti-Iraq war protest, 2003, 249, 259–260
Anzaldua, G., 188
A/Part of the Whole, 171
Apel, D., 107
Architect Magazine, 39
architects: design process and, 24–27, *25*, *26*; role of, 19–22
Architects' Renewal Committee in Harlem (ARCH), 47; Black Power utopia and, 57–66, *63–66*; democratic participation in, 53–57; reforming urban renewal, 48–53; unintended consequences of, 66–70, *70*
architecture: Children Village, Formosos do Araguaia, Brazil, 29–32, *30*, *32*; Common-unity, San Pablo Xalpa, Mexico, 36–39, *37–38*; Dreamhamar, Hamar, Norway, 27–29, *28*; El Guadual Children Center, *25*, 25–27, *26*; Equal Justice Initiative, Memorial for Peace and Justice, 32–35, *33*, *34*; evolution of, 19; future of public, 41–43; role of, 22–24; service learning pedagogy in education, 81–83; Stage, Dnipro, Ukraine, *39*, 39–41, *40*
Arnaud, N., 29
Artemesia Gallery *see Critical Messages: The Use of Public Media Art for Women*

262 Index

artistic practice projects, 134–136, *135*, 152; *Abeyance (Draves y Robles y Vargas)*, *135*, 147–151, *148*; Contact Points (2006-present), 136–144, *141–142*, *136*, *138*; *The horizon toward which we move always recedes before us*, 151–152, *152*; South of Market Community Action Network (2011-present), 144–147, *146*
Art of the Woman's Building, The, 156
Ashraf, H., 197, 199
Atget, E., *97*
Avgikos, J., 157

Ballard, J., 161, 167
Baraka, A., 58
Barker, R., 29
Baudelaire, C., 96
Baxandall, L., 166, 168
Beat, J., 123
Becker, H., 168
Bellavance, L., 164–165
Benjamin, W., 106, 115
Berlin Wall, 22
Betsky, A., 23, 38
Bitch Flicks, 197
Black Arts Movement, 58–66
Black Lives Matter, 249, 251
Black Power, 45
Black Power movement, 17; Black Power utopia and, 57–66, *63–66*; democratic participation in urban renewal and, 53–57; growth of, 45; reforming urban renewal, 48–53; spatial segregation and, 45–46; unintended consequences of, 66–70, *70*; urban renewal and, 46–48
Bless, N., 162, 165, *166*
bodies in space, 175–176, 255–256; *see also* protests
Bomb Desert, A, *164*
Bond, H. M., 54
Bond, Jean Carey, 54
Bond, J. Max, Jr., 47, 48, 53, 54; Black Power utopia and, 57–64
Bond, Julian, 54
borderlands, U.S./Mexico, 184–191, *185–187*, *190–191*
Both Sides Now: An International Exhibition Integrating Feminism and Leftist Politics, 156
Bowlby, R., 96
Brooklyn Jumbies, 123, 128, 131–132, *132*
Brown, D. S., 102
Bryan-Wilson, J., 189

Building and Dwelling: Ethics for the City, 6
Building Community: A New Future for Architecture Education and Practice, 81
built environment, 17–18
Burrington, I., 6
Butler, J., 241, 243
Butler, M., 197
Butler, S., 159, 164, 169

capitalism, 1, 94, 103, 106, 114–115
Care & Craft, 187–188
Carey, E., 157
Carmichael, S., 45, 47
censorship, 166–170
Center for Exploratory and Perpetual Arts (CEPA), 157
Centro Cultural Móvil: community partnership and reciprocity and, 85–86; conclusions on, 89–90; design as a form of activism and, 83–85; introduction to, 78–79; Latinx farmworkers in Vermont and, 79–81, *80*; opportunities and challenges in participatory design process and, 86–87; participatory design meetings for, 87–89, *88–89*, 91n6; service learning pedagogy in architectural education and, 81–83
Cervantes, R., 123
Chang, J., 151–152
Chicago Reader, 175
Children Village, Formosos do Araguaia, Brazil, 29–32, *30*, *32*
Chopra, D., 202
Churchill, W., 35–36
Civil Rights march, 1963, 249
Clement, R., 54
CodePink, 197
Cohen, A., 3
Common-unity, San Pablo Xalpa, Mexico, 36–39, *37–38*
Community Action Program, 50
Community development corporations (CDCs), 52–53, 69
community partnership and reciprocity, 85–86
Congress of Racial Equality, 52
Conical Intersect 3, *105*, *106*, 116
Contact Points (2006-present), 136–144, *141–142*, *136138*
Covid-19 pandemic, 190
Critical Messages: The Use of Public Media Art for Women, 155; as an exhibition seen and unseen, 158–166, *160–166*; brief

Index **263**

history of Artemisia and, 156; censorship and, 166–170; epilogue on, 172–176, *174*, *177*; evaluating impact of, 168–169; precedents for, 157–158; private made public in, 171–172

Croteau, M. E., 175

cyberspace, 4

David, A., 155, 156, 157, 158, 163, 167

Davis, J., 33

De Architectura, 20

Dear Men, While on the streets…, Maintain 5 feet distance. Thanks, 164, *165*

Death and Life of Great American Cities, The, 62, 96

Degas, E., 97

democracy and public space, 5–6

Demolished, 112–113

Demolition, 99–101, *101*

demolition art, 95–96; demolished houses in, 102–104, 112–113; on Detroit, 107–108; domestic spaces, *108–109*, 108–112; in modernizing cities, 114–116, *116*; open space in, 113–114, *114*; postwar loss of historic environments in, 102–104; rowhouses in, 101–102; skyscrapers in, 98, *99, 100*

Demolition: Forbidden City, Beijing, 115–116, *116*

design as form of activism, 83–85

design as product, 29; Children Village, Formosos do Araguaia, Brazil, 29–32, *30, 32*; Equal Justice Initiative, Memorial for Peace and Justice, 32–35, *33, 34*

design as program, 35–36; Common-unity, San Pablo Xalpa, Mexico, 36–39, *37–38*; Stage, Dnipro, Ukraine, *39*, 39–41, *40*

design process, 24–27; Dreamhamar, Hamar, Norway, 27–29, *28*; El Guadual Children Center, *25*, 25–27, *26*; participatory, 86–89, *88–89*, 91n6

Destruction of Lower Manhattan, The, 102

dialogical practice, 83

Dialogue with Demolition, 115

digital organizing, 255–256

Dimitrakaki, A., 111

Direct Action: Protest and the Reinvention of American Radicalism, 241, 243, 244

DiSalvo, J., 199

Drapiza, A., 146, *146*

Draves, V. M., 149–150

Dreamhamar, Hamar, Norway, 27–29, *28*

Du Bois, W. E. B., 54

Dunn, A., 7

East Harlem Triangle: Black Power utopia and, 57–66, *63–66*; democratic participation in, 53–57; unintended consequences in, 66–70, *70*; urban renewal in, 48–53

Ebrahimian, S., 208

Ecker, H., 157

Economic Opportunity Act of 1964, 50

El Guadual Children Center, *25*, 25–27, *26*

Ending Homelessness for People Living in Encampments, 234–235

End of Care, The, 113–114, *114*

England, M., 50

English, C., 157

Equal Justice Initiative, Memorial for Peace and Justice, 32–35, *33, 34*

Evans, R., 103

Expanding Commitment: Diverse Approaches to Socially Concerned Photography, 169

Farmer, J., 50

Faulkner, D., 156

"Fear is Our Gross National Product," 162, *163*

Feldman, D., 25

Felted/Woven Low Rod Chair, 189

Ferentz, N., 155, 157, 158, 163, 167

Fields, J., 51

Finkelstein, A., 257

Fire, M., 156

First International Hotel (I-Hotel), 136–144, *141–142*

Floyd, G., 8

food sharing, 238

For All You Folks Who Consider a Fetus, *174*, 174–175

Foscarinis, M., 193

Foucault, M., 6

Fraiman, S., 193

Freddie Mac, 228

freedom of public space, 5–6

Freire, P., 83

Gardner, F., 166, 168

Gardner-Hugget, J., 121

Gayle, A., Jr., 58

Gentileschi, A., 156

Ghana, 53–55

Ghost, *108*, 108–109

Gibson, D., 112

264 Index

Gillis, K. L., 172
Ginsburg, R. B., 176
Giovanni, N., 58
Goldstein, B. D., 17
Gonzales, D. P., 134, 136, *136*, 150
Gorsuch, N. M., 176
Granet, I., 158, 164, *165*, 175
Gran Fury, 175
Gray, J., 50
Griffin, T. L., 3
Guardian, The, 5
Guinness Book of World Records,
    184
Guys, C., 96

Habal, E., 140, *142*, 150
Habermas, J., 96
Halberstam, J., 104
Hamilton, C.V., 45, 47
Hardikar, A., 197
Harlem Commonwealth Council
    (HCC), 52
Harlem News, 53, 56
Harris, M., 230
Harvey, D., 1, 6, 7, 24, 117
Hassam, C., 94, 98, *100*
Hatch, C. R., 48–50, 52
Haussmann, G.-E., 96, 104
Helms, J., 175
Hendler-Voss, A., 86
Holzer, J., 158, 159, *162*, 163
homeless encampments *see* tent cities
Hōōz Responsible, 176
The horizon toward which we move always
    recedes before us, 151–152, *152*
Hornstein, S., 110
Horsfield, K., 168
House, 109, 109–112
Hovel and the Skyscraper, The, 98, *100*
How to Look at Women, 159, *160*
How to Read a Protest: The Art of Organizing
    and Resistance, 241, 244, 253
Hurwitz, H. M., 197–198, 199

information space, 4
Innis, R., 50, 55
Intervention: Indigo, 123–124, *124*; artists of,
    131–133, *132–133*; experience of being
    there for, 124–126, *125–126*; indigo
    color and, 126–127, *127–128*; stilt-
    dancers and ritual in, 128–130, *129–130*;
    transcommunality and, 130–131
Ishikawa, S., 139

Jacobs, J., 59–60, 62, 96
Jacobsen, C., 167
Jacoby, B., 83
Jameson, F., 111
Johnson, L. B., 50
Judith and Holofernes, 156
Jumbie Camp, 131

Kauffman, L. A., 5, 193, 241–246; on acts
    of faith, 253–255; on effect of protests
    on protesters, 246–248; on effect of
    protests on their object, 248–253
Kavanaugh, B., 176
Kelly, M., 156
Kester, G., 158, 172
King, M. L., Jr., 56, 243
Kissing Doesn't Kill, 170
Kohr, T., 233–234
ko Robinson, t., 121, 134, 137–139,
    140, 143
Kostof, S., 19
Kruger, B., 158, 162, 175

Lacy, S., 156
Latinx farmworkers *see* Centro
    Cultural Móvil
Lawson, L., 86
Lebron, M., 167, 168
Le Corbusier, 103
Ledesma, I., 125, 127
Lee, B. C., Jr., 23, 102–103
Lee, P., 102, 104
Lefebvre, H., 79
Letter from a Birmingham Jail, 243
Life Story, 165
Lifton, N., 168
Lippard, L., 156
Liu, J., 139, 153n2
Looking at Men, 156
Looking at Women, 156
Lopez Barrera, S., 17
Lyon, D., 102

M5, 157, 158
MacArthur, D., 159
Maddox, D., 3
Maharawal, M., 197, 199
Maison. Vue en perspective du pencement de la
    rue Domat, 97
Malagrino, S., *164*, 171
Malcolm X, 60
Manifestation at 12th and Vine, 166
Marin, J., 98, *99*

Martinez, D. J., 147–148
Martin v. Boise, 236–237, *237*
Matta-Clark, G., 94, 102–106, *105*, 110, 113, 116
Meyer, R., 170
Michaels, R., 159, *161*, 169
Migrant Justice, 80, 84, 85, 87
Mills, A., 230
Milosevic, S., 259
Mirth and Girth, 171
Mobilization for Survival, 167, 168
Moko Jumbie, 128
Montiel, R., 36–38
Moore, M., 168
Morton, K., 82
Ms. Blog, 197
Mullins, 110
Murphy, K. D., 17, 121
Murphy, M., 34

Napoleon III, 96, 104
Nation, The, 197
National Association for the Advancement of Colored People, 54
National Endowment for the Arts, 175
National Organization for Women, 250–251
National Urban League, 23
Neal, L., 58
Nelli, G., 17
Nelson, D. K., 171
neoliberalism, 1–2, 6, 7, 107
Nishio, L., 165, 176
Nkrumah, K., 54, 55
Notre Dame Cathedral, 42

Obama, B., 7, 175
Occupying Wall Street: The Inside Story, 204, 207
Occupy Wall Street, 6, 7, 35, 131, 193, 195, 223n1, 243; caring for the revolution and, 207–212; geography of, in lower Manhattan, 218–221, *219–220*; greater New York and, 221–222; in search of radical equality, 195–199; spatial strategy of, 217–218; status of female leaders in kitchen workgroup of, 199–203; status of kitchen in, 203–207
Orlofsky, J. J., 158

Palermo, G., 20
panhandling laws, 237–238
Parada, E., 159, 164, 169

Paris Spleen, 96
participatory design process: meetings in, 87–89, *88–89*, 91n6; opportunities and challenges in, 86–87
Pedagogy of the Oppressed, 83
Pepe, S., 121
Peters, B., 168
Piano, R., 104–105
Pinkel, S., 159, 162, *163*, 169
Piper, A., 156
Piss on Passivity, Piss on Patriarchy, 176, *177*
Planned Parenthood, 167–168, 176, 250
Pompidou, G., 104–105
private space: in demolition art, 95–96, 102–104, 112–113; public views of, 94–95, 106, *108–109*, 108–111, 171–172
privatization of public urban space, 2, *2*
protests, 175–176, 259–260; acts of faith and, 253–255; digital organizing versus bodies in space, 255–256; effectiveness of, 244–246; effect on their object, 248–253; effects on protesters, 246–248; introduction to, 241–246, *242, 245*; shaming through, 258–259; significant, 244; taking back public space, 257–258
public interest design, 84
public-private partnerships, 5–6
public space: action, praxis, representation in, 8–9; artists and, 121–122; in demolition art (*see* demolition art); fragility of, 1; ideology of freedom of, 5–6; intervention in (*see Intervention: Indigo*); neoliberalism and, 1–2, 6, 7; privatization of urban, 2, *2*; public sphere versus, 13n1; relationship to democracy, 5–6; struggle for, 3–4, 6–8; taking back, 257–258; virtual, 4–5

Quiñones, I. D., 25

Rabine, L., 150
rant art, 172
Rattle Your Rage, 175
Reagan, R., 2, 156, 159, 161, 167, 225, 245
Reed, I., 58
Revelle, B. J., 159, *160*, 164
Reyes, J., 121, *135, 146*, 149
Rinehart, L., 189–190
Robbins, M., 4
Robles, A., 145, 149–150
Rogers, R., 104–105
Rogers, S., 197
Rosen, K., 157, 158, 159, *161*, 165, 168

266 Index

Rosler, M., 156
Routes and Seasons, 140, *141*
rowhouses, 101–102
Rush, M., 157
Ruskin, J., 21

Salinas, E., 149
Sassen, S., 3, 13n3
Sassin, E., 17
Schumer, C., 258
Scott, D., 171–172, 175
Seaglove, I., 164
Seeking Spatial Justice, 6
Seltzer, S., 197, 199, 208
Sennett, R., 6
service learning, 81–83
Seven Lamps of Architecture, The, 21
shaming, 258–259
Shaw, G., 94, 112–114, *114*
Shaw, R., 170
Sherman, C., 157
Sign on a Truck, 163
Simmons, K., 52, 53, 55
SisterSerpents, 173–176, *174*, *177*
Smith, A., 165
Soja, E. W., 6
Solnit, R., 254
Soul of Leadership, The, 202
South of Market Community Action
    Network (2011-present), 144–147, *146*
spatial agency, 84
Spector, B., 155, 158
Splitting, 103–104
Stage, Dnipro, Ukraine, *39*, 39–41, *40*
State Womb, 175
Stevens, A. B., 197
Stevenson, B., 33–34
stilt dancers, 128–130, *129–130*
Stombly, G., 162
Stonecipher, T. W., 158
Streetfare Journal, The Magazine of the Rider,
    157, 167
Stroman, E., 226
Studio Ecosistema Urbano, 27–29, *28*
Subculture, 157, 158
Survival: UNEX sign, 162
Symes, A. L., 57

Tars, E., 193
Taussig, M., 202
Tension, *191*
tent cities, 224–226, *225*; case studies of
    non-enforcement approaches to, 234;

communities responding with punitive
law enforcement approaches to,
228–230, *229*; courts affirming the
rights of homeless persons and, 236–238,
237; ended through housing, 234–235;
evictions from, as not the best way to
protect health and safety, 233–234, *234*;
expense of evictions from, 230–231,
231; integrated as step toward addressing
homelessness, 235–236; law enforcement
threats not decreasing the number of
people on the streets and, *232*, 232–233;
rapid growth of, 226–228, *227–228*;
successful approaches to ending,
238–239
Tent City, USA: The Growth of America's
    Homeless Encampments and How
    Communities are Responding, 224
Thatcher, M., 2
Thermonuclear Gardens, 162
This is a Nice Neighborhood, 147–148
Thompson, 87
Thorpe, A., 84
Thrash, D., 94, 99–102, *101*, 113
Tile Hill, 112–113
transcommunality, 130–131
Trump, D., 2, 3, 5, 8, 175, 241, 244–245,
    258–259
Turner, J., 173–174
Turyn, A., 164, *165*
Twitter, 259

United States/Mexico borderlands,
    184–191, *185–187*, *190–191*
Unleash the Fury of Women as a Mighty Force
    for Revolution, 176, *177*
Untitled (You Body is a Battle Ground), 175
urban modernization, 94–95; American,
    98; in developing nations, 114–115; as
    dynamic process, 96, 106–108; Parisian,
    97, 97–98; *see also* demolition art
urban space, privatization of, 2, *2*
Ursprung, P., 103
Utrabo, G., 31

Vargas, J. A., 149–151
Venturi, R., 102
Vers Une Architecture, 103
Vidler, A., 111
Village Voice, 169
Villa Rica, *25*, 25–27, *26*
virtual space, 4–5
Vitruvius Pollio, M., 20, 21

Walker, C., 123, 129–130, *130*, 132–133, *133*
Walls Paper, 102–104, 113
War on Poverty, 50
Washington, H., 159, 171
"Watch your Step," 165–166
We Gon' Be Alright, 152
What Is the Proper Way to Display a U.S. Flag, 171–172
Whiteread, R., 94, *108–109*, 108–112, 113
Whitewalls, 155
Wilcox, P., 52, 55

Window Shopping, 157
Wise, M., 193
Wojnarowicz, D., 95
Women's March: 2017, 5, 7–8, *242*, 244–246, *245*, 250; 2018, 176, *177*

Yanukovych, V., 39
Young, W. M., Jr., 23

Zedillo Velasco, C., 36
Zero, A., 29–32
Zhang Dali, 94, 114–116, *116*

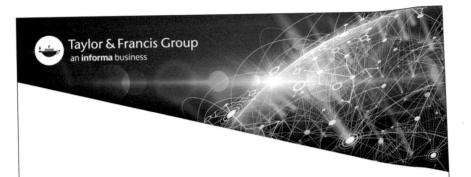